KOKOSCHKA

KOKOSCHKA

RÜDIGER GÖRNER

Kokoschka

The Untimely Modernist

Translated by Debra S Marmor and Herbert A Danner

First published by Haus Publishing in 2020
4 Cinnamon Row
London SW11 3TW
www.hauspublishing.com

First published in German as *Oskar Kokoschka: Jahrhundertkünstler*
Copyright © Paul Zsolnay Verlag Ges.m.b.H., Wien 2018
English-language copyright © Debra S Marmor and Herbert A Danner, 2020

A CIP catalogue record for this book is available from the British Library

ISBN: 978-1-912208-81-4
eISBN: 978-1-912208-82-1

Typeset in Garamond by MacGuru Ltd

Printed in the UK by Clays Ltd, Elcograf S.p.A.

The translation of this work was supported by a grant from the Goethe-Institut
which is funded by the German Ministry of Foreign Affairs.

Where my brush touches you, you are mine,
You are I, are more than I, I am yours,
Primordial beauty, Queen of the World!

Johann Wolfgang von Goethe
Des Künstlers Erdewallen (The Artist's Sojourn on Earth, 1773/1774)

The eye's practice in forms:
Presumably also the ear's and touch's.

Friedrich Nietzsche
Nachgelassene Fragmente (Posthumous Fragments, 1884)

I live at such high speed, Maia. We live so, we artists. I, for my
part, have lived through a whole lifetime in the few years we two
have known each other. I have come to realise that I am not at
all adapted for seeking happiness in indolent enjoyment. Life
does not shape itself that way for me and those like me. I must
go on working – producing one work after another – right up
to my dying day. [Forcing himself to continue.] That is why I
cannot get on with you any longer, Maia – not with you alone.

Professor Arnold Rubek, Sculptor, in:
Henrik Ibsen
When We Dead Awaken (1899)[1]

Contents

Preface to the English Edition

Nothing could be more humbling than contemplating the enigma of great works of art. And little could be more edifying – and sometimes sobering – than investigating the interrelations between them and the life of their originator. What is it that drives artists? And what constitutes their uniqueness?

Oskar Kokoschka's life comes across as having been as colourful as his paintings and vice versa. His colours generate shapes and these shapes challenge colours – for the benefit of the beholder's eyes.

This is an account of an extraordinary life conditioned by strong emotions and the 'will to art', determined by uprooting political circumstances, and fulfilled painting after painting, drawing after lithograph. It acknowledges that the visual arts are a celebration of vision, in both meanings of the word. Kokoschka was a continental European through and through with strong connections to Britain – not least due to his years in exile, spent mostly in London but also in Cornwall and Scotland. He was a towering figure among the German-speaking refugees from National Socialism and yet remained an outsider. He was highly political with strong sympathies for the Left and yet indulged in portraying members of the establishment. The reader will find a fair number of 'and yet' constructions in this text; they reflect the inner contradictions of this prickly character and hugely productive artist whose subjects ranged from distinctive faces to animals, cityscapes to large-scale mythological images.

Why should we remind ourselves of Kokoschka and why now? There is something deeply touching and overwhelming in the visual presence of his art and there are plenty of disturbing, if not upsetting, features of his life that concern us with undiminished significance. For instance, once again we find ourselves confronted with increasingly aggressive right-wing nationalism all across Europe, including Britain, not to speak of other parts of the globe, which makes this artist's political stance eminently relevant. Even though Kokoschka's art and writings bear witness to the heights and the unprecedented lows of the last century, he has remained an artist of our time. His emphasis on the absolute necessity of 'aesthetic education' could not be more topical in a political climate that suggests that education should serve merely utilitarian purposes. He was courageous enough to put the arts centre stage against all odds, and narrow-mindedness in particular.

What brought me to this extraordinary artist? The sheer evocativeness of his paintings had already struck me in my last years of grammar school when I came across a few reproductions of his works in the collection of our modest school library. I then found myself collecting press cuttings that dealt with Kokoschka's legacy following his death in 1980. And when I came to London as a student one year later, good fortune had it that I met former emigrants who still had personal recollections of Kokoschka. Furthermore, I found a piece on Kokoschka by the Prague-born British art historian Josef Paul Hodin, who had written a biographical study on this legendary artist back in 1966 based on his frequent encounters with him. It was published in the same magazine that contained pieces by other (former) exiles, among them the writer H G Adler, the artist Helga Michie, the academic Peter Pulzer and the gallerist Wolfgang Georg Fischer. But it was the great retrospective of Kokoschka's work in the Tate Gallery in 1986 that defined my impression of this extraordinary art. The man behind it remained rather opaque, though. The palette of texts on Kokoschka I had collected could only illuminate him to a certain extent. But it was not before I began work on biographical studies of the poets Rainer Maria Rilke and Georg Trakl some twenty years later that Kokoschka came back to me as a subject worthy of more thorough investigation. It involved retracing some of his locations – often the subjects of some of his most striking paintings – starting in London, then back to Vienna and Prague (visits to archives included, mainly Zürich, where most of his papers are kept), to Dresden and

Paris, Hamburg and Cologne, Lake Geneva and Salzburg. Finally, I visited Pöchlarn, Kokoschka's birthplace, that ancient district which appears sleepy, crushed by the Nibelungen legacy seemingly too big for this little village on the relentlessly flowing, at times dangerously flooding, Danube. I found it noteworthy that Pöchlarn and its immediate surroundings did not lend themselves to Kokoschka for artistic rendering of any significance. But what he did carry with him from his place of origin was the broad Lower Austrian dialect of this region, which never left him.

Kokoschka's paintings radiate a distinct urgency; his brushstrokes often betray inner tension, excitement and drama. These paintings mirror the sheer strength of his imagination even when, in later years, his voyages had reached somewhat calmer seas of outer and inner landscapes. Kokoschka's expression of restlessness – especially in his earlier work and during the period of political upheaval – is arresting, as is the sincerity of his writings and the humanist concern they reflect.

To the very end of his life, the human being took centre stage in his studio. It was the very source of Kokoschka's artistic quest. Apart from his other great artistic achievements, Kokoschka was – arguably – the greatest portraitist of the 20th century. His portraits were analytical to the point that his easel and canvas could be seen as equivalents to Freud's couch.

With Kokoschka we are made, in a Nietzschean sense, to *listen* to the rhetoric of colours and shapes, and to *see* the soundscapes of his subjects. For his art continues to teach us how to see differently, and this experience continues to be hugely gratifying and enriching, if not essential, for the ever-endangered humanising of our increasingly mechanistic world.

Rüdiger Görner
Kingston upon Thames, March 2020

Foundations, or the Journey to an Achievement of the Century

'Let us *see* how it all began.' With these words, Oskar Kokoschka enticed the readers of his autobiography[1] to follow the sometimes labyrinthine development of his life. In this, he is reminiscent of Johann Gottfried Herder's claim that man is reborn in every instant. 'Let us *see*' – Kokoschka loves to emphasise the purely visual of his childhood impressions. 'One gawks at the world before one is capable of comprehending the wonder of creation in light and shadow. It is not surprising that it can remain pitch dark all around us, if one has not experienced understanding along with sight' (ML, 31).

What had begun there? An artist's life that has many examples, but no parallels. A more-than-ninety-year insistence on the value of the person, on confirming the individual through the creative act in an age of the collective expropriation of the self or, as Kokoschka tended to emphasise in later interviews, the loss of individuality.

By and large, artists do not consciously prioritise giving expression to their time. Rather, they are burdened by time. What is called 'expression' can result from this condition. Every expression is preceded by an impression, a shaping of sorts. A yearning to communicate, or represent, this initial impression develops in artists. *That* is the primordial mimetic constellation underscoring creative work.

In the beginning, according to Kokoschka, he developed a sense or impression of space in order to visualise colours, flowers and scatter patterns on the walls – through the slats of his crib and the 'green fasteners' of the netting within. That is how the very person who would one day found a School of Seeing began his life – with masses of primal visual scenes. One is particularly noteworthy: pupil Oskar K, who is laid over his (female) teacher's knee and physically punished. According to the eighty-five-year-old artist, this gave him a first sexual experience, ornamented with unambiguous symbols because during this punishment he had 'stared at the [teacher's] gold bracelet that had the form of a serpent with red eyes and encircled her white [naked] arm' (ML, 34). The young Adam, punishingly seduced by the authoritarian yet erotically attractive older Eve. Apart from that, colours were the child's one and all. He was given a box of paints one Christmas.

> The paints tasted of honey; I often licked the paintbrush while I tinted the black and white pictures in the book of legends of antiquity. In life, everything is colourful, that is why I chose my favourite colours for colouring in: red, green, yellow, and blue. (ML, 39)

Favourite colours, but not the single *one* that dominated the work, like the pink of Giambattista Tiepolo.[2] Yet this effortlessness of the Rococo master appealed to Kokoschka early on and therefore also the high school of *sprezzatura*, or studied carelessness: the desire to create art in which the artful was not beheld.

One is accustomed to reading autobiographies with some reservation but can agree with Harry Graf Kessler, who wrote in December 1898:

> Autobiographies are actually the only biographies that are not worthless: because, for the individual, a fact in and of itself – rather than the impression a fact makes upon him – is never of importance; and only he himself can relate the perceptions he derived from the facts.[3]

'What is a biography?' Kokoschka asks right at the beginning of his autobiography and rhetorically speculates: 'Juggle with facts? Idealise?' (ML, 31). It becomes immediately clear that he hopes to show the colourfulness of life's truths in the depiction of his life because, at best, it can only deal with truths over one lifetime. And, despite its review of authentic sources, the impression remains that one is moving along the very edge of fictionalisation – no matter how much one tries to faithfully reconstruct atmosphere and event from the biographical material. After all, the primary objective in these attempts is to remain just to the personality in its time, to learn to understand it a bit better, and to show what this understanding means in the present day. In no way can Kokoschka's *Mein Leben* (*My Life*) qualify as a reliable biographical source, even though he was unquestionably trying to achieve the definitive interpretation of his life with this autobiography. This role instead belongs to his rich prose, which becomes apparent in that his narrative prose and life stories often get mixed in his, at times, highly literary work. In addition, *Mein Leben*, along with his other writings, confirms what the richness of his self-portraits says: Oskar Kokoschka, the multi-talented one, was capable of nearly everything – except self-awareness. Incidentally, Kokoschka freely admitted to art historian Werner Schmalenbach in March 1970 that his autobiography contained 'part real, part imaginary events and anecdotes', 'because I have no sense of the past any more than a notion of the future. I live in the moment'.[4]

With the title *Mein Leben*, Kokoschka naturally signals that art was contained in this life, even that 'Leben' ('life') in this context is the name for a lifelong creative work: the opus as life and the life as opus.

In the following pages, we examine 'man in his contradiction' (C F Meyer): in Kokoschka's case, the expressive Modernist, anti-conventionalist and at the same time avant-garde traditionalist; the emphatic pedagogue and critic of all things institutional; the exultant bound to his homeland; the opponent of all things ideological and yet one who, in exile, could take some pleasure from Soviet Communism, even if from afar; the colour virtuoso who decorated his studio in black during a very specific life crisis. We will show how this once iconoclastic and starving artist became a wealthy citizen of the world, but one who remained awake to artistic and political questions, and that, as a 'Lenin among artists', as he once referred to himself after 1919, Kokoschka understood how to derive his own style from the great, even overwhelming, artistic traditions while rejecting the abstract.

One could be tempted to precisely reconstruct the specific day or month or year in Kokoschka's life that encapsulates this so-called microhistory. But that would not do justice to this artist. It would be too forced, too contrived. What's more, it would have the appearance of wanting to compete with the photographs we have of Kokoschka in all manner of situations. After Pablo Picasso, he may have been the most photographed artist of his generation. One will also have to query what role this desire to be photographed had as part of a self-portrayal to which *Mein Leben* naturally belongs as well. Because someone who placed such importance on appearances, whether paired with 'insight' or not, also understood something of wanting to be seen – the vision of oneself.

Kokoschka was an artist of his time, and this biography takes account of this fact. At the same time, he stood out – not only because of his physical height but in terms of his artistic range, which included plays and stories as well as essays on art and politics. So many of these are 'untimely meditations' on Modernism, to use Nietzsche's famous phrase. Kokoschka was an artist who used his brush and pen to work against the tide if necessary – as every so often it was. Never afraid of spelling out uncomfortable truths about his time and artistic trends, Kokoschka should be seen as a rebel, if not a radical, who cherished nothing more than acquiring, and testing, new perspectives in all aspects of life and art.

Yet the term 'untimely modernist' also means that he was an artist of his century, full of contradictions and paradoxes. For the biographer, this raises possibilities and problems that exemplify the nature of Oskar Kokoschka's life's work and work life. They begin with the question of what criteria art uses to define 'Modernism', how the young Expressionist revealed himself in his middle period and whether the work of his later years recanted this original impetuous Modernism. Despite the burdens of ill-health (he was twice badly wounded during the First World War), Kokoschka managed to reach a near-biblical age. How did the length and breadth of his life impact his art? Must one view the work of his older years as traditionalist, or does it mirror a type of tradition that he built up over time through his work and passed on to innumerable students?

When considering the broader context of Kokoaschka's work in

Vienna's Modernism, there is the striking example of a highly acclaimed artist who, towards the end of his life, raised questions about his own work with its unintended radicalism, yet in the end created something never seen before. This refers to a fictional character, the unseen protagonist in the play *Der Tod des Tizian* (*The Death of Titian*) by the young Hugo von Hofmannsthal. Familiar with the hopes and machinations of the powerful, this ageing radical renaissance artist breaks with all convention in young Vienna and bets it all on his last card, thus risking his artistry. By contrast, Kokoschka continued to enjoy painting them – the mighty – in portraits. One has to ask what this incessant preoccupation with portraiture meant. Did it suggest a particular conception of humanist thought in Kokoschka, or was he merely siding with the 'political influencers' of his time?

Moreover, how was his criticism of abstraction – which became ever more prominent in Kokoschka's work after 1945 (comparable to that of the young painter and novelist Günter Grass, even) – to be understood and valued? After all, at some point, the thesis arose that avant-garde and abstraction are not only allies but are, in fact, dependent upon each other. Was it, too, a dogma, like that of the musical avant-garde with its atonality and literary Modernism with its broken inner monologue, speaking on over each other on stage, renunciation of a plotline and breakdown of lyrical materials? Asking these questions about Oskar Kokoschka is to move them into another light, specifically into persistent humanism, because Kokoschka continually questioned whether the abstract could be humanist or only represented a recent betrayal of the classics and thus man's visible inheritance.

Whoever considers this artist cannot avoid the complex doll, the life-sized anthropomorphic (or rather, *Alma-morphic*) egg that the artist laid in his own life and in future studies about him. In an age of discourse about gender, how does one treat the situation in which, after his separation from Alma Mahler, Kokoschka commissioned an Alma doll? Is it a crass case of a fetishised substitute love object – a doll he could caress and, in the end, decapitate? This question also raises (oppressive) reservations in the treatment of Kokoschka, the self-confessed humanist.

In the monumental Prophyläen project, *Die Kunst des 20. Jahrhunderts* (*Art of the 20th Century*, 1926), Carl Einstein calls him a 'two-sided talent'.[5] Furthermore:

A painter who restlessly drifts between original idea, particular emotional interpretation and ancient heritage; who occasionally epigonically satisfies inner overwhelmingness, entering in an almost conscious contest with the great masters and tries to rejuvenate the ancient riches of representation through novel sensibility.[6]

Einstein was even more explicit when he called Kokoschka a 'complicated talent' that enchants 'many undecided minds' 'because it comprises their foremost chaos and the restless inadequacy of the period.'[7]

And yet, what a body of work to be reviewed and considered! How rich his peculiarities, how impressive this ability to which genius was attributed early on, whether one felt it genuine, self-declared or a pretension-laden talent. One perceived Kokoschka's artistic faculty, thus, as an oeuvre which according to all evident influences seemed to be resolutely self-explanatory. Oskar Kokoschka – an Austrian from Bohemia on the sea of colourful surf, an artist for whom the creation of worlds around people's self-determination was a matter of intuition and common sense, a self-declared European humanist among artists of the modern movement – he and his work continue to be part of a lasting fascination.

So how should one construct a picture of an artist who so thoroughly understood how to portray himself and loved to be *photographed* (and it is worth emphasising the literal meaning of this word, *photos graphein*: 'writing in light' or 'written in light'), to be sketched? Could our picture of Oskar Kokoschka be more than the sum of all extant pictures of him? Or should it present something else, offering a different perspective of him?

As described, our subtitle employs the notion of 'untimeliness' as a measure of Kokoschka's personality and the character of his work. There is something exemplary about this vivid body of work and, at the same time, something unsettling, disturbing, reflecting a lifelong restlessness, which he was only able to put aside at the shores of Lake Geneva – or so it seems judging from his late paintings of that magic landscape that inspired so many, from Lord Byron, Percy and Mary Shelley to Nabokov.

Kokoschka was an artist of many things, most notably of the human face. For what interested him in respect of facial expressions was what these faces, including his very own, had had to 'face' in terms of personal fate and drastic features of their times. Kokoschka created in colour and form; he was a painter, a dramatist and narrator of the highest order, a (cultural) political author, essayist and autobiographer (one who understood how to record his life), and an important pedagogue as well. The most obvious of tasks suggests itself: to examine the interrelationships, the interdependence among these art forms – both in terms of content and stylistically. Had it not overburdened the subtitle of this book, it would also have included the word 'European', as his humanistic self-awareness was grounded in the depths (and abysses) of European consciousness, which did not stand in the way of Kokoschka's worldwide impact. Precisely because he admitted his middle-European roots throughout his life, he could be convincingly cosmopolitan.

Kokoschka referred to his multiple talents as his creative capital, as did Ernst Barlach, Wassily Kandinsky, Max Beckmann, Ludwig Meidner and Alfred Kubin. The relative proximity of literature and painting as demonstrated by Max Dauthendey ('a violet rain falls in the distance in an apricot-golden evening haze')[8] periodically alternates with the symbiosis of literature and music shaped by Wagner and Wagnerism. This closeness was found in verbal graphic symbols or poetic feasts of colour, in the rapture of colour adjectives. Barlach's early dramatic work – particularly in his drama *Der Tote Tag* (*The Dead Day*), which was published by Paul Cassirer in Berlin in 1912 with twenty-seven lithographs and premiered seven years later in Leipzig – has a thematic overlap with Kokoschka, even if it has a different emphasis; the son is unable to reconcile with his father, who remains invisible because the mother proves too dominant. Kokoschka, on the other hand, was haunted by a fatherhood denied to him. In Barlach's drama, as with Kokoschka, the 'murderer's hand' may strike at any time, yet in the end turns on itself when both mother and son die by suicide.[9]

In contrast to the contemporaries mentioned above, Kokoschka also had an impressive command of political theory and its history – from the social utilitarianism of one Jeremy Bentham to the problems of state sovereignty. No other artist of his stature was able to comment on political developments with such expertise. It should not come as a surprise to find in his political writings as early as 1935 the thesis that the totalitarian state 'which does not know the term human, only that of subject; its purpose, its *Lebensraum*, must lead to total war.'[10] Kokoschka's non-partisan political commitment was deeply anchored in humanistic principles. (We will return to the reasons he underestimated or did not want to examine Stalinism later.) From an aesthetic perspective, humanism and his total body of artwork converge in his convictions as a result of what one might call his education of the senses. The activation of the five senses and the development of sensual perception seemed to him to be most likely guaranteed through the interrelationship of art forms.

The entire creative approach of Kokoschka's work derived from the desire to express himself. Collage, in the mode of Kurt Schwitters, was not his thing, even if both artists identified with the magazine of Expressionism, *Der Sturm*, first published in 1910. To understand what Kokoschka did *not* wish, then, Schwitters' aesthetic principle is cited here.

> My goal is an all-embracing art form that brings together all forms of art into creative unity. I have pasted words and sentences together into poems in such a way that the order evolves into a rhythmic sketch. Conversely, I have pasted pictures and drawings on which sentences are meant to be read. I have hung pictures so that a sculptural relief develops in addition to the image effect. I did this to blur the boundaries of different art forms.[11]

Kokoschka, too, had expectations that were orientated around the all-embracing art form, but not through surrealistic parody. Pasting or nailing pieces together insulted his notion of creative imagination. The interplay of shapes and colours, their musical origins, rather than the blurring of boundaries, were much more important to him. Of course, Kokoschka in no way ruled out that his paintings could be 'read' and that his plays could also be visual events.

Being *en route* to becoming an artist of an untimely and Modernist nature means, in the first instance, a journey to a particular vision which manifests itself in Kokoschka's painting and which is intended to encourage and train the observer's gaze rather than steer it in any particular direction. This vision requires an engagement in the interplay of poetry and painting, portraiture and dialogue, the musical transformation of colour and critical aesthetic-political discourse. It also means allowing the places where this artist lived and worked to have an influence on his art. If you open yourself to examining the epic phenomenon called 'Kokoschka', you will learn much about the times in which he lived and his relationship to them.

Being *en route* as a way of life; Kokoschka was himself a migrant, like his great role model, the 17th-century educator and thinker Jan Amos Komenský, or Comenius, until he arrived in Villeneuve in 1953. We will have to determine whether and how his artistic style, together with his attitude to life, changed while on this journey. We will look at the artist Oskar Kokoschka's points of origin, places he lived and destinations he sought: Pöchlarn, Vienna, Berlin, Dresden, Prague, London, Salzburg and even Lake Geneva. We will need to shine a light on his portraits of people and animals together with those of cities and landscapes – and the associated doubts he had about the purpose of abstraction.

He was *en route* to becoming an artist who was an avant-gardist and considered a left-wing rebel even while in exile, yet who understood how to represent institutions – he was president of the Free German League of Culture in London during the Second World War, for example – and who had an (artistic) interest in the faces of the more or less powerful in politics and society, which is to say the physiognomy of power. Did he become a cultural conservative after 1945? Or did his concept for a School of Seeing, which he was able to put into practice at his Salzburg Academy, retain a subversive radicality that could be traced back to Max Imdahl's concept of a pure or 'seeing vision' and, in the Modern Era, to Alfred Lichtwark's deliberations about art history, also valued by Franz Kafka?[12] Is the description 'modern' appropriate in his case, or did his Modernism revert to restorative traditionalism? Did Kokoschka become captivated by the 'superstition of timelessness', to use Adorno's phrase, or did he remain a secessionist his entire life?

He was continually *en route*, but to where? So many different places would impact him. Looking at this artist's life can only ever be retrospective, no matter how hard one may try to occasionally use the present tense in order to bring him to life and declare him a contemporary. Nearly everything in the work of Oskar Kokoschka's life appears to be logically consistent, despite all the twists and turns and the seeming contradictions. However, that is the danger particular to biographies, that they suggest a logical sequence, with one thing simply leading to another. And yet, one knows no life proceeds in that way. It is rare enough to recognise turning points in one's own life. It is even rarer that before, during and after particular decisions, one has all the options available and understands that one either had a choice or did not. Even a creative person has phases of idleness that do not appear in any biography – periods of doubt and despair that only become tangible in the overcoming of them. One searches not for the logical and conclusive in a life, but rather the colourful, diverse and unexpected, particularly in the case of Oskar Kokoschka. As with Russian dolls, much is hidden in the life of this artist – one object of interest inside another – and yet he was able to live his life and continue his work by creating a vision of life in each painting, to equip it with eyes, because his most important works, *Der Mandrill* (*The Mandrill*) unquestionably among them, also observe the observer; no, they penetrate him, will not release him, follow him. These pictures keep us in their sight until we have learned to view them and everything else in a new way. What applies to Kokoschka's efforts also applies to what is known about his life: he created not just an engaged, but an engaging, art. That is what this study hopes to be: a journey towards an exceptional artist, however twisted, though not unfathomable, the path may be.

1

The Journey

En Route to a Life's Beginning

Kokoschka's beginnings in Pöchlarn in the Mostviertel on the south bank of the Danube, the place where he was born on 1 March 1886, remained important to him; in 1936 he wrote: 'My cradle stood [...] in the Bechelaren [i.e., Pöchlarn] of the Nibelungen, known to be the guardians of the Rhein treasure, the golden ones. When I was born, however, there were only devalued gulden receipts in the state treasury, which is why I learned early on to be independent and to work for my livelihood'.[1] This is a classic Kokoschka sentence, as he alludes to the historic-mythic past, slightly ridiculing it, associating it with contemporary problems (the relative monetary devaluation following the financial crisis in the 1870s with the loss of the state's gold reserves) and making it personal. The reference is to the 26th and 27th adventures of the *Nibelungenlied* (*Song of the Nibelungs*) in which the Nibelung kings and their entourage arriving from Worms are received as guests at the court of the Margrave Rüdiger. Together they will move on to Vienna, where Kriemhild will marry the Hun king, Etzel, only to then be killed in Gran (today, Esztergom). Pöchlarn was that little idyll of mythical chivalry before the catastrophe. Nearby, incidentally, is Artstetten Castle, which houses the tomb of Archduke Franz Ferdinand and his wife, the victims of Sarajevo, to whose philistine manner in matters of art the young Kokoschka, in turn, almost fell victim. But more on that later.

Oskar K only spent the first year of his life in Pöchlarn at 29 Regensburger Strasse; however, this was long enough for him to later mythologise his birthplace in an authentic, clearly rustic accent of his native region, especially in later television interviews. His father, Gustav Josef Kokoschka (1840–1923), who came from a Prague family with a long-standing goldsmith tradition, worked as a travelling clock salesman for a local jeweller. After Prague, the provincialism of Pöchlarn must have been difficult for him. Presumably, the family was in a holding pattern until Gustav – who, given his family tradition, must have considered himself in social decline – could find a better-paid job in Vienna. Nothing more specific, though, can be said on this – only that which Kokoschka comments on in his autobiography (ML, 39 f.). The kindest thing that Oskar K later said of his father appears in a letter to his mother on 27 July 1918 when he was visiting his convalescing son in Dresden: 'I admire [father's] mental freshness and his lively interest in everything and his memory. I prefer him as a companion to all my acquaintances here because he is so human.'²

Josef's parental home in Prague's Brentegasse 'with workshop and shop', should Oskar K have looked it up during his first visit to the capital of Bohemia, was that of a well-to-do patrician. Oskar's grandfather, Václav Kokoska, born 1810, arrived in Prague as a twenty-six-year-old goldsmith originally from the village of Racineves, about 65 kilometres northwest of Prague. In Prague, he married Therese Josefa Schütz, daughter of a local goldsmith. Kokoschka's father was born of this marriage in 1840. It must have been decided early on that he, too, would belong to the Guild of Goldsmiths. Oskar Kokoschka's future father-in-law Karel B Palkovsky was familiar with genealogical research and sought out these connections. Apparently, he wanted to know exactly to whom he was entrusting his very young daughter.

When Kokoschka discovered a picture in the Prague National Gallery of a goldsmith in his workshop, painted by Quido Manes (1828–1880) in the manner of Carl Spitzweg in 1861, he believed himself to be standing in front of a portrait of his grandfather Václav. The Kokoschkas were unquestionably respectable and so suitable subjects for portraiture. In fact, the composers Antonín Dvořák and František Smetana were guests in the Kokoschkas' town house in the Brentegasse, and father and grandfather helped with the restoration of the gothic St Wenceslas Chapel on the Hradčany, which illustrates their importance as craftsmen. Economic difficulties, the impact of the Vienna Stock Exchange crash of 1873 and the Bosnia Crisis after 1878 forced Gustav Kokoschka to sell his Prague family home and dissolve the business. But his appreciation for fine craftsmanship, which would soon be revealed in his second-born son, proved to be an enduring paternal legacy. In an article in the *Neuen Freien Presse* (*New Free Press*) on 28 August 1898, Adolf Loos soberingly observed: 'The public does not want a proud tradesman.' His thesis was that the real, undistorted can only be found in craftsmanship. For this he offered an ideal: 'The English brought us their wallpapers [...] Those are wallpapers not ashamed to be made of paper.' In other words, the English are no parvenus. 'Even his clothing is made of sheep's wool and unashamably so. If the leadership in fashion were left to the Viennese, we would weave this sheep's wool like velvet and satin.' Being a parvenu, then, is all about appearances. The young Kokoschka would soon set about demystifying this. Incidentally, it is worth noting that just after the First World War even *the* great anglophile of Vienna Modernism, Hugo von Hofmannsthal, emphasised *The Importance of Our Arts and Crafts to Reconstruction* (*Die Bedeutung unseres Kunstgewerbes für den Wiederaufbau*, 1919) in a lecture to the members of the Austrian Association of Craftsmen, and claimed that the applied arts had a role to play in creating identity, which in his opinion should moderately orientate itself against Otto Wagner's rejection of ornamentation on buildings.[3]

So, what did Kokoschka receive from his mother? Maria Romana (1861–1934), née Loidl, came from the deepest provinces, the Lower Austrian Hollenstein in the Ybbs Valley. It would appear she gave her son an interest in his native home, meaning a sense for the unadorned, simple and unpretentious. She insisted on the practical. Incidentally, she was likely to have found the somewhat larger Pöchlarn quite pleasant in contrast to Hollenstein. It is certainly significant that after her death in Vienna (which remained alien to her all her life) in 1934, both of her sons Oskar and Bohuslav (1892–1976) had her body transported back to Hollenstein, at considerable expense, for burial in a chapel built just for her in the mountain cemetery. Near-civil war-like conditions dominated in Austria the year that Maria died. She must have been particularly distressed when the government troops of the Engelbert Dollfuß regime opened fire on the Viennese working-class neighbourhood. In the month of her funeral, a coup by the Austrian National Socialists was thwarted, though Dollfuß fell victim to it. He was assassinated in the Office of the Federal Chancellor on 25 July 1934. As far as the First Republic was concerned, it now found itself on the edge of a Nibelungen-like ruin.

Where and under what circumstances Gustav Kokoschka and Maria Loidl met remains unknown. The extraordinary talent of their son Oskar must have also remained a mystery to them. At least his mother appeared to have admired him unreservedly, seeing him as a gift from God. In those petit bourgeois circumstances, one was accustomed to accept matters as gifts in whatever form they came. Two photographs handed down through the family show two people who could not have been more different: the father with an imposing beard and positively elegant appearance; the mother, withdrawn, seemingly shy, with a countrified round face, far from the feminine ideal of her time. They appeared to have borne the sorrow of their first child's early death together. Despite all that may be said, they encouraged their three children each in their individual way, and gave them a feeling of safety and security, even if the travelling salesman father, who in selling clocks might have appeared to little Oskar as dealing in time, was absent all too often.

The family name, *Kokoschka*, does not just sound Slavic; as КУКУШКА, *kukuschka*, it actually means *the cuckoo* in Russian. Indeed, in an early letter in which he – intentionally or not – falsely gave the year of his birth as 1887, Kokoschka referred to purported 'Russian ancestors' (Br I, 10).

One of Maria Loidl's brothers had a lumber mill near Pöchlarn. A devastating fire raged in the small town the night following Oskar's birth, which he later associated with the fire of Troy. A scar on his right hand, blamed on a glowing ember, ostensibly bore witness to this fire, as did his surprising admission: 'I love fire above all else' (ML, 41).

One of the four pre-Socratic elements, Promethean fire, was therefore placed in his crib and thus impressed the Nietzschean motto 'live dangerously' upon him. Birth and death practically joined in the supposed Pöchlarn fire catastrophe of Nibelungen – apocalyptic proportions on the night of 1 to 2 March 1886, in itself curious enough. At that point, in remote Sils Maria, Nietzsche had written:

I know whence I originate!
Like a flame insatiate
I anneal me and consume.
Light grows all that I conceive,
Embers everything I leave:
Certainty is I am flame.

This theme of beacon or fire sign would be reprised in his *Dionysos-Dithyramben* (*Dionysus-Dithyrambs*): 'My soul is itself a flame, / Insatiable for a few distances / Blazes upwards, upwards you still glow.' Since then, however, it has been proven that Kokoschka constructed a more than characteristic legend in order to be able to provide a point of origin for his later favourite colour, red.[4]

Vienna, the imperial capital, was only 100 miles in the near distance. Just one year after Oskar's birth, the family moved from Pöchlarn into the monarchy's centre. The move was overshadowed by the death of the two-and-a-half-year-old firstborn, Gustav. Beyond that, these first years in Vienna provided the Kokoschkas, or at least Oskar, with a rather idyllic period at the edge of the city where nothing but labyrinthine gardens, meadows and fields awaited the boy. Oskar K experienced the first intellectual imprinting at Währing's state secondary modern school which, unusually for its time in particular, offered modern foreign languages, something he drew from his entire life. Two teachers there were especially demanding of him: Johann Schober, the drawing instructor who saw the future artist in his pupil, and Dr Leon Kellner, of a rabbinical family from Czernowitz and former President of the Austrian Shakespeare Society, to whom Kokoschka owed his 'preference for England' (ML, 43). The teaching materials included

the *Illustrated London News*, which among other things had an essay
on the latest archaeological excavations with a picture of a half-naked
Aphrodite statue. In retrospect Kokoschka commented: 'Had I understood as a child that the Greeks worshipped goddesses, I would surely
have become a pious pagan and not a tepid Christian. That is how
my love for antique art awoke as a sensual experience' (ML, 44).
Kellner seems to have rated Oskar K particularly highly, as emerges
from a letter the pupil wrote to his teacher in December 1905, which
equally reveals a remarkable self-assessment: 'I cannot yet accept your
very kind offer to interest Vienna critics in my work, as I do not feel
ready, too unclear in my desires, to appear in public' (Br I, 5). One year
later, the mutual candour between teacher and pupil had apparently
increased further, as Oskar K felt free enough to write the following.

> I am not entirely satisfied in school presently. I had believed that as
> a specialised student I would be able develop myself entirely accord-
> ing to my wishes and on the basis of my specific inclinations. And
> I now have the feeling that those around us are not particularly
> invested in fostering individuality and allowing it to mature, but
> rather only have an eye toward the school's success and milking the
> system. (Br I, 6)

It may have been around 1898/1899 that the boy chorister Oskar K had,
according to him, his first profound, even existential, creative experience. It may have been partially responsible for his later placing such
great value on the interplay between the arts and their impact on the
development of the senses. In the Piarist Church Maria Treu in Vienna's Josefstadt, at whose organ Anton Bruckner delivered his practical
composition exam with bravura, the pubescent Oskar K felt literally
overwhelmed by the ceiling mural by Franz Anton Maulbertsch, the
master of Austrian late Baroque from Langenargen on Lake Con-
stance. It depicts the admission of Maria into heaven, wherein the con-
voluted figures, the fluidity of the representation and the emphasis on
colour over shape may have been the pivotal impression.

In one fell swoop of mild self-dramatisation Kokoschka combined the memory of this moment with being overwhelmed by his voice breaking – and 'in the middle of a solo in a mass by Mozart' to boot (ML, 46).

Vocal change with a play of colours; the ability to sing had deserted him, but not the ability to hear, even with his eyes, as Nietzsche once demanded. And, thus, the comprehensive School of Seeing had begun for him. In addition, he showed an interest in the elements and, thus, in chemistry. 'Originally I even wanted to study chemistry at one time because curiosity urged me to penetrate the world of cells, molecules, organic and inorganic matter, in the secrets of nature in a Faustian way' (ML, 45). But the teacher of natural sciences dissuaded him of this attempt to compare it with Faust. He had his above-mentioned drawing instructor Schober, who had recognised the extraordinary talent or even 'special inclination' of his pupil, to thank for a state stipend to study at the School of Decorative Arts. An unsuccessful applicant was supposedly named Adolf H. Particularly during his London exile, Kokoschka is supposed to have been preoccupied with this unverifiable situation in the form of a sense of (actual or feigned) guilt, as passed on by Elias Canetti.

[...] I hadn't been with him even half an hour, when he came out with a guilt that was monstrous: He was to blame for the war, for the fact that Hitler, who had actually wanted to become an artist, became a politician. Both, Oskar Kokoschka and Hitler, competed for the same stipend at the Vienna Academy. Kokoschka was accepted; Hitler turned away. Had Hitler been accepted instead of Kokoschka, he would never had gotten into politics; there would have been no National Socialist Party; war would not have broken out. In other words, Kokoschka was to blame for the war. He said this almost imploringly, with much more emphasis than he usually used; he also repeated it several times; came back to it in the course of the conversation, which had eventually turned to other things; and I had the disconcerting impression that he put himself in Hitler's position.[5]

A peculiar scene, even if one does not necessarily want to concur with Canetti's analysis. It once again demonstrates how psychologically entwined some victims felt with the primary perpetrator of this ideologically led, unique catastrophe of civilisation. The outstanding parallel case would be Thomas Mann's essay, fiercely debated in exile circles, from early 1939, *Ein Bruder* (or *Bruder Hitler*) (*A Brother* or *Brother Hitler*), in which he compares the 'Manipulation Principle' in art and politics and comes to the conclusion that a highly embarrassing relationship exists between an artist and a politician working with the means of the aesthetics of power. It was pointed out, however, that in any case the young Hitler would have likely read the scathing art critiques in the Viennese arts pages whose vocabulary would provide him with the catch words for the 'Verfolgung der Moderne' ('Persecution of the Modernist Movement') a quarter-century later.[6]

In contrast to Stefan Zweig, his senior by five years, Kokoschka did not later view the time prior to the First World War and the turn of the century as a 'world of security'.[7] He instead saw the upheavals as due to industrialisation, the lack of any sound financial policy at the time and the end of (arts and) crafts through the accelerated finishing processes in factories. Kokoschka's thesis that pre-war Austria represented a 'culture commonwealth' that took place in schools – the combination of multi-ethnic students and teaching staff – was similar to Zweig's view. 'Actually, I came to know my world in my modest secondary school in Währing in Vienna as well as a schoolboy in England at the same time learned of foreign continents where his parents administered colonies' (ML, 46).

1906 was the year the twenty-year-old Oskar K discovered the art of Japanese woodcuts[8] and, in the family of his maternal uncle Anton Loidl in the Lower Austrian Lassing, models for his awakening interest in portraiture. The portrait sketches created there in June 1906 of this family of chamber musicians only hint at musical instruments and notes, but it is these particular subtle suggestions which lend the portrait studies a discrete tone. This occurs most impressively in the study *Bauer Kupfer, vulgo Blachl* (*Farmer Kupfer, commonly known as 'Blachl'*), which shows a musician blowing the bass flugelhorn and makes his playing somewhat audio-visual. These studies, possibly together with his early Maulbertsch impression, prefigure what Kokoschka would produce in completed form in his 1920 created work *Die Macht der Musik* (*The Power of Music*).

Distortions and ripple effects – such things are easier to claim than definitively prove. Whatever is having a subliminal impact on the artist, what shapes him, only shows up from case to case, most acutely in the respective evolving work, but even then only in some aspects. For example, what does it mean that Kokoschka received his training at an applied arts school, and consequently associated himself with the Wiener Werkstätte, the equivalent of the Arts and Crafts Movement of William Morris? His instructor Carl Otto Czeschka had recognised the exceptional talent of his pupil Kokoschka and recommended him to Josef Hoffman at the Wiener Werkstätte. Together they worked against the spirit of the *l'art-pour-l'art* movement and demonstrated the practical meaning of art, its utility and most particularly its foundation in craftsmanship. Kokoschka produced painted postcards until 1908/1909, similarly stickers, fans, posters, book covers and illustrations, even *ex-libris* designs. The young artist gained great advantages through these manual skills – detailed knowledge of materials and technical processes – though he was able to break away from them in decisive, creatively inspired moments. Unlike many other fellow campaigners in these institutions, he did not remain entangled in the material. Consequently, it is apparent that Kokoschka's early portraits, such as the musician from Lassing, show no influence of the Werkstätte, though the illustrations for *Die träumenden Knaben* (*The Dreaming Boys*, 1907/1908), which Gustav Klimt deemed 'worthy of veneration', do. Fritz Waerndorfer (1868–1939), the cotton magnate and patron of the arts who was brought together with the Vienna Secessionists Josef Hoffmann, Gustav Klimt and Koloman Moser by Hermann Bahr, financed the founding of the Wiener Werkstätte and commissioned this storybook. Kokoschka later explained that this was about a coded love letter to his fellow student Lilith Lang (1891–1952). It was to become his first self-contained piece of graphic art. Also, for the first time, a love affair appeared in his work. When *Die träumenden Knaben* was published (1908), though, this relationship had already ended. It is worth dwelling a bit on this dream, which Kokoschka called a 'free picture composition' (ML, 52).

Who is dreaming what here? Not so much a boy as a twenty-one-year-old of love's temptations, more precisely of 'Li', at the very least one who 'recognised' himself and his body: 'and I fell down and dreamed of love' (DSW I, 11).[9] Exaggerations belong to this poetic fantasy: 'first I was the dancer of kings / in the thousand-stepped garden I danced the wishes of the sexes' (ibid); Kokoschka did not yet know Else Lasker-Schüler, but her *Nächte der Tino von Bagdad* (*The Nights of Tino from Baghdad*) was familiar with related 'dances'. But, to continue with Kokoschka's increasingly ecstatic poetry:

> danced the thin spring bushes
> before you Li
>   – maid your name tinkles like silver foil –
>   stepped out of the falls of cinnabar flowers
>   and yellow sulphur stars
> out of the spice gardens
> I already knew you and awaited you
>   on blue evenings upon my silver blanket
> out of the tangled bird forests of the north
>   and from the lakes of the red fish of the south
> I sensed you coming
> felt the gesture of the angular twist of your young body
> and understood the dark words of your skin
> (DSW I, 12; Mitchell, 4–5)

Atmospherically this poem is related to that of Richard Dehmel's *Verklärte Nacht* (*Transfigured Night*), which became the seminal atmospheric piece of the turn of the century when Arnold Schönberg set it to music (1902). However, Dehmel allowed himself far fewer word experiments. His poetry also did not have the daring verbal imagery which the young Kokoschka risked. This self dreams of approaching the 'young girl Li', yet then flees again 'into the gardens'. The line '[I] felt the gesture of the angular twist of your young body' is noteworthy with respect to the interlinking of visual and poetic works. This is where the poet Kokoschka interweaves an aesthetic principle of the trainee artist with the text; the 'angular' of the girl's boyish body is consistent with the beauty ideal of the Belgian artist George Minne, whom the young Kokoschka greatly admired.[10] Fifteen-year-old Lilith modelled for his nude studies at the time, when she often posed sleeping under veils. A youthful desire is expressed in this poem – and in the associated feverish dream pictures – which is hymn-like in its characteristic poetic language. Kokoschka's lithographs accompanying his Jugendstil piece provide visual counterparts. Hans Maria Wingler judges appropriately: 'Broad, melodically vibrating outlines encompass an entire archipelago of colour islands and allow tender figures of young boys and girls to rise like blossoms in a paradisical landscape.'[11]

Equally revealing here is the circumstance in which the poem's self makes dancing with the beloved its own. The athletic Lilith with her narrow Madonna-like face had subscribed to free dance, presumably influenced by Grete Wiesenthal, whom her brother was seeing at the time (they later married in 1910). In addition, Kokoschka designed a skirt with a black-and-white pattern for Lilith for one of her performances in arts and craft student circles. Lilith, in any event, was a bit of a story in herself. Kokoschka recalls she liked to wear a 'red, peasant-weave skirt such as people were not used to seeing in Vienna. Red is my favourite colour. I was in love with the girl' (ML, 52). The question must be asked: in love with the girl or the skirt or its red colour? Peter Altenberg, the pathological lover of girls, worshipped Lilith Lang and warned her of the 'super rascal' Kokoschka, whom he referred to as 'Herr K'. One may speculate whether this warning contributed to the ending of this relationship. The point was that Lilith Lang was supposed to marry the youngest son of the Ringstraße architect Emil von Förster soon thereafter, whilst Kokoschka became the best friend of Adolf Loos, the architect of Viennese Modernism and the sharpest critic of Ringstraße architecture. Vienna around 1910 thus presented itself as an almost incestuous network in almost every domain, with consequences for world culture.

En Route to Scandal: In the Name of Art

Kokoschka found Vienna constraining early on – very constraining. 'I can't stand it here any longer,' he wrote in a letter in the winter of 1907/1908, 'it is all so rigid, as if one had never heard an outcry. All relationships have such a dead, calculated predetermined course, and the people are all such incredible outcomes of their ilk, like marionettes [...]' (Br I, 7). He continues, 'I can't get out of the persistent narrow tension, I am often so hollow that I scream into the clenched duvet just to do something real' (Br I, 7). And three years before Jakob von Hoddis observed how 'the hat [flies] from [the citizen's] pointed head' in his poem *Weltende* (*End of the World*), the young Kokoschka described the surreal dimensions of bourgeois society more precisely: 'Hats stroll 175–186 cm above the ground and 15 cm below that clothes that drape as though alive and where it appears these drapes are all from the same monotonous theatre act, and I buy myself a false red beard between hat and clothing to disrupt this pathetic drapery theatre' (Br I, 7).

And yet, Kokoschka's craft proficiency and technical knowledge garnered him public attention in that occasionally oppressively restrictive Vienna. This good fortune stretched from designs and woodcuts to the making of fans. He would attain mastery in both fields. One might suppose the mere hand-colouring of glass slides of Vienna attractions might also have been in this mix. Today the originals are treated as precious objects because they capture an authentic look at the Vienna of the pre-war decade – the 'world of yesterday in colour'.[12]

A slide from 1913 is particularly characteristic. It shows the view from the Urania down on to the Franz-Josefs-Quay with the worn Aspernbrücke, a piece of discarded bridge-building history along the Danube Canal, whilst the foreground is determined by the new Franzensbrücke, where the two iron bridge spans project, or rather thrust themselves, into the picture like symbols of the technological modern movement.[13]

How often must the young Oskar K have crossed this bridge and gone along the quay with his long stride, following the Schottengasse and the other labyrinthine alleys of the First District? He would not have appeared lanky, and dandyish, more likely powerful, of substantial body size, usually well dressed, with the all-domineering face that rose from the wing collar. A photograph aptly shows Oskar K in the summer of 1909 as described: a half-veiled look due to a lazy left eyelid, an almost shaved head (supposedly why Vienna high society considered him a criminal) which lets his equally-high-as-wide forehead appear more prominent – an impressive twenty-three-year-old seemingly determined and dreamy, self-assured and pensive, while also scary as though something dark were lurking behind this face, which may have been just a mask. He wanted to be seen 'as a marked man' even though he soon would be ordering bespoke suits from Vienna's best gentlemen's tailor, Ebenstein (ML, 85).

What growing unrest fomented behind this face with its seemingly smooth planes? In the young Kokoschka, the material artist and technical reproduction processes expert were in conflict with the impetuous artist who had discovered the sense for the dramatic in himself and the momentum of colour, even forms, that broke new ground in his 1909 *Stilleben mit Ananas* (*Still Life with Pineapple*) – a result of his Van Gogh experience. At this time he was probably reading the writings of the aristocratic anarchist Prince Pjotr A Kropotkin (1842–1921), demonstrably his study *Moderne Wissenschaft und Anarchismus* (*Modern Science and Anarchism*, 1904).[14] In this work, Kropotkin outlines not just the obvious, that knowledge leads to the undermining of tradition, but also that the anarchist teaches the artist, above all else, the 'law of mutual assistance' which is essential for the 'progressive development' of man as well as fauna – a sentence Kokoschka highlights in his copy, in addition to passages criticising the state and its tendency to make political use of the education system. In Kropotkin, Kokoschka also found references to the brother of the poet Georg Büchner, Ludwig, and his deliberations on *Geistesleben der*

Thiere (*The Intellectual Life of Animals*, 1877) as well as on the topic *Liebe und Liebes-Leben in der Thierwelt* (*Love and Love Life in the Animal World*, 1885). We will see how prominently Kokoschka places animals in his paintings. Kropotkin went a step further, which Kokoschka highlighted for himself: the comparative anatomist '[T H] Huxley did not suspect that society [...] had existed among animals long before humans evolved.'[15] Comments such as these must have had a particular impact on the young Kokoschka as he consciously orientated himself along apparently naïve forms, wanting to make the primeval visible in order to confront the excessive refinement of his time. The defamatory label 'super rascal' undoubtedly described the circumstances. Through his art, Kokoschka wanted to become the leader of the 'young wild ones', meaning those who saw unbridled wildness as an anarchic power, of course simultaneously tamed by the sense of form, as primitively as it may have impacted the observer at first.

The years 1908 and 1909 offered Kokoschka two fora, the *Wiener Kunstschau* and the first *Internationale Kunstschau*, through which he was able to gain access to the public and to expert circles who saw in him *the* hope of modern art, among them Emil Orlik, Fritz Waerndorfer, Kolo Moser and Adolf Loos. A comparison of the exhibits with which Kokoschka was represented at both shows indicates the two sides of his swiftly maturing creative persona: in every sense woodcut-like in his prints and drawings, as, for example, *Die Traumtragenden* (*The Bearers of Dreams*) and *Die Baumwollpflückerin* (*The Cotton Picker*) (the latter also being the official poster for the art show at the Wiener Schwarzenbergplatz in 1908), as well as his 1909 pen-and-ink drawings and aquarelles illustrating the prose of *Der weiße Tiertöter* (*The White Animal Slayer*), his nude drawings, a self-portrait in the form of a painted terracotta sculpture and especially the oil portrait *Der Trancespieler* (*The Conjurer* or *Portrait of Ernst Reinhold*, later a great Shakespearean actor and reciter). Particularly noticeable in this portrait are the apparently immobilised, intense blue eyes from which something hypnotic emanates. The roughly painted left hand somewhat distracts the attention, which would otherwise be focused solely on the face and its eyes, while the other hand is merely intimated. The somewhat off-centre mouth tends to make the actor's personality appear more enigmatic than revealing. Another stroke of the brush merely hints at slight blue – that of the eyes and capturing the striking light-blue cravat – which flows around the shoulders and head. The contour of the colour attempts to determine the form – not the other way around. The artist's signature is found prominently in the upper-left half of the painting. It has signal value in the sense of, 'Look here, the great white hope of a new art.'

Kokoschka thematises 'hope' of an entirely different nature in a different, full-blown medium made available to him. This refers to the open-air theatre performance of his pieces *Mörder[,] Hoffnung der Frauen* (*Murder, the Hope of Women*) and *Sphinx und der Strohmann* (*Sphinx and Scarecrow*), staged on the side lines of the *Internationalen Kunstschau* by friends and students at the Kunstgewerbeschule (School of Arts and Crafts). They draw attention to the visual artist as a potentially scandalous dramatist. Even the poster was to thematise the scandal in a paradox manner: 'The man is blood red, that is the colour of life, but he lies dead in the lap of his wife who is white; that is the colour of death' (ML, 64).

Neither piece came about by chance. *Die träumenden Knaben* had prepared the way for them, or at least accompanied them, as did the prose sequence *Der weiße Tiertöter.* The rhapsodic nature of the poetry in *Die träumenden Knaben* was lost in the distinctly dialogue-based *Tiertöter* prose. It could have been called 'I and the Girl', in which the 'self' is reached through the seductive 'Woman in the Moon' – in a dream, of course. The ideal of the poem is never to have to awaken from this dream, in which milk flows like blood, tender devotion and animal desire blend into each other, woman-like children appear and falling in love with a 'nightmare' and copulation with the Moon Lady become possible. The dreamlike intimacy with the girl leads to an exchange of identities. The 'playing girl' says to the dreaming self of the poem: 'I will lay down beside you and do with you what must be done to make you the same as me' (DSW I, 23; Mitchell, 15).

From the perspective of the visual artist, the deformation of the physical, such as the reappearance of the Moon Lady, is of the greatest interest: 'Then she emerged from the water, her arms loaded with me, laid me down on the shore and pressed her fingers into my eyes and shaped my face in the dark earth, in the dust, which in its barrenness, moves love to leave it the mortal remains' (ibid; Mitchell, 15). Conspicuous here is the peculiar manner of articulating a process which could be called the interment of the self through the Moon Lady. The self, buried in this manner, sees his death and undertaker in a dream – or is she actually his murderess? 'Different in essence from me, feverish with expectation, my love-ghost, my soul, no longer bound by any earthly cloak, rose over my own body' (ibid; Mitchell, 15).

How had these forms of poetic expression prepared themselves in Kokoschka? The mystical-visionary of this love fantasy could have originated from a reading of Alfred Mombert's poetry, for example, *Die Schöpfung* (*The Creation*, 1897) or *Der Denker* (*The Thinker*, 1901). Mombert had connections to Prague circles, in particular to author and translator Emanuel Lešehrad. In 1908, Alban Berg set poems by Mombert to music as part of his song compositions Op. 2. It was also the year that Frank Wedekind's *Frühlings Erwachen* (*Spring's Awakening*) was performed at the Deutsche Volkstheater (in the spring) and the erotically loaded Paul Dukas opus *Ariane und Blaubart* (*Ariane and Bluebeard*) played at the Volksoper. Both of these, incidentally, made a significant impression on the young Alban Berg.[16] Or had Kokoschka encountered Richard Dehmel's poetry at that time? The poems *Weib und Welt* (*Woman and World*, 1901), *Lucifer* (1899) or the rhapsody *Die Verwandlungen der Venus* (*The Transformations of Venus*, 1907) come to mind.

As tempting as it might seem to read *Tiertöter* as a psychological study and put the text on the couch for analysis after a fashion, preferably together with the author as virtual analysis patient, that would be misguided. (We will treat Kokoschka's 'Puppe' ('Doll') differently; she will not be spared the couch here.) Also, the question as to whether the author's real dreams are mirrored in *Tiertöter* does not seem useful. The author is playing with pre-Expressionist clichés and rehearsing a verbal register that aims for only one thing: to achieve an intensity of expression and wording, give voice to the outrageous as well as explore euphemistic imagery. Already the title leads to ambiguity as this Self kills no animal, at most scaring away with a toss of a pebble the 'white bird' who seeks his attention. The title is better understood as: the Self kills the inner animal.

Mörder Hoffnung der Frauen, the second edition of which (1907/1916) Kokoschka dedicated to his 'loyal friend, Adolf Loos', seems to be a different case. The provocation, which this text must have represented for the tastes of the time, is intentional. This is not a rowdy berserker venting his fury; rather, in this scene the writer shows how thoroughly he understands poetic symbolism and verbal shock value which are further bolstered by detailed stage directions. They are in no way of epic length, as with Henrik Ibsen or Gerhart Hauptmann, but rather precise and to the point, including 'tower with a large, red iron cage-door' (DSW I, 35; Mitchell, 22) to which the key has gone missing.

It is not the battle of the sexes that is dramatised here, but rather the doom of the sexual. 'Loudly', the 'Woman' declares at the beginning of the scene: '[...] my eye gathers men's exultation, their stammering lust prowls round me like a beast' (DSW I, 35; Mitchell, 22). The 'Man', who is known to be an animal abuser and on whose account a young woman takes her own life 'because he left her a virgin' (Mitchell, 23), reacts to the challenge of her appearance by attempting to ban this female archetype with his glance. The breathless, intensifying sexual tension erupts in duplicate in that the Man has the Woman branded with a hot iron and she cuts him with a knife. One could say this leads to an Amfortas syndrome; the Man cannot live from then on and cannot die. His deliverance is not to be contemplated, even when it seems to him that the Woman is breastfeeding him with his own blood. The need for redemption turns around in the end. Despite his being seriously wounded, the Woman feels 'bound' by the love of this infernal Man (DSW I, 40; Mitchell, 25), until he pulls himself together, fatally touches her and then continues to murder indiscriminately.

One gets the impression of the young Kokoschka trying to discover how far he could go, how much he could stretch the limits of his imagination. Occasional poetic sprinklings are not meant to offset the gruesomeness; rather, they are meant to strengthen the contrast, such as when the 'Second Girl' begins, not by chance: 'Time a-singing, flowers ne'er before seen!' (DSW I, 36; Mitchell, 23).

The second edition grounds the gruesome events in feelings of fear and insecurity ('Who is the stranger who looked on me?'; Mitchell, 31). When the Man finds himself in 'convulsions', he is able to artic-ulate this in a painful song, which in 1916 sounds not just frivolous but rather simply true, particularly in view of the fact that the cast of the piece has been augmented by 'warriors': 'Senseless desire from horror to horror, Insatiable gyration in the void. Labour without birth, sunfall, heaving space' (DSW I, 48; Mitchell, 34). The expres-sion 'labour without birth' had taken on an existential meaning for Kokoschka at this time, to which we will return later.

On 4 July 1909 the public was able to see another piece by Koko-schka at the Freilichttheater, *Sphinx und Strohmann*, with the subtitle 'An Oddity'. Indeed, already the character descriptions left no doubt as to the curious nature of this offering: 'Hugh Avver, a gigantic revolv-ing straw head with arms and legs, carrying a pig's bladder on a string. Herr Indiarubberman, an educated contortionist. Female Soul called "Anima". Death, a normal living person' (DSW I, 54; Mitchell, 40). The 'Female Soul', moreover, appears as a parrot. In comparison to the first piece, *Sphinx und Strohmann* appears harmless, its cleverness only coming to the fore in the revision of 1917. It was the satyr play to *Mörder*, yet twice as long and as talkative as the previous tragedy. This piece even contains a visual artist thesis, which moves *avant la lettre* in the realm of the theatre of the absurd. The contortionist claims: 'The invention of perspective, merely an optical fraud by art historians' (Mitchell, 43). Furthermore, he determines: 'Give lust its head, con-science is dead' (DSW I, 63; Mitchell, 48). Of course, what that meant had yet to be demonstrated for the author. A somewhat subtler inter-pretation of the Sphinx as mythical-allegorical figure was put forth by Egon Friedell. In his 1912 book *Ecce Poeta*, which he dedicated 'to the dear O K', there is the following passage under the header 'The Poet and the Sphinx'.

In the poet we see the wise man, who recognises the Sphinx, meaning: he understands that she is Sphinx and must remain Sphinx. [...] He will not wish to unveil anything more: where there are veils, he will see veils; but he will show exactly where they are and why they are. And we will find a time all the more enlightened, the more riddles she has discovered. But they must be knowingly discovered, not fumblingly, accidentally and in a state of anxiety. That is the path of progress.[17]

Symbol is symbol is symbol – nothing more and nothing less. The culture critic Friedell warns here of overinterpretations, hasty decoding, which Kokoschka must have liked. Seeing what the situation is. The Viennese passions, however, would have been less likely to rise over the piece *Sphinx und Strohmann* than over *Mörder Hoffnung der Frauen* on that summer evening in 1909. From then on, Kokoschka was established as an enfant terrible, as a playwright and designer of frightening posters and illustrations, whether the Pietà poster or drawings for the *Mörder Hoffnung der Frauen* drama in the weekly journal *Der Sturm*. The murderer, with the dagger in his hand and his foot on the woman's body at chest height, unmistakably has the features of the artist; for the avoidance of any doubt, an O K tattoo adorns his left bicep.

2

Determination and Confusion

Additional Contours: An Anticipatory Image with a Rigid Pen

Woodcut-like, chiselled, berserker-like even, apparently ever-ready, with the cry of the decadents on his lips: *'Épater la bourgeoisie!'* ('Shock the bourgeoisie!'), submitting himself to art while immeasurably in love with life, idolised by women – that is how one imagines the young Oskar Kokoschka. He retained this forceful, disarming youthfulness and would enjoy citing and ironising the proclamation *'Épater la bourgeoisie!'* later as well, once civil society was well past being shocked by anything because it had ruined itself and its values in two world wars. The much-vaunted middle-class establishment had failed as an ideologically critical instrument.

As in Goethe's *Wanderjahren* (*Years of Wandering*), Kokoschka paused as a 'man of fifty years' (1936), asking himself how he saw himself. He no longer trusted conditions in his native Austria. Since the autumn of 1934, after the death of his mother, he had lived in Prague, as had his sister Berta Patocková (1889–1960) since 1918. As previously mentioned, it was the city of his father, who was a knowledgeable man and in his early years gave his son Oskar probably the most important gift for his future development in addition to the first paint box: a quadra-lingual edition of *Orbis sensualium pictus*, authored by the aforementioned Moravian theologian and pedagogue Johann Amos Comenius (1592–1670) and first published in 1658. The gift edition was from 1835. Book and author were to become guiding themes in Kokoschka's life and work. Comenius' compendium attempts to impart worldly wisdom through visual instruction. The complete title of the *Orbis pictus* was the key and would become so for Kokoschka: 'all the chief things that are in the world, and of men's employments therein.' This unique primer contained an educational programme culminating in the final entry on 'Humanitas', then translated as 'affability', meaning the ideal 'pleasant and sweet' of mutual friendship, i.e., in*sight* into relationships between people.[1]

But how did Kokoschka view himself? As a victim of his time? As a beneficiary of his art in the end? 'I received the police ban for my play *Mörder, Hoffnung der Frauen* at the same time as my conscription into the World War' (DSW III, 251). That was not quite consistent with historical fact, but perhaps with his mood at that time. Previously, Archduke Franz Ferdinand had been furious about Kokoschka's paintings (his taste in art was somewhat similar to that of the German Kaiser – his Austrian counterpart had none!). As a punishment, the exhibition site was converted into a market hall for vegetables by order of highest authorities.

How did Kokoschka feel when he had to admit to still being the bogey of the middle classes at age fifty? In the First World War, according to his own statement, he had 'not the heart to shoot down supposed enemies unknown to me, instead I saved the lives of several Russians by taking them prisoner, for which I was decorated. I also was shot in the head and stabbed in the lungs. Nevertheless, I did not have the feeling of having accomplished enough for culture and decided to return to my earlier vocation. I painted' (DSW III, 251/252). Consequently, he intermittently built up his 'house of cards in Germany', mostly in Dresden.

The war experience was defining, the injuries almost fatal (more on that later, when we consider a text associated with First World War literature that eclipses some with its naturalistic depictions– and that is saying something).

At fifty, Kokoschka found himself ostracised by Hans Hinkel, the notorious Staatskommissar and 'Reichskulturwalter' ('Keeper of Imperial Culture').[2] The artist responded with cries for a peace education in the style of Comenius. And in his fiftieth year Kokoschka would begin to write a play about this significant intellectual, which would keep him occupied into his seventies. Kokoschka moved into a studio in Prague in the tower wing of the Bellevue, a 'town house' built in the style of the 19th-century Dutch Renaissance, with views of the Vltava, Charles Bridge and Prague Castle.

In his fiftieth year, Kokoschka painted a portrait of the legendary politician and philosopher Thomas G Masaryk in his last months as president of Czechoslovakia. At his country estate in Lány they discussed Comenius and his notion of an education from the bottom up, a humanising of society through the idea of primary education. Masaryk assisted his portraitist in obtaining Czech citizenship (1935), as he did with Heinrich and later Thomas Mann. This, in turn, enabled Kokoschka to engage in political pursuits as the immigration law that was passed by the Czechoslovakian Parliament in June 1935 prohibited immigrant political activity. Incidentally, Kokoschka's portrait of Masaryk was first shown at the Carnegie Institute in Pittsburgh (USA) in October 1936 and was seen as a visual manifesto of a humanist.

In Kokoschka's fiftieth year, the *Prager Tagblatt* provided him with a forum. In addition, the year 1936 saw him as a member of the Czechoslovakian delegation to the Peace Congress in Brussels in September, where he gave a highly regarded speech. He promoted a 'league of international elementary schools', schools with democratic solidarity and of peaceful cooperation under the protection of the League of Nations. It was once again an attempt to translate Comenius into the 20th century and to design an emancipating peace pedagogy against the totalitarianism of the time (DSW IV, 171–189). Surprisingly, he did not assign art a specific role in this. However, he left himself in no doubt over the purpose of artwork. He saw in it the emulation of the 'miracle' of which 'every young girl of the common people is capable at any time: to conjure a life out of nothing'. And further: 'That is why only women and artists have respect for life', whilst 'so called "society" [...] takes an interest in the throttling of humanity' and thus 'indirectly or directly in wars' (DSW III, 255). Yes, he was obviously familiar with his *Faust*, where the women gardeners accompanied by mandolins in the second part sing: 'Then, the temperament of woman / Is so very close to Art'.[3]

He had met her prior to his fiftieth year, the Prague patrician's daughter Oldriska Palkovská, twenty-nine years his junior. He wrote his friend Anna Kallin about Olda: 'She is a well-behaved child, 2 m tall, 20 years old.'[4] He had recognised her in the late autumn of 1934, having first seen her as a six-year-old in Prague. 'You are my bride. We will marry', he is supposed to have said at the time, according to Elias Canetti, 'which the child never forgot'.[5] Canetti, cynically charming as ever, granted her a 'pretty horsey face', though it also 'reminds of one or the other face by Michelangelo'.[6]

Olda addressed her 'O K' formally her entire life and also used only this abbreviation when speaking to him. 'In the year 1941 Olda married me', Kokoschka recorded, leaving no doubt who had taken the initiative.[7] That was three years after their emigration to England, which Olda instigated after she had had sight of seizure lists in the autumn of 1938 (probably through her influential parents) that recorded the names of individuals at risk of deportation after the 'shattering of the Rump of Czechoslovakia' by the National Socialists. Olda became Kokoschka's vital support in the second half of his life. Canetti again: 'There she was, the slender giantess, always looking out for him without ever making the slightest fuss of herself, listened to him respectfully but not fawningly when he spoke to guests, became accustomed to his arabesque style of storytelling which always consisted of parenthetical leaps and in a chaotic manner often contained exceedingly original comments and observations.'[8]

Returning again to the beginnings of this artist's life, and his repeatedly seeing the colour red. What had Kokoschka written in the winter of 1907/1908? He had obtained a false red beard to *disrupt* the pathetic performance of a pleated fashion overdoing it with its hats and dresses. The colour red – signalling lust and passion, danger and death. Kokoschka painted entire bodies in red, for example, the Pietà's dead son (1909), motif for his unsympathetic poster for his play *Mörder Hoffnung der Frauen*. To Erwin Lang, his fellow student and Lilith's brother, Kokoschka mentioned what, for him, was an unsettling childhood experience: 'Through a grisly coincidence, my mother gave birth next to me in my early childhood; the blood made me faint. Ever since I cannot properly interact with people.' This sentence reads more disturbingly, half-cryptically, half-drastically formulated: 'Since then I intend to strike my parents dead or buy myself free' (both quotes: Br I, 9). This must have had to do with the birth of his brother. At the very least, it seems to refer to a primal experience (Kokoschka did not mention it in his autobiography) on which at least some of his fantasies fed. The blood-red of the sibling's birth became the parallel to the fire myth of his own birth night. Seen this way, it was only logical that he took Alma Mahler's (his Almi or Almili) fire-red nightgown (which she disliked anyway because of its colour). According to her, 'from then on he only hung around his studio dressed in it. He received appalled guests and stood in front of the mirror more than in front of his easel.'[9]

However, before Kokoschka found inspiration for such reflective self-examinations, prior to April 1912 and his first encounter with Alma Mahler, he was constantly on the move. Having become restless in Vienna, he made plans and asked his friend Lang: 'Can you go to Java, Persia and Norway with me in three years?' (Br I, 9). First it was Berlin's turn, then came the first trip to Switzerland (1909/1910) and the place that would become his home after exile in England: Montreux, in the canton of Vaud. At Adolf Loos' invitation he painted the portrait of the English chorus girl Bessie Bruce, Loos' ailing lover, in the Grand Hotel of the winter sports resort Les Avants in the Vaud Prealps. She was originally one of the Barrison Sisters, who appeared in the first night club in Vienna, the Casino de Paris, from 1905. With the exception of Bessie, the other sisters all married into financial or real nobility. Loos took pity on her then and made the sojourn in Switzerland possible so she could look for a cure for her dangerous lung disease. In addition, Loos tried to procure local portrait commissions among the wealthy, often unwell guests for his young artist friend. He even persuaded the scientist and ant specialist Auguste Forel, who he was acquainted with and who lived there, to pose for the young genius from Vienna. However, Forel rejected the result and thus also any payment. In such cases – and they were multiplying – Loos acquired his friend's painting. In this way he soon had at his

disposal one of the largest privately held Kokoschka distress collections. Kokoschka saw his subjects' illnesses, penetrated the mundane
facades and gave expression to exactly that scrutiny. Thus, the skull is
already visible in his portrait of the Conte Verona, and the painting of
Victoire de Montesquiou-Fezensac has something of a ghostly appearance, so waxenly transparent appear her face and cleavage. The portrait
of Bertha Eckstein-Diener, the lover of the Viennese doctor Theodor
Beer whose Villa Sangata near Vevey had been built by the Viennese
architect, came out altogether spooky. It became a pattern; homeown-
ers whose houses Loos had designed or arranged offered Kokoschka,
Loos' friend, accommodation for a short while and a portrait commission. Kokoschka presumably allowed himself to be appropriately
accoutred by the client as well, especially if they were in the fashion
industry. That is why photographs of Kokoschka around 1911 show
a fashionably dressed artist with dandyish tendencies far beyond his
actual modest means – at least when he had not just allowed his head
to be shaved in wanted-poster style.

But back to Bertha Eckstein-Diener, and that perhaps best through
the retrospective account Kokoschka noted down during his London
exile and in fact in his prose 'Erste Reise durch die Schweiz' ('First
Journey through Switzerland'), which sounds far more colourful than
the corresponding passage in *Mein Leben*.

> The lady I was supposed to paint was a devotee of the Rudolf-
> Steiner-sect. On arrival already, she gave me a bit of the creeps. I also
> had to constantly think of the money and how I was at the mercy
> of the whim of fate. The lady wandered around in a riding costume,
> with riding crop and a hat with feathers. [...] In the house there were
> a good many bedrooms, all decorated in different colour schemes.
> Mine was done in silver and gold, which presumably was a refer-
> ence to the worlds of the moon and sun but had the impact of a box
> of chocolates. [...] One night there were clamour and disturbance
> in the garden and house, voices became audible and lights were
> moving around outside. I came out of my room, where I had pre-
> ferred to lock myself in, and I was informed by the excited lady that

her husband [from whom she was divorced] was trying to have the child kidnapped which the police were able to prevent. In short, she poured her heart out to me, her fears and woes and soon turned out to be the successor of Madame Potiphar. I was afraid of her. What was I to do? I had begun to paint her picture. When she came too near me, I could only defend myself with Prussian blue with which I had intentionally besmeared my fingers. (DSW II, 87)

Curiously, the photo that her often absent lover Theodor Beer took of her shows an utterly sensitive woman, withdrawn, very beautiful – one might imagine a hidden hint of esoterism. A crass contrast, say, to Kokoschka's portrait of 'his' Frau Potiphar, which remained unfinished due to circumstances; she appears witch-like with a voraciously consuming, heated regard; the desirable body remains barely intimated. The open arms imply willingness to come together. Was Bertha really (also) thus, or did Kokoschka wish to see her so? As a contrast to the enchanting Bessie? She succumbed to tuberculosis a year after Kokoschka painted her portrait; her admirer felt 'she was consumptive and appeared so beautiful to me that I immediately fell deeply in love with her' (DSW II, 85). And: 'She was the embodiment of all things English, as no longer happens these days' (ML, 96).

An alternative to such morbid tranquillity was available, as the first European ice hockey tournament was also being held in Clarens at that time (January 1910). He wrote to Lotte Franzos in Vienna: 'Lots of Englishmen that one would like to beat to death because they are always screaming and flaunting strength' (Br I, 10). And further: 'It is such a nervous light hanging over everything [...] Now I want to move on, stay nowhere and have not yet finished settling the score with criticism and my family' (Br I, 11). Again, there is this latent hint of tensions with the parents (one recalls the 'beating to death' in the letter to Erwin Lang), only this time he equates parents and public criticism.

Lotte Franzos (1881–1957), who would become a loyal friend to him, was also among his private critics from time to time. Franzos, married to a wealthy solicitor, led an important Salon at Teinfaltstraße 3 in Vienna's First District. Kokoschka had first painted her portrait in

1909. Despite her disappointment with this portrait, which showed her with too much 'blotchy skin' and unflattering hands, she became an early confidante who understood how to support her Oskar effectively. The charcoal portrait of 1912 brings out the melancholic in her character, or it projects Kokoschka's own melancholy on this striking face. In March 1911 she, too, received a special gift from the artist, a fan made by him – a precursor, if you will, to the six extant fans dedicated to Alma Mahler. He felt free to report failures to Lotte Franzos, including a 'row' with Frank Wedekind in Munich in March 1911 in which neither obviously spared the other: '[...] he was megalomaniacal and I was coarse' (Br I, 16). After all, megalomania was part of the *Zeitgeist* of pre-war times, as the 'Café Größenwahn' ('Café Megalomania') in Berlin's West End illustrates; artists and politicians could not get enough of it. Even in love this mania could sprout unusual blossoms.

Unique Berlin

There was nowhere that Kokoschka felt less understood than in Vienna, which he called the 'city of lotus-eaters' (DSW II, 93). The journalistic art criticism there annoyed him immeasurably, and none of that would change. At best, he was derided like the comparable figure in music, Arnold Schönberg. Five years later, in March 1915, Kokoschka was to attest, more than ambiguously: '[...] today Schönberg is the only one who at least feels at home in his cul-de-sac' (Br I, 210). Art critics in Vienna, led by Adalbert Franz Seligmann in the *Neuen Freien Presse*, would not shy away from converting Max Nordau's catchword 'Entartung' ('degeneracy') and applying it to Kokoschka's works. In doing so, they anticipated what was to happen two-and-a-half decades later when the National Socialists banned his art, labelling it 'degenerate'. Kokoschka noted: 'The Viennese liberal press was a major power, of common mind with the modern dictators in that they slavishly catered to the public's basest instincts' (DSW II, 92). Yet Seligmann should be given credit for at least one thing, namely supporting art created by women. He, that conservatively influenced historical painter, even co-founded the Wiener Frauenkunstschule (Vienna Women's Academy of Art), where his benchmark was and remained the work of Tina Blau. Nevertheless, he showed himself to be surprisingly open-minded in his article about *Die Frau in der Secession* (*The Woman in the Secession*) exhibition of 1910 (from 11 November of that year) to the 'magnificent portraits by Therese Schwartze, the splendid leaves by Käthe Kollwitz and the "Rotonda" by Emma Ciardi'.

Kokoschka's friends and sponsors, led by Karl Kraus and Adolf Loos, had recognised in any case that the art of this tempestuous genius would be better appreciated in Berlin. That is why they advised him to make the trip to the second-most important metropolis of Modernism after Paris, and so he did in March or early April 1910 with introductions to Paul Cassirer and Herwarth Walden in his hand. Berlin was different, 'unique', as Kokoschka later recalled (ML, 117). It was the movement, the dynamic which filled him with enthusiasm. Its vehemence 'literally tore [the city] out from under' passers-by, according to Kokoschka, and further:

> In my memory Berlin seems to have been like a network of underground trains, elevated trains, railways and street cars, columns of hackney carriages, automobiles, motorcycles and push bikes, in addition the rotating neon signs, enormous flickering cinema palaces, loud speakers and coffee house orchestras, perhaps also six-day cycle races [...] And scraps of newspaper flying above the streets. All this kept the senses awake day and night. Just as the strewn spots of colour in an Impressionist painting do not yet make the picture that you can only begin to make out from a distance, it requires a proper perspective at a distance in time in the description of an experience, whose eye witness I was, in order to give others a mental image of this Prussian city whose inhabitants were apparently themselves surprised to have become metropolitans overnight. (ML, 117)

These attempts to gain distance generate a particularly intense perception of the city which, however, does not lead to an artistic view of it. Creative depictions of Berlin scenes by Kokoschka have not survived.

In any event, he felt he had arrived in the 20th century in Berlin. In contrast, 'in idyllic Austria' the civilising process of the technology revolution had been seemingly forgotten (ibid).

When painting a Viennese lady at the Swiss Villa Sangata, also known as Villa Karma, he put a stop to her advances using Prussian blue paint. Yet no blue was of use against the intrusiveness of the 'Prussian city', only the practice of survival skills under aggravated social conditions because Berlin, whilst being open-minded, the Mecca of Modernism where East met West, was also a tough place.

Kokoschka had brought two unusual experiences with him to Berlin: an idyllic one on Lake Geneva (it could have been lifted from a Stefan Zweig novella) and a hellish one in the form of a Canadian snake dancer in Vienna who gave her erotic performances at the Tabarin, the former St Anna Monastery in the Johannesgasse.

> On a wonderful early spring day – the sun burned down on the snow, the snow lay calmly sparkling – I saw a little girl on a wall. She was about 14 years old. She lay and enjoyed, without moving, the warmth. She looked at me long and strangely through her eye lashes. A fig tree stood nearby; it was like a fairy tale. I approached the delicate apparition and asked her what she was called. She said: Virginia. She would later become the daughter of my dreams in my starving imagination in Berlin [...]. (DSW II, 87)

The unspoilt and virginal attracted the seemingly still inexperienced young artist; it is not for nothing that he counted Peter Altenberg among his friends. Alice in Wonderland did not seem far off, even if he was to make bunny rabbits the subject of a still life and not of a story. It was the girl's glance that stayed with him and then became a fantasy.

The antithesis was provided on his return to Vienna from Switzerland – Kokoschka at the Tabarin, the building of the Akademie der bildenden Künste Wien (Vienna Academy of Fine Arts) in the time of Emperor Joseph II. During the Vormärz (as of 1840) it was converted into an experience house with 'subterranean wanderings around the world' as the main attraction before it became a multi-story music hall. Kokoschka saw this 'powerful' Canadian woman 'in a love-duel with a python' and commented: 'If the snake had been Lucifer himself, then he, the tempter, had to be continually reinvented since the beginning of Creation because with every performance she was able to free herself from its entanglement' (ML, 101). The following day, Oskar K dared to enter the elegant den of the lioness near the Hofburg. He wanted to experience the temptation, but not succumb to it. The performer, herself snake-like, stretched out on the divan, awaiting him as the next admirer. He compared the situation he found himself in with the scene called 'Liebestod' ('Love-Death') in *Tristan und Isolde* and took the appropriate action: 'She lay still, I kissed her hand and would have liked to throttle her, [but] took my leave and washed my hands immediately afterwards' (ML, 102).

And here it appears again, that latent momentary violence in the utterances of this artist, which, while mirroring his frustrations, points alarmingly to the potential realism of his play *Mörder Hoffnung der Frauen*, as well as the water-coloured pencil-and-ink drawing *Frauenmord* (*Murder of a Woman*, 1909). What was going through his mind? Were these idle artistic gestures and themes? And time and again Isolde. He described a chalk drawing of 1909 with the words: 'I am the voyeur at the makeshift bed of the European Isolde.'[10] This title alone earned a special treatment. Animal motifs surround the drawing next to a crescent moon and a vaguely suggested landscape. The self of the picture has the hand raised as for an oath; it imagines the dying Isolde naked, wearing a black veil, as if it wants to protect her.

For his farewell to Vienna Kraus and Loos dragged their young, inexperienced friend to the 'famous Salon of Madame Rosa' (ML, 102) where prostitutes were allocated to the highest bidders. 'I did not await the end of the auction, did not want to become a witness to a fate that certainly meant an end for the girl as a tubercular seamstress or a syphilitic prostitute. Why had I gone along?' (ML, 102). Indeed, why? There were no pictures to be acquired here, only infections. Did he want to emulate Henri de Toulouse-Lautrec? How close did he stand to Egon Schiele's abused bodies? He set down harrowing examples of that, for instance, in *Amokläufer* (*The Frenzied Attacker*, 1908/1909), illustrations for his own poetic texts and portrayals of self-inflicted wounds. In Madame Rosa's Salon, too, he must have explored resistance against temptation, denying the betrayal of his body, as close as he may have come to it. Yet these impressions and experiences accompanied him – and not just to Berlin, the 'watershed between the past and the future' (ML, 107).

Berlin – that meant once again winning clientele for portraits. Herwarth Walden, himself one of these sitters, published some of them in the *Sturm* portfolio of 1910. Richard Dehmel's, Paul Scheerbart's and Yvette Guilbert's faces are among them, some of them quick sketches; Kokoschka becomes a painter for hire. But he paints the portrait of a cat as well. For Christmas 1920, Walden published a pencil-and-ink drawing by Kokoschka under the heading *Geburt Christi* (*Birth of Christ*) in *Sturm* which brings to mind what he had almost suppressed in Berlin: the scenic, a tumultuous effort in which everything is literally chaotic. It was an impression that Kokoschka understood how to create through layering motifs and intense shadings. When he was to draw Dehmel, it had apparently been agreed that this was to be during a reading by the poet. Yet, Kokoschka wrote to him: 'In the hall it will be difficult to draw you because I am near-sighted and unsociable. [...] In January I have another exhibition at Cassirer's, I would like to do your portrait by then because I can do it better like Liebermann' (Br I, 14). His self-confidence had obviously increased, despite his being 'unsociable'. 'Better *like* Liebermann' – this formulation would have been promptly corrected by Karl Kraus, but Dehmel generously allowed this 'like' in the comparative to stand.

Regarding Karl Kraus. We have yet to come to Kokoschka's portrait of the poet and critic, but briefly: Kokoschka was to receive from him a most unusual book inscription. Kraus gave Kokoschka a copy of his volume *Worte in Versen* (*Words in Verses*) with this sarcastic poetic note under the date, 'April 1916':

To the embellisher
The best part is still innards.
How rosy Kokoschka paints some scoundrel!

To expose him, he does not succeed.
How differently Schattenstein. He paints at the dress![11]

This refers to Nikolaus Schattenstein (1877–1954), the portraitist of
Russian origin who was able to exhibit his painting *Lesender Knabe*
(*Lad Reading*) at the Künstlerhaus Wien in 1911. Schattenstein painted
Russian farmers as well as elegant ladies and tavern scenes; in his genre
of paintings he focused on fabrics and garments, supported by Kraus'
comment that he was painting 'at the dress'. Nevertheless, the artist continued to remain associated with the critic, at least as a reader, though
it is unclear whether he was even aware of Kraus' principle work, *Die
letzten Tage der Menschheit* (*The Last Days of Mankind*).[12]

No, it did not look good for Kokoschka in this period, even if he
was spared the hateful Viennese tirades about his art on the Spree and
Havel. In the autumn of 1910, he seems to have travelled to Weimar
specifically to make a portrait of Henry van de Velde, which did not
happen. Similar cancellations had a significant impact on his finances.
Shortly before Christmas, he wrote to Loos: 'I cannot, unfortunately,
leave Berlin. Schlieper [a further commission] was sufficient for rent
and 1 week, a second portrait went unpaid because it was not liked. I
have made 4 pictures in the last few days and now almost feel persecuted by grinning human heads so that all this portraiture sticks in my
craw' (Br I, 14 f).

The above-mentioned 'second portrait' is likely a reference to
that of the celebrated actress Tilla Durieux, later the wife of gallerist
Paul Cassirer, which turned out looking a bit cat-faced. Apparently,
she would have preferred to see herself immortalised as a seductress,
as Circe. Before she sat for him in her apartment, he had to help her
fiancé Cassirer with lacing her corset (ML, 115). The scene reminded
Kokoschka of Manet's 'famous painting *Nana*. I could not paint her
that way as Manet had already done that well' (ML, 166). The alternative was more modest and thus unsatisfactory – evidence of what
keeping to tradition can mean: self-defeat.

On Christmas Eve 1910 Kokoschka, now a reluctant starving artist,
admitted in a letter to Lotte Franzos in Vienna:

I am now so weak that I can no longer fake it. [...] I miss Vienna very much, though relationships have slipped away unnoticed and I will feel unsatisfied, if not thirstier, almost a stranger if I can return for a few days [...] my whole life is hell and I was initially an open, good young person and am now a spiteful weakling at the mercy of occasional sympathy. (Br I, 15)

He now contemplated returning to Vienna, also out of concern for his parents and two sisters. Berlin was to remain the centre of his universe: the world of Walden's *Der Sturm* (*The Storm*) was too inspiring and not at all comparable with Vienna's coffeehouse Modernism. Apparently in January 1911 it was Eugenie (Genia) Schwarzwald, not Lotte Franzos, who came to Berlin to enquire after the wellbeing of the former art teacher at her girls' school. It is unclear who made her aware of Kokoschka's situation. The Vienna education authority had forced the school to fire their art teacher after the 'scandals' provoked by him; in addition, there was an inspection which determined that Kokoschka used extremely liberal teaching methods, allowing the girls to draw what and how they wanted. The story goes that Genia Schwarzwald's intervention with the authorities, which she crowned with the words that Kokoschka was a genius and should not be measured by normal standards, was countered with the comment that geniuses are not anticipated in the lesson plan.

In any event, Genia seems to have offered Kokoschka her open home in Josefstädter Straße. There, in addition to Loos and Schönberg, Egon Wellesz and Rudolf Serkin, Hermann Broch and Georg Lukács, Rilke and Egon Friedell, anyone who was anyone – or was about to be – in Vienna's cultural or intellectual circles, kept company. Also, the prospect of an exhibition of his paintings at the 'Hagenbund' may have influenced Kokoschka's decision to settle in Vienna again despite everything. Back in Vienna, Kokoschka returned himself to public awareness through more than his art. In addition to further portraits (of Egon Wellesz, among others), religious motifs are noticeable – a self-portrait as St Sebastian and a crucifixion scene, both in the style of El Greco. Most importantly, the lecture *Vom Bewußtsein der Gesichte* (*On the Nature of Visions*) and the play *Der brennende Dornbusch* (*The Burning Bush*) are worth noting here.

So bold was the self-confidence of this artist that he, the former graduate of the arts school, thought nothing of portraying himself on a poster for the Wiener Akademische Verband für Literatur und Musik (Viennese Academic Society for Literature and Music) in order to advertise his lecture *Vom Bewußtsein der Gesichte* (*Consciousness of Vision*) which was to be delivered at the Ingenieur- und Architekten-verein (Society of Engineers and Architects) in Eschenbachgasse in the First District on 26 January 1912. The point of the poster is that it does not give the title of the lecture, it just shows the angular face of the artist in bold strokes and a broad shadowbox border, a hand pointing to himself with the words in bold capital letters written across his upper torso: LECTURE/OKOKOSCHKA.

Either the artist is giving a lecture about himself or the lettering has been vandalised by the audience into 'Oh, Kokoschka'. How did a twenty-six-year-old get to such a self-denunciation? How did he get to this text? In the oeuvre of this artist, the lecture *Vom Bewußtsein der Gesichte* may be considered a foundational text. Hence it is due special consideration.

With 'Gesichte' Kokoschka meant paradoxes: on the one hand, awareness experiencing itself, elements of life streaming towards consciousness – including that of the 'unborn' – with the aim of finding harmony within himself and to visualise this. On the other, it was about the 'visionary sinking back into the subconscious', as Walter Muschg believed.[13] For Kokoschka, consciousness was the 'grave of things' and at the same time the prerequisite for every perception. The 'Bewußtsein der Gesichte' equalled 'a deep dive into the waves and being winged in the air' (DSW III, 12). Consequently this 'consciousness' can label itself 'I' or 'you' and result in 'delusion'. And this 'delusion', according to Kokoschka, is then in 'all things that which is natural', be it 'nature, vision, life' itself. 'World' and 'I' were to him – almost Schopenhauer-like – the result of the intention towards reality *and* towards imagination. The religious element was not lacking. Kokoschka regarded himself as the artist-Christ: 'where there are two or three together in my name, I am among them.' Moreover, he already saw things happening to him 'and confessing on their own'. But what? 'I have,' so he lectures his audience, 'spoken with my face, rather than with its appearance' (all quotations in: DSW III, 12). Who among his listeners might have understood that? Who could have followed him – and what's more, all the way into his old age, which saw him found and lead a School of Seeing?

If it is safe to assume that Kokoschka tried to reveal the souls of the sitters in numerous of his portraits with his anticipatory fatalism, then it is likely this is also relevant to his play in five acts, *Der brennende Dornbusch* (1911) – because it appears as though he has predicted a special amorous experience for himself, the importance of which exists in the play's feminine perspective and tragedy. The male of the nameless protagonists lives at the expense of the Woman's strengths, drains her and yet is loved by her to the end. In the penultimate scene they communicate, seated on 'two rocky ledges' opposite one another. 'In the dark of the background,' the abyss between them, is the chorus which will preside over the final scene. When the Man speaks the stage is distinctly white; the Woman responds, red light 'alternating' with white (all quotations from: DSW I, 104; Mitchell, 101).

One of the Woman's attributes takes on the character of a guiding theme: her excessively long hair, which even 'trails on the floor behind her in ringlets' (Mitchell, 89). She sits on a chair at night, shivering, apparently clad only in her hair; she sleeps on and in her hair ('my woman's hair my nightdress', DSW I, 97; Mitchell, 94), and cries tears into her hair until it damply covers her eyes. This hair represents her seductive power and sexual potency, the symbolism of which 'the Man' perceives, suspecting that he will be destroyed by this asset of 'the Woman'. That is precisely why he pointedly disparages her by calling her a 'long-haired one'. She, in turn, yearns for him, even though he only mistreats her; no proximity can still this yearning. Because she repeatedly feels as though she is alone. Because she loves him unutterably, he is to remain 'untouched', though she also suffers with him as a result (DSW I, 107), and to such an extent that she herself becomes a self-consuming burning bush.

My body is a burning, fiery bush,
O you my man! Nourishing wind!
My breasts two tongues of fire,
O you, unwilling voice!
My hands hot wings,
My legs burning coals –
(DSW I, 104; Mitchell, 101)

He labels her a 'woman in childbed, hopelessly labouring! / Who, for weakness, does not dare to give birth!' (DSW I, 105; Mitchell, 101). She wants him to 'enter' her, extinguish her and thus 'deliver' her. In that he attempts this contrary to expectations, he sacrifices himself to her, falls into his own oblivion and dies 'quietly'. The woman watches the death of her standoffish lover and states without any apparent expression of sorrow: 'Silently a vision dissolves' (DSW I, 109). Does it dissolve or detach itself from reality? This question remains open, but the vision motif returns in the chorus at the end: 'Forced forth, there appears a vision, / a world to consciousness' (DSW I, 110; Mitchell, 106). Seen this way, in these closing words of the chorus, Kokoschka gave himself the keyword for his observations in the later lecture on *Bewußtsein der Gesichte*. Furthermore, he had designed a scenario of failed love in *Der brennende Dornbusch* which he would soon have to live through in reality. He himself would become an internally 'burning, fiery bush', though he would survive this situation even if in a miraculous way.

In the Throes of Love

Primal scene with Woman. Yet, unlike in the case of the supposed fire on Oskar's night of birth or the pool of blood at his brother's birth, this was about the all-or-nothing of love. Adam in Vienna and the reptilian Eve in the hellish paradise of a rear courtyard studio. Enter the barely thirty-three-year-old *femme fatale* and most desired widow of Vienna Alma Mahler into the life of the twenty-six-year-old artist. Put more accurately, Alma and Oskar each stepped into the life of the other. It would be superfluous to repeat the well-known, frequently novelised and cinematically embellished[14] scandalous history of the daughter of an eminent landscape artist, Emil Jakob Schindler. Alma was also the stepdaughter of Carl Moll, her father's student and friend of Gustav Klimt, who became one of the most important painters of Secessionist Vienna Jugendstil.

Moll lived the high life on the Hohen Warte in a patrician house with décor from the Makart era; he knew everyone and everyone knew him, a principle which his highly musical stepdaughter followed closely.

During her eight-year marriage to Gustav Mahler, Alma's musical talents lay fallow at his behest. In addition to the tangled amorous relationships in her parental home[15] (her mother Anna Sophie Schindler modelled unfaithfulness for her daughter – her father Emil Jakob Schindler suffered from this, just as Gustav Mahler would later from hers), Mahler's prohibition against her musical activities must have left the deepest scars in her psyche. Her early songs exhibit late romantic tonal overtones but show an utterly subtle feeling for storyline which she understood how to set to music effectively. She set to music poems by Heinrich Heine, Rainer Maria Rilke, Otto Julius Bierbaum and, in particular, Richard Dehmel. His poem *Die stille Stadt* (*The Silent City*) is one of her most impressive songs.

Stepfather Moll, in turn, was so impressed by the work of the 'young wild one' Oskar K, whose work on exhibit at the Vienna Hagenbund was so different to his own, that he had the ostracised Kokoschka paint his portrait. And the same was now to happen to stepdaughter Alma. By all accounts, to begin with Alma played and sang *Isoldes Liebestod* 'with great expression' as a warm-up for her poor artist protégé (ML, 129). Still, in September 1914 Kokoschka would write to her: 'Wagner is the marvellous composer. But *you* must play him (but only for me evermore)' (Br I, 180).

To Oskar K, Alma was instantly more of a Lilith than Lilith Lang previously: the demonic ancestress, feminine ideal and, of the previously mentioned women, probably most like the wild beauty Helen Ritscher who had appeared in his piece *Mörder Hoffnung der Frauen*, although far more cultured than this Maenad-like actress. They were on informal terms literally from one heartbeat to the next in that April of 1912, such that Oskar K wrote her notes upon letters repeatedly as one nearly lost, who threatened to 'rot' 'in the wilderness' (Br I, 30). By his own admission, 'life's ambiguity' drove him into the arms of his 'angelic woman' (Br I, 34). What awaited him there were physical delights of desired intensity, apparently an initial reversal of erotic magic into sexual fulfilment as well as the very opposite: rejection, withdrawal, demoralising waits for the next time, not to mention the presence of others in Alma's life. And the biggest of these presences, which Kokoschka painfully felt from the beginning, was not Zemlinsky or Gropius, but rather a dead man, an uber-dead man if you will: Gustav Mahler. Both Alma M and Oskar K could have recited to each other Goethe's poem, 'Fate, why did you grant us this depth, / Of insightful vision into our future':

> So that our love, earthly happiness,
> Is a thing we can trust in happily never?
> Why did you grant us such intuition,
> Such power to know each other's heart,
> To see, among life's scattered throng,
> The true relationship where we are?

And it continues:

> You knew every feature of my being,
> Saw the purest tremor of each nerve,
> With a single glance you could read me,
> Hard as I am for mortal eye to pierce
> (HA, I, 122)[16]

Of course, Kokoschka might hardly have felt in the mood for clarifying verses; Alma perhaps more so.

After 26 June 1912, just two-and-a-half months after the starry encounter on Hohen Warte, Kokoschka's nerves did not sound like strings; more likely, they were already stripped bare. The final notes of the premiere of Mahler's last symphony, his ninth, and celebrated by Schönberg and Berg as the dead master's transition to modern music, had just faded away in the great Musikvereinssaal zu Wien under the baton of the very young Bruno Walter, a recent discovery of Alma's, when Alma received the following letter from her ardent lover.

[Vienna, June 1912.]

Alma,

I cannot find peace with you, as long as I know a stranger, whether dead or alive, remains in you. Why have you invited me to a danse macabre and want me to mutely watch you for hours as you, intellectual slave, listen to the rhythms of the man or the man who was and must be alien to you and me, and in the knowledge that every syllable of the work hollows you out, spiritually and bodily. Whose fame and liberation never providing a release that would have come from himself.

I cannot see you on the day you have designated to the memory of this man because I cannot ever assimilate myself with this rigid complexity of feelings in you, which is amongst the strangest such that I can feel it too exactly even in the slightest stirring. Everything which I battle in you comes from that, whether it carries this or another name. You must begin a fundamentally new life with me, your girlhood, if we wish to be happy and forever at one with each other, Alma.

Oskar Kokoschka (Br I, 42)

Admittedly he immediately sent a second letter, in order to avoid the worst: 'Alma, my good angel, I write to you again because it would be a sin to afflict a grievance on you as it might have been contained in the vehemence of my first letter' (Br I, 43). Yet, Alma now had in writing confirmation of what perturbed her Oskar K so deeply: her past, namely her relationship to the art of the great Mahler.

Just as her late husband had prevented her from composing and practising her vocal art, so her latest lover wanted her to forget her previous life and become a maiden for him anew – Alma as Holy Virgin and unsullied muse who had waited only for him, the artist 'without dinner jacket and manners', as he once described himself to Ernst Lang (Br I, 6). In earlier letters, Kokoschka had also offered a considerable number of expressions in order to salvage her feminine origins for himself. Thus, he wished that she might find her 'bodily peace' in his 'presence' (Br I, 42). One month after the Mahler letter he wrote to her at the Dutch seaside resort of Scheveningen, overtly admonishing her: 'Don't fall back into your old errors, surrounding yourself with all manner of rabble that celebrates you as heiress' (Br I, 59). To him Alma's conduct – in Scheveningen she was taking a rest from his imprecations, and more such curative respites would follow – was already a sign of a 'confused character'. Among these behaviours was the connection with her lesbian friend, Henriette Amalie (Lilly) Lieser, who became an important source of support, particularly at that time. Lieser supported Schönberg financially and Alma morally. Her Jewish heritage apparently did not disturb Alma, the ever-increasingly notorious anti-Semite. After her deportation from Vienna, Lilly Lieser would perish in the Riga ghetto in December 1943.

Already by the end of July 1912, Oskar wished for – nay, tried to conjure up – a final tie: 'Should you have a love child from me, then Nature in all its greatness and goodness is being merciful and erasing everything horrible and will never tear us from another as we depend on and are supported by each other. You are now become healthy through me and I have found my peace in you, dearest. We now find the holiness of family; you will become Mother [...]' (Br I, 59).

Of course, she was already a mother, his (at times 'heavenly') Almili or – in Mozart-like escalation – Almilizi even, 'my little yellow hammer' and 'my dear sweet old little boy'. At the same time, it appears as though Kokoschka often took more loving care of Alma and Mahler's daughter Anna, also called 'Gucki', than did her birth mother. Apparently, this physical evidence of his Alma's 'previous life' seems to have disturbed Kokoschka less than Mahler's music and death mask.

The intensity of this ardour, as well as the jealousy bordering on the pathological, led Kokoschka into a frenzy of production which generated altogether over 450 pieces of visual art relating to Alma. Fortunately, the manic aspect of this emotional turmoil shows the lovers, whether individually or as a pair, in concentrated serenity. In April 1913, he admitted to Alma: 'I so yearn for a life where everything external breathes calm [...]' (Br I, 96). He would have to wait four decades for this 'calm'.

From the beginning, Kokoschka attempted to elevate the relationship with Alma into the sacred, but without allowing this metaphysical love to interfere with carnal pleasure. From his perspective, this love was about life and death, whereas Alma preferred to maintain the flirting game. Kokoschka was clearly prepared to risk everything for this relationship and to elevate it through delusional jealousy. Time and again he hectors his so much more experienced 'Almilizi' (that he should use the neuter diminutive speaks to his desire to possess it!).

> Please, my Almili, do not look at anyone, the men there will always stare at you because they are sexual animals, but I know that you will not betray me with even a glance. If someone, and be it even an acquaintance, a conductor or something similar, should want to approach, then no longer think of yourself as Frau Mahler, but rather my beloved woman, that you must bind me with your beauty and your spirit, not making me jealous so I do not become bitter and resigned. (Br I, 119)

It would be difficult to claim that Kokoschka had a positive image of his fellow men. He had placed the nameless type of 'Man' in his play *Der brennende Dornbusch*, as a brief note to Arnold Schönberg evidences, 'between the effeminate and brutishness' (Br I, 10).

There is much support for the idea that initially he may have seen his relationship with Alma as a means to escape the bounds of simply oppressive lust. At the same time, he wanted to bind Alma to him in that he tried to make clear to her that without her his art would have to die.

There have been repeated references to the, for Kokoschka, model nature of the calamitously tragic relationship between the sexes which Heinrich von Kleist nominally created in his tragedy, *Penthe-silea* (1808). This understanding is based on the proven early interest Kokoschka had in Kleist's work which still manifested itself in his exile, in particular in a contemplation of *Amphytrion* (1944). The Amazonian queen, Penthesilea, obsessed by a destructive love madness, tears apart her beloved Achilles. 'Kisses' and 'bites' have to rhyme here (in German) as they do in Kokoschka's piece *Mörder, Hoffnung der Frauen*.

One might also consider, however, an emotional configuration which Franz Grillparzer created in his tragedy *Des Meeres und der Liebe Wellen* (*The Waves of Sea and Love*). It is the transposition of the classical epic *Hero and Leander* by Musaios and dramatises the love of the future Aphrodite priestess Hero for the stranger, Leander, who appears out of nowhere. They have to separate on the grounds of the vow of chastity which Hero has taken; yet Leander swims through the sea under the protective cover of night back to Hero who lives in a tower in the temple complex. There she has placed a candle to guide Leander on his way. At the behest of the temple guards, who have discovered their relationship, the light is extinguished and thus Leander's death is assured. As we have seen, Kokoschka's *Mörder Hoffnung der Frauen* begins with a reversal of this tower-light configuration. Here it is 'the Man' who lives in the tower: 'Night sky; a tower with a large, red iron cage door; torches the only light; black ground rising to the tower in such a way that all characters can be seen in outline' (DSW I, 35; Mitchell, 22). Kokoschka's tower was to become his studio, which soon would have not only a 'black floor', but also black walls.

It seems a symbolic coincidence that the material was reprised in 1912, this time transposed to the arena of illegal sea trade, when the silent film drama *Des Meeres und der Liebe Wellen* came to the cinemas with Germany's answer to Asta Nielsen, the Dresdener Lissi Neb-uschka, in the starring role. What matters in any event is the love at first sight in which erotic attraction and emotional commitment are made instantaneously manifest. This 'first contact at a glance' (Christina von Braun) does not appear surpassable through any later physical touch.

It is sufficiently remarkable that in Alma Mahler-Werfel's memoir, *Mein Leben* (*My Life*, 1960), the relationship with Kokoschka takes up significantly more space than in his of the same title eleven years later. In his, Kokoschka includes an episode which shows how much his mother distrusted the relationship with Alma. One day she allowed herself a macabre joke in that she 'promenaded in front of Alma Mahler's house for several hours, her hand suspiciously moving in her coat pocket. Through a slightly open window she had seen the loitering Circe, as she referred to her, and later confessed to me how she frightened the poor thing' (ML, 132). This was because Alma seemed to believe she would carry out the threats expressed in her letter and shoot her, the Circe of Vienna. Kokoschka highlighted another incident in his recollections. He claimed it was not Carl Moll's stepdaughter, but rather a painting which Moll brought back from Italy, that first gave proper flight to his imagination – Titian's painting, *Venus mit dem Orgelspieler* (*Venus with the Organ Player*). Moll had left the painting with Kokoschka for a few months (before the First World War). This means he may have had it in sight as he worked on his *Windsbraut* (*Bride of the Wind* or *The Tempest*). Alma also would have seen it there, as would Georg Trakl.

Kokoschka described what was special about this painting as a 'triumph of light, the lumen over the volume' of the space, which he termed the 'luminosity' of a painting. Here, the light creates the space (ML, 133), a process he traced from Titian by way of Poussin to Ingres and Cézanne – a radiant evolution which leads all the way to him, Kokoschka. Unlike 'Cubism, which lacks light as movement', he claimed it had fostered Abstraction such that painting ended up, yet again, in the 'static vision' of the still life (ML, 133). Yet in that time Kokoschka also created two still lifes with motifs like *Katze, Hammel und Fisch* (*Cat, Lamb and Fish*), as well as *Hammel und Hyazinthe* (*Lamb and Hyacinth*). In this genre, life comes to a stop. To Kokoschka, still lifes were an expression of the fear that the world could withhold life, even make it impossible.[17] In them he saw proof of Henning Mankell's observation: 'One sees most artworks, or one hears them. In rare cases, however, I have the feeling of a pleasant scent wafting towards me. Occasionally I have even experienced a sense of unexpected taste.'[18] Kokoschka's above-mentioned still lifes have just such an impact.

According to Kokoschka two crucial issues stood between him and Alma: Gustav Mahler's death mask and her aborted child – 'my child', as he emphatically adds – even if he feared it would one day wear Mahler's features and not his (ML, 135). After the abortion, however, she seems to have come to see his art in a new light, for example, the lithographic sequence *Der gefesselte Kolumbus* (*The Bound Columbus*) and '*O Ewigkeit, du Donnerwort*' ('*O Eternity – Thou Word of Thunder*') based on the Bach Cantata (BWV 60). In the Columbus lithograph, Alma saw the death mask lying on the floor and the self-portrait of the artist robbed of his child looking out of his grave, 'slain by his own jealousy' (ML, 136). She saw the double portrait of the two of them, and he will have given her his three-part poem *Αλλοσ Μαχαρ* (*Anders ist glücklich, Happiness Comes from a Different Way*) to read: 'I am the poor summer's night, / which disappeared / and is crying from a crevasse.' The white bird and the bird-catcher meet. In the face of approaching 'dangers', the love nest seems to 'mysteriously' 'gird' itself – in order to achieve what?

> In the brightness of the sun's clear rays
> which, hot and strong, the world embrace,
> and unbolt the womb of forms to the night-dark ones,
> your net still spellbinds her who the herd's trail scorns.
> (DSW I, 26; Mitchell, 16)

Movement comes into play (of emotions): 'on the heels of winter gloom, / weary of wing, longing comes.' The wind rises, on which luck does as well. Yet the theme of violence is not missing in this poem either. Man and woman, both bird-like, 'are strangling a snake'. Yet she lets 'fall a scrap of paper' on which the Self of the poems reads the words: '"In other wise is happiness"' (all quotations from: DSW I, 28; Mitchell, 18). The seductive snake perishes and with it seduction itself, as in the meantime both have realised that happiness lies beyond physical satisfaction.

'Ghost ship hanging in the air, / may mast and anchor guide you there' (DSM I, 27; Mitchell, 17). The 'ghost ship' will become a 'wreck in the ocean' (ML, 137), on which the artist sees himself and Alma, those ultimate lovers, as devoted and not despairing castaways. With this poem he was already on the path to the painting *Die Windsbraut*. Alma and Oskar: these names were supposed to become the alpha and omega of love and its artistic expression, in which he – similar to Nietzsche – saw himself as a new Columbus and thus the discoverer of a love and a life in art.

Kokoschka and Alma were reunited at the end of July 1912, in the Swiss mountain village of Mürren, where nature provides for a 'drama' of a special kind; nearby, in the Lauterbrunnen Valley, there are the subterranean glacial Trümmelbach Falls, symbolising the invisible undercurrents of life. Alma was returning from Scheveningen and Oskar celebrated their reunion by working on his lover's great portrait, which he created as a new Giaconda based on Leonardo da Vinci. This is how creative immortalisations are executed. The painting shows him, as Heinz Spielmann aptly remarks, as a 'revolutionary secure in his traditions, who feels tied to his heritage especially when it pertains to his most personal interests'.[19] Mürren also provided the background for his painting *Heimsuchung (The Visitation)*, which depicts a markedly masculine woman in a state of anticipation. The dominance of the feminine in the work of that time (1912/1913) results from Kokoschka's realisation that woman as the bearer of new life has an unassailable advantage over man. Mürren, however, also gives him a different perception of landscapes. His *Alpenlandschaft bei Mürren (Alpine Landscape at Mürren*, 1912) depicts dramatic fissures, dominated by a sun that seems to whirl. This fissuring also framed the feminine *Doppelakt: Zwei Frauen (Double Act: Two Women)*, which can be taken as a template for his conception of the intimate togetherness of girlfriends Lilly Lieser and Alma Mahler. Oddly enough, here in Mürren, amidst the 'securely built Alps', to use Hölderlin's term, Alma and Kokoschka were able to see Colin Campbell's silent film *Kolumbus (The Coming of Columbus*, 1912), which examined the dangerous, daring nature of exploring the new, or 'other'. Was Kokoschka already imagining a ship on the ocean here, close to being wrecked? Alma, in contrast, tended to hear the new, rather than to see it. She called Stravinsky's *Petruschka* and *Le Sacre du Printemps* 'new countries of music'.[20] Kokoschka, on the other hand, saw only one thing: 'His eyes cried in rapture at Nijinsky's grace and beauty in movement'.[21]

Alma knew to largely hide her relationship with Oskar K from the Viennese public, which caused him to suffer. They became a moon couple and night their medium, though Oskar, much more attracted to the light, clearly felt as though he must suffocate from this shadowy existence demanded by Alma. It would be seven months after Mürren before they went away together again, this time to Italy in the spring of 1913 – by way of Venice and Padua all the way to Naples. They lived in a guest house with uninterrupted views of the Bay of Naples and Vesuvius. During their stay they apparently watched from their balcony a storm whipping up the sea. To Kokoschka the balcony seemed like a boat on the wild sea while the volcano erupts. He realised this visual idea in miniature on the seven middle segments of the third fan for Alma, in addition to two sketches that showed Alma resting on the balcony as well as both of them in repose. They proved to be preliminary studies for what would later become *Die Windsbraut* by Kokoschka's hand, one of the greatest paintings of the 20th century.

These fans for Alma literally fanned their love for each other, although it was in the nature of these intimate creations that the beloved would have her and Kokoschka's history before her eyes like a mirror while fanning herself – should she have ever used these works of art for cooling purposes. Kokoschka gave Alma fans of love and premonition: the story of her lucky moments, his adoration (he usually depicted himself kneeling in front of her), their inflaming each other (the flame is a key motif of the fans – even hinting at the self-devouring, bursting into flame of the fans!), but also of their separation, their no longer touching each other. These fans of Kokoschka's are pure poetry, adorned with multi-layered symbolism. These fans were construed as metaphors, specifically for the generalisation of the most personal, whereas Kokoschka could 'only draw what he had himself experienced'.[22]

Eyewitness to Art: Georg Trakl

Like a groom who writes to his bride and 'solemnly and lovingly' plans their wedding, Kokoschka reported the gradual completion of the painting he initially named 'Tristan und Isolde' to his 'wife' in April 1913. His first description of the masterpiece reads as follows.

> Both of us with a very strong calm expression, our hands folded together, along the edge in a half-circle a Bengali lit sea, water tower, mountains, lightning and moon. Until the idea crystallised again out of the fine details of the individual strokes that I wanted to express the mood initially, in that I now re-experienced it – which is a vow! In midst of nature's chaos, a person forever trusting the other and through faith attaching themselves to each other. Now it is purely a poetic work, requiring bringing a few areas that remain to life, as I have already captured the basic mood and dimension of expression so they no longer let me fumble around in suspense. (Br I, 94)

A (subsequently coloured-in) picture of love's tranquillity among the storm and fires of the world. Kokoschka admitted one witness to the emergence of this most significant depiction of love of the Modern Era, allegedly by way of Loos: Georg Trakl. Kokoschka recalls:

> My great painting that depicts me and my once so beloved woman on a wreck in the ocean was finished. Suddenly Trakl's voice broke the silence, a voice like a second self, the sibling you. So, my colours did not lie. My hand brought forth an embrace from the stormy shipwreck of my world. [...]
> Georg Trakl was burdened by grief for his late twin sister, to whom he was tied in more than brotherly love.
> His sorrow was like the moon that steps in front of the sun and darkens it. And suddenly he began to give voice to a poem: word for word, rhyme for rhyme he slowly mumbled to himself. Trakl gave shape to the odd poem *Die Nacht* [*The Night*] in front of my painting, until he could recite it by heart:

... Over dusky cliffs
The glowing bride of the wind
Plunges death-drunken

With a pale hand he pointed to the painting and named it *Die Windsbraut*. (ML, 137)[23]

Kokoschka clearly felt strongly about maintaining what can be called a private mythology. It may indeed have been a particular characteristic of Trakl's to bring forth verse spontaneously. Through Kokoschka's report we become witnesses to the gradual completion of a poem while we are viewing a painting. That this could not be a visual description in verse goes without saying; unexpected, however, was that this experience unleashed a desire in him, the poet, to later paint himself in the style of Kokoschka in the studio of a friend in Innsbruck.[24] In an interview in October 1950 Kokoschka commented on this scene, described in greater detail in *Mein Leben*, in which he went one step further.

> We painted *Die Windsbraut* together. Yes, Trakl painted, too, I once saw a portrait by him. At the time, though, when I was painting *Windsbraut*, which after an interim in the travelling exhibition *Entartete Kunst* [*Degenerate Art*] landed in the Basel Museum, Trakl was around me on a daily basis. I had a highly primitive studio and he sat dumbly on a beer barrel behind me.[25]

Even if one does not take this remark literally, the indelible impression of the intensity of the encounter remains. Kokoschka's relationship with Trakl can be traced back to the spring of 1909. The friends Georg Trakl, Karl Minnich and Franz Schwab had visited the Internationale Kunstschau (International Art Show) in Vienna in June 1909 and they, along with Kokoschka, signed a card sent to Erhard Buschbeck who had remained in Salzburg. As mentioned, Kokoschka was showing several pieces at this exhibition, including *Der weisse Tiertöter*, nude drawings, a painted fan and a painted sculpture representing himself. At the time the influential critic Ludwig Erik Tesar dedicated a lengthy article in the magazine *Kunstrevue* to Kokoschka's art, which was evidently still influenced by the Jugendstil of the Wiener Werkstätten.

The card to Buschbeck read like an anticipatory echo, as it were: 'Herewith we send you the pick of the Kunstschau! Oh splendour! Oh greatness! Oh eternal Kokoschka! (French: cochon! cochon!)' – meaning 'smut', referring to the pornographic drawings (presumably by Kokoschka) on the card. 'The pick of the Kunstschau' is thus obviously meant to be ironic – in the case of Kokoschka, self-irony. Here the 'young wild one' pipes up, but under the cover of classical verses from Goethe's *Faust II*, specifically Mephistopheles' ever-confident ironic words from the 'Imperial Palatinate' (in the writing on the card).

How merit and luck are linked together
These fools can't see, no, not a one:
If they'd the Philosopher's Stone, as ever,
There'd lack a philosopher for the stone.
(V. 5061–5064)[26]

It is always a possibility that Trakl saw the open-air performance of Kokoschka's scandalous play *Mörder Hoffnung der Frauen* in the context of the Kunstschau a month later, as he was still in Vienna at that time. At the very least he must have been aware of the reaction to this outrageous event.

However, the Trakl–Kokoschka network of relationships reveals yet another, far less ironic (if not existential), example. In early 1913 Trakl again wrote the often-cited lines to his friend Buschbeck: 'I drove past Hall like a dead man, a black town that crashed through me like an inferno through the damned.' The next paragraph reads: 'In Mühlau I walk in much beautiful sunshine and am still very wobbly. The Veronal granted me some sleep under Kokoschka's Franziska.'[27] This is a painting of Kokoschka's that does not exist. However, the riddle of Kokoschka's supposed Franziska portrait can be presumed solved.[28] It refers to a chalk lithograph portrait of the previously mentioned actress, Helen (Ilona) Ritscher (1888–1964), with which the

Akademische Verband für Literatur und Musik in Wien (Academic Society for Literature and Music in Vienna) advertised its Frank Wedekind Week. Among others, Wedekind's play *Franziska. Ein modernes Mysterium in fünf Akten* (*Franziska: A Modern Enigma in Five Acts*) was performed. In Trakl's eyes, the image of the woman and the name of the 'modern enigma' became one; it seems he owned one of these posters and hung it in his home in Innsbruck. It is a case of an associative, if not delirious, vision that accounts for Trakl's sentence. The synthesised namesake painting by Kokoschka–Wedekind apparently helped Trakl to find peace of mind from time to time. Nevertheless, there is also something ironic about the calming effect it had on Trakl as Wedekind's Franziska is one of his most restless characters. She is a sexually driven figure, thirsting for knowledge and life, who explodes the accepted conventional roles of Wilhelmine society.

It was Kokoschka's evocative representation of Ritscher, who played the role of 'Woman' in *Mörder Hoffnung der Frauen*, which instantaneously spoke to Trakl: the penetrating look, the demonic presence of the head, the 'curving, sweeping lines in the image' (Klaus Manger) that emphasised the actress' sensuousness, unquestionably the ideal casting for Wedekind's play and an ideal focus for Trakl's immensely inflamed imagination.

In literary circles, the *Windsbraut* motif also had an impact on the poetess Marie Luise Kaschnitz. In 1946, the year of her first post-war trip to Switzerland, she twice stood in front of this painting in Basel, and requested a postcard reproduction six years later. The following verse is found in her series *Tutzinger Gedichtkreis*.

All belonging to Earth. But the new,
Innate to the sparkling light and the Windsbraut,
Ephemeral as old Atlas long since,
Drifting through the clouds, homeless,
Dancing in magical shoes –[29]

She remarks on Kokoschka's painting even more explicitly in her lecture *Liebeslyrik heute* (*Lyrics of Love Today*, 1962) in which she compares the development of the lyric of 'rapturous, disembodiment with the visual arts'.

> You will understand what I mean if I remind you of a painting, in particular the painting of a Windsbraut by Kokoschka in which this Windsbraut drifts in a shell through the clouds, snuggled up to her serious and sad human lover. There the demonic being is still a woman, still has an earthly body and full lips and closes the eyes in eager yearning [...][30]

Notably enough, Kaschnitz saw this painting at the border of the abstract; in other words, precisely at that neuralgic point of Kokoschka's artistic sense. It remained important to Kaschnitz that Kokoschka denied himself this next step. In this she recognised a humane feat – as did he.

Alma: Finale without End?

How did Alma view her Oskar K in retrospect? At least as a genius, like all of her conquests before and after him. She never fell in love with someone beneath her; she owed herself that much. She loved the 'naughty, restive child in him', though questioned, 'Were we too similar? Our Catholicism came from the same sources, his clear and deliberate; mine still clouded by scepticism.' She speaks of their shared joy in the 'mystical events' of religious celebrations. However, her overall assessment of the young artist's appearance (who in many things was older than her) was unvarnished.

> As man and human being, Oskar Kokoschka is a most unusual mixture. Though nice to look at, something is off in the structure. He is tall and slender, but his hands are red and often swell up. The fingertips have such good blood circulation that when he trims his nails and cuts himself, the blood shoots out in an arc. His ears, though small and finely chiselled, stand out from his head. His

nose is somewhat broad and slightly swollen. The mouth is large, the lower part and chin jutting forward. The eyes are somewhat crooked so that his expression becomes a bit furtive. But as such the eyes are pretty. He carries his face very nobly. His gait is sloppy; he literally throws himself forward when walking.

The suit – clothing is a problem for him.[31]

Alma was likely just as accurate with a further remark: 'We massively rubbed each other raw.'[32] One could even claim they loved themselves raw. For example, what must she have thought of his setting a wedding date at the Döbling town hall in June 1913 without having consulted her beforehand? She fled – once again to Franzensbad – but returned to him again. They spent her birthday, 31 August, together in the Dolomites, near Cortina in Tre Croci, where both of them lived it up uninhibitedly for the duration of their stay. In her memoirs, Alma frames her entry for August 1913 with references to Otto Klemperer and Franz Schreker as well as, unexpectedly, to Gustav Mahler. And, again, the claim: 'Oskar Kokoschka fulfilled a life and destroyed it, at the same time.'[33] That this was equally true of her did not seem to occur to her. Unlike Oskar, who was set on exclusivity, Alma wanted to *live* the concurrence of different relationships.

The dimensions of *Windsbraut* (the measurements run to 1.75 by 2.25 metres) inspired in Kokoschka a wish for large surface areas. Murals and frescos began to interest him. Ironically enough, in April 1912, the month of his first encounter with Alma, he had received an invitation from Breslau to participate in the decoration of a crematorium dome. Detailed designs survive which also show that Kokoschka made suggestions for the architectural implementation, characteristically a Tower of Babel fantasy, which however came to nothing with the outbreak of the First World War. This major commission would have enabled Kokoschka to become financially independent, which was particularly important to him for Alma's sake. Yet it remains an extraordinary notion; their life together would have been built on a lucrative job at a 'temple of fire' (Spielmann). Flames everywhere – he created a wall mural above the fireplace in Alma's summer house at the Semmering that showed both of them rising from the fire. And in April 1914 he asked Herwarth Walden to procure a 'fresco commission' for him in the USA: 'I am ready for this my actual work and still have to daub little pictures again and again which can give me no satisfaction' (Br I, 158). He evidently wanted to become the Giotto or Maulbertsch of the Modernists. Above all, he was becoming 'ready' for the end of the relationship with Alma. The 'love storm' was threatened by the life-saving doldrums, even if he was not yet willing to see it that way in the spring of 1914.

In the period following, which reached long into the First World War, the love affair took on ever more bizarre forms. Kokoschka saw himself as a defeated knight in a love contest, a failed minstrel. 'Where is my dear wife?', he asked Alma in a letter of 10 May 1914. Nevertheless, he could also appear secretive: 'I have a quality no one else has and no one really knows, for which I had to take on three bloody devils, total loneliness, agonising jealousy (of everything for which you leave me) and voluntary abject poverty' (Br I, 159). A further sentence in this letter, a merely parenthetical thought, is as puzzling as this one 'quality': 'Because I have no roots.' He called Alma's world a 'completed world' in which there was no room for him nor for their child. Even worse: 'How I live now is beneath all – like an ugly doll's life' (Br I, 164). He searched for escape routes; better said, he imagined them. Barely had he finished reading a book about India by Rudyard Kipling than he set off there. But in June 1914 he wrote to Alfred Kubin: 'I unfortunately died today and will not be on this earth tomorrow' (Br I, 168).

The curious coincidence was that Kokoschka received a copy of August Stramm's *Du: Liebesgedichte* (*You: Love Poems*) from Herwarth Walden, who had published the collection. The volume opens with Stramm's poem *Liebeskampf* (*Battle of Love*), which apparently so spoke to Kokoschka that he felt he needed to correct a typographical error. He believed that the line 'Die rund runde hetze Welt!' ('The around round rushing world!') should read 'Hetze Welt!' (with a capital 'H'), thus more strongly emphasising the sense of being hounded. The poem ends with the convulsive lines:

In linked spasms
Press our hands
And our tears
Well
Into
The same stream!
Neither you!
Nor you!
The wanting stands!
Not
I![34]

Kokoschka noted in his copy, tersely and ominously: 'killed in action in France in World War, dec[orated] with Iron Cross.'[35]

Still, in February 1915, Kokoschka wrote to his 'Beloved', his 'You' and 'Dear Heart', as Alma's relationship with Walter Gropius regained its earlier passion. Accompanied by the inescapable Lilly Lieser, she had looked up her favourite bourgeois muse in Berlin in order to bend him to her will. Kokoschka was initially surprised by her epistolary distancing from him; even a telephone conversation proved unedifying. He believed her to have 'fallen into a Wagnerian madness' (Br I, 208) and suspected that the composer Hans Pfitzner was stalking her. One last time, he extolled himself to her: 'I am a completely different person than you Bachians, Brahmsians and Wagnerians' (Br I, 210). That was on 5 March 1915. To begin with he opted for the Officer Academy: 'I want in any event to be done with all the nonsense that is to be got through in this European insanity, so I can return to my beloved studio' (Br I, 220). By this time, Alma, his 'foolish sister', had keys to it. One month before her wedding to Gropius (on 18 August 1915; the divorce would follow five years later), Kokoschka realised that he had finally lost Alma: 'Now you have crossed the magical bridge and I remained behind in hopelessness, in the darkest epitome of self-deception' (Br I, 224). Previously he had said of himself he was 'crazy with anguish' and contemplated suicide over Alma (Br I, 222); he then decided to join up, which approached being the same thing as few illusions remained about the situation at the Austrian eastern front in July 1915. A love death was not granted to Oskar and Alma; rather, it was a death of their love. That would be a handy end point as a sentence, but let us be cautious with respect to the sources as there were sporadic echoes of their love in the years that followed, at least as far as Kokoschka was concerned. For example, he wrote to her from Prague on 16 December 1937:

> Alma, I also would like to see you and ask you what you think about life. Of the short life that we both still have ahead of us. I do not rant about our poor country; quite the opposite, I only say loving things about these poorest devils. That I could never tolerate the cream of society because I could not stand it anywhere, at least not with us where it was and remained particularly soulless and a road block – but that has nothing to do with the land and its people. It is lovely of you, how and what you write me, do not be frightened, think of all I have swallowed in my life and that it will probably not be any rosier for me in the future than previously. Being unusual does not go without its punishments.

> All my love, Your Oskar[36]

And when he described to her his brother's uncertain situation in Vienna shortly after the Second World War ('Bohi is a skeleton after he had frequent visitors from the Gestapo and rendered sixteen-hour donkey work on the land. Now he is allowed to live in an unheated room in our little house in the Liebhartstal with wife and a little angel of a child. The baby has not tasted milk other than from its mother's breast'), she sent a care package from New York. And again, Alma is quite present: the time of love from times gone past, whether in the recollection of this insatiable passion, of the 'Windsbraut', or of Trakl's poem of this title, which he now (in March 1946) says he had 'recently' found. Now she, the ever-unattainable, is again his 'most beloved Alma', as a recently discovered letter begins.

Dearest Alma[,] Thank you very much for your love. There has been no mention of the package and I am frantic as to whether it has been properly delivered. You are very kind. I knew I could depend on you. It is crazy in Vienna and they have shown the city no mercy. All of them. In that they are united! All! Some day you will tell me what you remember about me, of our life in a time when one still wanted to live and tasted everything until it ran out. Right? Do you have my 'Orpheus and Eurydice'? I recently found a poem by Georg Trakl about the 'Windsbraut' that he wrote while I painted you and me and the storm was already rising. Sometimes I think we set the world on fire because we were two gluttons. Do you remember how we put a fig and a banana into our life? You have probably forgotten everything after this long, long time. I never!

All... Oskar[37]

After Alma's death he heard from her daughter Anna: 'Mama's last years were increasingly a dream life – time and space had completely disappeared; it always rained and day and night; she was always searching for someone – different people and she was always alone. I am glad that it is over.'[38] And for a final peculiarity one did not have to wait long. Around 1971 a friend, Rathenau, told him about an auction in New York of a letter he wrote on 31 October 1913 to the *Berliner Börsen Curier*: 'I request to set the record straight that a marriage between Frau Maria Alma Mahler, the widow of composer Gustav Mahler, and me solely depends on the desire and discretion of Frau Maria Alma Mahler and request suppression of this widespread, misleading news.' What he had decried as 'misleading' in his letter at the time now proved profitable in the right way at the auction house.

3

Wartime Art

Injuries and Rilke in the Gap

As a dragoon of imposing stature but supposedly only a less-than-robust constitution, and appropriately kitted out by leading Viennese tailors Goldmann and Salatsch, with light-blue jacket, red breeches and golden helmet – this is how Kokoschka reported for cavalry training at the Kaserne Wiener Neustadt on 3 January 1915. He was dressed in signal colour as if begging to get shot and, furthermore, mounted on a horse which he financed in part with the proceeds of the sale of *Windsbraut* and in part with taking on additional debt. The photograph, which shows him in this get-up, could have been taken at a fancy-dress party had the circumstances not been so tragic. From a distance, Kokoschka is reminiscent of Gustav Klimt's 1903 painting *Der goldene Ritter* (*Das Leben ein Kampf*) (*The Golden Knight/Life is a Struggle*) – a stylised herald of individualism, an anachronism of stiff stature who has stumbled into the Modern Era. Incidentally, it was friend Loos who had recommended the cavalry to Kokoschka. The emotionally damaged artist then found himself in the Lower Austrian Moravian dragoon regiment 'Erzherzog Joseph' ('Archduke Joseph') Nr 15.

Kokoschka was apparently willing to lose himself to the world. It seemed to him as if the world conspired against him and declared war against *him*. His emotional state was as precarious as his financial one in the weeks and months before he was drafted, though 10,000 kroners had already been donated to him by an anonymous patron. The generous mystery man was Ludwig Wittgenstein, whose large inheritance (which embarrassed him and he wanted to be rid of) enabled this spirit of patronage. He had asked the publisher of the journal *Der Brenner*, Ludwig von Ficker, to distribute 100,000 kroners to deserving artists in need. Among these beneficiaries were Rainer Maria Rilke, Else Lasker-Schüler, Adolf Loos and Georg Trakl. However, Kokoschka had substantial obligations: his own subsistence and the overheads of his studio in Vienna (he was able to sub-let it later), a large dowry for his sister which he had to provide to enable her to marry, the material support of his father and mother, which he continued to provide in various ways and means until their deaths (1923 and 1934, respectively).

Thus, Kokoschka went to war as one already injured, a psychological invalid. He later would see the serious wounds which still lay ahead of him as the physical counterparts to the state he was in when he entered the war. He lived and loved despairingly in the months prior to enlistment and until his deployment to the front in Galicia. The six-month-long military training in Vienna Neustadt, with its well-known humiliations (although as an officer candidate he was not required to live in the barracks), was interspersed with letters to Alma, now sometimes addressed 'my dear foolish sister' (Br I, 221). He still could not accept that he had lost his 'Almi'. Yet what he held to be true in art he also began to recommend as a maxim to himself and Alma for love: 'I like: to gain control over one's own noisy nature, and for me art is of the highest order that only *he* who no longer has the intoxication can practice and understand' (Br I, 211). As far as the practicalities of life in military service were concerned, Kokoschka had no difficulties bluntly reporting to his friend, the writer Albert Ehrenstein:

> I rise daily at 4 o'clock, ride with the squadron from 7 – 12 o'clock until my kneecaps practically fall off over ditches and muck and ice, as if I was born on the horse, am roundly cursed by junior officers such that I have no right to complain, lunch break from 12 – 1 and from 2 – 6 drills = attack lines, shooting and similar jokes ordered by an overzealous Major, mixed with dreadful annoyances and swearing flowing out of the mouths of two bourgeois reserve

officers who, now that the fat is in the frying pan, carry themselves as if everyone else is not worth shit. (Br I, 212)

At this time, Kokoschka may have dimly suspected that this was but a mild foretaste of the Galician front. Kokoschka depicted himself as a casualty, shot in the heart, in numerous works he produced in 1914. A finger lying on a chest wound is an early gesture in the self-portraits which seems to presage the bayonet wound he received at the end of August 1915. And he depicted himself on the fifth fan for Alma, his birthday present to her on 31 August 1914, as a knight who is lanced through the heart by one of her three anonymous lovers. It is more than symbolic that his double injury, a shot to the head in addition to the bayonet stabbing, happened a year later and thus shortly before Alma's thirty-sixth birthday. Incidentally, in October of that year, Alma (as of 18 August 1915, married name Gropius) presciently composed the song *Der Erkennende* (*Recognition*), setting to music the poem by Franz Werfel, whom she would win for herself later, in 1917.

In the meantime, Kokoschka had proven himself as a cadet with 'very good nerves' and sharp eyes in the baptism by fire in Galicia. He saw 'shot-up villages', cemeteries, 'famous battle fields' (Br I, 226/227), among them Grodek, the sight of which Georg Trakl could not get over. To Loos he announced at the beginning of August 1916 to be 'so happy' 'that I am still alive' (Br I, 226). Yet, as he told Herwarth Walden, at all times, in the trenches and later in the hospital, he yearned for 'his' magazine *Der Sturm*. Kokoschka's survival instincts were awakened in the extreme conditions at the Galician front. And he would continue to need them.

However, in a postcard to Walden, Adolf Loos reported what happened. On 29 August 'O.K. [was] shot in the temple during an attack.' And further:

The bullet pierced the ear canal and exited at the nape of the neck. His horse also fell. He ended up under four dead horses, dragged himself out, a Cossack stabbed him in the chest with his lance. (Lung) Is bandaged by the Russians, taken prisoner and transported.

At a stop he bribes one of his guards with 100 rubles so they carry him off the train. Now lying under guard of the Russians at the station. After two days this is attacked by the Austrians, walls collapse, OK stays in one piece. The Austrians take the house and OK can hand over the remaining Russians as 'his' prisoners.[1]

An unparalleled dragoon drama. Contrary to all previous self-assessments, often bordering on the hypochondriacal, Kokoschka apparently had a good constitution. The type of care he received, in particular at the Palais Palffy on the Josefsplatz in Vienna, which had been repurposed as a hospital, provided the rest. The photo which shows him with a caregiver there bears witness to a patient whose spirits already enabled him to flirt shamelessly. The caregiver has a name: Comtesse Alexandrine Mensdorff-Dietrichstein. She also had psychiatric instincts. In his memoirs he reports that she took him for a drive 'in her pony cart in the park of her parents' country estate', 'where she tried to wean me from my fear of the forests, the panicky fear from which I had suffered since the sudden burst of fire in Russia' (ML, 162). The headwound had caused a minor brain dysfunction through which Kokoschka lost his sense of balance. He knowledgeably compared his condition to one suffering from beriberi: '[...] you turn in a circle and fall like the experimental chicken placed on a straight chalk line which has hypnotised it' (ibid).

The poems of August Stramm, who fell at Horodec on the Dnieper-Bug Canal on 1 September 1915, which were printed in *Sturm* with a dedication by Herwarth Walden, particularly spoke to Kokoschka during his convalescence. Among others, he will have read the poem *Granaten* (*Grenades*) in the September 1915 issue.

Knowledge falters
Mere guessing weaves, deceives
Deafness deafens gruesome wounds
Folding groping digging screaming
Shrilling whistling hissing buzzing
Splintering clapping

Creaking crunching
Blunting stamping
The sky taps
The stars are slagging
Time abhors
Stolid worlding duller space.[2]

Oddly enough, before his mobilisation, Kokoschka saw himself as a corpse, as a Christ taken down from the cross in the arms of his mother, as a knight hovering between heaven and earth, as one risen in the darkness of the world. In the midst of the dying, art lives on. Equally so for Kokoschka. Walden organised a special exhibition of his works in early 1916 in his Berlin *Sturm*-Galerie, including *Windsbraut* and *Stilleben mit Katze, Putto und Kaninchen* (*Still Life with Cat, Putto and Rabbit*), whereas Kokoschka tellingly writes 'Kind' ('child') instead of 'Putto' in a letter. Fritz Gurlitt printed, albeit with a delay bitterly lamented by Kokoschka, the lithographic series *Der gefesselte Kolumbus* (*Columbus Bound*) and the *Bach-Kantate* (*Bach Cantata*), which was particularly important to the artist. Kokoschka painted portraits of his caregiver with her sister and brother, his doctor the ear specialist Dr Heinrich von Neumann, as well as Hermann Schwarzwald and a *Dame mit Papagei* (*Lady with a Parrot*). With these he proved to himself his ability to carry on, particularly after the serious injury. In the spring, he met more frequently with Rilke, even if, rather surprisingly, he did not paint his portrait. An undated letter from that time by the poet demonstrates his familiarity with Kokoschka's lithographs, the *Columbus* sheets and the *Cantata*. In June 1918 he writes to Kokoschka that he repeatedly thinks of the *Cantata* and is 'persuaded by it in his heart of hearts'.[3] The letter also reveals that the Fürstin Marie von Thurn und Taxis owned 'the self-portrait from the *Cantata*' and apparently had kept it safe. 'How are you and what are you up to, dear friend?', Rilke asks, referring to his sojourn in Rodaun where he hoped to meet Kokoschka and 'Frau Loulou Albert'-Lazard, the model for the *Dame mit Papagei*. Of himself, Rilke says in this letter that he is sitting around 'otherwise uselessly' and asks Kokoschka,

'Has some form of destiny resulted from your military fate? And the work?'⁴ This interest stands in stark contrast to what he wrote to Lou Albert-Lazard on 4 March 1916: he 'preferred to [maintain] a most indifferent abeyance and a careful detachment from books, paintings and lively conversations.'⁵ Half-a-year later and Rilke would distance himself from Kokoschka. Katharina Kippenberg received a dismissive response when she asked the poet whether he would like Kokoschka to illustrate his new edition of the *Cornet* poem. And further: he now deemed Kokoschka's art 'destructive'; it had no 'nature' and was lacking a form that could adequately express his inner turmoil. He considered the visual artist's plays to be misguided for similar reasons. Yet Rilke's critique of Kokoschka was primarily directed at Expressionism in general, with which he seemed to identify the artist without reservation. Rilke's finding reads as follows: 'The expressionist, this suddenly explosive introvert, who pours the lava of his boiling soul over everything in order to insist that the coincidental shape into which the crust solidifies is the new, the future, the ultimate outline of being, is just hopeless...'⁶ Only someone who understands the other's art, even internalises its problematic nature or believes to have recognised it as his own, can write like that. Nevertheless, as late as April 1920, Rilke expressed himself admiringly of Kokoschka's 'great talent', albeit coupled with 'internal dangers', to which he adds, these may 'not be different from the general ones of the time'.

He had sent Kokoschka his poem *Haßzellen, stark im größten Liebeskreise* (*Cells of Hate, Strong in the Greatest Circle of Love*) at the end of April 1916, after a visit to the artist's studio (which Kokoschka used between hospital stays until his renewed mobilisation to the front). There Kokoschka gave him a pen-and-ink sketch *Christus am Ölberg* (*Agony in the Garden*). The painter, however, associated it with his 'macabre *Still-leben mit* [gehäutetem] *Hammel und Hyacinthe*' (*Still Life with* [skinned] *Lamb and Hyacinth*).⁷ Rilke to Kokoschka: 'I give you the sheet itself, as I have written it, so it is only with you [...] as I believe no one will understand it or identify with it better than you, perhaps you will find some parts to be strong and enjoyable [...].'⁸

Rilke may have guessed correctly, as there are lines and stanzas in this poem that will have affected Kokoschka. Alone the tension between the 'cells of hate' and the 'circle of love' or the verse 'Already our loving overbends / When facing hats and rows of houses' will have reminded him of the debilitating experience of love with Alma.[9] There will have been a reaction to a stanza such as this one:

> Innermost silence of statues: made of blue
> stones of the night, threatened by the scream of a peacock:
> shrunk spaces, pure headspace, no gazing
> can drag it across into the incurable red.[10]

Yet it is a further motif of this poem that must have resonated with Kokoschka, it being unusual for Rilke to emphasise a motif that he presents in the form of repetition.

> We have nothing else but what is there inside,
> we have all of it in there.
> How can we grasp what is in there,
> Given that even what is flying is in there.[11]

The wind does not blow as such; rather, it 'stands' 'internally'. And the same goes for 'falling', which doesn't fall, rather 'stands internally', as the poem later suggests.[12] Was not Kokoschka also concerned with this 'internal', with the uplifting internalisation of the wind for the couple in *Windsbraut*, and the own internal to which the 'wounds' in some self-portraits of the time provide access? At the very least, it seems appropriate to view Kokoschka's relationship with Trakl and Rilke in a similar light.

In the Palais Palffy, Kokoschka had a 'very notorious General', who was known only by the name 'the Hyena of Hospitals' (ML, 162), to thank for his earlier-than-expected release from this improvised hospital in the heart of Vienna. Though there could be no question of his being 'fit for field duty', he was sent back to the front. Safe administrative duty at headquarters was not to his liking; he simply could not stand this kind of service. This time (it was July 1916), he went as a liaison officer, not by horse but by train, to the Italian front, into the marshy Isonzo Valley which would soon become infamous. A new, heavy shrapnel wound would end his deployment in terror after barely two months. August Stramm had also found new means of expression for this in his poem *Schrapnell* (*Shrapnel*).

The sky casts clouds
And rattles to smoke.
Points flash.
Feet teeter flying pebbles.
Eyes giggle in the craze
And
Splay.[13]

Nevertheless, for Kokoschka this meant he was no longer fit for duty and it was the end of the war for him. A turning point loomed in his life.

Berlin, Dresden and Stockholm Interludes

By early September 1916 Kokoschka was again living in Berlin. In addition to Herwarth Walden, other gallerists and art dealers were now showing an interest in him, such as Wolfgang Gurlitt and Paul Cassirer. They contended for him almost 'like for a prima donna', he wrote to his parents, meaning perhaps an increasingly positive response to his work and he was sure to make use of it, particularly to secure his material livelihood and thus also to contribute something to his elderly parents' care, especially his increasingly frail father. The ups and downs of his 'dearest little brother' Bohuslav also worried him. In addition to seeking more favourable remuneration for his paintings and drawings, he hoped more than anything for a professorship at the art academy 'in Dresden or Darmstadt' in order to become financially independent. However, it was the extremely advantageous contract he signed with Galerie Cassirer in 1916 that provided him with relative financial independence until 1931, and commensurate artistic freedom.

The worried letters to his parents, his brother and the occasional friend from that time have something touching about them and contradict the impression of Kokoschka as an inveterate egotist. What is more, these letters show someone who is marked as a casualty by an injured body and soul. Contrary to all common sense, he wants to return to the front. His mood swings drastically in those weeks. To Albert Ehrenstein he remarks on wanting to make an end to all (suffering). In contrast, he writes to his mother in November 1916, from Berlin: 'If I have managed to survive in one piece so far, I don't want to get nailed now towards the end. [...] So I want to go to Dresden on 1st December to a sanatorium where I also have friends among the doctors who will protect me there for as long as possible' (Br I, 259). This was not entirely true as he did not have such friends in Dresden at that time. He met the doctor who was to become his friend, Fritz Neuberger, once he was in Dresden. It is likely that Albert Ehrenstein told him about Neuberger. Ehrenstein asked him to look after Kokoschka in Dresden, as he also did for the authors Walter Hasenclever and Iwar von Lücken, as well as for the actor Heinrich George. From December 1916, Kokoschka spent nearly nine months in Dresden-Loschwitz, in the spa district Weißer Hirsch, where during the war a military hospital was based in Heinrich Lahmann's then-world famous 'psychiatric sanatorium'. In his memoirs, Kokoschka describes the encounter with Neuberger at the Dresden train station as an unexpected event. He portrays the doctor with the Tolstoy beard as his mystagogue who literally leads him away from his suicidal desire to report back to the front, and into the world of natural healing through light and air, water and diet, because here in the spa district of Weißer Hirsch, Franz Kafka, Rainer Maria Rilke and Thomas Mann had taken their cures, as had the beautiful Gräfin Schwerin and members of the Austrian imperial household.

This Dr Neuberger, nicknamed 'Wonder Rabbi' by Hasenclever, would quickly become a confidant and advisor to Kokoschka, and not only in matters medical. Kokoschka portrayed him with a quick pencil; he drew the ensemble of friends, among them also the actress Käthe Richter, deep in silent conversation in a form of group portrait (1917/1918) – his most important painting from this period. Dr Neuberger's expert assessments provided the definitive confirmation of Hasenclever and Kokoschka's lack of fitness for duty.

The world of the Weißer Hirsch was an urban magic mountain or a Monte Verità on an Elbe sandstone elevation. A bizarre little crowd had gathered there[14] – mystics and Expressionists – though some of the doctors gave their patients a close run in their bizarreness. One thinks, for instance, of the neurologist Dr Heinrich Stadelmann who, following Lahmann's example, maintained a private sanitorium for the mentally ill (though, according to hearsay, some of the patients there pretended to be sick). George Grosz depicted him in great detail in his autobiographical novel *Ein kleines Ja und ein großes Nein* (*A Little Yes and a Big No*): 'His patients were like precious, exotic birds to him. [...] He constructed a ghost piano, came up with a totally new calendar system and invented his own mathematics.'[15]

In addition to the friendships with Käthe Richter, Walter Hasenclever and Fritz Neuberger, who was translating Honoré de Balzac's novel *Der Vetter Pons* (*Cousin Pons*) for the Kurt Wolff publishing house, the municipal Albert Theatre proved particularly stimulating for Kokoschka in this first Dresden period. Hasenclever's piece *Der Sohn* (*The Son*), which introduced the conflict between generations as a contemporary issue, premiered there in 1916. The Albert Theatre would now prove to be an aptly experimental stage for Kokoschka's dramatic efforts. Under his direction and with his set designs, he staged his plays *Mörder Hoffnung der Frauen* and *Hiob* (*Job*) there on 3 June 1917, with Käthe Richter and the young Ernst Deutsch in the lead roles. As well as praising what Kokoschka considered the 'very modernly led' Albert Theatre, Hasenclever championed his plays (Br I, 263). He wrote to his ill father, probably to cheer him up a bit and to impress him: 'The actors are very excited because the entire press from Berlin has to come over, as ever when something momentous is happening in the provinces' (Br I, 264). Though not all came, there were a few critics from Berlin, among them Paul Kornfeld. He judged:

Kokoschka's people express themselves not only through the word, but especially through gestures and movement; as the word speaks the contents of what needs saying, the movement communicates its spirit [...] We suspect a new style possibility, perhaps a new art form that most closely resembles the opera; the pantomime supported by the word.[16]

Director Kokoschka will have paid particular attention to the actors' movement sequences, as he had shown a strong interest early on in free dance as per Isadora Duncan, though it was more likely to have been Mary Wigman who stood before him in Dresden. These forms of physicality are expressed in the stage directions, as when he prescribes that the Woman should writhe 'on the steps like a dying animal', clenching 'her thighs and muscle[s]' (DSW I, 40; Mitchell, 28).

Another critic, Camill Hoffmann, emphasised the creative lighting effects of Kokoschka's direction, which were supposed to be more, and apparently also offered more, than simple lighting: 'The light, colossal, will be Kokoschka's most effective tool. White with intermittently red light on the scene, bright cones drop on the figures, glorioles twine around groups [...].'[17] The reference that a light figure ('cone') not only illuminates the action but becomes an actor in itself is revealing here. This also impressed another critic, who praised how the light 'at the right place and the right time' was part of the action on stage, and thereby speaks of a 'colour-musical allegorisation' of the plot.[18]

In a remarkably insightful review, this same Camill Hoffmann would point to the importance of colour for Kokoschka, specifically as the primary 'source of inspiration, capable of all transformations'. It was also Hoffmann who was the first to see a connection between Kokoschka's landscapes and his portraits – appropriately named 'human countenance' by him: '[...] one believes oneself drawn in [into these paintings is meant here, among others *Die Auswanderer* (*The Émigrés*)]; one does not stand on the outside observing, rather one senses history or a legend or a poem from the rhythm of the emerging mountains, houses, trees, paths.'[19] Added to this was now Kokoschka's work as a director, for which the critic had a particular eye, given his synaesthetic perspective.

Kokoschka's theatrically effective work with light showed Adolphe Appia's influence, whom the young artist was presumably introduced to by that Viennese master of light direction and professor at the Kunstgewerbeschule, Alfred Roller (1864–1935). Roller's Appian lighting design had already made its way into his production at the Vienna Hofoper – with the approval of its director, Gustav Mahler![20] There was also the oddity that in addition to the theatrical, Kokoschka also experienced the therapeutic meaning of light in Dresden, namely at the sanatorium on the Weißen Hirsch.

There would be further productions of his plays in Berlin by Max Reinhardt (1919) and in Frankfurt (1920 and 1921) where Heinrich George directed. Undoubtedly, in that period, Kokoschka became the primary provider of lighting design and a revivor of the idea of the synthesis of the arts through a marked shift in their elements; music was not the all-dominant medium, but rather the gestural communication and the work with light. Paul Hindemith's setting of *Mörder Hoffnung der Frauen* to music did not fundamentally change that, as the premiere of this sound-drama in the Württembergische Landestheater Stuttgart was with lighting effects and set design by Oskar Schlemmer.

It seems appropriate to make a small digression about a deleted and then reinstated comma, raised by the crucial question whether a comma separates 'Mörder' ('Murderer') from 'Hoffnung der Frauen' ('Hope of Women'). And would the murderer(s) thus be the perverse bearers of hope for all womankind? Kokoschka in no way treated this comma consistently. The first printing by Kurt Wolff set 'Mörder' as the main title and 'Hoffnung der Frauen' – still in capital letters but reduced in size by one point – as the subtitle. Hindemith insisted on the comma in his adaptation and therefore understood 'Hoffnung der Frauen' as definition of 'Mörder'. With or without the comma, and with or without music, this text remained controversial.

Incidentally, the performances of the plays *Der brennende Dornbusch* and *Hiob* at the Berliner Kammerspielen in 1919 took on the dimensions of a major theatre scandal. Kokoschka recalls:

At the time, Max Reinhardt feared for the iron curtain; the Schupo, thence the foot patrol police, had to separate the fighting supporters and opponents in the street. I put a masked head that could be removed on the actor Paul Graetz, who had the role of Job. As the uproar started at the end of the performance, I took my bows in front of the audience and held this empty skull of the dead Job lying on the stage up to their eyes, thumped on it and scornfully screamed at the audience: 'this is how empty your heads are!' (ML, 170)

This increasingly Europeanised Viennese artist from Pöchlarn was capable of scandal even in Berlin in the penultimate year of the First World War. In any case, it seemed that from then on, the dramatist and director Oskar Kokoschka was on an equal footing with the picture artist. Kokoschka seems to have taken his Dresden stage success as a pivotal inspiration for continuing those parallel efforts in his work. Previously he had taken up his earlier piece *Sphinx und Strohmann* again and renamed it *Hiob*. His reworked version of this burlesque piece, first staged in the open air in Vienna in the summer of 1909, had taken on a personal poignancy, belonging to his continued attempts to come to terms with his unresolved love affair with Alma Mahler, now Alma Gropius. As painfully grotesque as this relationship must have come to seem to him by that point, he still felt tied to her. To the uninitiated in this bizarre affair, the play frankly could only seem to be an example of surreal theatre, in which a pig's bladder filled to bursting symbolises the feminine Anima, Death appears as 'living normal person' and the Contortionist heightens the absurdity of the human condition. The main character, Herr Firdusi, becomes Job. If one can imagine this character with a 'gigantic revolving straw head with arms and legs, carrying a pig's bladder on a string' (DSW I, 54; Mitchell, 40), Job presents himself as a lovesick fool knocking on the door of his wife Anima in vain. Of course, both Job and Anima gradually grow a set of antlers in the course of the play, Firdusi's where an air pistol has wounded his head during a suicide attempt. It was hardly surprising that the DADA-Gallery in Zurich declared itself willing to support the performance, which took place in April 1917. Hugo Ball and Tristan Tzara appeared in the leading roles. Kokoschka had finally arrived in the literary Modernist movement, which is also evidenced by the fact that the Kurt Wolff publishing house brought out both pieces, *Der brennende Dornbusch* and *Mörder Hoffnung der Frauen* (now even referred to as plays), in the prestigious avant-garde series *Der jüngste Tag* (*The Newest Day*) as its forty-first edition.

Kokoschka continued to be afflicted with heartache and so for his *Hiob* drama he transferred the Anima, the Contortionist (now a type of Mephistopheles) and the Parrot from *Sphinx und Strohmann* – including entire passages word for word. With this he gave himself the signal, the torment continues: 'I had a wife, / She was my world!' (DSW I, 71; Mitchell, 66). This Job loves himself hand and foot (the German can be taken quite literally), whereas the Contortionist sees the whole situation as a quasi-scientific experiment.

In this period, likely the summer of 1917, in Dresden, Kokoschka began work on a new play, *Orpheus und Eurydike* (*Orpheus and Eurydice*); it would be his most important poetic-dramatic text to date. At the same time, he was occupied with illustrations for *Hiob*, the paintings *Liebespaar mit Katze* (*Lovers with Cat*) for which Käthe Richter and Walter Hasenclever posed, as they did in the winter of 1916/1917 (ML, 169), *Die Auswanderer* (depicting Käthe Richter, Fritz Neuberger and himself), as well as, presumably, the beginnings of the painting *Die Freunde* (*The Friends*), in which he turns his back to the observer and only offers a half-profile whereas usually he offered full-frontal views of himself. It is a creative work of the soul that Kokoschka delivers. Yet it is not a true processing, but rather a repeated effort to work through his continued fixation on Alma in all forms of expressive media available to him. This also includes an oral essay, which he simply calls a 'composition'. It wants to honour Amos Comenius, in renewed praise of his *Orbis Pictus* as a means of recognising the purpose of the world in pictures. However, the attempt leads Kokoschka to a story about a – no, *the* – 'red string'. The meaning of this was a 'necklace with blood-red glass pearls', a keepsake of Alma Mahler's, that he had given his mother – of all people – to keep safe when he was mobilised. In his memoirs, Kokoschka explains: 'My mother stuck it in a flower pot so she would not have to be reminded of blood' (ML, 145). He introduces the prose of 1917, which refers specifically to this episode, in a markedly circuitous manner.

> If I relate an incident that was told to me [...] as if it were my own, then I am venturing to hide a stranger in the first-person form; as no one knows him as I do, the reader only from the perspective of his good will. Who shows me a string that held meaning for him, as a madness no longer held truth for him in this life. (DSW III, 15)

In Kokoschka's palpably painful, alienated story the string is composed of stones which 'glow when they are held into the sun's fire'. The 'I' of the story is heavily wounded in the war, but is still able to write to his mother to request the red chain. She initially pretends not to be able to find the 'red string' cursed by her. Only once the aforementioned flower pot shatters in pieces does it reappear. She helps him to live on: 'Because the string is set for fire which came from the beloved and, without nourishment, diminished as I vied for her. Until the fire consumed me. Now my soul, despite her beloved appearance, shone from the embers' (DSW III, 16). In this chain of embers – at least in the story – the love stored within outshines all accumulated feelings of hate. Nevertheless, one notices the unusual sentence structure ('When death, this in winter was; as all burning life, in deep in the earth is buried?'). He allows one to decipher the meaning of the sentence in phases. It is supposed to be constructed from sentence pieces, just as Kokoschka would shortly put together the remembered, felt and caressed parts of Alma's body in the form of a doll.

But first, something else occurred, something totally unexpected. On 1 August he received an invitation from the Austrian foreign ministry to contribute to an exhibition in Stockholm on Austrian modern art. This self-portrayal of Austrian Modernism in pictorial art was in the context of the International Peace Conference meeting in neutral Sweden. He received the travel permit for mid-September. It is surprising in retrospect that such a thing was even possible in the middle of the war. For Kokoschka, in addition to a short trip north and a welcome distraction, this, most importantly, represented the first official government recognition of his art, which he however would perceive ambivalently. His parents were instructed to send 'immediately express highly insured dinner jacket complete, frock-coat including grey trousers, low patent leather shoes in two packages' to him in Dresden (Br I, 271).

Times had changed. Previously he had described himself in writing as being 'without dinner jacket and manners'. Now he wanted to travel as an up-and-coming man of the world because he would be meeting Stockholm's mayor and two Nobel Prize winners; he would paint their portraits, as well as Selma Lagerlöf's. After his visit 'with the author Lagerlöf' he felt 'once again armed, through her friendliness, to endure brutalities' (Br I, 275).

With Kokoschka, it was not just travel sickness, as his health was not the best despite the lengthy stay in Dresden's Weißer Hirsch. The first letter from Stockholm, dated 17 September 1917, went to his friend Albert Ehrenstein: 'Am quite worn out from the trip, much pain, not practical enough to orientate myself, cannot work, everything very expensive, very pretty, but terribly cold' (Br I, 273). The journey took him from Berlin by way of Saßnitz where he realised at the border that he required a passport, which forced him to return to Berlin to obtain the necessary document. In Saßnitz 'the train [was] pushed into the steamer', as he described to his parents, then crossed to Trelleborg, and finally from Malmö to Stockholm – a total of twenty-four hours' journey time.

He remained sceptical of Stockholm. He deemed the people withdrawn; the climate seemed unbearable. The cool north was not good for the fiery emotional person. He articulates matters to Ehrenstein.

I experience everything more in lead-grey and ash colours.

I have never been so miserable. My own countrymen here a tight ring of interests I am ill-disposed towards. [...]

The exhibition was also put together and represented to the public so unkindly (towards me). [...] A similar torture may await me in Copenhagen. It is grotesque. (Br I, 276)

He was spared Copenhagen. He yearned to be 'out' 'of this cold, heart-less loneliness'. He hoped for an attaché post at the Austrian delegation in Bern; however, intellectuals and artists from all over the crumbling Imperial and Royal Empire were drawn there and Kokoschka did not have sufficiently influential supporters to obtain such an appointment.

> All my life I was an outsider, alone, at best known as a comical fool at home, and now one believes one must drape a modern coat around oneself whilst abroad, but has so little confidence that one might cover everything up again and begin unhappily so one only harms me in a way that is difficult to make good again. The foreign market and suggestion of a first performance will take a devilishly long time if one is represented (that is, trampled) by such Viennese idiots. In addition, I have to spend at least two–three days in bed each week, with high fever, the lung just doesn't have the resistance anymore, devilish chest pains and I am certain that my strength and youth are gone, and also my health. (Br I, 276)

He seems resigned at the end of his two-month stay in Stockholm: '[...] I am so done in and so depressed that I already have horrific worries about the practical side of the journey. I wish I were already dead, if only to get some rest for once' (Br I, 278).

And yet, his stay in Stockholm was not a complete waste. Already familiar with Strindberg and Ibsen, he discovered Knut Hamsun for himself, in particular his novel *Pan*. Kokoschka identified with the main character as with no other literary figure; discharged from military service, Lieutenant Glahn cannot cope with life as a civilian; he is torn between two women, loses both and destroys himself in the process. Kokoschka would even sign some of his letters as 'Lieutenant Glahn'. Kokoschka's impact on women – it would increase further in later years – could be aptly described with one narrative phrase from *Pan*: 'A lady is supposed to have said: "When he looks at me, I am lost; it is as if he touched me." '[21]

Kokoschka's preferred reading material at the time indicates a preference for contrasts. In addition to Hamsun's *Pan*, he read and recommended the odes of Horace, as well as Stifter's novel *Nachsommer (Indian Summer)*, which he hoped to illustrate. *Nachsommer* brought him back to the country of his childhood, 'before the big time across the border came...', as he remarked, not without irony, when he recommended the novel to Alexandrine, Gräfin Khuenburg (Br I, 259). A comment to his brother Bohuslav, who was in the process of dedicating himself to literature – as well as, more importantly, to a dandified lifestyle – suggests that he found a too-intensive reading of Hamsun problematical. 'Stick to Stifter, so you avoid Knut Hamsun', he advises his 'old darling' in a letter written after his Sweden trip (Br I, 285).

It is hardly surprising that Kokoschka felt addressed by Stifter's novel *Der Nachsommer*, with its topography and atmosphere, in light of his multi-faceted connections to an area familiar to the artist, but also to the visual arts. Consequently the development of the main character, the artistically inclined geologist Heinrich Drendorf, has its beginning in the appreciation of the riot of colours in a rose arbour: 'The colours went from the pure white of the white roses through the yellowish and reddish white of the roses in between into the delicate red and in the crimson and the blueish and blackish red of the red roses [...]. Thus the colours bloomed in mixed confusion.'[22] Even the building sketches by his host, the ageing Freiherr von Risach, offers Drendorf a reason to contemplate the aspects of colour treatment as they relate to drawings – a question of lifelong importance to Kokoschka. 'The colours were always held so subordinated that the drawings did not become paintings, rather remained sketches that were lifted through colour.' The general conclusion follows.

> Where the colour has taken on another reality, it was placed with objectivity and mass, which, as I knew from experience, is so difficult to find, so that things appear as things and not as colourations. This is particularly the case with objects that have less defined colours, like stones, walls and such like, while those things of distinct colour are easier to treat, like flowers, butterflies, even some birds.[23]

This articulated something that had direct relevance, particularly for Kokoschka's landscapes and nature impressions. Yet in 1917 there was no colour-pure non-political zone. Just the opposite. Thus, in Stockholm, he presumably encountered Stefan Grossmann, the eminent journalist who introduced the Viennese *feuilleton* style to Berlin in the *Vossischen Zeitung* and would later publish the influential literary periodical *Das Tagebuch*. Through him it is likely that Kokoschka had access to the (socialist) peace conference of which, however, he only had sobering things to say. He met Carl Lindhagen, the mayor of Stockholm, and painted him, as well as the Nobel Prize winner Svante Arrhenius. And, on his own account, he was introduced to another Nobel Prize winner, the Austrian physiologist and neurologist Robert Bárány, who taught in Uppsala and who provided him with a new medical certificate that confirmed his unequivocal lack of fitness for duty.

He saw the powerful and the powerless around the edges of the peace conference, saw 'the newsreel films' in the cinematograph which 'in comparison to those of the countries at war had the advantage' 'that they did not heroise and did not bring idealised acts of war, but rather authentic pictures of the battle field to the public, which pleasantly gave one the creeps and rejoicing in one's own neutrality' (ML, 172). He took notice of the Belgian socialist Camille Huysmans; even more so of the 'Lion of Sweden', 'people's champion' and future prime minister of Sweden Hjalmar Branting, in whose study a concert grand piano and wastepaper basket stood on a polar bear skin next to a marble bust of Branting himself. Kokoschka noted how Branting was celebrated as a man of peace, while at the same time Swedish 'production of war materiel for both sides increased daily' (ML, 172). And then there were also 'the three wisemen from the East', 'an Indian, an Egyptian and a negro', who wandered around Stockholm, self-declared representatives of the colonies, who had heard something about the peace conference but were ignored by the official delegates. In his *Brief aus Stockholm* (*Letter from Stockholm*), dated winter 1917, Kokoschka depicts the scene of their encounter (DSW II, 143–152), which became so fixed in his mind that he also picked up on it in his autobiography. Kokoschka found himself at a dinner with Mayor Lindhagen, of whom it was said he sympathised with anarchists. The gathering could not have been more culturally diverse.

Furthermore, in the National Museum of Sweden Kokoschka marvelled at later works by Rembrandt and came across paintings by the Swedish artist Ernst Josephson (1851–1906), who wanted to become the Swedish Rembrandt. This artist (in the end suffering from hallucinations, paranoia and delusions of grandeur), who also made his mark as a lyricist,[24] must have particularly appealed to Kokoschka, based on his intense colours, his use of light and the mythological material of his paintings (although he also incorporated the world of work in his creations). Josephson's later drawings did not impress him any less. Kokoschka's expert opinion of them prevented the administration of the mental hospital, where the artist had died more than ten years previously, from burning the drawings found there.

Nevertheless, from an artistic perspective, one piece which Kokoschka did during his Stockholm weeks was of particular significance: his painting of the Stockholm harbour with a view to Strandvägen, created on a 'lofty elevation'. For the first time, in neutral Sweden, he honoured what he had sworn to himself in the trenches of Galicia and at the Isonzo front: to relinquish the mole-like perspective of the soldier and instead paint the cities of Europe with a broad view from the highest possible vantage point in order to give the magnificence of these cities and their culture a face.

From 21 November 1917 Kokoschka was back in Dresden in Teuscher's sanatorium, working on the painting *Die Freunde* (*The Friends*) and pursuing his interests in an academic professorship in Dresden or Darmstadt through his – by then – influential publisher Kurt Wolff. Though receiving outstanding medical care, Kokoschka felt himself to be on the precipice of a volcano or in the vicinity of Hades emotionally in the following months. That may also be why he began working on his play *Orpheus und Eurydike* again, a piece he had begun before Stockholm.

Once to Hades and Back, or Orpheus and Eurydice as Mystagogues

The material lent itself: lovers caught between life and the underworld, even though the classical mythological situations did not quite match those important to Kokoschka. However, myth lives through trans-formation, and so it does here. This play, *Orpheus und Eurydike*, was being written by an author who had come close to death more than once, who had loved passionately and who was still trying to 'uncover' the 'true relationship' between himself and Alma. Regardless of how clearly matters may have stood for Alma after her marriage to Gropius, Kokoschka still felt himself tied to her. In contrast to the myth, Koko-schka/Orpheus did not have to travel into Hades to bring Alma/Eury-dice back from the realm of the dead into that of the living. In his fantasy it was more her pulling on him, who saw himself as half-dead, as Alma stood squarely in the midst of life. In his eyes she was bursting with vitality whilst he starved, continuing to suffer emotionally and physically, all the while having to fend off suicidal tendencies which he could not (yet) conquer.

It speaks to the quality of the play's script, however hotly debated it was from the outset, that Kokoschka did not simply attempt to depict the problems of his own life. First and foremost, this three-act drama, clearly structured in scenes, intends to satisfy creative demands. Notable personal experiences are not incorporated in *Orpheus und Eurydike*. As a piece of dramatic literature, Kokoschka's work definitely meas-ures up to Jean Cocteau's *Orphée* (1925), though Kokoschka – heavily influenced by Rilke – was preoccupied with the death and rebirth of the *writer's* Orpheus. The triad of treatments of the Orpheus myth at that time was completed with Rilke's *Sonette an Orpheus* (*Sonnets to Orpheus*, 1925), which in turn declared transformation as the central theme.[25] Over fifty literary treatments of the Orpheus myth can be found across Europe between the late 1880s and early 1930s.[26]

Kokoschka's etchings for his play, but also the painting which shows Ernst Deutsch and Käthe Richter as Orpheus and Eurydice, function especially intensively as mutual elucidation of picture and text. This is particularly so when he portrays the Furies as the Devil, or Orpheus as an artist with a brush in his right hand whilst behind him an owl-like Eurydice partly emerges out of the shadow, and is partly rooted in it. In contrast to Orpheus, Eurydice directs her barely suggested glance towards the observer. It almost seems as though Eurydice has twisted Orpheus' head to the side as if she were manipulating him. Or does he just wish to concentrate on his art, his emblem?

It is one of the peculiarities of Kokoschka's struggle with this thematic complexity that he seriously questioned whether in future he should focus entirely on writing for the stage or at least rethink his artwork and its technique. This intent is expressed in an unpublished letter, of July 1923, to the composer Ernst Křenek in which Kokoschka writes: 'I think I will go to America in the autumn, if not then after the winter to build myself a new existence based on the theatre, and as a painter keep my works in progress secret for a time so I can make them really strong.'[27]

The idea for the drama goes back to the autumn of 1915 in the military hospital in Brünn; the actual writing of it must have followed between the end of 1916 and mid-1918; its premiere was on 2 February 1921 by courtesy of Heinrich George. In the midst of this artistic development process, Kokoschka was able to create not just expressive etchings, and pen-and-ink drawings of this mythical motif cycle, but also the painting of *Orpheus und Eurydike* on a ship where in the background – corresponding to Kokoschka's play – its helmsman dives into the sea. What he will find there is a skull with a ring between its teeth.

On the opera's opening night, critics were harsh particularly regarding the libretto. One critic called it a 'monstrosity' and found: 'The libretto is also reminiscent of some Cubist-Dadaist painter who makes a dog's dinner of colourful splotches and thick lines.'[28] The overall thrust of the critiques was that it was only Křenek's composition which made the piece comprehensible. The 'mood' of the opera was praised; its daring architecture and stirring music released the listener from the 'duress of the words'. Křenek was able to evoke the perceived abstraction of Kokoschka's language through the use of somewhat free contrapuntal structures.

However, let us recap the content and thus Kokoschka's piece. Three Furies function as representatives of Hades. They arrive to take Eurydice into the Shadowland, Hades' realm. Eurydice is torn between the fear of having to forget Orpheus and the desire for the dark stranger, the ruler of the underworld, who is pursuing her. Orpheus and Eurydice make their farewells; they are able to do so without embracing each other as Eurydice already belongs to the shadows. She is meant to remain with Hades for seven years; yet before the term expires Orpheus, driven by restlessness, descends into the underworld to retrieve his beloved wife. The condition is that he must overcome his distrust and may not ask her what kind of 'life' she led in the underworld. But the ship that is supposed to take them into the land of the living is a ship of the dead on which the Furies weave a net; on the journey Orpheus forces Eurydice to confess that she gradually forgot about him in the Orcus and eventually belonged to Hades. This confession is brought about through a ring which the helmsman finds in a skull when he dives into the water. This ring reveals to Orpheus his wife's betrayal. Not only can he not overcome his distrust; he is consumed by such a jealous rage that he kills Eurydice. In the third act Orpheus, now a lunatic, returns to the wreckage of his house. Playing his lyre, he rages against Nature and urges the people into the ways of iniquity; consequently, they rise up against him and murder him in the ruins of his house.

Hate lurks behind love; murderous urges germinate in distrust. Now it is Eurydice's turn to kill Orpheus in Orcus once again. Only those twice-killed erstwhile lovers can find peace in each other imparted by Psyche, who, for her part, tricked by the Furies, blinds her beloved Eros with a torch. She is the one, in Kokoschka's play, who finds Orpheus' lyre again and thus can grant a final harmony in death, just as her tears healed Eros' eyes in the end.

If Orpheus' manic dialogue has qualities reminiscent of Hamlet, then the master plan of this drama demonstrates that Kokoschka not only gave it a visual component, but also hoped for a musical transposition. That this was then accomplished by Ernst Křenek may be termed a particular coincidence, not just because Křenek himself was from Brünn, where Kokoschka designed his drama; this young composer also understood the effectiveness of cutting Kokoschka's drama down to libretto size. In addition, at the time of his collaboration with Kokoschka, Křenek was in a relationship with Anna Mahler and as an insider could instantly see through the symbolism of his (for a brief time) mother-in-law and Kokoschka in this life-and-death drama.

In Křenek's 'Erinnerungen an die Moderne' *Im Atem der Zeit* (*Self-Analysis*), extensive as it is readable, there are important accounts of Kokoschka in his Dresden period and of the work on the *Orpheus-und-Eurydike* opera which was completed in 1923/1924 (the premiere was then at the Kasseler Stadttheater on 27 November 1927).

> Kokoschka was a very good-looking man of indefinable age – in the fifteen years of my acquaintanceship with him he did not seem to change or, if anything, appeared younger each time. In fact, he was in his early thirties when I met him. He had a hesitant and unsettlingly volatile manner, spoke in a broad Viennese dialect which I hugely liked from the beginning even though it was very strenuous and often virtually impossible to follow his fantastical discourse. He had a lovely apartment, which had been provided to him by the state, in a charming rococo pavilion which the Saxony kings had built in a huge park bordering on the royal palace in Dresden.[29]

One can picture him: the artist king telling tales in Viennese dialect in the Saxon cultural metropolis; from 1919 he was even a professor at the Elbe-Florentine Kunstakademie. Křenek continues about this environment.

> Kokoschka lived there with a pretty, but not very refined woman [this refers to the Russian Jewess Anna Kallin, whom Kokoschka had met in art collector Ida Bienert's social circle] and a cook from Vienna or Bohemia, who addressed him as Herr Rittmeister [Mr Cavalry Captain], appropriate to the rank which he supposedly held in the War. He also told a story of how he had been wounded by a Russian lancer and had spent a time in Siberian captivity, but all these stories had something fishy about them, though never creating

the impression of boasting as they were told in such a way that one thought the narrator did not care whether one believed him as long as one respected his rich imagination.[30]

Křenek admitted that he did not understand anything of Kokoschka's Orpheus drama initially. He saw it at first as 'expressionistic blah-blah of the highest order',[31] until he then realised what the main theme was, specifically the 'problematic nature of fidelity and memory'[32] – a memory which becomes a burden and weighs so heavily that it makes continuing to live an impossibility. Orpheus, initially the survivor, eventually succumbs to his survival.

Kokoschka repeatedly indicated to Křenek how 'childishly' he was looking forward to his music for *Orpheus*.[33] This anticipation was then rewarded with a score which would count as one of Křenek's most important compositions. According to the composer this impact was also the result of that 'magical' chord (D-E-A), from which an atmospheric aura emanates and with which Křenek allows the opera to begin and end. He also uses this chord during the piece 'as a type of orientation point',[34] a tonal character which is not used as a recurring theme, but rather, one could say, as a matter of musical orientation.

Kokoschka's 'work on the myth' may have had a cathartic effect on him. In the sexualised Hades of his play Eros and Thanatos become one, whereas the central theme of the piece is the simultaneous repeated killing-off of love. The trauma of weaning from Alma received its dramatic-allegorical expression with the visually artistic (self-)analysis in *Orpheus und Eurydike*. Kokoschka obviously appeared to have overcome his self-centredness with this in that he was able to transform the problematic nature of his love life into a universal human-mythical story. However, the third form of this weaning process – literally turning Alma into a doll – seems to revert to self-centredness at first glance.

What did this this doll transformation of Alma Schindler-Mahler-Gropius represent? A sensual-manic fetish or an attempted metamorphosis? Perversion or the anatomisation of a love object?

The Doll Transformation, or Dollyfication of Alma Mahler-Gropius

Kokoschka tried to parallel this new attempt to articulate the myth with trying to visualise music, as happened in his painting *Die Macht der Musik* (*The Power of Music*) which he completed in the summer of 1919. The colour-intensive painting can equally be interpreted as an Orpheus allegory; whilst the shepherd's pipe in the right hand of the Orphean musician grows flowers, animals take flight and a large youth cowers in the corner. Here, too, Kokoschka suggests the myth. It is not the taming of the wild through music that is depicted here; rather, it is the powerful effect of music which is continued or further reinforced through the strong use of colour.

Kokoschka's reputation as an artist and the esteem in which he was held by then is also seen in the fact that the Dresdner Gemäldegalerie acquired this work as early as December of the same year. Kokoschka had now arrived, in every respect, in Dresden. On 18 August 1919 the Internal Affairs Ministry of Saxony appointed him Professor at the Dresdner Kunstakademie for a term of seven years and with an annual salary of nearly 5,000 Reichsmarks, a princely sum in those days. He moved into the home mentioned by Křenek, one of eight so-called cavalier houses, in December. His studio could not have been more centrally situated but also publically exposed, in the gardens behind the Brühl's Terrace above the Elbe from where he created his first Elbe-view paintings, among them *Dresden, Neustadt I* (*Dresden, Newtown I*). The perspective of the Dresden paintings that followed also showed that the artist found himself to be the equal of this city by then. They distinguish themselves through bright, saturated colours – in particular striking blue tones – and expansive projections. The painting's structure is technically defined by the palette knife. If the Elbe still seems particularly dark, Hades-like if you will, in *Dresden, Neustadt II*, it brightens noticeably in the further renditions of the series, becoming a mirror-like surface for the city, even picking up the light blue of the sky. Dresden had become his city, or so it seemed.

However, Kokoschka still had to cope with long-standing psychological issues. The weightiest of these, in every respect, continued to be Alma Mahler-Gropius. The summer of 1918 offered an unexpected opportunity for him to let this continuing painful emotional effort become tangible and redirect it to a life object. The encounter with the Stuttgart doll maker Hermine Moos led him to commission a life-sized, anatomically identical doll of his erstwhile lover. In his memoirs he claims to have been focused on the larger political picture in these last months of the war. His letters reveal nothing of the sort. Kokoschka was far more interested in the exactitude of reproducing Alma's body than in what was happening at the front or any internal tensions in the Empire. He himself provided anatomical sketches, advice and suggestions for the materials to use. His training in the *applied* arts emerged to his benefit once again. Because that was what this 'fetish', as he himself called the doll (Br I, 295), was supposed to be above all else: an art *object* with significant real-life relevance. And that is what Kokoschka had literally meant from the beginning, because this Alma doll was supposed to *live* with him.

In the history of dolls as a cultural phenomenon, this event is unique.[35] It is also fundamentally different to Rilke's interest in Lotte Pritzel's wax dolls and in their 'souls'. Rilke spoke of it, that things are grateful for tenderness. In this case, however, there was no hint of tenderness in describing the doll's materiality. Kokoschka's letters to Hermine Moos, taken together, provide an essay on the doll, but as a physical manifestation of a heartache addict's imagination and projection.

I am very curious about the stuffing, in my drawing I have broadly indicated the flat areas, the incipient hollows and wrinkles that are important to me, will the skin – on whose discovery and material, consistent with the character of the body parts, different expression I am most excited – will it all become richer, more tender, more human? Take one of Rubens' paintings of his wife, for example the two where she is shown as a young woman with her children, as the ideal. (Br I, 291)

He demanded the 'deception of magic' from Moos, to which even the organic attachment of the hair to the scalp belonged. According to Kokoschka's instructions, should the internal wall of the body be reinforced with 'boiled, paste blended paper mixture', then the doll maker should work the particularly sensual body parts of 'cotton pulp' with cotton wool. He wanted to be 'fooled' by the 'miraculous being', and that literally at any price (Br I, 293). In order to form an understanding of the precision Kokoschka provided in his information and instructions to his doll maker, a further longer passage from his letters is cited here.

> Pay attention to the dimensions of the head, of the neck, the rib cage, the rear and the limbs. And take to heart the contours of the body. For example, the line of the neck to the back, the curve of the belly. I only drew in the second leg, set at a slant, so you can see the form of the same from the inside, otherwise the entire figure is only intended in profile, so that the line of emphasis from the head to the instep of the foot enables an exact determination for your shaping of the body. Please permit my sense of touch to take pleasure in those places where layers of fat or muscle suddenly give way to a sinewy covering of skin, from which a piece of bone rises to the surface, for example, at the shin bone, the pelvic bone, the shoulder blade-collar bone and arm bones. The striation and layering of the fat and muscle bundles can be seen from the position of the white spots which I applied according to nature. (Br I, 294)

This was written on 20 August 1918, the day the great Anglo-French offensive to the south of Arras began. Kokoschka continues to worry about the 'flexibility of the joints' and the 'relative firmness and granularity' of the muscle meat on the legs and back of his love doll. Moos is to obtain fine, curly horsehair for which she is to purchase an old sofa and have the stuffing disinfected. The skin is to be made from 'fleece silk'. Special care is also to be given to the correct reproduction of the proportions of 'forehead, eyes, mouth in relation to the chin' (Br I, 296). As the end of the war approached, he was interested in the 'inner surfaces of the thighs'. He is moved by the mental image of his 'fantasy princess' that is meant to live with him in Dresden (Br I, 298). He wants to see photographs of his doll-lover in advance. Mid-November 1918 (the revolution is in progress), he leaves no doubt as to the urgency for the doll's completion: 'I repeat that my future happiness and peace of mind depend on holding this centre point of my life in my hands' (Br I, 299).

The longer Kokoschka has to wait on the tangible enchantment through the doll, the more detailed his instructions to the by-now-pitiable Hermine Moos become. The hands are to be like those of a 'riding Russian woman' or those of the dancer Karsavina. The cornea is to be glazed with nail polish. The skin as ripening peaches. The rhythm of the living form is to be maintained. The dead material is to be brought to life in a clever manner. The decoration is to be done with only 'powder, nut juice, fruit juices, gold dust, waxen skin' (Br I, 304). The breasts are to be 'even more detailed'. The nipples should not be prominent, rather slightly raised from the skin through roughing of the material.

Kokoschka refers to this nascent, but then forever available and docile, doll as his 'ghostlike lady companion' (Br I, 302). He credits his ability to remember his former lover's physicality, which he wants to become Alma's 'real presence', so to speak. This doll is to be portrait-like. The detailed colour presentation then forms the apex of instructions in the letter of 23 January 1919.

> In general I would ask you to tint the skin at the following places from the inside, in other words the skeleton side, in various hues so that the lustre and golden sheen of the velvet receives the varying shadow colouration, consistent with the natural flesh tones at different points on the body. In particular: spinal cord, shoulder blades, back of the neck to the head, arm pits, knee hollows, collar bones, shin bone, pubic bone, elbows, navel, hip bone: light saffron yellow.
>
> Buttock cleft, sacrum, eye sockets, instep, pudenda, inner upper arm lightly with natural nut colour.
>
> Belly, bottom, breasts, mons veneris, palms, soles, cheeks, nostrils,

calves, outer lower arm, outer thigh lightly pink with watered down red wine [...] (Br I, 306)

What does this reveal? The perversions of one posessed? Kokoschka himself provides a hint: only the 'woman' would be able to 'inspire' him to artworks (ibid). He evidently needed this doll for his eroticisation and inspiration.

The result could only disappoint him, and this disappointment was bottomless. In early 1919 Hermine Moos received a scathing assessment of her work: 'the outer shell is a polar bear skin, that would be suitable for a shaggy imitation bedside bear rug, but never for the suppleness and softness of a woman's skin, whereby we have always put the priority on tactile delusion' (Br I, 312).

And yet the doll as an aesthetic object of dubious artistic value fulfilled her purpose. She posed for Kokoschka and sat with him at his table; his domestic was to take care of her as 'lady in waiting, Reserl', and he went out with her; yes, she even accompanied him to the theatre. For a time, Kokoschka and his Alma doll must have been the talk of the town in Dresden. Apparently, in the summer of 1920, he grew weary of her. It is not certain whether he actually beheaded her, drenched her in red wine and threw her in a flower bed as he claims in his account *Briefe aus Dresden* (DSW II, 198). It is perfectly conceivable. In any event, she eventually landed on a garbage truck after a drunken night celebrating his farewell from his 'idée fixe' with friends. By then he had already met Daisy Spies and raved to her about the 'grâce d'imagination', the blessing of the imagination. Alice Graf and Lotte Mandl were among his new comforters, and the 'Russian' announced herself, if not on horseback, Anna Kallin.

Whilst not wishing to place too much importance on this doll episode, it suggests an analogue to E T A Hoffmann's famous tale *Der Sandmann* (*The Sandman*). In general, one can assume that youthful and less youthful Vienna was aware of Heinrich von Kleist's conversational essay *Über das Marionettentheater* (*On the Marionette Theatre*) and Hoffmann's tales. In Kokoschka's case, there may also have been familiarity with Ernst Jentsch's and Sigmund Freud's *Versuch über das Unheimliche* (*The Uncanny*), but that is not certain.[36] It is likely that Kokoschka wanted to exorcise Alma's uncanny (after-)effect through a minute description of the construction of his Alma doll. He apparently tried to get hold of her through this, to gain control over her, something which Alma denied him in real life. This construct, however, is related to that which the narrator in Hoffmann's tale explores in the example of Olympia, the artificial daughter of Professor Spalanzani, with whom Nathanael falls fatally in love. He refuses to accept her fabrication until it comes to a catastrophe, the destruction of this feminine automaton and the onset of Nathanael's insanity. The actual shock for Nathanael is the insight that a lifeless doll is 'his' Olympia, whom he had previously – perhaps against his better judgement – held to be a young woman of unapproachable beauty.[37] Whilst Nathanael is unwilling to accept reality, Kokoschka simultaneously behaved in a similar way to both Spalanzani *and* Nathanael; he commissioned the doll's construction, treated her half as art object, half as Alma's replica which he – somehow – *wanted* to fall in love with anew. It is specifically because the mimetic reconstruction of Alma as a doll failed so miserably that Kokoschka reacted so angrily. His ideal and thus his self-delusion missed the mark. He had no other choice but to carry on with a parody of his desired illusion. That he incorporated the deformed Alma doll into social contexts is entirely consistent with Spalanzani's behaviour, who also introduced his artificial daughter Olympia at a social occasion.

But returning to the reality of Kokoschka's life, Alma Mahler-Gropius demanded the return of her letters in June 1919. In an undated telegram, perhaps sent at the time Kokoschka took receipt of his dismal doll, Alma confirmed: 'That alone really belongs to us, what we experienced, whatever it may be, as we perceived it. Internally, that is where it is kept' (Br I, 314) – *internally* – in contrast to any anatomical details.

Nevertheless, he ascribed a certain long-term meaning to the Alma doll in November 1919: 'because I have my doll who will one day come alive at Lake Geneva, under the fervour of my perception' (Br II, 8). Yet this inadequate doll could in no way replace Alma. But, and this is significant, the doll turned into an object of his art in the shape of a striking painting based on numerous studies. Later, on 27 May 1921, Kokoschka wrote to her, out of the blue and in the middle of his relationship with Anna Kallin; it is probably his most beautiful letter to Alma. One can only cite it in full.

Alma,

I am sitting in front of the painting I once did of the two of us, in which we look so discouraged and you are giving me the ring. By coincidence it came into my hands because there will be an exhibition of my most important works here, a form of overview of my life to date. And the owner did not want to put it in strangers' hands until the opening. Now it is in my green pavilion and I see you and toast you [with] Spanish red wine and do not think that you have betrayed me, don't believe you have forgotten what secretly ties us since I was injured. It is our fault that we were so foolish to have preferred an even greater, abstract love to such a great love.

Life rolls by so furiously fast. I have given everything away, your ring, your red necklace, your coat, even my memory in which I brought our experiences to the stage. But today I am alone again, and it seems to me you are thinking of me and as if all that I valued nothing could come up against the secret power that goes from heart to heart, which always returns until one of us is dead.

If you were as brave as I, so we would only now begin to live and love each other.

I will travel to Spain shortly.

An everlasting happiness in each other. (Br II, 22)

As a visual artist, Kokoschka could not help but create an image of the Other. The paintings of Alma and himself – here he refers to the double portrait of March 1913, which was supposed to represent their engagement – interpreted and transfigured them. But now he saw himself with them and was thus confronted with her as a part of, but separate from, his life's work to date – briefly sharing her life with him again, if only as a picture. He toasts her while not wishing to acknowledge her 'true' character. The visual presence he has created of her allows him to repress her 'betrayal'.

What of that he had brought to the stage as a playwright – he alludes to his play *Orpheus und Eurydike* – he dresses in mythology and not really as a double act or portrait. One who 'gifts' his 'memory' to the stage can only do this in a transformed manner. In contrast, a visual artwork, in particular one which rejects abstraction and exposes itself to the eye, naturally denies a dramatic further development of the one depicted which is appropriate to the stage.

He still seemed to believe in a new start with Alma, even if his grammar emphasises the unreal ('were... would... begin'). *In other wise is happiness* from 1913 had become *An everlasting happiness in each other* – that also signalled at least a significant change in Kokoschka's feelings.

The double Alma surrogate, doll and painting, were soon no longer sufficient. The presence of Anna Kallin, who became his 'Malina', proved to be transitional (until 1925) as new inspiration for his loving and working – even if the paintings which show her with her erotic-seeming girlfriend, Alice Graf-Lahmann, would not attain the intensity and virtuosity of the Alma portraits, nor even the pencil sketches. An important exception is the portrait sketch of Kallin from 1921 with the handwritten notation: 'Take this along and leave me the painting.' It shows a woman suffering, the opposite of Alma bursting with vitality; the look is turned inwards. Kallin does not seem conceivable as a model for nude drawing, whereas Alma, even clothed, seems naked.

There was one thing Kokoschka attested to at that time, something crucial, that would carry him through dangers in the future: 'Levity [to be understood as lightness of being] and imagination like a graceful woman'. He had been born 'to lead a fairy tale life, a life that I love so much and embrace with all fire'. He no longer wished to be a man of passion and pain. 'My breast hurts. Yes! But it could be a sweet pain like lust that makes me sing like my god Mozart, and not, as one advises here, "running to the doctor"!' (Br II, 7 f).

However, he was not free from prejudices; the worst of these he shared with his erstwhile Alma, of all people, the real one, not the doll: 'I can't take it anymore here in Germany. Nor in Vienna. There are too many thinking and reasoning Jews there, and the others are blinkered and degenerated by misery and abandoned by the Graces!' (Br II, 8). Is that how an artist dedicated to the humanism of Comenius speaks, or was that simply glibness, if not a 'customary' expression of anti-Semitic sentiments? Who did he think he was? In November 1919 at least, when he expressed these idiocies, a 'charming magician'.

The doll and Kokoschka's fixation on it would later – into old age – become his 'little dollies', more or less profane muses and female students; the 'wild man' of the art world had become, for some, an irresistible charmer.

4

Pre-Schooling Vision

Between Times in the Florence on the Elbe

In November 1919 the Dresden Secession was founded.[1] Otto Dix belonged, as did the writer Konrad Felixmüller and the art critic Will Grohmann. Emil Richter's art salon became an important exhibition space for the Dresden Secessionists. Oskar Kokoschka was elected an honorary member but did not contribute anything to the exhibitions of the Dresden Secession. He kept his distance in his little cavalier's house. By then his reputation far exceeded that of a (mere) Expressionist or Secessionist. The art critic Wilhelm Hausenstein had anointed him as the living heir of Matthias Grünewald, even though Kokoschka cried: 'No, I don't want thorns, cross or pain anymore, enough, enough, enough with this!' (Br II, 7).

The Secession had made the potential for political unrest after the November Revolution (1918) its own and tried to render the concept artistically. In the Secession's founding month, the extravagant, if not wildly eccentric, poetess and muse to the late Franz Marc, Else Lasker-Schüler, gave a recitation in Dresden. It is unclear whether Kokoschka was present. It is not idle to speculate that she would have fascinated him – at the very least as a truly colourful subject for a portrait.

In September 1919 the first German Protestant Convention was held in Dresden. Kokoschka was aware of this, at least to some extent. It explains why he wrote to his friends Carl Georg Heise and Hans Mardersteig, whose portraits he had done, that he was ready to leave the 'Christian protestant' paradise 'to a German of the Reich' (Br II, 8). Far more important to him was the experience of 'seeing' in Dresden, where his paintings were created, and then bearing witness. They do not show the actual points of interest, not the Zwinger Palace, the Semper Opera or the Frauenkirche; rather, they integrate the Dresden Neustadt into the landscape. Landscape and cityscape are interwoven and placed under the primacy of mostly unmixed colours. It is a perspective that Heinrich von Kleist, who was becoming increasingly more important to Kokoschka, had described in a letter from May 1801.

> I looked down upon the lovely Elbe valley from the high bank, it lay like a painting by Claude Lorrain at my feet – it seemed to me like a landscape embroidered on a carpet, green acres, villages, a broad stream that quickly turns to kiss Dresden a[nd] it kissed it, quickly flees again – and the mighty wreath of mountains that encircle the carpet like arabesque border – and the pure blue Italian sky that floated over the entire area [...].[2]

With respect to Kleist, by the way, a thought expressed in a letter written half-a-year earlier can be interpreted as a precursor to Kokoschka's School of Seeing.

> Seeing and hearing [...] all people can do, but to perceive, that means to grasp the impression of the sense with the soul a[nd] think, that is something not nearly all can do. They have nothing but the dead eye, a[nd] that perceives so little of the picture of nature, like the mirror surface of the sea the picture of the sky. The soul must be active otherwise all appearances of nature are lost, even if they impacted on all senses [...].[3]

But back to Kokoschka's Dresden. The freshly minted Professor, as he could now call himself, stepped into the public eye when a painting by Rubens in the Dresden Zwinger Palace was damaged during the Kapp Putsch in March 1920. He came forward with an appeal *An die Einwohnerschaft Dresdens* (*To the Residents of Dresden*) which, with its mixture of acknowledgement, surreal attitude and superior wit, belongs in every collection of German pamphlets.

To all here who in future intend to argue their political theories, regardless of left, right or centre radical, with shooting irons, I direct the beseeching request not to hold such planned warlike exercises in front of the Art Gallery of the Zwinger Palace, but rather at the firing ranges on the heath where human culture will not be endangered. On Monday, the 15th March, a masterpiece of Rubens' was injured by a bullet. As paintings do not have the opportunity to escape from there, where they are no longer under the protection of mankind and also because the entente could thus justify a raid on our gallery because we have no taste for paintings, it would then fall upon the artists of Dresden, who tremble and shake with me and are aware that they would themselves not be capable of creating such masterpieces should those entrusted to us be destroyed, the responsibility to put a stop to the robbing of the poor future people of its holiest goods by all imaginable means. Surely in the future the German people will find more joy and sense in viewing the rescued paintings than in all the views of the politicising Germans today. I do not dare hope that my counter proposal will ring through; it provides that in the German Republic, as in classical times, *in future feuds would be settled in duels between political leaders*, as in the *Circus*, made more impressive through the Homerian ranting and raving of the parties they lead. Which would then be less harmful and less confusing than the currently typical methods.

Oskar Kokoschka
Professor at the Academy of Fine Arts in Dresden (DSW IV, 31 f)

In Berlin George Grosz and John Heartfield thereupon labelled him an 'art nobody'. Kokoschka himself explained to his parents at the end of this turbulent month: 'The Germans are such that they immediately want to beat each other to death for all their self-opinionatedness. They just do not have eyes, only ideas that are not viable, because they do not want to see the life that is so beautiful, but only themselves and then some other elaborate state, humanity or truth or the devil only knows what they call it' (Br II, 13).

What can we derive from this statement? On the one hand, it

confirms Kokoschka's notion that paintings are alive because they can be *injured*. On the other hand, he believes he can defuse conflicts like this through the classical artist's gesture, namely irony, even Homeric laughter. And, in addition, his conviction that everything depends on the schooling of the eyes is stirring here; it would henceforth determine his pedagogy. Comenius would remain at the core of this conviction for Kokoschka. This can be taken from a far-reaching speech on the *Orbis pictus* which he had already drafted in 1919. Kokoschka's tendency to rather woodcut-like debate is noticeable in this text. It was apparently intended as a settling of matters past. In the war, the earth was 'crucified' and God 'consumed'. The purpose crawled 'out of Logos' balls' and called itself Christ. 'We murder on articles of faith! Croak for ten commandments (increased by fourteen points)' (DSW IV, 11) – referring to those of the American President Wilson that, among others, included the people's right to self-determination which had just been denied to Kokoschka's native country Austria. And he feels himself robbed of his homeland: 'Homeland! Mother! My homeland – I can't find Mozart's Austria anymore: deforested, pillaged, leaving a state of English and emigrants from other countries' trade and morality clerks, oh, we homeless!' (DSW IV, 17).

It took him several more attempts to arrive at the point where he felt himself anchored. In the pictorial world view of Comenius 'the purpose from a "child's perspective" should be our spiritual power [...]' (DSW IV, 19), he proclaimed, even if he had previously rejected the 'superstition of the future', as well as the cast of the (biblical) Prophets. The world did not consist of states, but of illustrations. Yet Kokoschka's confession to interpreting the world through pictures unexpectedly also became a plea for the emancipation of the mother from the 'Baal of Purpose', who impregnated her so she would 'bear armies' for the 'world's trenches' (DSW IV, 19).

Kokoschka's text is riddled with a marked use of sexual metaphors – from the testicles of Logos to the emasculated Priapus. In the end, however, this 'preamble' also becomes a manifesto, appeal and prophecy of quite Old Testament eloquence; one can hardly miss the mocking irony in this final rhetorical outburst:

Extol, you mouth, but as final home – paternal and maternal limbs, which are the beginning and ending of all. Now the eternal curse is buried, its purpose fulfilled, we are redeemed. Kyrie eleison! [Lord, have mercy!] Pan is risen, little Jesus and the genii and fairies! Now I want to open the books of the world for you. And there are no words, only many pretty pictures in it.

Throw away the stone, perhaps your laughter has moved heaven. (DSW IV, 29)

Kokoschka was notably serious, however, with a comment to Anna Kallin, about his work being a prophecy: 'war and wound' was in him before 1914, as his work consisted of 'nothing but pictures speaking of his actions' (Br II, 24). His challenge was to 'justify the world of love'. He wished to show that 'a woman is pure', 'beyond all doubt, noble, that she can love, can believe to the greatest depth without allowing herself to be unfaithful through others nor through herself' (Br II, 25).

His work was having ever more impact, for example, in April 1922 at the Biennale in Venice where Kokoschka (along with Liebermann, Slevogt and Corinth) was able to show twelve paintings. He encountered a rainy Venice, describing it to Alice Lahmann, his 'Colibri', as a 'damned middle-class nest of ruins, full of nooks and crannies' in which he got lost a thousand times. He was irritated that Anna Kallin, his 'Niuta', did not travel with him. All the while her girlfriend, Alice, was markedly rising in his favour. He closes the letter he wrote to her from the Hotel Bauer-Grünwald in Venice with the phrase 'I kiss your knee' and signs with 'in devotion your Lieutenant Glahn', once more identifying with the main character in Hamsun's *Pan* novel. He would kiss more than Alice's admirable knees for a long time, throughout the 1920s and 1930s, alternating between Anna, Alice and, later, Marguerite Loeb as well as various nameless others.

He must have been surprised that the German pavilion in Venice was decorated in black, just like his studio in Vienna had once been. This, however, provided a contrasting effect to his 'new burning pictures', as he later wrote to his parents (Br II, 43). He escaped the Venetian rain with a trip to Florence where Michelangelo's 'David' 'simply floored' him (Br II, 44). 'I almost always had to weep with every object, so majestic, so much and beautiful this genius created' (ibid).

Thereafter he seems to have taken measure of the art in Florence. Having returned to Dresden, he worked on another self-portrait and declared to his parents: 'My paintings are becoming beautiful like Old Masters. In ten years, when all this modern crap is outmoded, I will be truly discovered by the greater world and then all the effort and sacrifice will be rewarded' (Br II, 45). Now, he realised that was more or less what his parents wished to hear, but 'all this modern crap' was altogether too harsh a verdict for the honorary member of the Dresden Secession.

Nevertheless, with this comment Kokoschka rather bluntly expressed how constraining Dresden had become for him, because he believed he had now outgrown himself. To his father he declared himself to be the most important living artist. With his 'nomad of the heart' Anna Kallin, he felt forced into the unknown (Br II, 55). One of the many sketches in his letters shows him (just the head and hand) writing the word 'longing'; overhead hinted-at migratory birds fly over the ocean in the direction of palm trees. Africa entrenches itself in him as perspective. (French) Switzerland or Paris came under consideration as tangible destinations and possible places to settle. Initially, however, he remained challenged in Dresden. On 12 December, Paul Hindemith's opera based on Kokoschka's piece *Mörder Hoffnung der Frauen* was performed under his direction, with his stage sets and comma in the title under the musical direction of Fritz Busch, together with *Arlequino* by Ferruccio Busoni and *Petruschka* by Igor Stravinsky. For a final time, Kokoschka made plans in this context with respect to Alma Mahler-Gropius. He writes to her on 9 October 1922 that he can imagine his *Orpheus* in a version by Alexander Skrjabin, or a new 'masterpiece' by him at the Metropolitan Opera House which he furnishes with the significant addendum: '[...] so you are happy about me once more' (Br II, 60). He still wanted to impress his Alma which – in the midst of his numerous Dresden love affairs – may have surprised him more than anyone. Later he summed up: 'I could pretty much get away with anything in Dresden in those days' (ML, 192). This would soon include extended absences, as well as the ostentatious threat to the state authorities that he would relinquish his post if the residence permit for his Russian girlfriend Anna Kallin was not extended.

But then she was the one, to Kokoschka's annoyance, who travelled alone to London (to see her father). Kokoschka and Anna then spent the summer exploring Switzerland: Zurich and Lucerne, Les Avants, Montreux and Blonay where the painting *Lac Léman I* was created in the early autumn. Meanwhile there was consternation in the Saxony interior ministry about their most famous art professor, such that they granted him a two-year sabbatical with full salary. Never before nor in the future would Kokoschka be treated more generously by public officials than in Dresden at the time. Only in July 1927 did the officials reach the end of their tether. Kokoschka, the restless, was relieved of his office and replaced by Otto Dix.

Kokoschka – profoundly disillusioned with Europe – yearned for the unknown, something else, preferably exotic: 'I would like to be a negro king and run off all the European money bags and travelling tradesmen, and wake up the negroes. I would find that worthy and exciting enough; to exile these loathsome citizens from Europe alone, where to continue living, they have to trade pens, stamps and little gelatine prints until they are carried to the graveyards' (Br II, 81). Anna, whom he would caricature naked in his next letter, was to keep a look out for African-language books in London.

However, this half-feigned, half-serious African exoticism did not blind Kokoschka to the reality of a hyperinflation-tormented Germany: 'The banknotes printed by the state now had the value of autumn foliage falling from the trees' (ML, 194). Before the end of the Ruhr Strike against the French Occupation Kokoschka submitted an article that apparently seemed to the *Berliner Tagblatt* to be too explosive to publish. Modelled on Montesquieu's *Persische Briefe* (*Persian Letters*), Kokoschka imagined himself as one from 'Tabriz in Persia', writing about the situation in the Ruhr as an outsider. This *Persische Brief* of 1923 was drafted by an artist with noticeably sharp political knowledge, who could even comprehend the mechanisms of the political economy of the time. In quoting Lord Curzon that the Allied

Powers had 'floated to victory upon a wave of oil' in the First World War, Kokoschka lays bare the British machinations that aided them to a quasi-monopoly over crude oil. In addition, he points out that England has a vital interest in preventing a German–French compromise so that it can continue to pit both countries against each other. This (also linguistically) astounding polemic (DSW IV, 33–39), as skewed as some of the individual arguments may be, shows Kokoschka as politically aware. In a letter to Anna Kallin as early as September 1921 he had spoken of himself – though ironically – as a future 'statesman of a novel character', jokingly based on the triumphant progress of his kind of Expressionism, which he had launched into the world in 1907 (Br II, 33). Yet something was beginning to emerge here which would later take shape in Kokoschka's interest in painting portraits of leading political figures. It was an aesthetic-political drive that took its place next to his credo of the (new) seeing and in the idea of mutual understanding, based on Comenius or rather emulating a vision for education. That allowed him to consider painting the Reichspräsident Paul von Hindenburg in the Hotel Adlon in Berlin in January 1926 (Br II, 150), although this came to nothing.

The view of political affairs – and this should not be underestimated, particularly in the times that followed –was also essentially related to Kokoschka's credo for seeing. The look at social conditions and the tendency to romanticise the political translated itself into Kokoschka's visual artworks, though not with anything nearly approaching the radicality of Dix, Beckmann or Grosz. But this perspective never lost its sharpness; it led to allegorical transpositions until the end and was crystallised particularly in the signalling nature of his colour treatment. The light, bright colouring that defines so many of his paintings – including his Dresden scenes – can also be seen as an alternative to a sickening world. Also ensnared in this is the (justifiable) accusation of escapism in the neo-baroque splendour of colours in many of his paintings from his Dresden period. He wished to gain views of the world and their conditions through his travels.

A Dream Picture and Travel Pictures, Euro-African

The now forty-year-old Kokoschka felt like travelling to the Orient in the spring of 1924, perhaps in Ehrenstein's company. He wanted to turn his back on the old world, particularly after his father's death on 23 October 1923. But this old world initially continued to hold him fast, owing to public recognition for his work. In Berlin, the leading Galerie Goldschmidt-Wallerstein displayed his paintings, lithographs and watercolours in March 1924. In the same month, Galerie Goltz showed his graphic work. Wilhelm Hausenstein wrote enthusiastically about Kokoschka's art in the *Münchner Allgemeinen Zeitung*. And in June/July, the Neue Galerie in Vienna honoured him with an extensive selection of his works, which it augmented in October. It showed seventeen early paintings and thus made up for what Vienna had missed out on with respect to Kokoschka for thirteen years. It was as if they wanted to bind him to the old Europe, this recalcitrant Modernist and magician of colours and shapes on the verge of their dissolution. Yet this very exhibition would end in a scandal of a completely different nature, with an assassination attempt on his art that would catapult him out of Vienna. The *Neue Wiener Journal* reported on this on 26 October 1924 and printed Kokoschka's open letter to the director of the Neue Galerie, Otto Kallir-Nirenstein (who was quite positively disposed towards him), which left very little to be desired in terms of clarity. In the letter, he references the wanton damage done to one of his earlier paintings.

> [...] symptomatic of a sterile, wanton thirst for glory of an entire society which is nourished by a press averse to all things creative, which in 1907 – began to spout venom about these same paintings, whilst the public befouled them; who denounced me as often as I nevertheless tried to function as an instructor at schools for children, apprentices, art students, to the authorities.

The outrage at this vandalism was mixed with the feeling of no longer wishing to live in Vienna. Kokoschka saw himself validated in his uprootedness, a feeling that had not let go of him since his war experiences. In any event, making arrangements after his father's death kept him in Vienna. This included as a priority his concern for the family's wellbeing and grief, a worry that would remain with him. He wrote to his beloved Anna Kallin:

> If you could have only seen a little of things here, the misery, the helplessness and the heart stopping end, and that one always has to lie to keep the mother from seeing anything, so she doesn't go mad, and then this God damned ghastliness with a corpse in your arms and having to hide [it] for a night and a day until all the socially proper hygiene business is taken care of in all piety, then you yourself smell so badly that you want to flee from others and from yourself. (Br II, 92)

Initially his father was interred in a temporary crypt, then cremated; Oskar apparently had to make all the arrangements himself. He further reports:

> My brother spent every night for three weeks awake with the father; you can imagine how shattered he his. Do you know, a little talent such as I have must be dearly, too dearly, paid for by the parents with a life that is not quite normal and not quite insane. Everything hopeless, complicated and tragic at home [derives] from that. Why should I even bother to poke my nose into the psyche of a South Seas aboriginal who has survived the extinction of his race? I have that in my own house and in my own head. (Br II, 92 f)

Yet this work of mourning also had a literary fallout. In Kokoschka's estate there is a short, undated piece of prose which survives in his own handwriting, as well as copies (presumably by Anna Kallin), and begins with the note: 'In the night before my father died, I had this dream [...].' This could be a purely fictional reference or an authentic testimonial. The text itself is at least sufficiently remarkable that it should be shared here.

A Dream

Enveloped by the dawn, illuminated from treetop to treetop, a park sloping into the distance, beautiful and joyful, planted for the benefit of the eyes.

Although life failed to mirror this reflection, to which this was to attest, they created living pictures, the dreamlike that attached themselves did not spoil appearances. Just as the sun's rays only brokenly appear in manifold colours to the waking mind, so the drowsing sensation that was able to design a world in moments does not receive its confirmation from consciousness. Anxiousness, with all its half-tints, places its Yes? and No? in this arch until it fades, as soundlessly as a cry without an echo, as soundlessly as shadows glide.

Across the avenue cobbled with large blocks of stone, mute monks in cowls hurriedly pull up a dusty black hearse, leaving it standing across the street so that this is blocked on the left side and the eye is arrested by the blinded glass panes, forced to look into the coach in which a dead priest is laid out, under random yellowed paper flowers and carelessly strewn icons of saints. With the simplicity of the thoughts of death's exposure realised, from which the straying curiosity recoils shudderingly, I opened my eyes in the dream and, unconscious, confusedly reached with my hands into the void. But now lads are gently bringing near the dreamer in person on an open bier from the castle on the right side of the park. He now lies, without being able to move, a second time here and in a martyr-like pose. On one side an arm and a foot tensed, the other half of the body relaxed, totally revealed and allows this doubling of mine to see what anyone in a less helpless situation would have avoided showing out of modesty. From a hole in the cadaverous chest, from which fresh blood flows which is constantly washed away with sponges by the lads, an overlooked drop runs forth and causes unbearable new pains; the bloody heart hangs from the chest cavity and beats like the hammer of a melting bell that swings in a void in a sounding, falling apart tower. And under the drawn forehead burning desires still want to turn to the world. The large tired eyes united with an inaudible sigh have just expressed a wish. This is adhered to by the attendants as quickly as he fiercely demands. The single movement by this mute picture of martyrdom, was a look that emitted like lightning from lead grey eye sockets and motivated the others. The bier is lowered down, the lads draw back before a third vehicle, which is driven up soundlessly over the moss of the park by girls with proud movements, pulls next to the dreamer's bier. Advancing in front of the young women is an aromatic cloud of incense wafting across the entire landscape, while an inexpressible lustre shines forth from the display cart which becomes ever more intense. On it lies, shrouded under a cloak, adorned with delicate pictures under a mound of fresh, white, intensely fragrant blossoms, a stone which breaks light into all colours. No one knows what it is like when a glance and act and being emigrates from the fabric of human nature, after such a unique shock which death is, and perhaps enters a different principle. Does someone teach an order of reality without breaking with nature through the human? In human consciousness experienced to date, we would have to stop believing in the beyond that the human soul is a magical act of earth's love, and do Nature's spirits leave an area in order to settle in another? The invalid's eyes closed after the excitement[;] he had found sleep which had eluded him and the morning dream, which had measured only a few steps from cradle to hearse, was at an end.

In Kokoschka's handwriting the last sentence reads: 'He was carried into the castle as I awoke.' Moreover, the girls here are, of course, angels. This is about a surreal processing of a mourning experience, a literary transcendence that nevertheless remains concrete and expressive.

Let us now add an overdue word on Kokoschka's friend and contemporary, the poet Albert Ehrenstein. He may be considered one of the most important representatives of literary Expressionism in Austria.[4] As an avowed anti-nationalist, he focused on a poetic revolution of attitudes. With his nihilistically influenced tale *Tubutsch* (1911), he created his alter ego whose only attraction lies in his onomatopoeic name. Tubutsch consists of void and wasteland; for Kokoschka, however, the text was sufficiently appealing to provide it with illustrations. Even in retrospect, these drawings remained important to Kokoschka, because they – according to him – presaged his lithographs for *Bachkantate* and *Columbus* or at least influenced them. He indignantly made Edith Hoffmann-Yapou aware of this when she sent him proofs of a monograph on his work for review or, better said, endorsement. She had overlooked his illustrations for *Tubutsch* (Br III, 126).

Ehrenstein was noticed early on by Karl Kraus, who published a poem in the *Fackel* (*Wanderers Lied*; *Wanderer's Song*); courtesy of Kokoschka's arrangements, he was also able to publish in the periodicals by Herwarth Walden and Franz Pfempfert, *Der Sturm* and *Die Aktion*. Ehrenstein maintained himself as Kokoschka's advisor and travel companion during the 1920s. An anti-militarist declared unfit for military service, he spent the first two years of the war working in the Vienna War Archive. Afterwards, he worked alongside Johannes R Becher as an editor at Kurt Wolff's publishing house.

However, he met with no true success. His decline was precipitated by his hopeless love of actress Elisabeth Bergner, to whose breakthrough he contributed. After 1933 he felt himself only tolerated as a hunted quarry. He, too, took Czech citizenship, and travelled across the Soviet Union in 1934 having apparently failed to persuade Kokoschka to accompany him there. A tough immigrant's fate followed, mostly in the USA, where Ehrenstein never really settled. Occasionally supported by Thomas Mann, Richard Hülsenbeck and George Grosz, he led a miserable existence. Kokoschka lacked the means and opportunities to help him over the long term. Ehrenstein's brother Carl, who lived in England, could only receive the ashes of his brother who died in a New York's paupers' hospital on Welfare Island and inter them in Bromley Hill Cemetery in London. The Tubutsch nihilism had long caught up with him.

For Kokoschka's fortieth birthday, Ehrenstein had honoured his friend with a poem and short essay. With this he wanted to bring the artist's beginnings in Expressionism into renewed awareness and at the same time introduce him as the essential primal force in modern painting and literature. The poem, titled *Oskar Kokoschka*, reads:

You are one of those imbued with the light
of the rising red sun;
Whatever is ghosting black in darkness
will move away from you towards the turning of clouds.

Quietness sways to the bench of rotting
chaos measures the abyss of mountains
life is pregnant in the low
but not so craving love:
Creation only endows you with creating;
hovering in the heavy storm of light
protecting the ether in pure breathing.[5]

The following essay begins emphatically: 'In the beginning was Oskar Kokoschka.' As a poet, according to Ehrenstein, he is 'a wild romantic'; as a painter and illustrator, in contrast, already a classicist. In this piece, Ehrenstein sees 'rainbows swooshing into each other, waterfalls, fast dramas' and names their originator in Expressionistic manner an 'explosionist' driven by the subconscious. Ehrenstein's resume could not have been more grandiose, yet with an acute observation which would be continued as a theme in the illustrations for his *Tubutsch*.

Kokoschka has drawn himself often and, in many guises, is to be found as the 'bound Columbus' as well as in his Bach portfolio – he bows deeply before all greatness. His stature is not talent, rather genius; his possibilities extend far beyond what he might accomplish as painter and writer. Yet who in an Austria grazed bare, who in a savaged Germany can give him the means, the space and the time to create the frescoes that he dreams of, to build the massive Egyptian structures that he envisions – giant statues flanking the Panama Canal.[6]

Kokoschka, the colossus – that is how his friend Tubutsch alias Albert Ehrenstein saw him in 1926. Of course, Kokoschka could not be bothered to even come close to such an impressive dedication for the writer in turn.

But returning to Kokoschka's travels in the mid-1920s. As an old European through and through, he initially sensed the Orient in Venice and later in the south of France. And he returned to Venice in April 1924. He settled into the Hotel Danieli with an uninterrupted view of Santa Maria della Salute and the Punta della Dogana, the old customs building Dogana da Mar. 'From the balcony of my hotel I painted the "Dogana" with the silhouette of the Giudecca from two different windows, two different aspects, so that I had a doubly wide view, an experiment that I often later repeated' (ML, 198). For him maritime breadth (he would also appreciate it later on visits to Hamburg and Lübeck) would connect itself in Venice to his 'oriental dream' with caravans, Bedouins, oases and spices.[7]

After a further stay in Florence where he painted the banks of the Arno and three months in Vienna, Kokoschka's next target was Paris. Here a pattern emerged that would remain until his move to Prague in 1934. Vienna, Berlin, occasionally Hamburg and Zurich, become places for stopovers. He returned once more to Dresden in early 1925. The known became a springboard into the unknown.

Kokoschka continued to run into influential promoters during this period. Among them were the former director of the Imperial Library in Vienna, Jan Slivinsky, who made his studio apartment at the Quai d'Orsay in Paris available to Kokoschka; similarly the Frankfurt banker and art dealer Jakob Goldschmidt supported his travels and arranged his stay at the Grand Hotel in Monte Carlo where his first actual travel painting, the harbour of Monte Carlo, was done at the end of February 1925.

It is perfectly imaginable that Kokoschka was already living and working according to the principle of Comenius at this time: 'Seeing [is] the prerequisite to the ability to understand', as he claims in *Mein Leben* (ML, 203). Although in his case, this seeing immediately translated into visual art views, which for their part meant insights into unfamiliar surroundings and cultures. On the other hand, it was also true that Kokoschka represented not only the legendary beauty of these places, but also their dark sides. In mid-November he wrote to his friend Lotte Mandl from the restaurant in the Hotel Foyot (once frequented by Rilke and later by Joseph Roth, and where he now bumped into his composer friend, Ernst Křenek).

> Yesterday he and I [he is Adolf Loos, who accompanied him to Paris along with the painter Sebastian Isepp] took a little prostitute to the hospital because she was deathly ill. If you are not staying at the Ritz or Claridge's, you only now begin to see how much wretchedness there is, and a deep depression and feeling of impotence to be able to help is my lot, where others think to find sensations and orgies. I am very unhappy and even a little repulsed by life in general. (Br II, 99 f)[8]

In Paris Loos irritated him with his get-up-and-go spirit. Kokoschka was drawn to London, but had to go to the south, to Monte Carlo, Nice, Marseille, Avignon, Aigues-Mortes, Vernet-les-Bains, Toulouse, and then from Bordeaux to Lisbon via Madrid by train on 14 April. The trips were not without stress; the train from Madrid to Lisbon (without sleeping car) took twenty-two hours, as he informed his sister (Br II, 109). And further: 'the city [Lisbon] itself is not very big because of too frequent earthquakes, but very garish. No women on the street.' One believed oneself already in South America. But in Portugal he was also reminded of the Balkans. Increasingly the city pleased him, became a synaesthetic experience for him. He writes to Gräfin Alexandrine Khuenburg – he calls her 'dear sister Aline' – from the Avenida Palace Hotel.

> [...] if you could see this ocean! The air sweeps to South America, the vegetation is immense, the land is so green, at least the southern half, as like the birches in bud in May at home. The Tagus is rosy and the light so forceful that you think you are hearing or smelling it. And herds of horses and a rich earth and the people, the farmers and fishermen like real people born of a woman's body, not confec-tioned in the factory of the world. (Br II, 110)

Yet, Kokoschka idealises here. The First Republic, founded in 1910, experienced its agonies. President Bernadino Machado lacked the instruments of power to save the Republic. Kokoschka vaguely recalls 'unrests' in *Mein Leben*, which forced his premature return to Madrid. Portugal was on the way to becoming a quasi-fascist corporatist state, the Estado Novo, which augured what lay ahead for Kokoschka's Austrian homeland. In a letter written to his mother from Madrid, the son already describes the volatile events in a mixture of playing down and dramatising; a 'revolution' apparently 'came over night' like a thunder storm,

> and I was in a teensy bit of danger, as there was shooting over the houses from the left and right of the city like in a real war. Houses got grenades in the walls, many people were injured, twelve dead, and the entire lark lasted two days and two nights. Of course, one could not go out on the street. (Br II, 111)

Does one forgive his use of the word 'lark' in this context? In his memoirs he even claims he wanted to paint the city from the Lisbon fortress as the unrest broke out. He was already 'installed' with his painting tools, for which the 'fortress commandant' proved himself to be 'very helpful' and recommended he 'return to Lisbon through the battle lines with a safety detail. [...] So I left my large canvas for another painter' (ML, 203).

The artist's orderly retreat from the Portuguese revolution led him all the way to the Palace Hotel in Madrid and to studies in the Escorial and Prado, where he could spend the time alone(!); for all that he allowed himself nightly beach strolls with a Spanish conquest whose identity remains unknown. 'I want to remain in Spain for a year, Velazquez is that good', he announced to his brother. (Br II, 112) What disgusted him about Spain were the bull fights which he refers to as a 'cowardly, revolting affair' (Br II, 116).

Always these views from hotel room windows. From the Palace Hotel he overlooked the Plaza Cánovas del Castillo and interpreted what he saw onto his canvas. It is a seeing that does not abstract from the physical reference; rather, it transposes the concrete. The objects remain recognisable from their outlines; the people are only outlined as though they are mere shadows of themselves – similarly in his paintings of Notre-Dame in Bordeaux or the Louvre from late spring 1925. Kokoschka seemed almost addicted to seeing more different locations: Sevilla, Granada, Aranjuez, Toledo and Biarritz, where his romance with Marguerite Loeb awaited him – an amorous interlude that would lead to his most tender letters addressed to his 'Tamariske' as he called her, referencing a delicate Mediterranean shrub with feathery blossoms.

At the Savoy Hotel in Paris, competing for his favour and love, in addition to his 'Tamariske' ('I kiss you all over'; Br II, 131), were Anna Kallin, the 'Indra' of his memoirs who used to sing the letter scene aria from Tchaikovsky's *Eugen Onegin* to him with her 'soft, stirring voice' (ML, 196), and Alice Lehmann, his 'only, dearest Colibri'. More precisely, their images competed in him. Nothing and no one forced him to make a decision for *the one* from his female menagerie – least of all himself. But Paris was spoiled for him, not least because of the broken nose he suffered there. A caricature in a letter to Marguerite Loeb showing him in the clinic being looked after by raven-like doctors speaks to Kokoschka's enduring self-irony in any situation. He comments on this: 'I am proud that I have aligned everything already on my body. And I had a fever, for days, like a sheep' (Br II, 128 f). He refers to the x-ray for 400 francs as a 'wonderful life-sized skull of mine' (ibid), similar to the internal archetype for his innumerable self-portraits. He could have likened himself to Rodin's sculpture *L'homme au nez cassé* (1863), in which the principles 'art must be true to life' and 'blemish before grace' found their manifestation and to which Kokoschka was a definite subscriber by then.

In the end he was very glad to escape Paris. Together with Jakob Goldschmidt he continued on to Holland, the atmosphere of which he could not praise enough. He lets his mother know: 'Holland is the most beautiful I have seen so far. I am glad that I am gone from that grimy Paris' (Br II, 134). Scheveningen cured him of the Paris experience. He now equated the metropolis on the Seine to a 'dirty, dumb,

miserable, immoral, narrow-minded nest' (Br II, 135). He only knew
how to help himself by painting a landscape while lying in his hotel
bed. As exaggerated as this judgement seems, in Holland he knew
himself to be in the land of Van Gogh, with whom critics repeatedly connected him. As evidence of this, he claimed to have created
a 'charming flower painting with the sea as background' on the 'first
afternoon' in the spa hotel in Scheveningen. Yet, by mid-July 1925 we
find the travel-hungry artist, imbued with a 'passionate need for love',
in the Abbotsford Hotel, 4 Upper Montague Street, London. He came
to London for its use as a motif and for a 'discussion' with Anna Kallin
who was staying with her parents there. His mother was first to hear
the critical news: '[...] in the first hour I arrived in London I immediately found the place for painting. On the 10th floor on the Thames.
The entire river and a city 10x as big as Vienna. The first painting is
finished.' Even the reunion with Anna Kallin appeared to pale next to
this impression. After all, his 'Tamariske', his 'miracle', was waiting for
him in Amsterdam. Nevertheless, he does not write to her of any kind
of impressions of London, no descriptions of street scenes or buildings
– all his observations had gone into his paintings. Instead he yearns for
something else.

> If it were in any way possible, then quickly and often send me pic-
> tures of yourself, with lots of skin, and also of your toes, and spe-
> cifically your eyes and hair. And all around, also your back, and also
> send me a few hairs. I have already often held the little cache of your
> hair in my hand such that it is almost useless, and your stockings,
> too. Drink a lot of milk, you must be awfully healthy and lazy for
> me. (Br II, 140)

From a distance this long wishlist is reminiscent of the doll descriptions he had sent to Hermine Moos. Then he was in Amsterdam, but
soon wanted to make a 'hop to Switzerland, in order to recover from
the thousand canals, that don't smell good, but are pretty' (Br II, 141);
presumably he also wanted to write to 'Tamariske' from a distance
again. Kokoschka was not the first, nor the last, to find that absence

made his heart grow fonder. By August he was already in the Grand Hotel Kronenhof-Bellavista in Pontresina; after that in Vienna again where he lodged at the Hotel Bristol like a guest in his own city, before he returned to Vienna towards the end of 1925, only to soon travel once again to Berlin and, in early March of the following year, to London.

Kokoschka travelled in order to paint. Being on the road became an essential prerequisite for creativity for him, but also a lifestyle. He needed – also emotionally – freedom of movement. But he could not do so without amorous involvements. They inspired him, gave his colours and shapes special emotional values. He repeatedly complained about his 'poor hearing', yet he could write to Anna Kallin that it gave him a pang when he heard the Australian soprano Nellie Melba and believed, 'it is your sound in Dresden' (Br II, 142). Soon he, too, would reside in the Savoy Hotel, where 'the' Melba stayed in 1892/1893 and the dessert Peach Melba was invented by the head chef Escoffier after a performance of *Lohengrin*. By mid-March 1926 Kokoschka was living on the eighth floor of the Savoy with uninterrupted views over London: 'I have to live up here because I can paint a picture with the widest view over the Thames' (Br II, 152).

Earlier in February 1926, in Berlin, he found the time to send fan mail to the Jewish-Russian actress and co-founder of the legendary Habima Theatre, Hanna Rowina, in which he parodies Yiddish sentence structure.

> Dear Madam Rowina,
> The 20th Century means the end of male criminal's history. *On this will follow the good fortune*: the founding of a series of women's states, between both cycles a gender of sybils and prophetesses and Amazonians will rise at the beginning of which they, great artist Chana Rowina, will burn your glowing heart. In admiration, I am your
>
> Oskar Kokoschka (Br II, 152; author's emphasis)

As far as London is concerned there is nothing in his letters about the city itself. But we are somewhat better informed about this second London sojourn through a report by the art critic Josef Bard,[9] who refers to Kokoschka as his 'friend from Vienna back in those days'. It was an unexpected reunion during the crossing from the Hook of Holland to Harwich. Bard immediately noticed Kokoschka: an elegant appearance among the other business travellers, bank clerks and students. Bard particularly mentions the sales representatives of German manufacturers of shoe arch supports, which apparently were a scarce commodity in England at that time.

Despite Kokoschka's bowler hat, in Bard's eyes he resembled a Melanesian god perhaps from Papua New Guinea, the Solomon Islands or Vanuatu – a godlike figure who could not understand that one no longer offered sacrifices of throbbing human hearts to the gods. And then his head. It is as ghostly as his paintings. Once seen, never forgotten. The paintings are painfully exact when they show these irregular faces that look as though the artist has ripped away their mask. And then these never-before-seen colours, the colours resembling past dreams.

Later Bard visited his friend in his apartment at the Savoy, high above London's rooftops with its uninterrupted views of the Thames. There Kokoschka teased from the metropolis a very unusual colourfulness in its intensity, wherein, in Bard's eyes, he painted the palaces and factories as ruins at the same time as having a promising future. He shows – and this characterisation of Kokoschka's first London paintings is particularly apt – how the sun pushes its light through the damp atmosphere, illustrating the silver-blue breadth of the city as well as the vibrating green lines, the dragon's-blood red and the white.

Bard describes Kokoschka's work methods at the time. He did not stay at it for long stretches, rather from time to time created a large-scale picture within a few days and then fell into lethargy. He hired one of the Savoy's messenger boys to wash out his brushes daily, for which he paid him extra, since he had learned how poor the young man was and that he had to care for a sick wife and seven ailing children. Because of this, Kokoschka felt more compelled to work every day, otherwise he would also have a guilty conscience about his assistant, who only earnt money if there were brushes to clean.

At this time Kokoschka painted George the mandrill and Ranji the tigon, a cross between a lion and a tiger, in London Zoo. Yet Bard believed Kokoschka was by no means a socialite. In (English) society, he remained leftish. What he gave forth sounded 'obscure'. His strong Viennese accent was not very helpful. There was something abrupt about his speech that often puzzled his fellow countrymen. This was also reflected in his plays. Bard suggested that one had to close one's ears to the conventional meaning of words in order to even come close to understanding this theatrical way of speaking; it was best to listen with half-closed eyes. However, among friends, he seems to have been much more relaxed. Bard reports of long strolls through the city and of Kokoschka's eye for the beauty and elegance of English women. He would later portray them in the guise of Posy Croft. What Kokoschka attempted to capture – according to Bard – was the immediacy of expression, even when he turned to Bible stories, such as in *Lot und seine Töchter* (*Lot and His Daughters*), a theme that presaged his later penchant for *König Lear* (*King Lear*).

As to the topic of Kokoschka in society, he reveals himself on this in a letter to his mother written from London in mid-March 1926.

> Tonight, I was in a true English intellectual gathering (which is unbelievably difficult for a foreigner, because English high society does not receive anyone who is not well screened) for the first time in my life. And I almost fainted for shame because I did not understand a single word of the conversation. *I would have to live a whole year in London, otherwise I will never make it in this world.* I have nothing to wear, am naturally again in the greatest difficulty because I cannot touch my painstakingly saved up money, rather have to increase it so we have our pension this year. I could paint an English bishop, if I could at least speak English, from Westminster Abbey! My heart is squeezed like that of a school boy, and that despite the fact I am already such an old stick. Bohi [Bohuslav], please learn English!!! Mother, all money is wasted if Bohi is not better educated. We in Vienna are like the negroes or untamed in comparison to the real world of the English. (Br II, 153; author's emphasis)

I would have to live a whole year in London... There was no possible way of knowing that in a little more than ten years' time this would become a fateful reality – and not for one year, but for sixteen.

Again and again, Tower Bridge; again and again the play of light on the Thames, a busy river, an artery of modern hustle and bustle and thus offering a mythical panorama – that is how Kokoschka presents London around 1925/1926. And out in the suburbs, in Richmond, on the terrace high above the middle reaches of the Thames, Kokoschka achieves an elegant idyll, captured in intense lilac-hued pastel colours. It is the same famous Thames view in Richmond that Constable and Turner had featured before him. As always in Kokoschka's land- and cityscapes, the people remain suggested as though taken from his joy of portraiture. A stylishly dressed English lady, only hinted at, a boater and sun shade, and a rider enjoying the view from horseback suffice to visualise a symbiosis of nature and gentility. Virginia Woolf was also living in Richmond at this time and it does not require much imagination to see her in this picture. A landscape representation of this relaxed, bucolic type is virtually unique in Kokoschka's oeuvre because his landscapes normally also show drama – for example, a stormy atmosphere over Lake Geneva or the Scotland paintings of 1929, *Dulsie Bridge* and *Plodda Falls*. The maritime counterpart to the serenity of nature at this time can be found in his painting *Die Küste bei Dover* (*The Coast at Dover*). It demonstrates just how much these coastal landscapes of white cliffs impressed him. Shadow-like tones of black at the picture's left edge and a slightly stormy cloud scene, contrasting with glistening sunlight, lend the painting a suspense-laden hue which the summery late afternoon atmosphere of the Richmond terrace painting lacks.

The London months of 1926 brought new inspiration from animals. In Richmond Park he painted a group of red deer at a water trough. His visit to London Zoo, in Regent's Park, generated the most amazing animal portraits of Modernist art. He painted the dancer and singer Adele Astaire (later Lady Cavendish), and shortly afterwards the diva of German-Hungarian silent films, Elza Temáry – each with a dog. Kokoschka had already shown the creature as a trespasser on civilisation in an unexpectedly ironic manner in his second portrait of Karl Kraus (1925). Here there is a large insect, half-dragonfly, half-bumble bee queen, that distracts the critic and writer from his book or manuscript. The result is a surprised expression of his emphatically pale face alienated by nature. In the London of 1926, however, the animalistic-creature-esque gained a new dimension for Kokoschka. Apparently in May the director of London Zoo, Julian Huxley, gave him permission to paint the tigon and the mandrill before the zoo opened. In *Mein Leben*, Kokoschka further embellishes this episode, wherein he does not neglect to mention that the important biologist, behaviouralist and humanist Huxley also refers to him in a paper on suicide. More apt would have been a mention of Ludwig Meidner, who had created a painting titled *Der Selbstmörder* (*The Suicide*) in 1912. Oddly enough, Thomas G Masaryk, whose portrait Kokoschka would paint ten years hence, also drafted a study on suicide, on the basis of which he was granted his PhD. The connection to Huxley would become meaningful for Kokoschka in other ways during the years of his English exile.

Kokoschka's fascination for the archaic expressed itself in his interest in the mandrill and the tigon. His friend Bard recalled a joint visit to the British Museum. Kokoschka wished to see the collection of Neolithic stone tools. He apparently claimed to be a distant descendant of these Stone Age people. He wanted to connect to his ancestors through these tools and he supposedly came close to destroying a display case in order to lift a stone hammer. The mandrill and tigon also offered an outlet for Kokoschka's desire for the exotic, as demonstrated by the background of his *Mandrill* which teems with a tropical blaze of colour.

Yet it was not the tropics that were his goal; rather, it was the desert. He would have to wait on it until early 1928, and it on him. Because for him, the International Art Exhibition in Dresden in the summer of 1926 lay between London and the desert, as did additional stays in Paris, Vienna and Berlin; the premiere of Ernst Křenek's opera based on Kokoschka's play *Orpheus und Eurydike* in Kassel; major retrospectives in Berlin and most importantly Zurich; another stay in Venice;

the great Mont Blanc painting of October 1927; and in the subsequent visits to Lyon, Blois (the city fascinated him due to its pure histori- cal architecture) and, again, Paris. At this time Kokoschka was repre- sented in nearly all major museums and galleries in Germany and also, increasingly, across Europe, particularly in the Netherlands, France, Italy and Switzerland. By the time he separated himself from Europe and boarded the ship in Marseilles to 'Carthage', with Helmut Lütgen (the Hamburg art dealer who managed the Amsterdam branch of Galerie Cassirer), Kokoschka had already become a phenomenon of the European art scene. Never lacking a grand gesture or even a subtle hint, Kokoschka does not shy from an obvious reference in *Mein Leben*.

> Carthage! That was what was to be read on the board at the quay in large French and Arabic letters. My dream of the Orient had been fulfilled. From here Hannibal once set out to attack the dangerous Roman Empire in an historic adventurous campaign across Spain and endless marches across the ice fields of the Alps – where I had just previously frozen while painting [...] We encountered two lads, tall moors in white shirts. Each held a twiglet of jasmine under the nose; with their little fingers linked, they led each other in the sand. (ML, 213)

In reading the letters from this time (1926/1927), one gains the impres- sion that in his eyes two events were and remained formative: the memory of the London stay (Anna Kallin provides him with Mack- intosh Toffees and in Berlin he buys 'gramophone disks' of *The St Matthew's Passion* with the 'Westminster Abby Choir' (Br II, 157)) and the nature and art experience of Mont Blanc, Monte Rosa and Little St Bernhard. He becomes a 'real climbing enthusiast' in the glaciers, mountain gorges and scree. At Chamonix he even digs up a 'giant gentian' and sends it to his mother in Vienna (Br II, 162–167). Yet in the midst of his mountain wanderings in snow and cold, which primarily serve the search for motifs, he does not forget to write to Alma Mahler-Gropius and ask her for the latest photographs; it is 19

October 1927. She comes to mind even – or especially – here in the highest alpine regions.

In December 1927, his thoughts long since turned to North Africa, he lunched with the Duchesse Clermont-Tonnerre and attended a musical evening at Comte de Rambaud's, after a 'music tea at a banker's wife's, who collects aristocrats' (Br II, 174). To mother and brother he makes known, as ever self-mockingly: 'I am very posh, slender, shyly make very good remarks and discretely make great advertising for myself', especially to Comte de Rambaud, who proves to be a great Picasso collector – 'hopefully not always', as Kokoschka smugly notes (Br II, 172 and 174). There were apparently also plans to commission him to paint the interior of the Salle Pleyel. Yet Tunis awaited.

Kokoschka *Ante Portas*

What do locations mean to a visual artist? Sources of motifs, spacial possibilities, unfolding of perspectives; encounters happen at locations and, in the best cases, end in portraits. Kokoschka's art thrived on changing locations between 1928 and 1934; it was the only constant in his life in those days. However, he did not rush from city to city, landscape to landscape; rather, he concentrated on that which he saw as fundamental from place to place. In Tunis, well dressed and wearing a hat, he painted on the roof of a bazaar shop, until the unceasing rain made this impossible for him and also soaked the roof to the point of collapse. His mood usually sank to a low when he could not leave his hotel due to weather conditions and had to entertain himself. The only aid in those cases was to work on a self-portrait as interiors apparently did not interest him. Yet the absence of self-portraits during his three-month stay in the North African Orient is noticeable. It would appear that the new impressions managed to distract him from himself, even during persistent rain.

He used the Transatlantique hotel chain, which at the time reached from Tunis, Gabes, El Kantara, Touggourt and Tozeur all the way to Biskra, Algiers and Fez. That meant he travelled visibly as a European and did not try to dive into the local culture. A photo, taken in the desert near El Kantara, shows him in coat and tie in conversation with Bedouins, and that in front of an automobile which his driver (likely Helmut Lütgen) guards. He reports on an obligatory camel ride on 26 January 1928: 'Much more comfortable than on horseback' (Br II, 183). Other than that: 'The cities themselves are boring, lots of square little boxes. But the desert!' (ibid). At least preparatory, perhaps accompanying, reading material was available to him – exploring Morocco through the American novelist and confidante of Henry James, Edith Wharton.[10] Later Kokoschka would also grapple with the writings of leading pan-Africanist George Padmore,[11] as well as the memoirs of Abd el-Krim, which centred on the so-called Rif War in Morocco (1920–1926) that France and Spain led against Moroccan tribes.[12] In general, Kokoschka's deep interest in the scandal of colonialism stands out, demonstrated by the numerous relevant books in his library that he had worked his way through.

As early as 1923 he had hinted at how he imagined an oriental figure in a watercolour he painted in Dresden: sensuous outlines of a girl with a large jug on her head, unveiled, looking sadly into the unknown. In Biskra he was then affected by the genuine Bedouins. They seemed unapproachable, unfathomable and at the same time seductive. From Touggourt he writes: 'Am healthy, and in the evening I drink my peppermint tea with somewhat loose women in the dance café (Arabic) here with the other natives. The conversation with my special girlfriend, who looks like a little Ottakringer beer glass, is conducted in Arabic' (Br II, 193). He coquettishly mentions the 'bad temptations' that awaited him in this dance café to Anna Kallin, although he claims he let himself be admitted to a 'male cloister' so that he could avoid them and paint – men (Br II, 191).

In Tozeur he painted on the minaret, and in Temacine he painted the portrait of a Bedouin prince, the Marabout. He saw Carthage and noticed something quirky in the bazaar in Tunis: old men in the marketplace 'love their suspenders', though on 'naked legs' without socks (Br II, 177).

Once again Kokoschka's language abilities are confirmed by his remarks. He is able to flirt and converse in Arabic after a short time. The language of his letters is a feast of oriental pictures, although without relinquishing distance through self-mockery. *Tausend und eine Nacht* (*One Thousand and One Nights*) becomes the stereotypical standard by which Kokoschka, too, measures impressions: almond blossoms next to eucalyptus, palms and oranges. Add to that a 'labyrinth of spice-silk-slipper-goldsmith shops, that all lie in tunnels' (Br II, 176). He remarks on thick-bodied women, 'Thank God, veiled', in 'white bloomers'. The ethnic pluralism visibly impresses him: 'Negros, Berbers, Turks, Jews.' We will refrain from commenting on the fact that he wrote right across chest height of the three Bedouin women dressed in white on the picture postcard.

An experience of singular nature awaited him on the island of Djerba off the Tunisian coast. As far as is known, his correspondence does not mention it. *Djerba*, a tale written in 1930 and reworked in 1956, and the relevant passage in *Mein Leben* paint this episode all the more richly in differing ways, whereby the narrative embellishment in the autobiography seems shortened, though more colourful. In Jerusalem Kokoschka had heard of the Jewish community on Djerba, which traces back to the diaspora following the destruction of the Temple. In addition to an 'age-old synagogue' the 'prettiest Jewish girls' are there (ML, 223). The goddess Calypso, who seduced Odysseus, is said to have lived there during Homeric times – reason enough for Kokoschka to have sought out this isle. In *Mein Leben* he reports that immediately upon his arrival at the marketplace of Houmt Souk, the little capital city of Djerba island, he saw a group of women with water jugs at the well. Among them was 'a young maiden of such grace, that I immediately determined to paint her as Madonna in memory of Titian's Assunta in Venice' (ML, 223). In the tale, the first-person narrator arranges a kind of beauty contest with the local council; the one he declares the winner is to have her portrait painted by him. The mayor's foster daughter, the nameless beauty, is held back by her father. When she eventually shows herself, the narrator believes himself entranced. He wants to paint her immediately but requests that she turn her eyes towards him, forgetting that in this culture any reference to the eyes is considered a bad omen and responded to with a sign against evil. The beauty responds with a faint; she withdraws from posing for him, and is brought to the mainland by her family where she is to remain hidden. With the help of a sorcerer, however, the narrator is able to find her [...] but in a state of sleepwalking. When he speaks to her, she takes fright and withdraws from him again. When he grasps her hand, he suddenly becomes aware of the absurdity of his intent: 'It was the eyes which she kept closed why everything now seemed so perverse to me and I no longer wanted anything from this being which an alien had forced into coming' (DSW II, 240).

In the tale, as in reality, a portrait thus did not come into being. Instead, in the narrative Kokoschka is able to provide a poignant description of the non-existent painting.

Sapphire blue, rose red and gold combined themselves in the brocade of her trousers over the crossed legs. From the little vest embroidered with blinking little silver disks, the deep neckline of which allowed me to see her small breasts bedded in a muslin nest like a pair of turtle doves, my glance moved on and let itself be bound by the allure of the hieratic head jewellery of gold, enamel and filigree work by the local jeweller, which crowned her thick black hair, when my eye eventually slid to the duller, ordinary colours of the relative's garb. A reflection of the light that emitted from the confused girl fell on the women like the sun's last ray touches the earth already shrouded in deep night. The light still played in the folds of the carpets on the walls and the floor, until the spell of love, once more glimmering in the velvet shadows, finally extinguished in the background. (DSW II, 233 f)

One can almost speak of a pictorial narrative here, rare enough among visual artists. Of course, this shunning of the eyes must have been particularly alien for Kokoschka, for whom the primacy of seeing and looking were of tantamount importance. And yet he only mentions it in connection with the Djerba episode, which nevertheless taught him something else. A missionary had told him that in this culture one could not make images of anything that had a shadow. That is why Arabs much preferred to paint abstract patterns. Kokoschka, who fought against the abstract his entire life, must have found that alien as well. However, his fascination with the unknown, with otherness, outweighed his growing discontent about conditions in Europe. Kokoschka's acquaintance with Richard von Coudenhove-Kalergi, which can be dated to early 1931, was also of little help. His conception of a Pan-Europa could at no time replace Kokoschka's pedagogically orientated, Comenius-based understanding of community in Europe. Hence, it is telling that there are none of Coudenhove's Pan-Europa writings in the library of Kokoschka's estate, only the aphorisms with a dedication to him, *Gebote des Lebens* (*Commandments of Life*) and *Los vom Materialismus!* (*Get Rid of Materialism!*), both 1931.

The artist's view was always the priority for Kokoschka. Whatever he painted, he always measured against the great role models, even in North Africa. He writes to Anna Kallin: 'My painting is finished. As good as a Rubens sketch. With a real line like a Fragonard. And I would be jealous if another had painted it again' (Br II, 191). For example, Picasso. That was the advantage he had over them, Dix, Picasso and Schiele – the real desert experience, the proximity to Bedouins. His mother and brother heard: 'It is really fantastic now, I paint a blue-black Arabian prince in his palace in the middle of the desert [...]' (Br II, 192). What the South Seas were to Gaugin, so now the desert was to Kokoschka: a space for familiarisation, meaning an area in which one's own expectations of the foreign are confronted with its reality, from which a hybrid form then develops. In the case of Kokoschka, this would be the portraits (of the Marabout and the Bedouin girl), which only reveal traces of what had been characteristic to date for this artist in the manner of their portrayal. There are, however, no hints of a mystical desert experience in Kokoschka. He is free of desert romance. He knows how to contain the glimpse into the vastness of the desert and the canopy of stars stretched over it.

In Algiers Kokoschka was already thinking of Sevilla again; on arriving there, of Madrid, where he was overcome by a kind of Habsburg nostalgia. He refers to Emperor Charles V as his 'favourite emperor', the 'truly last great person as sovereign' (Br II, 198). That was also how his friend Ernst Křenek saw him; at least that was how he would depict him in his most important opera, his Opus 73 *Karl V* (*Charles V*), of 1938. Reflecting further on Charles V and his origins, Kokoschka was overcome by a genealogical fantasy distantly reminiscent of one by Alexander Lernet-Holenia, who convincingly entertained the myth of having been the offspring of a Habsburg Archduke, which finally earned him the right to take residence in Vienna's Hofburg. Kokoschka writes:

> His [Charles V's] mother was also Joanna the Mad, who I am crazy about by the way, because she shared my necrophilia and love of dolls with her entire family and left it to her heirs. Based on that, perhaps [...] I am directly a bastard of the Habsburgs, like Don Juan d'Austria, from Frances I and my grandmother; did I inherit it from her – such matters often reappear again later? (Br II, 198)

He who fears having to remain without offspring (the numerous yearning mother-and-child depictions or allusions in Kokoschka's letters and paintings speak for themselves!), compensates for this fear with fanciful genealogies.

As mentioned, his own person is of less interest as a subject for self-portraits in this period. But that did not preclude the occasional self-examination. From Madrid he enlightens Anna Kallin about himself.

> My character is not consistent, but rather far-sighted and basically despairing. I notice far too much and fail in helping. I confuse the drive for action with the end result, and thus everything gets delayed for the other because I cause everything to happen with a too mechanical impulse. Whoever near to me does not lead their own life, is lost if he depends on me, because I gawp a long time without leaping after the drowning person. I am not a coward, but comfortable like a deep-sea newt and nature-shy. (Br II, 200 f)

Self-knowledge of this sort most frequently occurs with specific word choices; for example, he refers to himself here as 'far-sighted'. Also, the usage, to be understood literally, of the phrase 'notice far too much' could suggest a certain scepticism with regard to the self-tutelage in seeing. Perhaps it was too much for his seeing, from time to time, precisely *because* he did not want to learn, never mind about himself.

In his loneliness, which was a constant travel companion, he had become wistful, could not rest, found himself sometimes here then there, needed the hunt for emotional highs, and wanted to let himself be intoxicated by sensory impressions. Because: 'Everything can become a sensory perception', as he informed Anna Kallin in the same letter.

And once again he found himself on the road – after a rained-out Spain in May 1928 to an even rainier Ireland a month later. He travelled the west coast of this notoriously damp island whose (then) dirty hotels unnerved him, wanting to see 'whether many clouds from the ocean will still come apart here' (Br II, 205). They did not do him this favour. In addition, there seemed to be only 'old witches' in Killarney, where he stayed a couple of days. 'And I so desperately need chambermaids, milkmaids, fisherwomen, shepherdesses', he admits to Anna Kallin of all people, who was used to hearing this from him by then (Br II, 205). But on all these travels she remained a dependable correspondent, to whom he could be more open than to anyone else.

Dublin, Oxford, London, Vienna, soon Brindisi, Alexandria, then Cairo in March 1929 where no chambermaids or Bedouin girls comforted him; instead he painted a Sphinx 'as if I had an affair with her' (Br II, 208). But then it was the turn of an 'Egyptian beauty', whom he wanted to paint more than anything in the world. That came to nothing, 'though she would have liked to pose'. And why? Because he could not offer this spoilt beauty 'an oasis when she wanted to be alone with me, or because I could not have a Rolls Royce waiting to abduct her at her door, like the French banker's son (a poet), who won the contest' (Br II, 213). Soon he found himself in Jerusalem where he wrote these remarkable words in the guestbook: 'I wish fulfilment of the ideal to all coming home to this land' (Br II, 210). And although a word should be said here about Kokoschka's relationship to Jews, we will make up for it when we meet him in his English exile. He visited

Damascus, Athens, Istanbul, Venice and Zurich, followed by Inverness and Strathglass in Scotland – all that still in 1929, then in the first half of 1930 having longer stays in Rome and Paris following a stopover in Tunis.

In Damascus he summarises: 'My trip so far is terribly barren of results. I have fallen out with myself and would like to become a Muslim, seriously. There are also beautiful and pure wenches here' (Br II, 211). Yet Damascus did not offer much in the way of exhilaration for him. He describes a city 'shot up' in the war, which had risen again as a purely industrial city. And in the 'blessed Land', in Palestine, the British administration allowed the 'perversion of pretty Arab girls into starving plantation coolies' in order to help increase exports (Br II, 213).

This constant travel was by no means 'barren of results', even if no masterpieces were produced in this period. Yet the paintings done in Scotland count among the most impressive testaments to Kokoschka's examination of the wildness of nature, and that despite his claiming – as previously mentioned – to be 'nature-shy'.

One gets the distinct impression that he only regained his equilibrium in the second half of 1930 and began to rediscover (if not reinvent) himself. To Anna Kallin he confesses to health complaints, the price of his vagabondage: 'This constant gypsying around, without wanting anything and working too little are making me homesick' (Br II, 222). Even so, Kokoschka had formed a picture of the world for himself through this intensive travel activity, and had cultivated visual and verbal dealings with strangers through his own outlook. Hence it can be seen as consistent with this that Kokoschka considered 'painting together' a 'great wandering exhibition' clear around the world from New York to Shanghai. He is thinking, as he writes to his friend Ehrenstein, of 'a type of New World Symphony similar to the one by the Czech composer Dvořák. All the most important heads and different peoples and landscapes and cities and manmade constructions' (Br II, 278).

He considered 'an epic poem of wakening reason'; once again he had in mind an 'instructive picture book' in the form of his paintings of world leaders and that also because he had studied Robert Briffault's *The Mothers* (1931), a new version of Bachofen's matriarchy idea, to which Kokoschka felt himself bound. In the context of *The Mothers*, he had drafted a remarkable text, *Totem und Tabu. Denkübungen eines Zynikers (Totem and Taboo: Mental Exercises of a Cynic).*[13] It should be mentioned here that Kokoschka was also highly likely to have interested his friend Albert Ehrenstein in the idea of a matriarchy. Ehrenstein not only picked it up, but followed and developed it far more extensively than his artist friend, and over a significantly longer period of time.[14] Strangely enough, until then, Kokoschka had been omitted from the remarkably long line of prominent Bachofen readers.[15]

Back in an Increasingly Alien Europe: Political Optics in the Century of Deceptions

While in Rome Kokoschka had asked his girlfriend Anna Kallin to send him nude photos. The first letter he wrote from Paris after his North African expedition also demanded 'a quite sensuous letter with explicit photos' of her (Br II, 227). He yearned for his Russian Mirli, but above all for inspiration. His studio was in the Rue Delambre above that of the English portraitist Augustus John (1878–1961), who introduced him to James Joyce. Kokoschka would learn to prefer the art of John's more talented sister, Gwen.

Kokoschka found himself on the return journey into the European, but not on a retreat into the personal. Quite the opposite. His public presence was to grow considerably in the 1930s – in both creative *and* political arenas.

The Kunsthalle Mannheim showed a major retrospective of his work in early 1931. Max Liebermann dubbed him the 'born artist' of his generation and in February, the Parisian Galerie Bonjean showed six of Kokoschka's paintings; international critics compared them with Tintoretto and El Greco. This presentation was topped in March when the Galerie Georges Petit in Paris staged a solo exhibition of Kokoschka's work. Consequently, he was that much more aggravated when he received notice from the art dealership Cassirer that they would be reducing his monthly fixed allowance significantly. It led to a dispute, in part carried out in the public media, and eventually to a rift with his most important business partner to date. It is revealing for Kokoschka's self-awareness that he could not keep up with the demands of the art dealership to serve the market with more pleasing creations. His detailed letter to the proprietors of the Cassirer Art Dealership goes beyond a veritable critique of the practices and machinations of the art trade. In another letter from that time he injects his self-awareness on an economic point: 'In any case, a piece from me is a healthier invest-ment than all your state and private papers!' (Br II, 240). He would remain correct in that.

Wherever Kokoschka stayed, he was considered successful, if not established, though he expended considerable energy on catapulting himself back out of that established-ness. He belonged to the art scene of the avant-garde, was familiar with its own unique rules and simul-taneously scorned them. Growing political astuteness increasingly expressed itself in moral courage, for example, when in an 'open letter' in the *Frankfurter Zeitung* on 8 June 1933 he defended Max Lieber-mann, who had been forced to step down from the Prussian Academy of Fine Arts by the new authorities on the basis of the 'Aryan para-graph'. In this he paid tribute to Liebermann (the choice of words could not have been more pointed) the *artist* as a '*Führer* into freedom, into the light', and directly alluded to the book burning of 10 May, but also of his conviction that 'all fatherlands are rooted in the lap of Mother Nature Earth': 'Fires of joy and not funeral pyres are lit for this divine Mother, to whom the thorn, vine and rose are dedicated' (Br II, 263).

Despite broad public recognition prior to 1933, Kokoschka was at odds with his fellow Austrians and Germans. In June 1931 we read: 'The Germans are really impossible and have no concept of human, personal worth!' (Br II, 234). Yet the disturbing anti-Semitic attitude immediately follows in the next sentence: 'I will now make a major assassination attempt against the entire Jewish orientated world! I am drawing the "Holy Mass" and taking out all pagan themes and starting afresh. The Pope will excommunicate me and all mercantile thinking traditional shitheads' (Br II, 234). After that followed the *eli-eli-lama-asabtani* (*My God, my God, why hast Thou forsaken me*) gesture: 'Why has everyone left me so alone?' – and so on, in a letter to his beloved Alice Lahmann, his 'Colibri', written in the Villa des Camélias in the Fourteenth Arrondissement in Paris. Still, in October 1932 he proposed – unsuccessfully – a major exhibition in Paris of Max Liebermann's work as a contribution towards German-French understanding.

What bothered him about the German and Austrian mentality on his own behalf was the, as Kokoschka saw it, deep-seated hostility against art. In consolation he quotes Dürer's words written in Venice to his friend Pirkheimer: 'Here I am a gentleman, in Germany a parasite' (Br II, 242). In contrast to the other arts, the visual arts are more dependent on dealers (consequently also on exorbitant increases in value!).

On a previously unknown scale for Kokoschka, in-depth political views in the form of speeches and essays moved into the foreground between 1932 and 1938 – significantly from Vienna and after 1934 from Prague. They impress with their commitment and expertise, spanning from Comenius to Thomas Paine and Jeremy Bentham, from political theory to sociology. No visual artist of Modernism or the established avant-garde spoke out politically with such competence. What initially appears more like boasting, arguing with broad strokes and at best ambiguous in his letters takes on sharp contours in the essays. To Ehrenstein in May 1932 he comments: '[...] Mussolini admired my paintings in Venice, who four or five years ago had done a furious about-face and railed, such that the *Berliner Tagblatt* feared political entanglements on my part' (Br II, 255). He gives Alice Lahmann a quite elementary justification for his interest in the matriarchy: 'I have always been created anew by women. What strength a loyal woman has to kindle the best in one!' (Br II, 252). His personal word on the Austrian Ständestaat (corporative state) of 1934 barely sounds reflective.

The Austr. Constitution, which begins with the profession to Christianity and logically leads to the performance of the Watschentanz, is the theatricalisation of the Christian word: If someone slaps you on the right cheek, turn to them the other cheek also – what was sanctioned as an official miracle play, that is a farce performed by men! (Br II, 274)

Occasionally he thinks of Alma again, understandably, particularly on his return to Vienna. From Vienna he reports to Albert Ehrenstein: 'Werfel has conjured a veritable palace for Frau Mahler for 600,000 Schilling on the Hohen Warte. All are flourishing, only I am dying out!' (Br II, 269). Now, Kokoschka would endure the longest, and that was in part because he recognised where his Austria was heading earlier than others did. However, one thing should not be overlooked for all Kokoschka's criticism of the remnants of Kakania (imperial Austria): he criticised as an Austrian patriot. It was specifically this attitude which would prompt him, in the spring of 1938, to produce a five-page printed document, *Ansuchen an den Haager Schiedsgerichtshof um eine Feststellung des Ex-lex-Zustandes in Österreich unter dem Regime des Herrn von Schuschnigg* (*Application to the Hague Court of Arbitration for a Determination on the Ex-Lex State of Affairs in Austria Under the Regime of Herr von Schuschnigg*) which lodged a protest against the violation of international law in the 'Anschluss' ('Annexation') of Austria to the German Reich – a unique document by, let us say, a public private individual. It should not be called self-conceit that this artist still believed in 1938 one could use the medium of international law against political-ideological self-aggrandisement, if not pure megalomania. Kokoschka derived legality and legitimacy directly from the political theory of Thomas Paine and his alignment with the rights of men.

Kokoschka increasingly viewed the honing of political perspective as a moral responsibility at a time which he had long regarded as the Era of Deceptions. Ernest H Gombrich records that on his last visit to London in 1970 Kokoschka told him: 'That was the dumbest period there's ever been.'[16] By this he meant primarily the inhuman acceleration of technical development, and the expropriation of manual labour and independent thought.

Kokoschka's statements on art and politics blend into each other in terms of content, particularly in the 1930s. This becomes apparent when he repeats specific formulations and theses in different contexts, for example, his appeal for education reform based on the principles of humanism – that is, changing awareness in the sense of free coopera-tion. One is well advised to treat the written commentaries, broadcast lectures, views and essays (some of them resemble treatises) produced in Vienna and Prague between 1931 and 1938 as a unit. He certainly did in-depth research on this complex of themes, including a thor-ough study of Viktor von Weizsäcker's lectures *Seelenbehandlung und Seelenführung* (*Treatment and Stewardship of the Spirit*) of 1926. The notes in his copy lead to the conclusion that Kokoschka conducted a detailed analysis of the theses of this medical anthropologist and expo-nent of psychosomatic medicine, among whose main theories was that experience reconfigures biological developments and thus intellectu-ally repeats the experience. In his third lecture, Weizsäcker speaks of 'one of the most shattering experiences of an educator, that the student can become the opposite of his educator'. Only in the primal bond with the mother, according to Weizsäcker and noted with signs of agree-ment by Kokoschka, are the 'vital impulse and meaningfully spiritual undifferentiated'.[17] Their separation is then the primary reason for the disassociation of the student from the teacher as the non-mother.

Let us now move on to a more precise reading of the previously mentioned 'Denkübungen eines Zynikers', *Totem und Tabu* (1933). Written twenty years after Sigmund Freud's eponymous treatise,[18] this document contains one the most positive comments Kokoschka makes about Freud. Later he found him more irritating ('Again and again this Freud!') when a proximity to Freud's psychoanalysis was ascribed to his early pictorial work.[19] It is of course entirely possible that Kokoschka only really read Freud for the first time around 1930. At least in *Totem und Tabu* he deems it useful if one applies Freud's 'Neuroses and Sexuality', the 'dream research, psychopathology and the results of the psychoanalytic ego and character research' to the 'fields of the humanities': 'ethnology, anthropology, ethnopsychology, sociology, mythology, religious studies, cultural psychology and peda-gogy' (DSW IV, 53).

These 'Denkübungen' ('mental exercises') by no means make Kokoschka out as a cynic, as he referred to himself, but as an artist who
wanted to gain practice in discourses on cultural philosophy and politics. His guiding principle was derived from his pedagogic objective,
namely an enhancement of the primary school which should teach
a language that enabled individual pupils to 'think for themselves'.
In *Totem und Tabu* he focuses on the historical development of the
interconnection between speech and thought as well as the interplay of individual speech and societal communication, wherein he
also uses Freudian terminologically when he claims, 'not the "I" and
"You", rather the "It" now appears as the first pronoun' (DSW IV, 46).
However, first Kokoschka focuses on the relativisation of the principle of statehood. In the assertion of the 'sovereign state' he sees the
foundation being created for the 'Führer Principle' which violates all
individuality (DSW IV, 56). This principle is bolstered by the mono-
theistic religions and their 'humanity murdering myth of the primacy
of man', which is based on the suppression of the 'race of mothers'.
In doing so, as a pedagogue, he recommends not only a Comenius-
orientated globalisation of primary education, but also the study of
Mary Wollstonecraft's thought-provoking *Forderung der Frauenrechte*
(*A Vindication of the Rights of Woman: With Strictures on Political and
Moral Subjects*) of 1792. At the time, Kokoschka put it on a level with
the French Revolution. With reference to his own times, he further
writes:

> Twenty years after the outbreak of the World War, over the bat-
> tlefield of millions of unknown soldiers who lie there as the law
> required, the Academy, which was supposed to be responsible for
> the dissemination of the Enlightenment, was preaching the bank-
> ruptcy of democracy, myth of the state, restoration of the hierarchy.
> (DSW IV, 57)

It would seem that he had not only read Freud, James Frazer and John
Stuart Mill (*Die Unterdrückung der Frauen; The Subjection of Women*,
1869) at the time, but also the increasingly infamous political theorist

Carl Schmitt. Primarily, however, he had focused on Thomas Paine and thus the concept of the 'welfare state'. He spoke on this a year later (1934) and attempted a principle-based critique of Engelbert Doll-fuß's Austrian Ständestaat and its clerico-authoritarian manifesto.

Political necessity made Kokoschka intellectually curious. Paine interested him in a form of social awareness developed consistently on the principle of the rights of man which not only respected indi-viduality but encouraged it. With Hume, he was fascinated by his 'empirical, *impressionistic* concept' of the 'I as a bundle of experiences', to which Kokoschka could directly relate. He correctly recognised in it the rationale for Hume's anti-dogmatic position. At the same time, he doubted that the highly praised sciences always stood in the service of objective findings. On the contrary, he saw them as suppliers to ideological thought. Kokoschka speaks of the tendency of the sciences towards a 'cultivation of images that produce a disregard for reality' and which promote the political ideological aims of the state (DSW IV, 70). In this respect, what was already happening in National Socialist Germany in 1934 educated his critical eye for the other side of the border. However, Kokoschka also saw that a state as orientated towards orthodox religiosity as the Austrian Ständestaat would leave the door wide open to this kind of ideology.

Only as an aside does Kokoschka mention in his essay on Thomas Paine a philosopher who had clearly inspired him in many respects: Hans Vaihinger (1852–1933) and his *Philosophie des Als Ob* (*The Phi-losophy of 'As If'*, 1911), one of the most widespread philosophy works in the 1920s.[20] As a declared Kantian (Vaihinger had formed the first Kant Society in 1904), he reduced the pretensions of the scientific world to interpretation, which was consistent with Kokoschka's think-ing: 'The human image of the world is an immense web of fictions full of logical contradictions, that is of scientific fabrications for practical purposes or of inadequate, subjective, visual conceptions whose con-fluence with reality is precluded from the outset.'[21]

Kokoschka concluded from theses such as these that the modern state had made use of these scientific fictions, with the greatest fiction of all being the belief in its sovereignty. Kokoschka saw in it the first step towards a totalitarian state and the worship of force, as he explains in his 1935 essay *Zweierlei Recht* (*Dual Right*). Deeply worried, he asks: 'Will the coining of the myth of blood and soil as the basis for a concept of species only for a parliamentary term remain without tragic consequences?' (DSW IV, 119). The advancing technicisation of the state was to have led to the point that it deployed its 'machinery' against 'the principle of human confraternity'. Based on such insights, one would not be able to deny Kokoschka's political shrewdness.

He decisively turns against a continuing 'deification of the state' originating with Hegel; yes, he sees in the 'modern state' an 'absurdity' (DSW IV, 190). With Jeremy Bentham he goes into battle against a state fetishism, bidding farewell to the principle of social welfare whose 'artificial superstructure' now (1935/1936) allows an excess of totalitarianism on a scale unheard of even in the era of imperialism. Accordingly, he asks what the League of Nations will learn from the 'Abyssinian Adventure' of 1935 through which fascist Italy wanted to propel itself into the circle of European superpower states. Kokoschka comments:

Imperial maths, which harmoniously inserted the calculation of ballistic curves into the spirit of the Fatherland in schools, has no interest in mentioning that thanks to the shots fired in Sarajevo the national armaments industry earned twenty thousand dollars for every single casualty of the World War. (DSW IV, 157)

The artist castigates the absurd logic of the inhumanity of the politics of power. For Kokoschka, the only way out of these political power contexts of delusion was the '*via lucis*': Johann Amos Comenius' path of light and his plan for the international education of the people for the purpose of promoting peace. This now pushed itself into Kokoschka's perception next to the *Orbis Pictus* ideal. According to Kokoschka, 'the mothers' of the Eleusinian Mysteries should now have a say again (DSW IV, 82). Mothers should teach in this type of primary school, according to Kokoschka in a speech given in Budapest in 1934. He expresses himself similarly in the same year in a speech to

the Österreichischen Werkbund – and this under civil-war-like conditions in Vienna when government troops fired on workers' housing
estates, which had been built in the outer suburbs on the recommen-
dations of Adolf Loos, because the bourgeois factions suspected 'communist fortresses' there. In his memoirs Kokoschka goes so far as to
claim that his mother died of the psychological ramifications of this
shattering conflict.

In the 1970s Kokoschka had again looked through these texts
that originated four decades earlier, but did not change them sub-
stantially; they only received a new title in some cases. That suggests
that he remained convinced of their unchanged importance – not
to mention topicality. And it would not be difficult to create a connection between Kokoschka's Comenius-derived theses of the 1930s
and Robert Jungk's as well as Ludwig von Friedeburg's peace education designs of the 1960s and 1970s. And who would want to seriously
claim that the urgency of this endeavour has become obsolete in the
meantime?

Vagaries of Understanding: Thomas Mann and Oskar Kokoschka

'I never drew Thomas Mann, only attempted two illustrations for his
David legend, which I gave up on because I preferred the German of
the Lutheran Bible to his German, as I wrote him at the time when I
sent him back his manuscript' (Br IV, 222). What Kokoschka discloses
at the turn of 1969/1970 to the befriended art publisher (and cousin of
the former Reich foreign minister) Ernst Rathenau, whose house published Kokoschka's drawings in five volumes between 1935 and 1977,
surprises just as much as does the enthusiastic word by Thomas Mann
on the artist in 1933.

Kokoschka's recall is a bit errant here. On the one hand, it is not
about visual works for a 'David legend', but rather illustrations for the
first part of the tetralogy *Joseph und seine Brüder* (*Joseph and His Brothers*). And, on the other, such a letter in which Kokoschka bickers with
Mann is not recorded, not noted in the author's diary and thus was

presumably never written. What is on record, however, is a recently
discovered letter from Kokoschka to Thomas Mann, probably written
in early 1934 and on the stationery of the Grand Hotel Hungaria in
Budapest, where he stayed from 15 January to 6 May. Thomas Mann
mentions in his diary having responded to this letter on 20 January,
in a 'nervously tormented' mood, though this must have referred to
his general state of mind in this still early phase of exile.[22] Both illustrations were in reference to *Die Geschichten Jakobs* (*The Stories of
Jacob*) and episodes in it from 'Part Four: The Flight', *Jizchaks Tod*
(*Isaac's Death*) from 'Urgeblök' ('Primal Bleating'), as well as *Jaakob
und Rahel* (*Jacob and Rachel*) from 'Jaakob kommt zu Laban' ('Jacob
Joins Laban'). Illustrations and text excerpts appeared, together with
Thomas Mann's acknowledgement of Kokoschka, in an edition of the
magazine *Der Wiener Kunstwanderer* dedicated to both of them and
edited by Wolfgang Born (1893–1949).[23] The essay on Kokoschka was
in the form of a letter to Born, with whom Thomas Mann had been in
touch ever since his lithographs for *Tod in Venedig* (*Death in Venice*)
of 1921.[24]

Oskar Kokoschka and Thomas Mann – did 'Man of the Moment'
and 'Hearing Man' meet here, where misunderstandings were una-
voidable? Or are we talking about source material, which puts a
question mark over the much-clichéd opposition 'artifical' and 'not
sufficiently art-like'?[25] In his brief introduction, which he called 'pro-
grammatic', Born compares both artists, who could not have presented
a greater contrast based on their origins and development. Born notes,
however, 'that both stepped out of their accustomed *lebensraum* at
about the same time in order to go in search of new sources of experience in the Orient.' What prompted them to do that? Little in their
artistic careers to that point, but in both cases clearly an inner need for
the dissolution of boundaries, which expressed itself in more or less
extended sojourns in these regions. Born goes on:

> It may be five years since Thomas Mann travelled to Egypt and
> Syria, the settings for his novel about the biblical Joseph. At about
> the same time Kokoschka was painting his Bedouin pictures at the

edge of the Sahara and, in Palestine, the holy veduta of Jerusalem. The Goethe of the West–Eastern Divan had taught people that the Orient and Occident were no longer separable – a deeply romantic notion: exploding borders and cosmopolitan.[26]

The 19th century showed itself 'unequal to this range of vision' and the 'champions of self-sufficiency' (aka the Nationalists) defended themselves 'more fiercely than ever against the flooding of their laborious dams'. Against this, so Born suggests, art – now in the form of Kokoschka's paintings and drawings and the first part of Mann's *Joseph* tetralogy – knew how to perpetuate Goethe's legacy.

By all accounts, Born must have been the intermediary between 'painter and bard'. What exactly this interaction provoked remains in the darkness of the relationship's basis.

Under the date of 9 November 1933 Thomas Mann notes in his diary:

> [...] Letter from Born, Vienna, which thanks for the letter about Kokoschka and relates the beneficial impact on the artist. In Germany his paintings have been shown in a 'chamber of horrors'. He suffers from economic difficulties, and the loss of his manager P Cassirer has apparently rendered him quite helpless. He has repeatedly discarded the sketches for Jacob and done them anew. Insecurity has seized him. He overpaints and ruins, according to Born, superb paintings.[27]

At this point in time Thomas Mann had not yet seen the two drawings for the *Geschichten Jaakobs*. He carelessly closed his open letter about Kokoschka's art with the comment that he might find 'the idea of an illustrated complete edition acceptable' for his tetralogy. He would not have to see these latest drawings of Kokoschka's to know from whom he would 'wish more pictures for "Joseph"'.[28] Thomas Mann's disappointment was thus so much greater when he had both of Kokoschka's pieces of work in front of him. In his diary he notes: 'The booklet of the "Viennese art wanderer" with my letter and Kokoschka's drawings for Jizchaks Tod und Rahel am Brunnen arrived. The first one is odd, the second alien and inappropriate for me.'[29]

The enthusiasm for Kokoschka's art which his letter essay spoke of, where he claimed to have already recognised for 'some time' this artist as the 'epitome of modern painting', evaporated. In the oeuvre of Thomas Mann, this enthusiastic faith in a contemporary visual artist is so unusual that this letter about Kokoschka deserves closer scrutiny.

Little, in fact nothing, in Thomas Mann's work during the autumn of 1933 hints at an intense dispute with Kokoschka. And yet several of his comments about the artist's work sound well-founded and do not create the impression that this was about a marginal odd job or act of courtesy, but rather a realisation that had matured in him for 'some time'. And he immediately gives more specific information on what so binds him to Kokoschka.

> I love, understand, admire the picturesque art nowadays quite especially in him, and to being with that is *just* a matter for the eyes, a sensual liking of his colour, his form, the pleasant impression that these paintings are a *jewel of the world*, and the egotistical wish to own the one or another of them as a *jewel for one's own life*, for a daily *feast for the eyes*. (X, 914; author's emphasis)

As mentioned, this cannot be about evaluating these comments in relation to Thomas Mann's appreciation of art. At issue is only what is of use in our context: his view of Kokoschka. And this is characterised by the wish for acquisition in a symbolic and tangible sense. Alongside that the sensual experience of this art is appealing, which for its part can only be 'jewellery' – of the 'world' and his own. However, Kokoschka's painting does not represent a world of his own. It serves for the edification of the feast for the eyes.

> I love their noble colourfulness, the rich polyphony of their tints, the all-encompassing daring and breadth of their composition, the wonderful curve, which, as the painting 'Lyon' of 1927 shows it, a river, a street from impassioned proximity in the foreground and

environment to a colourfully gathering twilight in the distance. (X, 914)

He is interested in the characteristic techniques in Kokoschka's representational art, which are particularly exemplified in the portrait of Lyon, painted from a house in the Jardin des Chatreux above the Saône; the tension between near and far, typical of this genre in Kokoschka's work, is captured as much as reinforced by the shapes (here the curve) and colour gradients.

> But the sensory affirmation, the pleasure has cognitive reasons I soon found out. It is – to repeat a preferred, even beloved by the Romantics, word – sympathy, the harmony with certain cultural wishes, needs, tendencies, that I find expressed in these paintings, the agreement to a personality synthesis, that easily, naturally playfully and as if in a dream creates an accord reconciling elements, spheres and levels that are often descried as unreconcilable. Should I reduce what I mean to a snappy, almost humorous set phrase? Civilised magic – its like seems to be realised in Kokoschka's pictures. (X, 914 f)

Mann did not personally know Kokoschka and there would be no future opportunity for them to get to know each other. And yet Thomas Mann claimed nothing less than a Goethean 'elective affinity' with this younger artist, eleven years his junior. The sensory only commands value if it is based on cognitive prerequisites. Here, Thomas Mann transferred this fundamental conviction to the art experience in Kokoschka's work. And he even managed what was for him the ever-important condensing of a thought or descriptive passage to the *one* word, the *one* set phrase, in this case, the 'civilised magic'. In Mann's text, it becomes a bridgehead or crossing between Kokoschka's work and his own. As magic emanates from visual art of this kind, it can also 'decorate with pictures' a book that has dedicated itself to the 'unification of myth and psychology' – in other words, the *Joseph* project.

Here is a modern spirit and creator, who, loyal to the evolutionary stage on which life has placed him, without a trace of backwards snobbism and undignified longing for the primitive, nevertheless becomes the observer in that he sees; an insider despite and for all his undeniably lofty civilised behaviour and his late taste; a masterful dreamer, a master of exact imagination in whose entrancing work the spirit of nature and reality become transparent for the cognitive. With one word: an artist and so neither an intellectual nor a creature of dullness [...]. (X, 915)

From seeing to observing – what Thomas Mann singles out here as a particular characteristic of Kokoschka's work may actually be labelled as the artist's key concern; the same applies to the specific mixture of precision and dreamlike fantasy, one orientated on an object's metamorphosis into a 'transparent' for 'civilised behaviour' and thus the cognitive.

It is scarcely surprising how much Kokoschka must have felt boosted by *this* appraisal from such an illustrious source. The above-mentioned, originally six-page response by Kokoschka in no way matched what the artist remembered thirty-six years later. That he would think of taking issue with Mann's verbal quality is acknowledged, though not without some irony in view of the highly erratic German which Kokoschka took advantage of in this letter to the exiled German winner of the Nobel Prize for Literature. In other words, it burdened him with what was in many places such a stumbling German, in addition to omissions. The letter is cited here in full because it offers important insights into Kokoschka's thinking at the time (early 1934). One could speak of writing in broad – and at times incoherent – brushstrokes.

Grand Hotel, HUNGARIA, BUDAPEST[30]

[no date]

Dear Herr Thomas Mann,
It has been some weeks since your kind
letter about me appeared and from many

sides you will have received comments on
it and I myself, who is most affected,
cannot find the redeeming word to write
you dear master, graciousness, insight are
not apt enough, how happily turned
upside down
[p 2]
overflowing, all the more unexpectedly
was for me. That you, dear Herr Thomas
Mann, knew so much of my life, that you
could be in a position to so precisely
comment on a subject matter, which a
person, the one who is endowed with the
second sight, and no other, to really grasp,
to have the ability to see, has truly
touched the roots of my being and this
touch also made me extremely happy. I
must also be allowed to say this:
[p 3]
At no other time, insofar as it is
graspable to me, has the isolation of
people, who deal with the development,
forming of perceptions and faces, been
driven farther than in ours, and the thinner
the dividing wall was the more
unrelenting the border, drawn more
acutely against the other. Depending on
the cultural group, that the artist
transcends, he will be seen as a pariah, a
fool or a saint by the others. In your
Joseph novel that represents an enduring
human landscape, you have, dear master,
you have brought the future alive from the
material of the past and the culture no
longer circles in the present as it has about

your spontaneous opinion to my regret!
'still too fragmentary' work. Always in
the temptation to once again know my
boundaries, ever yet again throwing off
another skin, not yet naked, shame and
honesty prevent my admitting that I am
already the one who lives under my name
and daily die away under my hands, in
front of my eyes, dissolving into dusty
yesterday! And such is an echo, that
shatters me unbelievably, because I only
at the edges, border areas of human
behaviour fleeing, never confronted, only
[p 5]
their, the only in our experience possible
places, your Joseph story is already the
future, I already hear the moaning,
mankind's cries of labour, which no
longer overcome, which no longer want to
rebel against the conception, which has
conceived and must give birth. I would be
so happy if you would rightly interpret my
muddled babble
[p 6]
more simply, clearer.
I would be glad if I were allowed to draw
the contours of your face and your words,
as you suggest such in the cited letter, are
like a promise?
I beg you dear Herr Thomas Mann
to graciously accept the assurance of my
heartfelt thanks and I am with all best
wishes

Your Oskar Kokoschka

Kokoschka feels recognised and understood, and so completely that he falls into 'muddled babble' – for his standards sufficiently unusual. He sees himself as an artist working in 'loneliness', who has found his most subtle interpreter in Thomas Mann. He, however, hears humanity's 'cries of labour' in the 'Joseph story', and this coming-of-age novel based on the biblical myth must have seemed like a literary counterpart to his own ideal of humanity.

If Thomas Mann conceptualised Kokoschka as the ideal of a visual artist in his appraisal, in which 'common sense and dreams' meet and join, then Kokoschka portrays himself as totally vulnerable whilst virtually flaying himself in front of Thomas Mann: '[...] Shame and honesty prevent my admitting that I am already the one who lives under my name and daily die away under my hands, in front of my eyes, dissolving into dusty yesterday!' An admission that in Thomas Mann's eyes must have confirmed Wolfgang Born's assessment of Kokoschka's condition at the time. Because here was someone writing who was insecure in himself; one who was watching himself perish.

Oddly enough, after that Thomas Mann lost any interest in Kokoschka; the reverse is also true. And yet a diary entry of Mann's shows that they continued to be in agreement in one respect without knowing it, namely in the assessment of Dollfuß-ian Austro-fascism. Under 13 February 1934 he enters the following judgement of the situation, which was almost identical to Kokoschka's view.

> By crushing Marxism, Dollfuß wants 'to free up the army to fight National Socialism.' The civic press celebrates the victory of the state's authority that is won with all military means. It seems madness that a government opposed to Nazism annihilates its natural ally, and the attitude of the bourgeoisie is as idiotic as it was in Germany.[31]

For Kokoschka this double idiocy was the reason for leaving Austria.

Views from Prague's Windows

He only wanted to stay a couple of weeks.[32] He had Asia, Mongolia and China in mind as his next travel destinations. But his intentions became four Prague years, replete with further political activities, further growth in his artistic capital, in which political commentary and creative credo directly connected. But he also had worries about his sister who lived nearby, for his brother in the house of their deceased parents out in the sixteenth Vienna District in Liebhartstal, not to mention what he had left behind in Vienna: once again more debts and sheer despair at the situation in Austria. By contrast Prague was to bring him unexpected luck. Kokoschka in Prague; this new phase of life began with a curious incident.

> I had come to Prague in the late summer of 1934. To begin with I purchased [...] a cart-load of stinging nettles from which I had daily deliveries to my room. Stinging nettles are a known home remedy against rheumatism which I had suffered from since Paris. Early in the morning I laid them on the floor and rolled my naked body in them until I was covered in blisters. After two weeks I was immune to the irritation, the herbs no longer had any effect, yet I was cured. (ML, 238 f)

Drastic remedies were known to be Kokoschka's thing. And thus, one may believe even this episode. Did he also retell it in the upper-class house of Herr Dr Palkovsky, who knew of him through Galerie Cassirer and valued the familiar work of the – by now – almost fifty-year-old artist? The scene is reminiscent of the one in Carl Moll's house on the Hohen Warte in Vienna: the guest falls in love with the daughter of the house, only this time not with a *femme fatale* known all over town, but with the soon-to-be solicitor with an affinity for art history, Olda. She, and less so the nettles, would eventually prove to be Kokoschka's actual remedy, although the two things did not exactly have the same stormy beginning.

The distant lover in London, Anna Kallin, was apparently the first to learn of Olda, who was about to depart for London. Kokoschka now expected this of his Mirli.

> Miss Palkovská will be arriving in London for the first time and will be living near you with a friend. She is a well-behaved child, 2 m tall, 20 years old and in the event she should ask for information or for protection under your wings, do it for me, please? When she errs, then instruct her, tell her what one generally does not know about life and accept her into the order of women which should guard my last days. (Br III, 19)

Because, as the letter says, women are his 'support'. He repeats his request at the end, which becomes ever more urgent in the letters following, that Mirli should send him 'naked photographs' of herself. 'Send me naked photographs' initially remains the refrain in his letters to Anna. We have not searched for them in the estate and also do not know whether the comparatively small Anna Kallin introduced her young, inexperienced two-metre rival into the blessings of womanhood and could convey to her what it meant to be among the women who were chosen to be the 'support' of this great artist. In Kokoschka's revealing language, these women now became – in good Viennese dialect – his 'Pupperln' (dollies), for whom he was so interested in travelling to Shanghai in order 'to still see the thousand pretty young ladies on the flower boats' (Br III, 224). This attitude was not quite consistent with the noble image of women that he had designed in his political writings. Or were these 'Pupperln' to be derivations of the one, his misshapen Alma doll?

In Prague, the setting of the premiere of the Mozart opera *Don Giovanni* (1787), one might have expected Kokoschka to specifically favour this opera by his darling composer. However, he remained faithful to the *Zauberflöte* (*The Magic Flute*) and thus to the playing with transformations, the alternating between light and shadow, but also the secretive in relationships between people. At this time, he saw himself as an 'Un' – his word for a being that was neither man nor woman nor child (Br III, 26).

Prague, the city of his father, pleased him: 'In the four years between 1934 and autumn 1938, I painted sixteen landscapes, mostly in Prague and from continually different places, from where I could gain a glimpse of the Vltava; because this river, like the Thames, has enchanted me' (ML, 239). And that apparently more so than the Danube. 'I then painted one last picture of Prague from memory in London, and called it "Nostalgia"' (ibid).

In the main, Kokoschka appears to have perceived Prague as Joseph Roth depicted it in a *feuilleton* from 1932, though he initially noticed the policemen, who 'had been stuck into an English police uniform'. And further:

Yes, it is all a bit new in Prague and smells of international political varnish. It sometimes displaces the broad world-historical scent. Because the city has not yet found the right balance. It tends a bit towards the new, a bit towards the old side. It wants to be a capital city and it wants to be an old historic cultural site. It goes into tomorrow and looks at yesterday, even the day before yesterday. One can feel as it is becoming. As a result, it is delightfully interesting and always current. It is small in scale and strives into the expanse. It is a European hope. It has brought forth men who have a European perspective.[33]

There was indeed much to admire, which further inspired Kokoschka to political activism:[34] the Czechoslovak Republic, born of the Peace and initially also of the peaceful coexistence of diverse ethnic groups, in part of the Jewish faith (Czechs, Moravians, Slovaks and Germans), a republic which at first glance seemed ideally cosmopolitan. In its daring plurality some held it be the successor state to the k u k (Imperial and Royal) Monarchy. And that was primarily driven by Thomas G Masaryk, the president – an elderly, luminous figure, son of a manorial coachman but with an aristocratic bearing, highly educated, a long-serving k u k civil servant of the highest rank and something of a living legend. Masaryk, the physically suffering sage, geriatric eighty-six-year-old statesman of European stature, a monarch who had no need for a crown, was, of course, not exactly an advocate of the matriarchate for which Kokoschka longed.

Kokoschka had his studio in a tower on the banks of the Vltava. There were huge acacias along the embankment, the favourite tree of the Freemasons. Kokoschka suspected, ever leaning towards the legend of the *Zauberflöte* as a masonic opera, that his tower room was once the secret meeting place of the Prague Freemasons. He was forever searching for new viewpoints to paint, he recalls in *Mein Leben*. Every view of Prague meant being able to ignore Vienna and the conditions there.

In Vienna, where he himself, as he writes, 'almost became a politician' in light of the circumstances there, he sees in the autumn of 1934, already from the Prague perspective, predominantly 'princely gigolos, liberal canon crusaders and cardinals' whipping boys'. In addition, he sees the 'blood suckers' at work who print everything (primarily Franz Werfel, Emil Ludwig, Max Brod and Stefan Zweig), just not the manuscripts by his brother 'Bohi' and his, Oskar's, works, which they only know 'from looking away', as he quotes the words of an Austrian envoy (Br III, 7 and 17). Rather surprised, he informs his friend Ehrenstein that he has recently (in the summer of 1935) received 'an invitation with Hitlerheil from the Prussian Academy' – and that two years before he would once again find himself amongst the artists who were proscribed as 'degenerate', and whose works were supposed to be held up to ridicule at the personal behest of Hitler.

Kokoschka nevertheless unswervingly held fast to the 'International Primary School Project' based on the model of Comenius, and does so even in a letter of 11 July 1935 to his top dolly in London, Mirli, alias Anna Kallin, in which he also denounces the 'negligence of England' in the matters of 'Hitler's naval rearmament', Mussolini's Abyssinian War and the 'Habsburg Putsch'. Once again he beseeches her for the urgent forwarding of (additional) revealing photos. Yet he leaves no doubt on one thing. His 'Masaryk picture' was more important to him than anything else – his portrait of the Czechoslovakian president, once also admired by Rilke. He describes his personally historic image composition to Ehrenstein with the following words: the president's expression would be '[...] vibrant and hypnotic', 'and then there is also a pretty view toward the Hradschin and on the other side on a Torah scroll the "Orbis pictus" with two striking hands which are holding it, and in the background the burning Hus' (Br III, 22).

The light that falls on Masaryk's countenance in the portrait, which renders him almost transparent but also brings a discrete gleam to the eyes, is the light of Comenius' *via lucis* and the one that makes his Prague shimmer. It is the light of a philosopher of the Enlightenment, wise with age, in whom the history of this city and country literally find their embodiment. Soon after the completion of this multi-portrait (Masaryk, Comenius, Prague), Kokoschka must have begun the 'secret work' on his 'Komensky piece'[35] – in the bathroom by candlelight during the blackout drills in Prague, as he recalls in a letter (Br III, 76). A few weeks prior to his emigration from Prague he rationalised this work as follows: 'At some point the day will come, when my obsession, the primary school without state intervention, will be made the rallying cry for a global reconciliation' (ibid). Such a Comenius school for the nations seemed to him the prerequisite for his actual utopia, a culture in a 'world without a state', as he comments to Ehrenstein (Br III, 54). The Comenius drama and the romanticised memory of Prague, which lived with him in the form of Olda, would accompany him, now a Czech citizen courtesy of Masaryk's intervention, into his English exile.

But before this occurred in the second half of October 1938, Kokoschka reached a turning point on the Vltava, almost perfectly timed to coincide with his fiftieth birthday. He was now at the mid-point of his life. One can picture them, the scenes in this phase of Kokoschka's life, perhaps at Lány (the president's country estate) where the conversation between artist and statesman became ever more intimate, or in the studio tower where Kokoschka let his Prague shine as a city's portrait had never done before. Or the encounter with Olda, whose first acid test must have been to pose nude for him for a nymph painting. The long-since-inducted Anna Kallin received the following appraisal of his state of mind in August 1936.

Aside from that there is a well-behaved dolly here [meaning Olda], who has become a bit too set on me and made me half-insane with jealousy in the last year, in a state of suspended animation, cramp and all sorts of hysterical illnesses. If I were to go far away, so she says, she would not suffer from this, but she cannot know that I have yet other dollies that I dote on. I have to do this though, because I otherwise would not know that I am alive and become melancholic with the continual strain, building houses of cards with pictures, only to live in the past or future eternity, a dubious one, and only to work for others in the present. (Br III, 35)

Yet it is not the nude studies from this time that characterise the picture of the artist Kokoschka in the Prague years; rather, it is the scenes of Prague or views from windows that lead us to suspect that this city is most notably inhabited by colours. It is an intense colourfulness that, next to the Masaryk portrait, marks the one of Olda Palkovská which took him two years to complete (1935–1937), but also his 1937 self-portrait as a 'degenerate artist'. In the case of the latter, the noticeably light colours (Kokoschka in a light-blue jersey!) take on a resistance against the darkness of the times. Hopeful green shadings surround both portraits, while the image of Olda Palkovská incorporates Kokoschka, in typical manner, as a small (naked) faun-like figure into the background. It certainly is apparent that he shows Olda as the female equivalent to himself, so to speak; the similarity of the facial features and proportions is too obvious. It could be a sibling image.

It would be an error to see an idealisation of the times in these works, as they find contemporaneous critical expressions in his military drawings on the Spanish Civil War (*La Passionara* and *Federico García Lorca*) which he wanted to see distributed on behalf of 'the republican side'. In the case of the poet, Kokoschka labelled the drawing for the avoidance of any doubt: 'The murdered Spanish folk poet Federico García Lorca. N. P. All reproduction rights allowed for Spanish unions defending the rights of the Spanish people against the fascist powers' (Br III, 52 and 53).

Kokoschka had unequivocally taken sides. Manoeuvring in political questions remained alien to him. That showed itself with abundant clarity when he spoke as a Czechoslovakian delegate at the Brussels Peace Congress in September 1936 and in his (at the time unpublished) opinion piece on the infamy of the *Entartete Kunst* (*Degenerate Art*) exhibition in Munich in 1937, a comment on his self-portrait of that year.

The Brussels speech, with its plea for a reassessment of education ('every new society needs a new education'), became Kokoschka's cultural-political creed. The tenor of it is: 'The origins of our current crisis lead back to the time before the World War. Misdirection of the masses in the state school is to blame' (DSW IV, 175). He condemns an education system that is bound to the dogma of the state and backs delusion instead of a vision leading to an understanding of circumstances and things. World education begins, according to Kokoschka, with the rehabilitation of the five senses. Consequently, he calls for a 'reasonable education, the development of the five senses of man'; the 'lost natural talent of observation' should be given back to the individual and, with it, the 'opportunity to rationally evaluate his observations' (DSW IV, 177). He rejects the misuse of schools as a place for paramilitary training.

> The primary school as a preparation for life as an adult must nurture activity; and, based on the intentions of its creator, it may in no event be an institution where national ideology, war myth and 'heroic' self-sacrifice are taught. (DSW IV, 177)

Kokoschka clearly recognises that splitting off that which a specific civilisation considers rational from sensuality, imagination and feeling (this going back to the pre-Socratic Demokrit)[36] would lead to the ruin of man. Thus, the artist pleads for the reconciliation of the rational with the emotional culture in the name of Comenius.

One year later, in his response to the barbaric action *Entartete Kunst*, Kokoschka tellingly emphasises Hitler's speech on the opening of the 'Hauses der Deutschen Kunst' ('House of German Art') in Munich on 19 July 1937 (he only refers to him as the 'little man' named 'Schnock'), particularly that part in which this new 'Nero' accuses the artists of the modern movement of 'eye defects', even inherited 'horrible visual defects', and does so 'in front of an auditorium of invited international ceremonial guests, the tops of the authorities, the military, the crème de la crème, foreign journalists, the diplomatic corps [...]' (DSW III, 266).

Kokoschka's appraisal can be read literally.

> Our little man has not even understood what is unambiguously explained in his primary school reader: that seeing is a conscious act. If seeing were just a knee-jerk reaction of the stimulated optic nerve and nothing else, then indeed the art of painting would limit itself to the simple 'copying' of a 'template' delivered to the retina. But the crassest materialism, even the nationally dependent sciences in modern text books do not dare to claim that. (DSW III, 271)

Even if Kokoschka did not publish this 1937 composition, this same assertion became public, at least in part, through a letter of 3 August 1937 to the Austrian federal chancellor Kurt von Schuschnigg.

The reason for Kokoschka's letter was his urgent plea, though not granted, not to return his paintings that were on loan from German galleries for an exhibition on contemporary art in Vienna. For sound reasons he feared their immediate confiscation in the German Reich.

From Prague, he lectured the embattled chancellor on Vienna's Ball-hausplatz: 'seeing is an act of consciousness', which he was prevented from communicating to the 'decorator' and 'little man' from Braunau. It is noteworthy that Kokoschka even delved into this ridiculous argument of Hitler's and thus commented to Schuschnigg:

> To want to bring the inner vision of the creative artist into a causative relationship with suspected disruptions of sight capability is all the more absurd when one considers that within the logic of this theory supported by the German Reichskanzler lies, for example, allowing Beethoven to be silenced by the law enforcement agencies of his Reich's interior ministry, if he had had the bad luck to

live and work within the authority of this Chancellor as Beethoven
was known to have suffered from an organic hearing problem and
also engendered the heftiest opposition from some of his influential
contemporaries with his musical compositions. (DSW III, 50)

In February 1938, the most significant contemporary artist, at least of
Austria, was no longer focused on lecturing Schuschnigg. Now he was
indicting him and, as a Czech citizen in Prague exile, in the form of
the aforementioned *Application to the Hague Court of Arbitration* for
a 'Determination on the State of Lawlessness in Austria' (DSW IV,
201–205). In it he queried the legitimacy of Schuschnigg's negotiations with Hitler and attempted to put a stop to these dangerous activities through the international legal process, given that the Guarantor
Powers of the Versailles and Saint-Germain treaties were not willing to
do so. The process was without precedent and it is hard to know what
to be more amazed at: the naiveté of the artist or his obvious unwavering belief in the power of the law.

After the 'Anschluss' (Annexation) was implemented, the situation
in Czechoslovakia escalated with ominous rapidity. 'The cosmopolitan society in Prague suddenly dissolved into nothing. Everyone had
a plan, not I', Kokoschka recalled (ML, 248). Prague's windows began
to close. France was not an option for him; he distrusted the country.
Switzerland seemed equally threatening to him. Everything pointed
to London. The departure into the second emigration succeeded,
largely due to Olda's legal knowledge and her decisiveness, despite the
'unbelievable difficulties on the part of the bureaucracy, which made
any form of freedom of movement seem impossible'. Both took along
the colours of the golden city and memories of the Vltava with them
into English exile. There they once again found entry in a picture of
this ancient European city, a Prague nostalgia, a symphony in colours.
In the foreground sits a barely recognisable couple, a hinted-at swan
nearby as if it were preparing itself to take the couple into the distance,
away over the city ablaze in colour, the Charles Bridge and the Hradschin – right into the middle of the unknown.

Interim Status

Kokoschka does not make it easy for us to consider him in the context of his times. The new Seeing, with which the new objectivity identified itself as a project, comes closest to his efforts, although he was far off from the constructivist principles of this art direction. The montage, increasingly popular in the 1920s, remained alien to him. The pure object, the representation of the thing as a thing, appeared in Kokoschka's (early) still lifes at best, though it had already disappeared from his work in his Dresden period. Only the doll offers a unique reference point here. The objectification of a (once beloved) individual is achieved in it, though not the unemotional handling of it. It remained emotionally occupied.

The 'nouvelle objectivité', which Félix Bertaux discovered in the contemporary art of the Germany of the 1920s, also barely applies to Kokoschka's work. Rather, one gets the impression as if Kokoschka enabled the colour to find its shape, usually at the edge of its dissolving.

As decisively as Kokoschka condemned the abstract, he would have had difficulty signing off on Raoul Hausmann's appeal *Rückkehr zur Gegenständlichkeit (Return to Representativeness)* published in the *Dada Almanach* of 1920. There were sentences in it such as: 'Art is a matter for the nation [...] In the end a race forms a tendency to practicality in eating [...] the German, next to soups and sandwiches and his beer, has only accomplished a nauseating darkening of things, called Expressionism [...] The first Expressionist, a person who invented the "inner freedom", was a gluttonous and drunken Saxon, Martin Luther.'[37] Kokoschka was not interested in Hausmann's dumpling aesthetic. Verism, new naturalism: catchwords of this type were meaningless to him. Cityscapes, landscapes and portraits were Kokoschka's arenas for expressing himself – and those with an unimagined breadth of variation and depth of expression.

Precisely for this reason it will be important to take a closer look at his principle of the portrait, because it is in this genre that his renunciation of the new objectivity, for example, the portrait art of

Max Beckmann, Christian Schad, Otto Dix and Rudolf Schlichter or Georg Schrimpf, becomes particularly apparent.

Kokoschka was not interested in 'photographic faces', to use a term of Siegfried Kracauer's.[38] For Kokoschka, physiognomy pertained not just to the surface of a facial expression but also traces of the emotional – as the late Gottfried Benn said, the 'sketched self'.

5

Exile in England

London Calling

The ground in England – at least in London – seemed fertile for the art banned in Hitler's Germany. The art critic Herbert Read, but also the director of the National Gallery Kenneth Clark and John Rothenstein, who led the Tate Gallery, were largely responsible for this. Kokoschka contacted them shortly after his and Olda's arrival in London on 19 October 1938. Thanks to his Czech citizenship, he could handle even the most difficult hurdle more easily than his fellow German-speaking migrants: passport control, which he had feared (Br III, 82). Even a three-month residence permit was granted to him immediately. The memory of that exhibition in the Leicester Gallery in July 1928, when Kokoschka did not sell a single one of the thirty-six oil paintings on display, had been forgotten in the meantime.

After that, interest in the German avant-garde of the visual arts was catered for primarily by the *Twentieth Century German Art* exhibition, which opened in the New Burlington Galleries exactly three months before Kokoschka's arrival in London with a lecture by another prominent victim of Nazi barbarising of the art scene and London immigrant, Max Beckmann. The lecture was entitled *Über meine Malerei* (*About My Painting*) and had the character of a manifesto.[1] Perhaps in order not to upset his English hosts, Beckmann quickly emphasised (in the second sentence) that he had never 'engaged politically in any form' – a somewhat bizarre statement given that the best part of his art consisted of severe social, and at least by obvious implication political, criticism. He underlined the necessity for an artist to penetrate the visible in order to bring the invisible into the light of day. Beckmann named shaping space through painting as his primary objective. He spoke of the 'translation of an object into the abstract of the surface through the means of painting'. He answered the question repeatedly arising, as it did for Kokoschka, of the problem of abstraction as follows: 'I therefore hardly need non-representational things, as I find the given object already sufficiently unreal and I can only make it representational by means of painting.' Furthermore, he sees the carving out of the 'self' as a critical challenge: 'Becoming a "self" is always the urge of all bodiless souls. I search for this "self" in life – and in my painting.' He must search for wisdom, according to Beckmann, with his eyes: 'I particularly emphasise eyes, as nothing would be sillier and more irrelevant as a cerebrally painted world view without the terrible furore of the sense for every form of beauty and ugliness of the visible.' This work of the eyes was related to that of Kokoschka's Comenius-inspired creed of seeing, coupled with a veritable 'belief in the thing' in Beckmann.

Kokoschka, who had little time for such a 'belief in the thing', was after all represented at this exhibition with nineteen pieces, among them seven oil paintings and the *Selbstbildnis als 'entarteter' Künstler* (*Self-portrait as 'Degenerate' Artist*). Despite his good contacts ('From above this is all going swimmingly', Br III, 83), Kokoschka soon sensed that he was 'simply tolerated' in England. He mistrusted the 'Chamberitlers', his term in a letter to friend Ehrenstein for the Appeasers (Br III, 86) who enabled Hitler in his defiance of international law and inhuman conduct. He accurately recognised what both ideological systems stood for: the 'horrific attempt to propagate a new species of homo Anthropos: the totally servile domesticated citizens of Europe' (Br III, 85).

Though Kokoschka could not expect to immediately paint Britain's head of state, as in Czechoslovakia (King George VI's artistic sense was only modestly developed), in July 1939 he could nevertheless imagine painting the first Viscount Norwich, Alfred Duff Cooper, who impressed him less as a salon prowler and member of the literati than as an upstanding opponent of Chamberlain's appeasement policy. Cooper had resigned his post as First Lord of the Admiralty in protest against the Munich Agreement. Kokoschka wanted to persuade even him of his 'school reform plans' as an alternative to war. In general, in England, Kokoschka was once again reminded of Comenius, whose own exile had led him to England for a short time and is even said to have wanted to interest Parliament in his pedagogical-pansophist reform ideas in the name of humanism. That was in 1641. The escalating conflict between Crown and Parliament, as well as the emergence of Cromwell, were blamed for the parliamentarians' loss of interest in Comenius, his humanistic reform programme and the Bohemian–Moravian Resistance against the Habsburgs. Comenius had to leave England only one year later. Even though Kokoschka could not gain access to British government circles, this fate – to again be driven away – was spared him at least. He could remain, and that even after the British declaration of war against Hitler's Reich, without being sent to an internment camp for *enemy aliens*. As difficult as his beginnings in London were, from a boarding house to an initially quite modest rented flat, he and Olda led a relatively privileged existence. And, unlike the numerous writers in English exile, he did not suffer from a language barrier as his medium for expression, like that of music, was not dependent on a *particular* language.

In general, Oskar and Olda: what a pair! They were conspicuous on the London scene. Edith Hoffmann-Yapou, the art historian originally from Vienna who had already emigrated to England in 1934 and was the first biographer of Kokoschka, described the two from personal experience as a couple that did everything together.

> Kokoschka pretended to be a helpless foreigner who did not allow her a moment to leave him on his own. He, the large, broad shouldered painter in his tweed suit with lightly greying, absurdly short haircut, somehow ageless with apelike facial features; and she, the even larger young woman who appeared Pallas [Athena]-like in bespoke tailored outfits and conducted herself towards him with the friendly serenity of a sensitive mother; they both soon became a regular feature in this new circle that rapidly formed around Kokoschka.[2]

Olda literally developed into Kokoschka's other half, who completed his sentences in conversations (he preferred the suggestiveness of half-sentences!) and became his second memory, whereby she even remembered things in Kokoschka's life that had happened before she was born. She connected, arranged, took care of the important things in life, protected him from undesirable visitors and intrusive questioners. She seems to have put her own interests into the background, even if her strength of character repeatedly proved itself. Politically, she leaned to the left, while driven by an almost natural cosmopolitanism just like Kokoschka. This expressed itself in her multilingualism (in London she even took Chinese lessons), though she never lost her relatively hard Slavic accent. She corrected Kokoschka's English in his uncompromising political essays, but (as far as we know) held no conversations with gallerists or potential portrait clients. That remained Kokoschka's domain.

Despite the New Burlington Galleries and the strenuous efforts of gallerists and critics, Kokoschka of course found a predominantly traditionalist-oriented art scene in London. Prior to the First World War Roger Fry had championed the European modernists from Van Gogh all the way to the Cubists, and from Cézanne to the Fauvists. Wyndham Lewis and Ezra Pound promoted Vorticism in 1913, which had energy and expression as its subjects. Yet in portraiture the legacy of Singer Sargent and Augustus John continued to set the standard.

Other forms of Expressionism were awakening as Kokoschka returned for his longest sojourn on English soil, for example, in the young Henry Moore, in Barbara Hepworth, Ben Nicolson and Graham Sutherland. Nevertheless, in his eighth year in England Kokoschka soberingly summarised in a letter to Arnold Schönberg: Art has 'absolutely no soil and roots' in England (Br III, 175).

In the autumn of 1938, the signs for Kokoschka seemed 'hopeful' against all expectations, yet the reality of daily life in London looked quite different initially. Depressingly shabby lodgings (among them was a boarding house in Belsize Avenue, followed by a somewhat better flat at 45a King Henry's Road in Hampstead, which a small loan enabled him to let) and often insufficient funds for the basics, which included oil paints, left him melancholic at times. Olda found the living situation so depressing that they felt compelled to escape to Cornwall, at the beginning of August 1939. Meagre accommodation was found in Polperro. 'Because of the tall child who was not accustomed to such miserable living conditions, I had to return to nature a bit in hopes for a little sunshine' (Br III, 93), even if it rained incessantly for the present.

Yet Kokoschka would not have been Kokoschka if, despite these hardships in his and Olda's first nine months in London exile, he had not got involved in various activities. In November 1938 he created his painting of Prague *Nostalgia* from memory, and participated in the founding of the Freien Deutschen Kulturbund (Free German League of Culture) which was inaugurated with John Heartfield (one of the co-founders of the Oskar-Kokoschka-Bund in Prague) on 1 March 1939. The literary critic Alfred Kerr and Stefan Zweig were other prominent members.[3] As early as 20 June the Bund laid on an exhibition to which Kokoschka was able to contribute his paintings *Prague-Nostalgia, Sommer (Summer)*, the portrait of Michael Croft and the *Selbstbildnis als 'entarteter' Künstler*. The commission to paint Michael Croft, the son of Henry Page Croft who became Under-Secretary of State for War in Churchill's first Cabinet in 1940 and was elevated to the first Baron Croft, was procured for him by Fred Uhlman (1901–1985), the jurist, writer and painter originally from Stuttgart.[4] In 1936, Uhlman – after years of exile in Paris and on the Costa Brava – married Diana Croft, Michael's sister; he was one of the few examples of Jewish-German emigrants marrying into the upper echelons of English society. However, Uhlman's father-in-law, Henry Page Croft, considered this marriage of his daughter to a Jewish emigrant, and an artist of all things, to be social suicide.[5] Uhlman said of this in his memoirs: 'I was *déclassé*, uprooted, and in almost every respect the last kind of person he cared to know. His roots were deep down in the English soil; he belonged to a society and a class which looked at everybody not British with suspicion.'[6] In the late spring of 1939 Kokoschka was then also able to paint the portrait of Ulman's sister-in-law, Posy Croft – these were the last portrait commissions to reach Kokoschka until he painted the Soviet ambassador to London, Ivan Maisky, in 1942/1943.[7] The Croft commissions enabled Kokoschka, via friends who had emigrated to Switzerland, to send financial support to his brother Bohuslav who had remained in Vienna and suffered from the repressive measures there. Uhlman was interned in the notorious Hutchinson Camp on the Isle of Man for six months from June 1940, where he met Kurt Schwitters, after which he founded the Freien Deutschen Kulturbund. However, he later distanced himself from its communist infiltration and thus also from Kokoschka, whose radical tilt to the left irritated him. Uhlman remembers Kokoschka as follows.

> I admire Kokoschka the painter. He was fascinating to talk to, a wonderful actor, charming as only a Viennese can be. He was always in need of an audience, admiration and complete submission. He hated Picasso. One day he showed me one of his early paintings and asked: 'Don't you see?' I couldn't see anything. 'Don't you see?' repeated Kokoschka. 'He has got everything from me (*er hat alles von mir*), everything.'[8]

By contrast, Uhlman is not mentioned once in Kokoschka's *Mein Leben*. Uhlman's break with him must have been painful for Kokoschka, as he believed he had a certain affinity, even a budding friendship, with the educated young artist from Swabia. For Kokoschka, such behaviour – from Uhlman's perspective of course only too understandable – bordered on betrayal.[9]

Kokoschka's *Michael Croft* portrait continued a style direction that he had previously tried out in multiple forms. The portrait's subject is not the only part of the painting's statement; the surrounding context also shapes the painting's message – in this case the painting of the subject's father, Henry Page Croft, in the background, as well as the dog of the house which is meant to be somewhat reminiscent of the English lion. The intensity of the suit's cobalt blue is particularly noticeable, as are the emphatic brushstrokes which stand in contrast to the rather soft facial features of the sitter. The portrait of the sister

Posy is different, but complementary; no melancholy overshadows her. The light blue of her deeply cut dress and the lightness of her face's colour suggest openness. Michael's expression appears veiled, almost insecure – he'd even removed his spectacles. In contrast, Posy requires no spectacles. Her expression is free and undisguised; both of them are again masterpieces of characterising (not psychologising) portrait art.

Incidentally, the aged and ill Sigmund Freud did not live far from King Henry's Road, in Maresfield Gardens, Frognal. But for Koko-schka no path led to Freud, who had become president of the newly founded 'Austrian Centre – Associations of Austria'. While Kokoschka appeared there occasionally, he felt closer to the Freie Deutschen Kul-turbund; he was supposed to succeed Alfred Kerr as president in the summer of 1941. However, Kokoschka and Kerr – can one imagine the two in the same room of the involuntary survival society named Exile? Nothing had been more alien to Kerr as a critic than the style of Expres-sionistic theatre of Kokoschka's early career. How did Kokoschka see him now; how would he have painted him if Kerr had allowed him to do his portrait? As a brother of Karl Kraus in exile?

Undoubtedly Kokoschka pursued a public presence, belonged to high-ranking 'artists' committees', and did not shy away from (semi-) official interventions, particularly in matters pertaining to the intern-ment of German-speaking artists after the outbreak of the Second World War, which we will return to later.

Among many similar requests was one from the 'Chelsea Commit-tee for Spanish Relief', of 29 October 1939. They wished to mount an exhibition of British and continental European art in the former home of James Abbott McNeill Whistler in Chelsea, where works by German, Austrian, Czech, Spanish and Polish artists would be put up for sale. Kokoschka was meant to lead the organising committee.[10] He also acted as the most prominent adviser to the 'Artists' International Association', for whose great exhibition *For Liberty* he created a paint-ing: *What We Are Fighting For*.[11]

He was increasingly haunted by the problem of internment and the manner in which the British authorities handled it in the early phases. This chapter in British domestic policy,[12] which is known to have been modelled on similar practices in the First World War,[13] apparently threatened to have consequences for Kokoschka also. It appears he drafted a declaration (which is no longer available) on this topic around 1940/1941 that he provided to his acquaintance the author John Rayner Heppenstall (1911–1981) for critical review. Heppenstall's reaction is available and shows that he emphatically advised Kokoschka against publication. He held the text to be 'entirely misconceived' and feared that this declaration would damage Kokoschka in the short and long term. Apparently, Kokoschka had claimed that refugees in England had fewer rights than 'dogs and cats'.

That Kokoschka turned to Heppenstall is revealing on two counts. First, it shows how well connected he was only two years after his flight to England. Second, Kokoschka immediately orientated himself, even in English exile, towards literary Modernism as, after the publication of his first novel *The Blaze of Noon* (1939), Heppenstall (a friend of George Orwell and Dylan Thomas) was counted among the 'Modernists' of contemporary British authors and was paving the way for the 'Anti-Novel', later represented by writers such as Anthony Burgess, Angela Carter, B S Johnson and Eva Figes.

Kokoschka's draft of a protest declaration about the treatment of internees may have also coincided with his interceding with the authorities regarding the release of the Jewish fellow exile and artist colleague Ludwig Meidner, a matter which Kokoschka apparently pursued intensively. Meidner was interned as an enemy alien on the Isle of Man. On 6 January 1941, Kokoschka received the following notification from the relevant authorities in the British Home Office: 'With reference to your letter of the 11th October [1940] regarding the internment of Mr Ludwig Meidner I am directed by the Secretary of State to inform you that instructions have now been given for Mr Meidner's release.'[14] To date, no further indications of connections between Kokoschka and Meidner in exile in England have been found, other than that both were interested in the poetic and visual work by William Blake. It is also unclear whether Meidner was ever made aware of the fact that he had Kokoschka to thank for his early release from the internment camp. There are, however, later signs of

Meidner's true veneration of Kokoschka, for example, in his birthday greetings of 3 February 1961: 'Esteemed *Master*: I finally have been able to obtain your address – so I can take great joy [...] and wish you in English: Many happy returns! – *your grateful humble* painter Ludwig Meidner.'[15] The 'painter' congratulates the 'Master' – that is also the perspective from which Meidner writes to their mutual friend, Ernest Rathenau, on 27 May 1965, about Kokoschka's graphic work.

> I was always an admirer of the 'K'-ish drawing skill and I am no less so today, it provides us so much beauty and truth, like no work of the present and the last hundred years, perhaps excepting Menzel, who remains in the background for the time being but will soon step back into the foreground. 'K', by contrast, is a radical innovator, who does not in the least eschew tradition a[nd] that, too, is the great thing about him. Should you personally meet the Master some time, would you please report to him of my greatest, undiminished admiration.[16]

Rathenau had immediately redirected this letter of Meidner's to Villeneuve, where upon Kokoschka shared his astonishment with him: 'Meidner's letter was touching, I had no idea he thought so highly of me' (Br IV, 170).

No, in reality it did not exist, the secret society of exiles. Despite shared survival problems, distances were frequently maintained even when their (artistic) interests would have suggested a beneficial exchange. The English expression *too close for comfort* is quite apt, at least with respect to Kokoschka's behaviour. Were there alternatives to London? What about other parts of Britain?

Escapes to Cornwall and Scotland, or Solace of the Countryside

Consider Polperro, for example, on the south coast of Cornwall. Smugglers and (crab) fishermen were at home in this tranquil place. It is picturesque how the little houses densely cover the hillside and cluster around the harbour, which stands dry during the ebb tide and only offers the boats silt because the water level drops by three-and-a-half metres. It is difficult to imagine a starker contrast to London for Kokoschka and Olda. They arrived here at the beginning of August 1939 and initially stayed at Harbour View; later they moved up the hill into Cliff End Cottage with a view of the sea, which Kokoschka had hoped to cross to the USA. But the American Consul in London had not approved his visa, despite the fact that the Dean of the University of Chicago had endorsed it by telephone.

So then, off to Polperro. Here lived Uli Nimptsch (1897–1977), the sculptor originally from Berlin who had one thing in common with Kokoschka: the representation of the human body, or, expressed more accurately, the human through the representation of its body. They became friends, and helped each other precisely because Nimptsch was not a painter and Kokoschka not a sculptor.

In addition to a first oil painting of the village, the six-part water-colour series *Polperro*, which feels like a dive into the landscape, issued from Kokoschka's hand in rapid succession. The colours of the sea and coastal landscape melt into each other, while gull, eel and cat in addition to occasional people represent the living beings in a scenery, in which the landscape has the starring role.

Nevertheless, Kokoschka and Olda's thoughts repeatedly wandered back to their relatives, to Prague, now the capital city of the Protectorate of Bohemia and Moravia, to Vienna-Liebhartstal, where Kokoschka feared a 'strange Nazi made himself comfortable' (Br III, 96) and may have dumped the parental home and its contents. He discovered that the Kunstmuseum Basel had acquired his *Windsbraut* in Berlin. And in Lucerne, in the Grand Hotel National, the art dealer Theodor Fischer auctioned over a hundred 'degenerate' artworks confiscated from German museums, among them nine paintings by Kokoschka; apparently the Reich was trying to raise foreign currency in this manner.

In Polperro, seemingly far from the war, Kokoschka was also troubled by political thoughts.

I am cut off from everything due to the war situation, from my family about which I am very, very anxious, from my friends, from every sphere of activity and of course serious pecuniary concerns are my guests again, as usual!! It is very depressing to be entombed alive so to speak and it would do me good if a voice that gives me courage were to get through to me on occasion. All the people one meets here show such a self-evident indifference that can only be excused through their total lack of awareness of continental fates.[17]

In addition, Kokoschka finds: '[...] everywhere is equally unsafe, unpleasant and equally inviting of suicide' (Br III, 94). He also played with suicidal thoughts for another reason at this time. Through the grapevine, he had heard that his brother Bohuslav, for whom he continued to feel responsible, was being evicted from the parental home in Vienna-Liebhartstal due to reprisals by the Nazis and forced to work 'on the land as a farmhand'. Kokoschka admitted to Joseph Paul Hodin, the Czech art historian, who had also emigrated to England and was to write major studies on Ben Nicolson, Barbara Hepworth and, in 1966, on Kokoschka himself: 'For me that is almost a motive for suicide [...]'[18] He remained bitter about British policy in the first weeks of the war, as can be seen from a letter written in Polperro to Anna Kallin.

Nazi-Germany already belongs to history, what remains is this militarised and armed heap of tramps who await their fodder from Moscow. All of this has been brought on by the city folks and reactionary lords, only we believe that it is about war or peace or fatherland and duty and right. As such it is in truth the undisguised intellectual poverty of the so-called democrats who nurtured reactionary forces for years to start up the war industry because one feared the unemployed, a question that will be disastrous until this entire war scam is truly at an end as a result of the general European bankruptcy. *Leave the nursery and come here to us.* I cannot go to London, would not know what to live on from there as all my collectors are dead or broke and America hopelessly distant. [...] I will yet have to thank the English for their wise policy. And you will scold why I would not rather leave this land where I do not fulfil my duties as guest? (Br III, 95 f; author's emphasis)

A *ménage à trois* in Polperro to defy the world's state of affairs? One suspects that Olda would not have been happy about this, she who courageously and unflinchingly earned an extra income for them by producing baked goods from her Czech homeland in her tiny kitchen and selling them. Later (presumably 1941) the artist and pedagogue Hilde Goldschmidt (1897–1980), who had been Kokoschka's student in Dresden in 1920, came to Polperro to visit, which to all appearances did not seem to cause any complications. She lived with her mother in Kitzbühel before she was forced to leave the Austrian 'Ostmark' for England in early 1939. After 1954 she would teach at Kokoschka's Summer School for Seeing in Salzburg.[19] Kokoschka's later confidant and biographer, J P Hodin, dedicated a monograph study to Goldschmidt's work.[20]

The early period in Polperro generated, already in the second painting, a political allegory – or should one perhaps say a landscape painting, which turned into an allegory under Kokoschka's hand? This reference is to *Die Krabbe* (*The Crab*), a motif that outgrew itself into an oversized creature. This crab guards Cornwall's beach; it turns away foreigners like the swimmer who has escaped from the sinking ship in the background in search of rescue. No invader or mere asylum seeker would be a match for this crab and its defensive weapons. Kokoschka had named this crab 'Chamberlain after Munich', thus referencing the appeasement policy which first and foremost focused on saving Britain while letting Austria and Czechoslovakia sink, as well as showing arrivals from these lands blatant contempt.[21]

One may deem this allegory unfair in light of the relatively liberal immigration policy Britain practised between 1905 and 1938, as the number of refugees grew six-fold to 70,000 within a few months and the ability to provide care for the immigrants became a real problem. It was at this time that Anthony Eden made his infamous statement: 'The boat is full.'[22] Kokoschka himself, as mentioned, did not need to fear legal difficulties on the basis of his Czech passport. Most importantly, he was spared internment in 1940, though his friend Uli Nimptsch was not. However, Kokoschka was able to obtain the endorsement of the Countess of Drogheda for the artist and thus his early release. Towards the end of the war, Kokoschka created a portrait of the Countess that would be one of his most impressive from this period.

Die Krabbe also evidenced that even the innocent landscape, a sandy bay in Cornwall, was no longer free from politics, even if it offered more consolation than the city. And that is exactly where he and Olda had to return when even Cornwall was declared a military exclusion zone for 'aliens'. Yet before that he reminded himself of the twelfth edition (1939) of Sheldon Warren Cheney's influential (in the USA) study *Primer of Modern Art*, which waxed lyrical about Kokoschka. Had he possibly spotted a copy in remote Polperro, perhaps among Uli Nimptsch's books? Again, here was a glimmer of hope, even if the reproductions of his pictures bothered him. He complained that the book brought 'only the old, hundred-fold used few photos that were already well known' (Br III, 99). He had made a similar criticism some time earlier about black-and-white reproductions of colour paintings, which were the order of the day for stingy publishers.

London – that meant accommodation at the Strand Palace Hotel initially, which sounds luxurious but in fact was not. It ate up their remaining reserves, and it was Kathleen, Countess of Drogheda who took pity on them and arranged a furnished house for them at 17 Boundary Road in St John's Wood, which they moved into on 18 July 1940. As a first act, Kokoschka painted a bouquet of flowers – unusually light, jolly and summery. On 7 September the Blitz on London began, which lasted until May 1941. Olda's parents, who periodically lived with the as-yet-unwed pair, found St John's Wood too precarious. Kokoschka himself seemed absolutely fearless. Cellar or air raid shelter, for example, in the deep-lying Tube stations and tunnels (one need only think of Henry Moore's charcoal drawings) – Kokoschka never sought them out, even later during the V-1 and V-2 attacks on London in 1944. He justified this with the rationale that he would likely develop pulmonary illness as a result of his bayonet wound from the First World War – a reasonable assumption supported by the countless other examples.

In the autumn of 1940, he wrote to Hilde Goldschmidt – who had found employment in a shoe factory – a letter which presumably quite accurately reflects his inner disposition through a mixture of irony, bitter earnestness and calculated optimism.

Dear Hilde,
Since you have made it so easy with the letter writing, I must do it [...]. I wish you in the coming year a prospering shoe production process, is in any event more sensible than making munitions, people will always need shoes. From time to time, reach for a brush and paints – and for me. All my love

Your OK

NB In a bad mood, no money. Yesterday I gave a lecture at the free culture league in English and sold a water colour for 25 pounds, gifted it to the 'Interned' for whose benefit the Christmas event is.
    No longer have a telephone, the bill is still unpaid, hence blocked, but am still in Boundary Rd (the rates are paid there for 3 weeks). Bitch of a life! But it doesn't matter, have experienced worse in 30 years of fame [...] There was always more coverage (including material) on my paintings than on any and all state papers, industrial share certificates, but the people are muggins even in an economic sense. Peace on their remains. I will rise again – Amen

OK

A short time later, Anna Kallin heard similar, though to a degree more pointed, thoughts.

All my loved ones are in part in migration, in part in occupied countries, I am spinning in my head in all wind directions and find myself – dreadfully alone [...] My palette is hanging on a nail, never before,

not even during the earlier World War have I been so – not at all –
needed. No one needs culture, no one knows what that is, no one
believes that you can make money with it. I also do not wish to go
to America, because the same story will come there tomorrow, the
day after, but it will come [...] and that is why I am not sending you
seasons' greetings, but only my inherent love and tenderness as ever

Your Un

And yet his belief in the Comenius education project remained awake
in him – in Polperro he had managed to complete a first draft of his
piece about his Moravian idol. And his by now broadly uncompromisingly politically motivated art began to find downright spectacular
expression in those weeks (end of 1940), namely in his painting *Das
rote Ei* (*The Red Egg*). It again deals with a political allegory; its resolution, however – unlike that in *Die Krabbe* – is delivered unambiguously. With this painting, Kokoschka pillories the Munich Agreement
post festum in that he captures a step that in his view enabled Hitler to
unleash the Second World War. Kokoschka quite obviously regarded
the Agreement as a total failure of the Western powers and the sacrifice of Czech interests. What he depicts is the consuming of Czechoslovakia by the signatories of the Agreement; the Czech 'roast chicken'
flies away in this allegory with no chance of survival (the silhouette
of Prague burns in the background). It leaves behind a red egg laid
in haste, a symbol of death on which the liquidators of Czechoslovakia will feast. The trenchancy of this representation is reminiscent of
Heartfield and Grosz, while the famous caricaturist of the late-18th-
century James Gillray may have stood as godfather[23] and probably also
Pieter Brueghel, as already suggested by Edith Hoffmann-Yapou.[24]

Before Kokoschka's next departure into the countryside, this time
to Scotland (1942), he created the painting *Anschluß – Alice in Wonderland* (*Annexation – Alice in Wonderland*). The horror has seized
the cityscape. Alice, naked except for a fig leaf and a little Red Cross
bandage, appears unusually disengaged; she points to the barbed-
wire fence encircling her. Behind her stands a baroque altar with a

war-damaged Madonna; a small child in the foreground wears a gas mask, while in the background London, with the Stock Exchange visible, burns. The middle ground is dominated by three air raid wardens, strangely wearing English, German and French steel helmets, in the style of the three Confucian monkeys – a clerical one covering his ears, a Wehrmacht soldier who points to the naked Alice and covers his mouth, and an Englishman in a suit and flat steel helmet who covers his eyes – loosely based on the Japanese saying 'mizaru, kikazaru, iwazaru'. Or as the *analects* of Confucius say: 'What is not consistent with the law of beauty [= appropriate behaviour], do not *look* upon it; what is not consistent with the law of beauty, do not *listen* to it; what is not consistent with the law of beauty, do not *speak* of it; what is not consistent with the law of beauty, do not *do* it.'[25] In front of the Englishman is a sheet of paper labelled 'Our Times/1934' which suggests that the artist continued to tie the tragedy of Austria to the Ständestaat under Dollfuß. It is a political allegory, similar to the earlier painting *Loreley* (1941/1942) which pillories naval power as much as British imperialism; it shows an emphatically ugly-looking Queen Victoria as Loreley sitting at the side, holding Ireland in the form of a green frog in her hand whilst the river (or more appropriately ocean) waves under a sky seared by lightning bolts swallow ships and crews. An octopus holds Neptune's trident like a beacon of destruction or power having become weakened in the face of nature's forces.

What Kokoschka created here are disturbing political fantasies. However, Kokoschka had started work on *Loreley* in Scotland in the autumn of 1941 as a landscape painting and then rededicated its theme back in London.

These fantasies were thanks to Kokoschka's predicament in his London flat. Edith Hoffmann-Yapou provides the following comment by the artist: 'What else can I do in this hole? I have to invent my motifs. But I hunger to *see* something again.'[26] And this renewed and liberating seeing, after the oppressive and stifling life in London, was offered to him by Scotland as it had been in the summer of 1929.

Before he travelled to Elrig near Port William in the early autumn of 1941, at the invitation of his long-time friend Czech economist Emil

Korner, Kokoschka availed himself for the first and last time of a Tube station repurposed into an air raid shelter. The occasion was appropriate. It was 15 May 1941 when he and Olda Palkovská exchanged their 'I do's' at the Hampstead registry office, which was housed in this underground shelter. As such one could refer to their stay in Scotland as their honeymoon trip, even if Port William, in contrast to Polperro, was anything but charming or even romantic. As dreary as the village and harbour seemed, Kokoschka discovered a natural alternative world to a self-destructive civilisation. Between 1941 and 1946 the Kokoschkas would travel to Scotland six times in total, later going even farther north to Ullapool; they were particularly taken by the northwest coast of Scotland. In and around Elrig in the autumn of 1941 Kokoschka immediately began with watercolours which are reminiscent of the flower studies he had worked on previously. In addition, there were other motifs: 'wild flowers, fruits, vegetables, fish, seafood and game.'27

Political Worries of an Exiled Artist-Activist

What brought him back from there to London was primarily the celebration of the 300th anniversary of Comenius' stay in England, which was to take place in Cambridge. His contribution was the essay *Comenius, the English Revolution and our Present Plight*. Within this, Kokoschka left no doubt as to the importance of 1641 for the year 1941. The core statement of his contemplations ran:

> The determination of the democratic people to not allow this crusade against fascism to pale into victory parades, but to see it replaced by a long-lasting peace can perhaps be promoted best by concentrating on how the individual can be freed from his embeddedness in an education for national purposes. (DSW IV, 237)

This plea for a consistent peace education in the midst of war must have brought Kokoschka at least polite applause at the event in Cambridge. Yet he would not allow himself to be deterred from his conviction that the war against fascism and National Socialism was only worthwhile and could only be won in the long term if the implementation of an international education programme for a peaceful coexistence became the guiding principle for conflict resolution. The publicist–essayist endeavours and lively lecturing he pursued in the years 1942 and 1943 were consistent with just this desire. Let us bring to mind his themes: *Children's Art Exhibition, Die Wahrheit is unteilbar (Truth is Indivisible), Was erwarten wir vom Theater? (What Do We Expect of the Theatre?), Opening of the Institute for Science and Learning of the Free German League of Culture, Exhibition of the Anti-Nazi Committee, Fast Vergessen (Almost Forgotten*, about contemporary Austria), *Comenius, the English Revolution and our Present Plight, Ansprache zur 25. Jahresfeier der Sowjet-Union (Address on the 25th Anniversary Celebration of the Soviet Union)* as well as the address *The War as Seen by Children*, written in 1942 and given in early 1943. He clearly recognised the relationship between peace education and art pedagogy founded in an internationalist awareness that would be decisive for both areas.

The Maisky Episode

The childlike perspective – how a child sees – was important to Kokoschka. Of course, he always wrote and spoke as an artist. He surprisingly defined the artist as follows.

> An artist differentiates himself from the average politician in that he is not a romantic, that he sees the world as it naturally always renews itself whilst the politician often does not understand what he sees and flees into irrational thinking, grasping for ideologies in order to explain the flight of appearances. (DSW IV, 242)

With these words, on 25 October 1942, he began his *Ansprache zur 25. Jahresfeier der Sowjet-Union* as president of the Freien Deutschen Kulturbund in London's Conway Hall, which was met by this organisation rather ambivalently. He further explained in this speech:

Because, if human common sense were not able to repeatedly, in the critical last moment, save the individual from his estrangement from the surrounding world, which generates the cramp, panic, hate, because man is able to overcome the dividing shallowness from the I to the We, and in this act of common sense repeats the act of human birth, mankind would have long since rotted away in superstition. (DSW IV, 244)

Was Kokoschka inclined, therefore, to surround his portraits of individuals with references to other and therefore social and natural contexts? This was no plea for a collectivism à la the Soviet Union, but rather a rational treatment, which was clearly intended to be critical of ideology – particularly when one reads it in conjunction with the initial quote.

The thirty-plus portrait sittings with the Soviet Ambassador to Great Britain Ivan Maisky, who was appointed to the Court of St James as early as 1932 and thus the doyen of foreign diplomats at the turn of 1942/1943, were tedious and protracted for Kokoschka. Even in his major television interview about his life and work in 1966, Kokoschka mentioned this episode as something especially difficult. That was because Maisky was closed and taciturn and read *The Times* most of the time, behind which he liked to disappear. Kokoschka is supposed to have told him then that he himself had already read the back page of the paper; he could now safely turn the paper around.

The portrait shows Maisky sitting at the desk without the newspaper, but with his gaze fixed on his documents, pondering, with an all-mastering head and massive upper body; in the background – exactly as in the case of the Masaryk portrait – is another figure, though not Comenius, but rather a frozen image of Lenin in orator pose, the right hand stretched out towards a globe which in turn lightly touches Maisky's head. Maisky's head and the globe seem like counterparts, which appears to indicate that this diplomat has something worldwide in mind. Globe and Lenin-figure thus are something of a speech bubble through which the taciturn Maisky seems to speak.

It is a portrait of absolute presence: Maisky as the eminent intermediary between East and West, between Churchill and Stalin.[28] It could not have been anticipated at the time of this portrait that the star of star diplomats was already sinking in the Kremlin. From 1941 Maisky's primary mission was to convince Churchill, and through him also Roosevelt, of the necessity of building up a second front against Hitler's Germany, which Stalin raised ever more urgently at this time. As a second front still had not come about, even by 1943, the Kremlin lost patience with Maisky; he was recalled in mid-September and ordered back to Moscow. Although Maisky drastically reduced his private correspondence in the last two years of his tenure – one of the few private letters was received by the former British prime minister Lloyd George on his eightieth birthday – the connection to his por-traitist was important enough to the recalled Soviet ambassador that he wrote to him under the date of 11 September 1943:

> On the eve of my departure for the U.S.S.R., I wish to express to you my most sincere gratitude for your efforts in painting my por-trait and for all your great patience with me, as I must confess quite frankly I was a very bad sitter.
>
> I am also very thankful to you for your generous action in con-tributing your fee for this portrait to the Stalingrad fund.
>
> I very much appreciate my meetings with you and our talks during the sittings.
>
> In reiterating my thanks to you, may I send you all good wishes for the future.
>
> Yours very sincerely, I. Maisky[29]

This letter demonstrates not only the esteem in which Maisky held the artist, it also attests to Kokoschka's generosity in donating the honorarium of 1,000 pounds sterling to the Stalingrad Hospital Fund, despite the fact that Kokoschka himself was dependent on every pound at the time. Kokoschka had made a condition of his donation that both sides, the wounded Soviet soldiers as well as the German prisoners, should be helped. What actually happened to this consider-able contribution remains uncertain.

The first connection to the Maiskys came about as a result of Koko-schka's preliminary sketches for the *Comforts Fund for Women and Children of Soviet Russia* in the autumn of 1941. They were intended as advertising posters which Madame Maisky, the patroness of this relief fund for mothers and children in need in the Soviet Union, disliked. She desired less representation of the sufferers than Koko-schka had provided, and more pictures of the 'heroic resistance against the Nazis'.[30] This was communicated to Kokoschka in writing on 31 December by the chair of the committee Dorothee Martin, who also promptly corrupted his name ('Dear Mr Kokorschka' [sic]). Indicative of the artist's self-awareness was his response by return.

> My dear Mrs Martin
> Regretfully I received my poster from you because I was so glad to think of having been useful to the common sake.
>   I hope you will find easily some work to the approvement of Madame Maisky from the war artists of which there is an official organisation build up [sic] by Sir Kenneth Clark, the director of the National Gallery.
>   I am sorry to say as an artist I believe rather in a more human appeal to men and I have good reasons to stick to this belief.[31]

Presumably Kokoschka did not know that it was owing to the said Kenneth Clark and not just his Czech passport that he was spared internment, as in June 1940 the Chief Constable of Cornwall enquired of Clark whether the artist resident in Polperro might be a German spy after all. Clark responded that Kokoschka was far 'too dreamy and undependable', just an artist through and through, to be of any use to the Nazis.[32]

Kokoschka would write to the Soviet ambassador from time to time, for example, to congratulate him on the conclusion of the Anglo–Soviet Mutual Assistance Agreement of June 1942. In general, Kokoschka's pro-Soviet position in exile during the war appears tinted with a different, personal light. Of course, his opinions with respect to the Soviet Union were more likely to coincide with those of Roosevelt, who, to Churchill's chagrin, was known to be far more generously disposed towards Stalin. It is unclear who instigated the portrait of Maisky. Kokoschka specifically noted that it was not a commission. The industrialist Henry Dreyfuss, chairman of the Celanese Company, acquired it for the said sum and made it available to the Tate Gallery on permanent loan. Yet initially there was also a plan to advertise the portrait for a type of collective subscription in order to make it available to the Leningrad Museum of Modern Art – a plan that even the British Foreign Secretary Anthony Eden approved of in his letter of 10 June 1943 to his colleague (and friend of Kokoschka) Major Edward Beddington-Behrens. However, on presentation of the portrait Eden withdrew for diplomatic reasons. They consisted primarily of Eden correctly sensing what effect such a gift would have on the Soviets; Maisky, who as mentioned previously had long passed the zenith of his influence, could not be honoured in this manner in a public museum in the Soviet Union. And despite the Mutual Assistance Agreement, the Anglo–Soviet friendship remained more than fragile. Hence due to diplomatic considerations the Maisky portrait remained in London. And even there it became a political issue and intermittently a bone of contention between the National Gallery (Kenneth Clark), and the Tate Gallery and its director (John Rothenstein). The question was whether Kokoschka's Maisky portrait could be shown in the context of the *War Artists Exhibition* in the National Gallery, where there was a preference to not show items on loan, though this painting was on loan to the Tate by the buyer (Dreyfus). In addition, the Board of Trustees of the Tate had to decide whether they could accept Dreyfus' de-facto gift of this painting. And as if that were not enough, the Foreign Office, in the form of Beddington-Behrens, tried to secure the copyright for reproductions for itself. Apparently Kokoschka's painting continued to be of diplomatic interest and a means of future symbolic acts on the part of Britain towards the Soviet Union. It was eventually decided that the presence of this portrait of the former Soviet ambassador in one of the most important London galleries fulfilled its objective of symbolising the Anglo–Soviet partnership more effectively than it could have ever done in Leningrad.

Either way, on 27 September 1943 John Rothenstein could advise the much-admired Kokoschka that the Board of Trustees of the Tate would welcome seeing him represented more prominently in its collection through his *Maisky* – 'certainly a most vivid portrait'. And he recalled the donation of Kokoschka's painting *Polperro II* by the Czech president-in-exile, Beneš. Kokoschka's *Maisky* could then also be seen in the *War Artists Exhibition* at the National Gallery; its Board of Trustees, Kenneth Clark emphasised in a letter to the Foreign Office, enthusiastically welcomed its acceptance and not for some political reasons, rather 'because it was a vital piece of painting by a great artist'.[33]

The Maisky episode shows one thing more than clearly in Kokoschka's exile: his art had become a political issue, even if the director of the National Gallery attempted to gloss over it. By contrast, Kokoschka unquestionably had no objections at this time.

Education Above All Else

It was his speech on the founding of the Freien Deutschen Kulturbund's Institute for Science and Learning that crystallised the core of his educational utopia out of the confusion of the times. With few words, Kokoschka constructed a type of pedagogical utopia through which fascism was meant to be overcome once and for all: a global community of intellectuals, scientists and educators, carried by a 'spirit of federation', specifically in the sense of a medieval guild. Once more Kokoschka evoked the virtues of the arts and crafts of that time. This global community was to serve building a global democracy, and in this, of course, he violated a key commandment of science – namely its purposeless character – in that he demanded that science be transmitted with respect to its 'social relevance'. Once again, Comenius, whom he celebrated as the founder of a peace pedagogy, served as a shining example. Kokoschka even went so far as to suggest that the tragedy of two world wars within twenty years was the result of a totally misguided pedagogy in all countries, namely an education in unvarnished nationalism. Letters from that time speak a similar language, whether they are to the also-exiled-in-London author Anna Maria Jokl (called 'Joke-line' by Kokoschka): 'You are an ingenious woman with a glowing, red heart' (Br III, 105), to Paul Westheim in exile in Mexico, to Sydney and Violet Schiff or to the editors of *The Times*. To Westheim he spoke of a universally raging 'misunderstood Darwinism as substitute' for 'lost values' (Br III, 110). As early as 1942, in an open letter to the publishers of numerous British daily newspapers, he demanded the 'Re-education of the Nazi youth' as the most important task after the end of the war. At the time Kokoschka also began to ask himself anew what Austria's future could be and mean. His reflections must have been stimulated primarily by Julius Braunthal and his book *Need Germany Survive?* Braunthal, who likewise had been living in exile in England since 1938, belonged to the political Left. Between 1927 and 1934 he was editor-in-chief of the popular Viennese daily newspaper *Das Kleine Blatt* (*The Little Gazette*), as well as the illustrated *Der Kuckuck* (*The Cuckoo*). His study *The Tragedy of Austria* (London: 1948) was among the most important analyses of the Austrian psyche in the early post-war period. Its tenor ran: Austria could only redefine itself culturally in that its self-determination lay in overcoming nationalism in an exemplary fashion, by exposing its paradoxes. Once Stalin's intent to reconstitute Austria as a state after the war became clear, this must have been a further reason for Kokoschka to see an uncompromising ray of hope in the form of the Soviet Union.

Yet Kokoschka never left any doubt that he commented on political events first and foremost as an artist. He derived this calling from his unique position, which he never really questioned: 'What eye witness is more dependable than the artist who does not just see the kaleidoscopic world of the average person but searches for the sense, the reasons and backgrounds in the world of the senses!' (Br III, 140).

Cause to consider the reciprocal relationship between political circumstances and one's own person, one's own efforts, was offered at this time not just by Edith Hoffmann-Yapou's intention to draft an all-encompassing monograph on Kokoschka, but also the unexpected reconnection with Paul Westheim, whom Kokoschka had met probably around 1918, as the best interpreter of his works in a long time.

Westheim's study[34] at the time impressed in its regard for motif-stylis-
tic relationships (into the middle of the 1920s). He was the first to give
prominence and emphasis to the baroque in Kokoschka's art, that the
object in it is granted its rightful space.[35] The chemist in Kokoschka was
to have been fascinated from the beginning by the 'riddle of alembic',
which in his case was to have led to a 'modelling with colour material'.[36]
Westheim saw a clear intent to objectivise in all the experientialism of
this art, yes objectification at work, and spoke of the 'translation of
the loose rhythmic of the two-dimensional into colour.'[37] In addition,
Westheim coined a phrase which remained relevant to Kokoschka's
art – especially for his sketching, whether with charcoal or crayon –
and in particular also for the work created in Scotland during the exile
period: the 'harmony of the line'.[38] Even if one cannot assume a causal
relationship with 'Fülle des Wohllauts' ('Abundance of harmony') in
Thomas Mann's novel *Der Zauberberg* (*The Magic Mountain*), we may
speak here of an 'elective affinity' between the visual and the literary in
the broadest sense of the word, as the lines, drawn and written, reveal
intense vibrations. For Westheim, it was particularly the lithographic
translations of the Bach Cantata with their 'contrast of undulations
and surges'[39] that were an example of this 'harmony of the line' in this
artist's oeuvre.

There were too many sharp, jarring notes. As such, the memory of
Westheim's thesis must have been a balm occasionally. The worst 'dis-
sonances' were the howling of sirens, the impacts of the bombs, the
hissing and whistling particularly of the V-1 rockets over London
and the knowledge of the destruction of Dresden, for which Kokoschka could not forgive the British military. He felt himself at the
end of culture often enough. He wrote to the artist Marie-Louise von
Motesiczky, whom he portrayed so impressively, on 24 October 1944.

Now the Stars-and-Stripes cannibals have also destroyed Salzburg,
but they meant Berchtesgaden, they say. The cathedral gone, the
Mozart House as well – the area will have blown up along with it.
'But the theatre (which Poelzig snuck in like a salad bowl for Herr
Reinhardt deceased) is preserved for the after world.' Why should

such witness to a better past also remain standing? Better to make a clean sweep of things for the cannibals. (Br III, 139)

The bit about the cannibals was unjust, admittedly, but this quotation mirrors Kokoschka's despair of the – as it seemed to him – unsalvageable state of cultural matters. This was soon joined by a complete disillusionment about the post-war period, in particular about the position of Czechoslovakia, for the reconstitution of which he had held such great hopes. He denounced – also in an open letter to *The Times* in September 1945 – Edvard Beneš' policy, under the protection of the four victorious powers and mocking international law, of expelling Sudeten Germans, which Kokoschka viewed as a purely racist measure. At the same time, he openly condemned the British-proffered solution of sending war refugees home again in order to gain valuable living space for the British (Br III, 150–152). Totally disillusioned for a time, he wrote to Josef Hodin:

> [...] I believe that whole business of democracy was a superstition. There is only nationalism, which is identical with fascism. [...] We are going to Ullapool where I try to sketch something so I will think better thoughts. Flowers, grasshoppers, grass, children, little girls and sheep. As long as the atom bomb still spares all of this. (Br III, 154)

He did get to thinking better thoughts in Ullapool, as brief as the sojourn was this time, thoughts which were again ignited by seeing, and by his translating this seeing into his work. He was not yet to know that the 'salad bowl' on the Salzach, his expression for the bastion-like castle fortification towering over Salzburg, would play a crucial role in this. Already by this time Kokoschka supported a theory pertaining to Austria which helps to explain why he would find resonance so quickly in the Austria of the post-war period – quite in contrast to his Vienna experiences before 1934; in tune with Soviet opinion, he now claimed, the country had been 'the first casualty of the Nazis' (Br III, 155). This also became the leading theme of his comprehensive confessional letter to Willi Scholz, who had fought against the Dollfuß regime as a Communist Party member and who emigrated to London by way of Prague after his imprisonment. He immediately returned to Austria after the war and led the Communist daily newspaper *Die Wahrheit* (*The Truth*) up until the Hungarian Uprising, which caused him to leave the Party in 1957.

This letter shows just how much Austria had remained at the centre of Kokoschka's political thinking. He now believed the country would be 'on the way to true democracy' if it knew to regenerate itself from the 'green Styria' – from the land – as 'the city person is no longer led by natural instinct'. And further: 'Democracy is the knowledge of the dependence of societal form on the conditions of the outside world. Democracy must lead as assuredly as instinct' (Br III, 156–159). Accordingly, Kokoschka was hoping that democratic behaviour would be internalised.

In addition, we learn that the artist wrote 'broadcasts to Vienna', which were rejected by the 'BBC censor'. The same fate apparently befell him with the Moscow censor (Br III, 159). He was done with London by the late autumn of 1945. The city was 'suffocating', he complained, once again on the grounds of the 'ignorance and blindness with which one looks toward the future in this country, too' (Br III, 160). Yet he fluctuated in his assessments. To Augustus John he claimed that England resembled his old Austria in light of the revival of music, theatre and art (Br III, 170), whereas barely two months later he attested in a letter to Schönberg that England had neither 'ground nor roots' for art. The tone of his letters at this time (1946/1947) remained decidedly manifesto-like. A stranger – a certain Fritz Schahlecker from Tübingen – sent him drawings from a prisoner-of-war camp for comment. Kokoschka responded: 'You are genuine in your drawings, yet it appears to me that they tend towards an idealised view, as would result if one found oneself in the centre of a world that one is attempting to build up.' He advises him to take into account 'the face of the next, the other' in shaping a new worldview. By contrast he rejects the 'materialistic attitude' which 'experienced its complete manifestation in fascism' because this ordering of things evolved 'from individual egotism which also resulted in the national limitation' (Br III, 176 and 177). Kokoschka held nationalism to be the spawn of a paradox, namely an enhanced individualism that represented itself as something collective. Humanism was as lost to him as the 'modern art of the now', that tends to 'dry Formalism', as Kokoschka's letter to a young painter claimed.

Suffer the Little Children...

There is another thing that can be taken from this letter of Kokoschka's to a former Wehrmacht soldier: the unreserved commitment to the issue of children by this artist who himself remained childless. Again and again he emphasises there could be no more important task than 'to create a better world for children' (Br III, 177). Kokoschka, who was robbed of fatherhood through abortion by Alma Mahler-Gropius, and who from the beginning created life drawings of boys and girls and even later repeatedly painted girls,[40] noticeably dedicated himself to the problems and suffering of children in his decidedly political paintings and, above all, in the clarion-call posters he had produced since the Spanish Civil War. Yet the painting *Spielende Kinder* (*Children at Play*) of 1909 seems to be uniquely lacking in political commentary, even if there is a sense of resignation and thus scepticism about the future. In fact, these two children – a boy and a girl, who may be siblings – are not playing. The boy appears sunken into himself; lost in thought, he peers at the girl, whose glance is vaguely turned to the observer and thus suggests openness. They lie half propped up next to each other, a hint of a *Windsbraut* motif yet with an air of innocence. The colours are more matte than glowing; the brown tending towards red playing around them does not allow an impression of light-heartedness or even cheerfulness to arise.

The child, suffering under the megalomania of so-called adults, pushes into the foreground of this pertinent pictorial theme in Kokoschka's works in the ensuing period, accompanied, as we have seen, by letters and essays on children's art and the child's view of the war.

The intensity of Kokoschka's representations of children in need is reminiscent of those in the oeuvre of Käthe Kollwitz and was first employed in his poster *Helft den baskischen Kindern* (*Help the Basque Children*, 1937) created in Prague. It shows a mother attempting to seek safety with her little one in her arms whilst reaching for her older child, who – apparently mortally wounded – falls behind and becomes a shadow. Dead children lie scattered. A fighter aircraft dominates the scene and a fallen cross. Prague shines in the background – an overly obvious suggestion that Czechoslovakia could be the next Spain. The dead child lying in the dead mother's lap also stands in the centre of the important political allegory of 1943 *What We are Fighting For* (Kunsthaus Zurich). The representatives of power and impotence, collaborators (Marshal Pétain), financiers (Hjalmar Schacht), the clergy, a seemingly uninvolved Gandhi in a rickshaw and a bust of Voltaire, with reference to his *Candide* and his slogan of 'the best of all possible worlds', surround an arena of horror. Machines process the dead; a crucified Judas laments mutely. The proceeds of this painting's sale were to be sent from Basel in 1947 to the starving children of Vienna, as per Kokoschka's express request.

Kokoschka gave the starving children of Vienna all of his active compassion. At the end of 1945 he created a cover for a concert programme for their benefit, which is as poignant as his depiction *Christus tröstet die hungrigen Kinder* (*Christ Comforts the Hungry Children*, 1945/1946). The cover again shows a despairing mother holding her half-starved, apathetic child. It is marked by stigmata on the hands and feet. In the background we see a cross with the inscription 'Xmas in Vienna!' A further variation of the *Ecce-homo* gesture is seen in the drawing which shows Christ half stepping down from the cross towards the children. The cross inscription is now more precise: 'In Memory of the Children of Europe Who Have to Die of Cold and Hunger This Xmas'.[41] He reacts similarly to the news of floods in Lower Austria and his home town of Pöchlarn in July 1954. Once again, the children in the flood area received his undivided attention.

Human solidarity, fraternity, sorority, not fratricide – that is what Kokoschka saw emerging from the pictures of the emigrant children that were exhibited under his aegis in London in 1943. He emphasised, despite all his reservations about England, that such an exhibition in these dark times could only be possible in a 'free democracy'. Through this collaboration of children from the most diverse backgrounds, he believed a primary objective of Comenius to be achieved: togetherness through art, born of mutual respect, which could not be learned early enough. In an artistic regard this sense for children was mirrored in the often childlike expression of his pictures which had already shaped his early works.

Where to Turn?

Was Kokoschka familiar with the church hymn in Franz Schubert's *Deutsche Messe* (*German Mass*) 'Where should I turn to?' Because this question summarises the need to settle down from which Kokoschka suffered after 1945. There was barely a letter in which he did not mention this question. The concern for the wellbeing of his sister continued to occupy him. In addition, he sensed that he had not put down any real roots after seven years in exile on the British Isles – despite the inspiring beauty of the Scottish and Cornish landscapes. It also did not help that his landlord explained to him, 'that he does not tolerate "foreigners" in his empire and counsels us to "go home" immediately to make room for soldiers who so gloriously freed us [...] Am curious about our "soldiers" who are supposed to live in Park Lane!!' (Br III, 160).

And yet despite his discontent with London and English conditions, and his doubt as to the interest of this culture in the profound, 'going home' was not an option for this learned cosmopolitan. In Prague, conditions darkened visibly. What he learned about the machinations of Edvard Beneš (who under tacit approval of the Allies was intent on finishing off the Sudeten Germans) Kokoschka compared with the genocide of the Armenians by the Turks (1916) (Br III, 179). Everywhere he looked he saw Hitler's nationalist seed showing signs of sprouting again, the old thought patterns of nationalism and racism newly at work. He acknowledged that he was putting off, if not alienating, friends with such views, particularly in the case of Jack and Mina Carney, and excused his occasionally exaggerated judgements with being a 'victim of depression'. He realised that he would be all the more vulnerable without Olda whenever he was separated from her for a longer period of time, such as in Switzerland in the late summer of 1947 and two years later in the USA. He must have been most surprised that he was not confronted with greater difficulties there – in Pittsfield, Minneapolis and New York – during the Red Scare proclaimed by McCarthy.

Kokoschka considered Mexico for himself and Olda. Paul Westheim lived there. The USA made overtures to him – galleries and museums as well as Minneapolis University, to say nothing of the female students. He wrote to Olda; she had long since become his 'little sweet', in case she could have forgotten.

> I look quite good when I've had my hair cut, the ladies are crazy for me and the men listen to me. But I think of my little sweet, do something for the longer and shorter term simultaneously and beg you, only to be healthy and rested so we have a great future together. The past no longer counts because I am too interested in tomorrow. This land will soon be all mine. (Br III, 230 f)

As far as the United States was concerned this prediction proved hasty and overreaching, but Switzerland emerged as a possible future destination. From Basel, where the Kunsthalle bestowed an important retrospective on him, he announced to his sister: 'In 9 days in Basel I have achieved a thousand times more than in 9 years in London' (Br III, 182). He still considered himself to be 'on walkabout' – and that 'since 1930' (Br III, 183). In Lugano, too, he was initially overcome by alienation – in this case about the 'shabby Kurort palaces' that 'ruin a magnificent landscape', something that 'had seemed possible only in England' to him (Br III, 184). Yet then he saw Sierre, the valley of the Rhône, the Muzot's 'tower' where Rilke was able to reside to the end of his life, courtesy of its owner Werner Reinhardt, and for whose portrait

Kokoschka now prepared himself. 'The landscape is right, very austere, rocky, great depths, vineyards to the scree, old houses' (Br III, 185). He was convinced of one thing: after ten years of a 'mostly grim life in exile' he now needed to find possibilities for himself 'which allow me to do that which most interests me under the best circumstances – to live for my art' (Br III, 189). One could easily forget that this artist, who asks himself again and again which way he should turn to ensure the continuation of his work, which in his eyes would be comparable to a new beginning, was by now over sixty years old.

Several letters from this time support the aesthetic dimension of this new orientation: in which direction should he turn his art (and himself in it)? 'Art is a fumbling, an exploration into the field of morality, and it is neither a luxury of the rich nor a rigid Formalism as it follows from the theory of the academy', as it says in his letter to the previously mentioned illustrator released from English imprisonment (Br III, 177). On his forays through Switzerland in the late summer of 1947 he saw the Matterhorn from the balcony of the Hotel Riffelalp near Zermatt, whose drama he painted as it 'towers over all the glaciers and abysses into the sky'. In doing so he felt 'like a Chinese hermit who has left the world behind and searches for the perpetual balancing between one's own nothing and the absolute' (Br III, 190). The result for him was a new perspective and technique: '[...] painting is completely different, transparent as glass with many sudden, ambush-like, colourful surprises and enormous depth and height. These effects are a result of the clear axial position, focal point in its intersection under the picture's horizon' (Br III, 191). To speak of a merely aesthetic self-positioning in a transitional phase in life is not really appropriate, particularly not when one views these utterances in relation to his large-sized double portrait of John and Betty Cowles produced in Minneapolis, and the letter laying out the foundation of his creative self-awareness 'to an American student' who asked him about his similarity to El Greco. In it, Kokoschka counted El Greco among the Expressionist painters, whereas he ascribed his own origins to the Austrian baroque. What emerged here was a new foundation of specific principles on which Kokoschka's last long phase of work was to rest, for example, the baroque use of colour in cityscapes, the perspective of being present through a conscious culture of seeing and – once again – the portrait as an expression of being together, because a direct path leads from the Cowles portrait to the markedly brighter, and in its intimacy of course even more intense, double portrait *Olda und Oskar Kokoschka* of 1963.

6

The Portrait as a Form of Representation

'[...] no portrait can be any good unless the artist produces it in its true sense.'[1]

The (Self-)Portrait as Biography, Along with a Few Retrospective Views

It is always 'faces'. In Hebrew – as the contemporary writer Barbara Honigmann points out – the face only appears in the plural and is combined with the verb 'to turn' or 'to turn itself'. The face is the seeing and seen. And she quotes a phrase from Emmanuel Lévinas, which could also be used in reference to Kokoschka: 'The art consists in finding the face again.'[2] Another reference applies to Kokoschka's portraiture, this time from Max Liebermann. He responded to one of the people he had portrayed, who complained that there was minimal resemblance, 'The portrait resembles you more than you do!'[3] Does the truth appear to us in the face of a person or does it distort it?

One does not need to be a proponent of physiognomics in order to find faces fascinating and to see in them either an essence or a mask. However, only in a portrait do faces become works of art. 'I think I will do many portraits,' Oskar Kokoschka announced to his parents from the Isonzo front on 21 July 1916 (Br I, 242). 'I have painted three pictures, amongst them a self-portrait, naked. Look like a man-eating Apollo!' (Br II, 117). That is how he views himself in a letter written to his mother from Paris in May 1925.

What determined that an artist would concentrate so intensively on portraits as Kokoschka did – dedicating his primary work to so-called human images, even? Human images show the picture of a person. That sounds self-evident, even tautological, yet it reveals a deeper truth about the manner of a particular art and the self-perception of an artist. As late as 1961 Kokoschka still spoke of it and, as so often, somewhat coquettishly. In doing so, he shared quite specific information: 'I content myself with painting portraits because I can do it and see my way to the human, a mirror which shows me when and where and who and what I am' (DSW III, 283).

It is worth turning this personal statement inside-out because in it is hidden the assumption that portraiture is a constraint, but one that allows a focus on the essence of humanness. Portraits, not just in and of themselves, are 'mirrors'; thus, they are reflections through which an 'I' is fixed in time and space. Portraits *show* identity and bear witness to an act that is artistic as well as humane. Kokoschka's statement acknowledges that, even in a portrait of another, the self-determination of the artist becomes visible. He lets himself be recognised in every portrait, 'when and where and who and what *I* am'. I paint others and myself, so I am.

Portraits bear witness to a series of encounters between artist and model. A few elemental questions play a determining role in portraiture and, most importantly, in judging a portrait: how does the artist encounter the other, the one to be portrayed? Where does the counterpart begin in portraiture and what of the artist is carried into the portrait of the other? Which picture of the person is thus created?

And yet caution is called for in the use of the term 'human image', which belongs to the clichés of the 1950s. The problem 'is less the person than the image, the fact that the artist is set an ideological challenge so that the person even fits into the picture', as Anselm Haverkamp leads us to consider.[4] The human image belongs to the linguistic register of 'Occident', 'Humanism', 'Reconstruction' and thus to a conservative cultural restorative mindset. Yet Kokoschka's portraits definitely show the person as he is and seems, but not how he should be; therefore, he understood the idea of human images as something more specific – and definitely not as something that ideologically fixes the person.

As early as 1926 Carl Einstein ascribed Kokoschka with a special affinity for portraits in his (somewhat premature) overview *Die Kunst des 20. Jahrhunderts* (*Art of the 20th Century*): 'Hardly an artist of this generation has equally relentlessly done one thing: painting people, the individual persons [...].'[5] And further to the general importance of this genre: 'The portrait attests to the wish of the person to set a constant image, resistant to changes over time and hopeless death, and thus to preserve eternity for themselves.'[6] To ward off death through a portrait: that of course does not occur in Kokoschka's early portraits, as they repeatedly and noticeably show people doomed to die.

By the way, Kokoschka himself was rarely portrayed by another hand. A remarkable exception is a drawing by Emil Orlik. It shows the artist not in front of an easel, but rather directing, in a heavy, somewhat oversized coat with his distinctive head in sharp profile, forearm slightly raised, issuing stage directions.[7] According to Kokoschka, a model's desire 'for immortalisation' as the 'most human hope' is expressed in the reflectiveness of a portrait (DSW III, 282). Portraits and self-portraits are found throughout Kokoschka's work in a quantity that allows us to surmise that he also always saw his own and the personality of others as a mirror of time. He even believed that the 'problem of modern painting', whether and how 'to fill the vacuum of the present time', could be 'solved in portraiture' (ibid). And that could only mean the question of the meaning of personality in Modernism.

The artist protests against collectivism through portraiture. Though that, too, is not true in the absolute. Kokoschka's *Prometheus* fantasy (1950) or his triptych *Die Thermopylen* (*The Thermopylae*, 1954) want to be panoramas of time, but not in the sense of the peasants' revolt panoramas by the likes of Werner Tübke. Individuals literally fall out of these paintings, step out of them – and, in the case of *Prometheus*, in the gestalt of the artist's self-portrait.

Yet there are also imaginary portraits in Kokoschka's works, for example, that of Vincenzo Pallotti (1961/1962). Before Pallotti was canonised during the Second Vatican Council, Kokoschka was asked to create a portrait of him, in particular on the basis of his death mask, referred to as a 'handful of clay' by Kokoschka. The artist summarised his task precisely: 'How do I breathe life into the ashes so that this mask becomes a face again, which looks us in the eye, reminding us that we, too, are called to aid our neighbour?' (DSW III, 285). What Kokoschka also brought back to life in this 'portrait' were unmistakeably his own facial features in addition to his massive hands. The imaginary portrait from the reanimated mask of the man who died in 1850 became an act of self-identification.

By the summer of 1909 at the latest, Adolf Loos had urged Kokoschka to concentrate on painting portraits. In October of that year, he painted Loos as well as Karl Kraus and Peter Altenberg. Later, presumably in the summer of 1919, Kokoschka was also to draw Loos' second wife – the dancer, actress and operetta singer Elsie Altmann-Loos. Kokoschka had set the name 'Ariel' above the drawing, characterising it as the spirit of the air or the rebelling angel, even the punisher of demons. The focus of the drawing, which hangs in the Loos flat in the Wien Museum today, is Elsie's eyes; they practically act as attention-grabbers. The face only seems to exist because of these eyes; it resembles a field of vision on which the observer thinks he is seeing the two charcoal-black eyes grow.

Kokoschka shows the face and appearance of a young but mature woman and thus not Loos' ideal: the child bride. His first wife, Lina, had an affair with a juvenile, an eighteen-year-old grammar school pupil called Heinz Lang. She abruptly but belatedly broke off the affair with her young, passionate lover when Loos discovered the pair's love letters. At Peter Altenberg's suggestion, Lang then committed suicide, far from Vienna in the English provincial town of Kidderminster, waiting for his Lina in vain. The scandal was the talk of the town, and it is no surprise that Arthur Schnitzler took up this material and constructed a play out of it. However, out of consideration for his friend Altenberg, he did not bring his tragi-comedy *Das Wort* (*The Word*: the harm that a single word can cause) to the stage. The premiere was not until 1969 in the theatre in Josefstadt.

Loos and his women in the legendary snow-white bedroom, which, however, would become the less-pure setting for his paedophilic tendencies. In 1928 he was in court, accused of the 'crime of consummated and attempted defilement as well as consummated and attempted seduction into fornication', perpetrated on three girls between eight and ten years of age.[8] The paedophilic abysses of Viennese Modernism are mirrored in the behaviour of Peter Altenberg, but also in the pictorial work of Gustav Klimt, Egon Schiele and the early Oskar Kokoschka. Intellectually accomplished artists and artistically inclined intellectuals seemed almost collectively under the spell of the ideal of the naïve, childlike woman, the crass contrast to what a Bertha von Suttner or the pedagogue Eugenie Schwarzwald represented: emancipation through the education of feminine consciousness. It was bizarre enough that Loos also tried to justify his scandalous behaviour pedagogically; education by sexual abuse is the formula to be gleaned from his testimony in court. However, he also claimed another reason for why perversions of this type were so widespread at the time in Vienna, when he grotesquely seemed to blame the willingness of the children in his testimony: 'The entire immorality of the children is a function of living conditions being so miserable and that 80% of children lie in one bed with adults.'[9]

Loos – who unquestionably considered himself to be a missionary; who followed a thoroughly noble concept of social housing *and* the furthering of artists (in other words, the selected few); who knew how to dispose of the remnants of the 19th century in terms of building style and interior design – came unstuck because of his fixation on the mother and sexual perversions. And yet, even as he was exposed through the trial five years before his death, friends remained loyal to him – whether through genuine loyalty or guilt at their own immorality is anyone's guess.

In any event, on the other side of the white (or dark) bedroom, in the smoke-filled coffee houses of Vienna, Kokoschka, by his own admission, primarily studied 'faces', such as those of Arnold Schönberg, Peter Altenberg and Anton von Weber. In Berlin the 'currents of life' naturally revealed themselves to him, transmitted through Herwarth Walden and Paul Cassirer, in the Café des Westens on the Kurfürstendamm (also called Café Größenwahn: Café Megalomania). He had met Walden earlier in Vienna when he was meeting with Karl

Kraus to discuss his planned magazine *Der Sturm*. (Kraus' *Die Fackel* published an interview portrait of Kokoschka in March 1909, the first in-depth appraisal of his work.) But, for Kokoschka, Walden also brought the connection to his wife, Else Lasker-Schüler – after Bessie Bruce the most exalted woman whom Kokoschka had encountered to date. Remarkably, the relationship to Lasker-Schüler did not develop as he claimed not to want to paint her portrait.

In Berlin Kokoschka saw the face of bohemian society – he, whose play *Mörder Hoffnung der Frauen* (1907) brought scenic Expressionism to life. In other words, he created a kind of *connecting link* 'between Vienna Modernism and Expressionism',[10] a position that he also embodied himself. George Grosz recalled an incident in the Berliner Panoptikum in which Kokoschka sat among the wax figures of murderers and dangerous criminals only to leap out at the terrified visitors.

Kokoschka escaped the wild goings-on in Berlin and returned to the then relatively sleepy Vienna, the context in which his erstwhile friend, the Viennese artist Max Oppenheimer (1885–1954), tried to emulate him is a reflection of his fame as an artist – Wassily Kandinsky would call him 'one of ours' to Franz Marc. Lasker-Schüler took Kokoschka's part and levelled a serious accusation of plagiarism against Oppenheimer. When Oppenheimer exhibited in the Munich Galerie Thannhauser in May 1911 (six months prior to the first presentation of the Blauen Reiter (Blue Riders) there, a group of prominent artists), Erich Mühsam commented very critically in his diary about the 'chap' with his 'shameless trap' and upbraided him as an 'archetype of a Prague Jew boy' with whom, to his amazement, Heinrich Mann was still friends – though the latter was no longer friends with Kokoschka.[11] This by no means covers everything about the much vilified Oppenheimer. That he was stylistically influenced by Kokoschka, by Egon Schiele (who in turn painted Oppenheimer's portrait in 1910) and by Albert Paris Gütersloh – and also, initially, by Van Gogh – is without question. The artistic closeness between Kokoschka and Schiele for a time is comparable, though Kokoschka readily denied it or at least attempted to radically minimise it. Oppenheimer, too, subscribed to portraiture and painted Thomas and Heinrich Mann, Arnold Schönberg and Tilla Durieux. Like Kokoschka, he began to grapple pictorially with music, which led to his large-scale painting *Die Symphonie* (pertaining to Gustav Mahler's *Vierte Symphonie* (*Fourth Symphony*)). The time seems right to view Oppenheimer as more than an Expressionist plagiarist. He unquestionably belongs with those previously mentioned, along with Richard Gerstl, as part of the Viennese art avant-garde around 1910. The title of his autobiography alone – *Menschen finden ihren Maler* (*People Find Their Painter*), written in exile in the USA – is indicative of the centrality of the portrait in his work.

Interest in the portrait received critical acclaim in Vienna in the form of an essay by Georg Simmel on the *Aesthetik des Porträts* (*Aesthetic of the Portrait*), which appeared in the *Neuen Freien Presse* on 22 April 1905. It is hardly likely that as an erstwhile student at the Kunstgewerbeschule zu Wien, Oskar Kokoschka (who was instructed in anatomical drawing by Hermann Heller, among others) did not take notice of this prominently placed article. In his article about the portrait, Simmel – who four years earlier had expounded on *Die ästhetische Bedeutung des Gesichts* (*The Aesthetic Meaning of the Face*) in the obscure (from a Viennese perspective) Hamburg weekly of German culture *Der Lotse* – laid out a type of critical manifesto for the representation of individuals as a cultural phenomenon. There are assertions in it that must have continued to have an effect on Kokoschka well into his last writings on (portrait) art. At least a close affinity becomes apparent between Simmel and Kokoschka's reflections. Take these statements by Simmel: 'From the totality of the person, in which the usual representation of his appearance and all that we know of his emotions, differences included, the portrait reveals it [...]'. The person's appearance 'represented in its purest form is the primary function of the portrait.' 'Thus, a strict connection between the features of a face develops, of which the artist convinces us through his manner of representing it.' 'No theory may decree away the ever elevated and often fulfilled demand of the portrait to represent the soul by way of the body.'[12] In an earlier piece, Simmel had emphasised the face, which has something of the 'peninsular' about it in relation to the rest of the body.[13] The 'plasticity of the face' speaks for being able to see the 'geometric location of the inner person'. Significantly, Simmel criticised the 'broad, expansive gesticulations of baroque figures'. He called them 'repugnant, because they disavow the intrinsically human: the implicit preoccupation of every detail under the power of the central I.'[14] Kokoschka certainly would not have followed him in this critique of the baroque had he been familiar with the essay *The Aesthetic Meaning of the Face*, as he was impressed by the broad-sweeping nature of the baroque, for example, in the works of Franz Anton Maulbertsch, who remained a lifelong role model.

Furthermore, Simmel derived a negative aesthetic judgement from the destruction of facial symmetry which directed itself against the avant-garde practice of portraiture or representation of people and anticipated a central criticism of Expressionism: 'Where [the de-spiritualisation of the face] more or less occurs, in mouths agape and eyes wide open, it is not only especially unaesthetic, but exactly these two movements are, as is now understandable, the expression of "despiritualising" emotional paralysis, the momentary loss of emotional domination of our selves.'[15] What might be meant by this is exemplified in the fifty-two self-portrait busts by Franz Xaver Messerschmidt (1736–1783), which are known by the title *Charakterköpfe* (*Character Heads*) or 'Kopf-Stücke' ('Head Pieces').[16] The problem with these distorted facial representations became acute in Modernism in the art of Edvard Munch, which was particularly valued by Kokoschka. Even in a 1953 essay, Kokoschka recalled his 'Expressionistic' period, 'which gave *gestalt* to the frightening contemporary face of modern man' and had the effect of a shock (DSW III, 173). The digression on Kandinsky in this essay about Munch was like a pot-shot. 'Kandinsky's programme' sacrificed the 'ability for conscious seeing', according to Kokoschka: looking back. One thing certainly belonged to this 'programme': the abstraction of the face. Kandinsky's faces became empty around 1910; more precisely, they emptied themselves of their features as, for example, in his *Intérieur mit zwei Frauen* (*Interior with Two Women*). At the time, he left the portraits – even the one showing him – to his lover, the artist Gabriele Münter (1877–1962). The likeness showed itself in his studies for *Improvisationen* (*Improvisations*), for example, in his fifth, also from 1910, which abstracts from the religious theme and attributes a barely recognisable veil to the Holy Virgin at bottom edge of the painting, but without granting her a face. The fading of facial features is also found in Odilon Redon's work at this time, for example, his painting *Ophèlia au milieu des fleurs* (1905–1908), and corresponds to a tendency that Kokoschka rejected for himself on principle. We dare to hypothesise, and will expand on this in another context, that Kokoschka's displeasure regarding the abstraction of tangible motifs and thus from the recognisable living environment made it impossible for him to abstract from his real-life experiences and thus also from himself. He developed a parallel Modernism in the visual arts that wanted to create sensory engagement by emphasising the humanly graspable.

At the same time as Gottfried Benn (*Lyrik des expressionistischen Jahrzehnts, Lyricism of the Expressionist Decade*, 1955), Kokoschka took stock of Expressionism in his essay on Munch. His findings turned out to be considerably more conversational than Benn's: 'Expressionism is a construct of experience, and as such it can be communicated, albeit only indirectly at times, as a message from the I to the You. As with love, it needs two for this. Expressionism does not live in the ivory tower; it turns to the next one it awakens' (DSW, 175).

Kokoschka's art was never uncontroversial. That also applied to his portraits. For instance, when Harry Graf Kessler, the great authority on Modernism and cultural mediator between France, Britain and Germany in the first two decades of the 20th century, visited Zurich in July 1927, he went to the Kunsthaus, which was showing a Kokoschka exhibition. In his diary he noted his ambivalent impression.

His [Kokoschka's] talent lies in capturing the most subtle and most tender of human expressions, namely in eyes, mouth, hands. But he dresses and marks that with a totally unrelated fragility and brutality.[17]

This tension between subtlety and ham-fistedness actually does define a large portion of Kokoschka's portraiture. Consequently, the hands of a sitter may seem paw-like and the facial features rich in contours. However, much depended on the medium. Pencil and India ink – for example, in his early work – render sharper, more naturalistic contours than the work with charcoal and crayon which began to dominate the portraits after 1912. Pencil and ink enabled him to mould the facial features, not unlike working with oil paints or oil pastels. Corrections, overpainting and erasing are possible with these media, and Kokoschka made liberal use of these possibilities, which could lead to outright colour layering in oil portraits. In contrast, few of his watercolour portraits remain, despite his recommending the use of watercolours to his students – even in capturing body shapes – if not actually requiring it.

Preliminary studies for portraits were the exception. For Kokoschka, the spontaneous impression of a person, which then crystallised in the process, was important. A significant exception is formed by the over 150 studies for the painting *Frau in Blau* (*Woman in Blue*, 1919), created in a period of three months, which literally formed the basis for the notorious Alma doll. On the one hand, the *Frau in Blau* represents 'Anima', the libidinously insatiable; on the other hand, however, it represents her objectified – and thus restrained – opposite. In particular the chalk drawings are striking due to their special plasticity and thus anticipate the impression of the oil painting. Then again there are pen-and-ink sketches among these studies, which make do with body outlines and in this way objectify the seductress.[18]

News from the Ego and More 'Images of People'

'The ego inundates the world in Expressionism', we read in Paul Hatvani's *Versuch über den Expressionismus* (*Essay on Expressionism*).[19] The ego centres, even multiplies itself, wants to seem omnipresent and play to the gallery. This phenomenon has existed since the Renaissance and was first reflected on in this historical context by

Jacob Burckhardt.[20] Wilhelm Waetzoldt, with whose writings Koko-schka must have been familiar at the latest via his Dresden period, transposes Burkhardt's approach into Modernism in his study *Die Kunst des Porträts* (*The Art of the Portrait*, 1908). The 'intimate mono-logue-like manifestation of the personality' shows itself in a portrait, according to Waetzoldt.[21]

Friedrich Gundolf scorned this phenomenon. In 1922 he used the phrase 'unleashed ego-nesses'. Though the term was actually coined during the rise of Subjectivism around 1800 (particularly with respect to Heinrich von Kleist),[22] it certainly also pertained to the zeitgeist in the visual arts of the 1920s and belonged therefore to the climate in which one (self-)portrait after the other came into being under Koko-schka's hand.

The 'inner being' showing in the face of the sitter (even more so the artist's), but also the perceived mask-like aspect of the face seemed especially to fascinate Kokoschka. By way of example, this shows itself in his painting *Mutter und Kind* (*Mother and Child*, 1934), which shows the mother (Trudl) with a Japanese Noh mask, thereby dis-guising herself to her child. He was no less preoccupied with the respective background to the face, which he seldomly disregarded in his portraits and populated with characteristic things that could be found in his rich collections.[23] Yet, in so doing, he never went so far as to represent the portrayed artist as an imposter.[24] One is more likely to gain the impression that the seriousness with which Kokoschka pursued portraiture was related to the position that Hegel took with his hypothesis of the 'dissolution of the romantic art form'. Art, he held in his *Vorlesungen zur Ästhetik* (*Lectures on Aesthetics*), hence-forth dissipates 'completely in the image of portraits'. Hegel called this process 'the subjective creative imitation of the available'.[25] And, in fact, Kokoschka's art seems to have developed in this manner, even if dogmatic standards and objectives were never the issue in his case – with the exception of the ideology of humanism, in whose service he was increasingly willing to act.

This impression that Kokoschka's art blossomed in portraiture deepens when one views the cityscapes and landscapes,[26] but also the animal paintings (especially the *Mandrill*), as portraits. Arguably, his over 150 sketches of the *Frau in Blau* amounted to but one portrait.

These paintings – whether of Prague, Dover or Lake Geneva – become character mirrors of the respective city- and landscapes. The people enter into them and blossom, as conversely the individual portrait of a person emerges from such landscapes; the portrait of Masaryk in his Prague setting is one of many such examples. Yet Kokoschka insinuated another dimension of this genre with these landscape and city contexts of his sitters, and also with the things he incorporated; in a portrait he represented snippets of the subject's biography. This biographical component dominates in his self-portraits, and also in those portraits of people that he painted multiple times and in different phases of their lives and mythologised, such as Alma Mahler and, in particular, his wife Olda. His self-portraiture could have ended with the *Triptychon* of 1950, created in London for Antoine Graf Seilern, as he already sees himself in the underworld in the third painting, *Hades und Persephone*. Yet numerous self-portraits followed on from this negative apotheosis of the self, mostly sketches, although none of them were able to attain the enchanting intensity of the Fiesole self-portrait of 1948. It may be that the artist surprised himself while painting his own portrait because he holds on tightly to a long paintbrush with both hands, as if clinging to an art tool, while the strikingly light eyes are fixed on the observer. A Wotan-like presence emanates from this self-portrait, and the long brush could also be a walking stick. This face emerged from quick, assured strokes, which in places have something bristly about them, that know no hesitation or doubt. In general, these self-portraits have nothing unflinching about them, not even the *Selbstbildnis als 'entarteter' Künstler* (1937). Soft features are rarely seen, such as in *Selbstbildnis mit Mütze* (*Self-portrait with Cap*, 1932) in which green tones dominate, a colour that is infrequently used in his self-portraits. More often the artist appears confident: purposeful, clear-sighted and full of certainty.

However, that applies to all of his sitters. By having their portraits painted, they gain individuality and presence, which Kokoschka confers on them. Through the act of being painted their personality strengthens, and a bit of Kokoschaka's own is added too – regardless of whether it is Henry Pearlman, the Countess of Drogheda or Valerie Goulding. Kokoschka is present in the composition of all the faces he has painted. This entirely characteristic effect of his portraiture becomes obvious when one experiences several of his portraits gathered together in a *single* exhibition space. They conduct a dialogue, literally on the same eye level: the Fiesole self-portrait with the *Marabou* (*Marabout*), *Mutter mit Kind* (*Mother with Child*, 1921), *Araberinnen mit Kind* (*Arab Women with Child*, 1929) and the noticeably carefully crafted painting of Olda (without child!). It is particularly interesting to eavesdrop on the conversation in the great hall of the *Fondation Oskar Kokoschka* in the Musée Jenisch in Vevey between *his* Bedouin prince from the late 1920s, the *Marabou*, and himself in Fiesole in 1948; it is also about a dialogue of forms and painting techniques. The *Marabou* characterises a horizontal brushstroke; the self-portrait is orientated along the vertical. The yellow and ochre shades enmesh the Marabout, whose left hand suggests openness, whereas the facial expression almost remains caught in itself. By contrast, the Fiesole self-portrait speaks of free expression, wherein a characteristic of later work is already suggested; the colours, which are becoming increasingly vivid, form a living body of work. In addition, unexpected colour accents and lightning-like illuminations enliven the painting, as is also the case in the later portrait of Lady Mary Dunn (1973).[27] There is definitely no case for serenity or sage (self-)transcendence in Kokoschka's later work. On the contrary, Expressionist remnants and mythological gestures intertwine and enable the lucid colours to find their vividness.

One unique feature of Kokoschka's portraiture – particularly in his later work – is the double portrait, whether of the siblings *Michael und Posy Croft* (1938/1939), the painting *The Duke and Duchess of Hamilton* (1969) or *Olda und Oskar Kokoschka* (1963). Of particular significance among his double portraits is the *Portrait of Mr and Mrs John Cowles* (1949) – Kokoschka commented at length about this large-format double portrait in letters to Olda.

'I paint every day for about three hours,' he wrote to Olda from Minneapolis in mid-September 1949, 'but then I have so many whiskeys in a row that it becomes too much even for me' (Br III, 230). He combs through John Cowles' extensive library, attends horse shows ('I practically cried that I cannot ride anymore'; ibid) and falls for a newlywed 'sweet 20-year-old Hungarian with long blonde tresses and blue eyes'. In addition, he speaks at the local university and promptly receives the offer, 'to return every year for 3 months as political, philosophical and moral leaven'.

The well-remunerated task in Minneapolis, in any event, was to paint John and Elizabeth Cowles. And in order to be able to complete this painting successfully, Kokoschka even completely forgoes his beloved whiskey, 'to be fresher the next morning, though I miss alcohol very much, when I am finished with the work' (Br III, 233).

In early October 1949, he can inform Olda with relief, after forty sittings and three times 'painting over [...] the entire story', he has 'pulled it off' and has 'no doubts' about the painting. The work was done, even if in retrospect it would prove to be more of a preparatory exercise for the large, multi-part paintings that still lay ahead of him. What now follows as explanation and commentary may apply as a key to his portraiture in general: the repeated 'painting over' had to be done, according to Kokoschka, 'because the paint work was not dense enough and the individual elements were not painted enough, meaning invented in colour' (Br III, 233). And further:

> Even a nose or corner of the eye, arms, body, room always has to be invented by the painter, as if such a thing had never existed before. [...] Now you have to have two older people, who drank too much whisky the night before, miming a harmonious married couple (as poor actors), smiling and cheerful, for company all day whilst painting. So you can imagine, how glad one is, when one sees the whole day finally drawing to an end and with sudden warmth and benevolence looks down upon one's self-made Adam and Eve and this human couple is now called upon to rise and go forth into the world on my word. Because, basically, I have created them, right, Sweetness? (Br III, 233)

The imagined portrait – Kokoschka never expressed himself about this genre more surprisingly than here. The hoped-for effect did not fail to materialise, as he was able to report to his 'Sweetness' soon afterwards. He had also taken appropriate care of the frame. His demanding clientele apparently expected complete customer service.

> You must know that my hysteria was over on the same day that I showed the painting. Betty sobbed beforehand, after all she is 50 and knows that her first spring is past, and men preserve better because they don't have to carry the four children they have here themselves. But on the other hand there is so much composition, so many surprising relationships, spirit and colour and determination and richness on this canvas that Betty is resigned to it, especially because it makes a huge impact on John. He looked at it three more times in the night. I had also had a Georgian frame made that fits exactly to the fireplace of the same period (the same relief), and painted it today with the negro chauffeur Randolph, who is a factotum for everything. In a few days the Minneapolitans will give their opinion at a 'house-warming party' and becoming accustomed to the guest will follow [...]. (Br III, 234)

Incidentally the comment about the factotum named Randolph was in no way meant disparagingly. One can discern from his Minneapolis correspondence that Kokoschka was 'very [interested] in the negro question' and in early October 1949 attended 'a meeting of the sleeper car and porter union (the most important negro organisation)' because he recognised 'the every help that one can give this highly talented people represents a service for the humanitarian solution of social conflicts. Not the communists alone should address these questions' (Br III, 232).

This also reveals that Kokoschka never forgot his humanist commitment and his curiosity about 'the other'. The correspondence also shows that he was not prepared to share the act of creation with the recipients, but rather to include the observer – in the sense of Wolfgang Kemp – in the painting through the act of creation.[28] His measure remained the convincing invention of a colour-dominant artistic fact. And such a situation could just as well be a face that became something new in a portrait, according to Kokoschka. 'All faces derive from the world of thought,' he claimed in a conversation with Nicole Milhaud, the wife of the composer, in 1966. For Kokoschka, faces were the result of the notion of 'pictures from the soul'.[29] Kokoschka's comment in a letter to Johannes Fürst Schwarzenberg of October 1949 that his painting in essence is nothing other 'than the state of my consciousness expressed in faces' merges into this picture – in visions that are mirrored in faces (Br III, 236). Around the same time, Kokoschka admitted to art dealer and friend Walter Feilchenfeldt that the work on this double portrait drove him to the edge of a nervous breakdown. Though the painting was 'completed to the greatest satisfaction of the victims' (Br III, 234), he certainly saw himself also as the sacrifice to his own creativity – and that from the outset.

There was more stressful portrait painting – this time in Zurich, which nearly disappeared for days on end in the December fog. His victim was the industrialist and collector Georg Bührle – Kokoschka again took a closer look at himself. He could not report anything good to his 'dearest Hold [Sweetness]': 'When I was done with my 6 hours at Bührle's and saw myself in the mirror whilst washing my hands, I had a completely distorted face like a mask, the eyes wide open like two pieces of glass and the mouth as of dough from all the concentration [...]. I hardly wish to speak to anyone' (Br III, 259). The Bührle portrait proved to be a work of hurdles. The subject (he owned the world's largest private collection of Impressionist paintings) was apparently not in agreement with all aspects of the picture. Kokoschka, believing he had completed the portrait before Christmas 1951, found himself forced to seek Bührle out again in April of the following year to rework the disputed parts. Bührle's family continued to remain sceptical. When the first public exhibition of part of Bührle's collection opened its doors in July 1959, one-and-a-half years after the death of its owner, the portrait created by Kokoschka was missing.

Bührle's wealth (he took Swiss citizenship in 1937) came from his armaments company, to which he converted the former machine tool factory Oerlikon after 1924. He supplied half the world – friend and foe alike – with arms, cannons and anti-aircraft guns: to Chiang Kai-shek during the civil war in China and to China's enemy Japan, later to Great Britain, France, the Baltic states, Czechoslovakia, Turkey and the Soviet Union, North as well as South America and, between 1941 and 1944 (sanctioned by the Swiss authorities for good or evil), to Hitler's Germany. As early as 1947, Bührle emerged as a winner of the Cold War and made major business deals with the USA.

That Bührle invested a large portion of his wealth in art might be interpreted as a way of easing his conscience.[30] None of that appears to have disturbed Kokoschka. A commission was a commission (particularly in the post-war years) and everyone had a face. His portrait of the highly cultured armaments magnate shows a distinguished Biedermann (that is, a man of bourgeois respectability) but without the arsonists (to slightly modify the title of Max Frisch's famous play), in his office in Zurich-Oerlikon.[31] The economy of gesture appears to suggest that the sitter wanted to say something; the facial expression is markedly calm, his glance is directed towards the artist. On his right is an Egyptian symbol of power, the bust of a pharaoh with nemes headdress as part of the royal regalia. Behind that, raised, is a pot plant growing somewhat wild, and partially hidden by the plant and a quite mighty head is a painting within the painting: Franz Hodler's view of Lake Geneva. For Kokoschka, this was a prefiguration, namely his relocation to Villeneuve: *pictura est omen*.

Blue tones dominate the portrait. The presence of the pharaoh bust creates the impression of a double portrait. Yet Bührle dominates the scene as patriarch, Croesus and art connoisseur. The somewhat rampant plant in the background may suggest that in the imagination of the sitter there is a less ordered world to be found than is suggested by outer appearances, which shows a person full of composure and superiority.

In any event, Kokoschka's portraiture may have been motivated by his interest in the 'inner person' from early on. That explains what we have pointed to previously: the transparency in his early portraits due to his 'X-ray vision'. As a result, the impression could also develop that

Kokoschka may have seen the inner crimes of his sitter and already included their (lethal) fate in the picture, especially in his images of Bessie Bruce-Loos, Montesquiou-Fezensac and the Conte Verona created around 1910. An early affinity with Egon Schiele's portrait is difficult to dispute, yet it would be inappropriate to reduce it to that alone. The uniqueness of Kokoschka's portraiture lies specifically in an astonishing development in his representation of the person – from the wounded self all the way to the image of women bursting with life.

Among artists, he initially painted the portraits of authors in the ambit of the Expressionist house magazine *Der Sturm*; yet between the Hasenclever portrait from the early Dresden period and the later portraits of Carl Zuckmayer, Agatha Christie and Ezra Pound, there are – unlike in the portraiture work of his admirer Ludwig Meidner – hardly any more writers, excepting his portrait of Claire Goll (1926), which represents less the poet and much more the *femme fatale* successor to Alma Mahler-Gropius. There is a photograph that shows the two at the Parisian Villa des Camélias in 1930/1931, which clearly speaks to an intimate relationship. Significance is found in a letter of Claire's to her (justifiably) ever-jealous poet husband Iwan from the summer of 1927. In it she labels Kokoschka a 'predator', that her Siamese cat Fan-Fan immediately smelt upon coming home.

> I am sitting for K or rather I am laying, but am feeling so sad [...].
> So, I am laying. You well know that I cannot sit still. Perhaps the
> moment is also coming for K, as he has thrown the shredded draw-
> ings at my feet. [...] Being at K's gives me the creeps. Perhaps because
> the studio is furnished with Expressionist despair and – hunger.[32]

Kokoschka was supposed to have looked so cadaverous, according to Claire Goll, that he looked 'moon-coloured', but was too proud to eat the tartlets she had brought along with her. What did she perceive in him? 'Nothing but tragedy and chaos. Uncontrollable explosive material', followed by the somewhat feigned pious hope: 'I hope K does not devour me and I will soon *lay* again for you.'[33] What did Kokoschka see in her? Something gently coquettish that consists primarily of cross-hatched contours in his drawing, with an open face and half-open mouth and the head leisurely propped up by the right hand. The expression of the sitter reveals anticipation and readiness on the path to fulfilment.

Musicians in the Picture

He valued being around musicians, even if he did not usually paint their portraits. His circle of friends – particularly in his final home in Villeneuve, which he called the Villa Delphin – included Swjiatoslaw Richter as well as Wilhelm Kempff, from whom a handwritten programme for a private concert still exists:[34] Bach's Fugue in D major from the first part of the *Wohltemperierten Klaviers* (*The Well-Tempered Clavier*), Beethoven's Sonata Opus 14 as well as the 2nd Movement of Opus 110, in addition to a piano transposition of Gluck's *Klage des Orpheus* (*Plaint of Orpheus*) and *Reigen der seligen Geister* (*Dance of the Blessed Spirits*). An encounter with Paul Hindemith was planned but did not take place.

But how does one make a painting ring with sound? How does one transpose notes into the picture? By painting the portrait of Arnold Schönberg and showing him playing the cello without showing the cello, as Kokoschka did in 1924?

It took a relatively long time before the theme of music in Kokoschka's work was recognised for its own intrinsic value, though it is now difficult to deny its dominance. This pertains, on the one hand (as previously discussed), to the musical treatment of dramatic poems by Ernst Křenek (*Orpheus und Euridyke*, 1925) and Gottfried von Einem (*Die träumenden Knaben*, 1971) and, on the other, to the two paintings in the set of motifs *Die Macht der Musik* (*The Power of Music*, 1918–1920 and 1966–1976), the double portrait *David und Saul* (1966) and the lithographs *Das Konzert I–V* (1921) which depict a sole listener in a portrait-like manner, as well as the nine-part lithographic cycle, based on the Bach Choral Cantata, of a text by Johannes Rist, *O Ewigkeit, du Donnerwort* (*O Eternity, Thou Word of Thunder*) (BWV 20)

(1916/1917). One should also examine Kokoschka's production and set designs for opera performances, ranging from Mozart's *Zauberflöte* (*The Magic Flute*) to Verdi's *Maskenball* (*A Masked Ball*). But this only speaks to the relationship between music and portrait, more specifically the portrait carried *into* the music, especially the self-portrayal in the cantata cycle after Bach. As a fourth lithograph they encompass a self-portrait without context with markedly open – hearing, as it were – eyes and in contrast to the choral cantata a recognisably closed mouth. The sixth lithograph, the *Wanderer im Gewitter* (*Wanderer in the Thunderstorm*), also carries Kokoschka's facial features, but above all the seventh lithograph, with the woman leading the man (also an Alma–Oskar allegory like the eighth image, in which a Kokoschka likeness vainly tries to raise his head from the grave whilst an enthroned Alma-woman weights down the burial mound, a pattern that repeats the entombment theme in the ninth picture in the lithograph series).

Before we turn to Kokoschka's musician portraits, let us examine the pattern here which we have already encountered in connection with Křenek's *Orpheus* opera based on Kokoschka's piece: the painter-poet's sense of pleasure on the prospect of being set to music and thus gaining access to a medium into which he could not directly insert himself creatively. This happened when Gottfried von Einem expressed an interest in setting *Die träumenden Knaben* to music. The project begins to take shape in the summer of 1971. Von Einem announces: 'Frau Furtwängler wrote to me yesterday that I should <u>press the button</u> on composing her lovely text from "Träumenden Knaben" in God's and her name.'[35] He did not yet know whether his eleven-part selection would turn into a song cycle for mezzo soprano or an *a capella* composition or orchestral piece. The recognition, however, that this piece, as Kokoschka let him know, was about a 'love letter', was important to him, which made the 'undertaking even more attractive' for him. And von Einem adds: '[...] It still aggrieves me to this day that I could not carry through my plan to perform your "Orpheus" with Křenek's music in Salzburg around 1950. It is Křenek's, all the more bitter, best opera!' Then readings from Kokoschka's memoirs *Mein Leben* occur in between. Von Einem writes to him soothingly, after

an ensuing close reading on 16 September 1971, whereby he succeeds –
literally – in harmonising a core concern of Kokoschka's with his own
composition principles.

> I calmly read your memoirs in August. The quiet, passionately
> restrained insight that your work and this book allowed to develop
> is inspiring. Every sentence is an opus, like an honest currency
> flourishing with gold. I also marvel at the tenderness as well as the
> serious passages, without wanting to wish for anything else. That
> your rejection of abstract painting sounds almost like my rejection
> of inadequately appealing systems of composition is all of a piece.
> If dissonance is emancipated, not only would consonance be lost
> but the form that derives from both tensions. I value mathematical
> formulations but not the scientific process which such a calculation
> seems to warrant.

An additional feedback loop from the setting to music of Kokoschka's
play to his visual creative work arose again, in fact, two years after von
Einem completed his composition of Opus 41 (1972) for mixed choir,
clarinet and bassoon: '[...] Yesterday I again looked at your illustrations for "Träumenden Knaben" and was enchanted. What unbelievable intuition, what strength to grasp the timeless and to sublimate
youth!'[36]
Kokoschka's relationship to the music of Werner Egk is no less
revealing, in particular to his opera *Irische Legende* (*Irish Legend*,
1955). As a student of Carl Orff's and promoted by Furtwängler, Egk
became one of the most innovative opera composers next to Gottfried
von Einem and the young Hans Werner Henze. He told Kokoschka
that listeners of his *Irische Legende* (the opera is based on the tale *The
Countess Cathleen* by William Butler Years) must have been reminded
of his tale *Ann Eliza Reed*. Accordingly, he begged of Kokoschka 'five
ink drawings or lithos' for his opera, a request that Kokoschka fulfilled for him almost immediately. This demonstrates the intense and
productive interrelationship of Kokoschka and composers, even if in
these two cases (von Einem and Egk) it did not lead to portraits.

To view music in a portrait (specifically also the listeners in the *Konzert* cycle), lending its abstraction a face – in other words, looking the effect of music in the face – must have also motivated Kokoschka's numerous portraits of practising musicians. One should also add that in the case of the Bach Cantata of 1723, Leo Kestenberg – a student of Ferruccio Busoni, who adored Kokoschka's *Orpheus and Eurydike* drama – had spoken with him about Bach's music.[37]

When Kokoschka portrayed the power, or in the sense of Kleist's legend of St Cecilia the 'might', of music, he chose as an emblem for it a wind instrument, a kind of shepherd's pipe or trumpet. The second painting of this type also leads in the title 'Morgen und Abend' ('Morning and Evening'), wherein the music is assigned to the morning. The evening shows itself in feminine shape, being only receptive and hearing more or less rapturously. It has been suggested that the dark-orange hues that play around or stream from the instrument in this second painting (1966–1976) are meant to represent 'the sound'. This seems overly bold because once again Kokoschka was focused on translating an abstract quality, the music, into a figurative arrangement.

The development process for the painting, of unusually long duration for Kokoschka, suggests a late but intense wrestling with the topic of music, perhaps happening in stages. One can imagine that his conversation with Nicole Milhaud about his relationship to music, theatre and art education – which took place in April 1966 in Cadenabbia, where Kokoschka created the portrait of Konrad Adenauer – may have at least aided in provoking this engagement with music. In this conversation, Kokoschka once again reiterates his relationship to musical life in his time: his friendship with Anton von Webern, which is mirrored in two portraits; his formative musical experience as chorister in the Piaristenkirche zu Wien and the vision of heaven as promoted by Maulbertsch's ceiling fresco there combined with the abruptness of his voice breaking; the *Tristan und Isolde* performance at the Wiener Staatsoper under the direction of Gustav Mahler (the double portrait *Die Windsbraut*, which was originally supposed to be titled *Tristan und Isolde*, could thus also be seen as an attempt at a pictorial transposition of a musical art work); as well as the later friendship with Wilhelm Furtwängler, who began to ruminate in front of the *Thermopylen* triptych in his studio at the Villa Delphin in Villeneuve. In his obituary of Furtwängler in January 1955, Kokoschka became more explicit: this conductor 'was a visionary. As he began to speak, actually began to think out loud, in front of the painting of the Thermopylae, clear and determined, but not as of this world any longer, I suddenly believed then to be witnessing a secret mission for my guest' (Br VI, 40).

The painting *Saul und David*, which Kokoschka gifted to the Tel Aviv Museum, also falls in the year 1966. It attests again to the effect of the harp-playing David, in other words the might of music, on the power seeker Saul who lets his spear rest and becomes contemplative in the face of music. Animal images of monkey and peacock, as well as an overall lighthearted atmosphere, reinforced by David's smile and Saul's unusually pensive grin, allow one to suspect an intentional reference to the Orpheus myth.

The conversation about music from 1966 includes Kokoschka's renewed acknowledgement of Mozart, but also of Shakespeare in music, and Beethoven, because they knew every little emotion of human experience, as well as Bach, whose harmonies he compared to the eternal patterns in abstract-geometric Islamic art. In any case, Kokoschka only has positive comments to make on the abstract theme in the context of Bach and Schönberg.

> Schönberg's ears, his sense of hearing, his imagination must have been in a world of highest mathematics. In my opinion, Bach communicates the best impression of that which is meant by 'abstract'. Because every appearance is abstract, and we know nothing of that which is in reality.[38]

However, this does not provide much insight into Kokoschka's creative practices in his treatment of music. He was eighty years old before he acquired a piano for his house in Villeneuve, on which great performers such as Wilhelm Kempff and Andor Foldes played for him. The latter played Beethoven's *Pathétique* for him one day; the pianist later put on record that Kokoschka grabbed a piece of paper after the first few bars and handed him, Foldes, a finished portrait sketch at the end.[39] Music triggered a creative process in Kokoschka that usually focused on the image of the trigger – that is, the performer. Yehudi Menuhin saw in Kokoschka the herald of a 'humane message'; the London and landscape pictures appealed to Menuhin the most, though 'over time' Kokoschka disregarded the detail in favour of the 'colour' of the 'weight and the form'.[40] It is this humanism that brought Kokoschka into contact with the great cellist and uncompromising opponent of Franco, Pablo (Pau) Casals. The two portraits he did of Casals in Sierre in the autumn of 1954 reflect the quiet brilliance of this humanist at the cello. In both cases, the image composition orientates itself around the interplay between the bodies of the instrument and the instrumentalist. The horizontal bow forms the lower edge of the picture, while the second portrait draws the practitioner closer in, appropriately enlarging the instrument and allowing the scroll to distinctly tower above the head of the performer. Yet the details (in the sense of Menuhin's comment) do not become any more visible – except the strings, which literally appear tangible. The bald, powerful head of the artist, the upper half of the cello and – as in Kokoschka's self-portraits – the paw-like gripping elderly hands, dominate the painting. The face, recognisable more as a result of the graduated light colours than the contouring, seems both open and closed at the same time. It thus only responds to the playing music in that – as with the background – it seems brightened. It almost seems as though the sounds emanate from the cello like a halo. Beyond that, the face of the portrayed performer remains untouched by the music. However, the proximity of the cello's neck to the face and left ear, as well as the similarity in body shape with that of the cello – reinforced further by the related vertical brushstrokes in applying the blue and brown tones for clothing and wood – speak to the great intimacy between soloist and instrument. The cellist eavesdrops on the music that he is bringing forth from his instrument, an impression also evoked by the many photographs of Casals playing. The face resembles Casals so unmistakeably that it, conversely, appears to be composed from mere intimations. It appears concentrated and yet consists of the traces of deep life experiences. The paintbrush obviously did not want to succumb to a smoothing-out of the facial features.

In Kokoschka's work, however, there are also portraits of musicians that cause one to forget that music was their metier. His images of Michael Tippett (1963), whom he personally valued highly (perhaps also because Anna Kallin introduced them to each other), do not suggest, even with the merest charcoal line, Tippett the composer of the oratorio *A Child of Our Time* (1944).

In musician portraits – and this may have driven his special interest in this genre – Kokoschka was able to translate the abstract of music into the objectively human, seeing the person behind the notes. Thus, in light of his otherwise passionate rejection of anything abstract in art, Kokoschka's open ear for Anton von Webern and Arnold Schönberg is thoroughly surprising. When he hears the third and fourth string quartets by Schönberg, he feels compelled to write a letter of homage.

> Bach, Beethoven and Schönberg are the last composers who can build a musical construct which can stand for an organic world, as such must hold true as nature creates, for example, in crystal, in the plant, in the living being. All music around them is either galvanised, artificially motivated made-up folklore (which can no longer be considered thinking since the iron wagon of progress has made one country after the other, one continent after the other 'equal') or purely abstract tone geometry with queer sounds and odd effects in order to attract the listener. (Br III, 226 f)

When all's said and done, Kokoschka was definitely conscious of this idiosyncratic tension in his relationship to Modernism. That he should use music, in particular, to try to make it clearer without allowing an unresolvable inner contradiction to come out of it is nevertheless astonishing. He clearly succeeded at this in his letter of November 1962 to an 'unknown high school graduate', characteristically written with educational intent and as an equivalent to understanding his imperative 'learn to see'. First, Kokoschka's finding: 'In no epoch of mankind was representative art [...] object-less. A lack of objects is equivalent to formless-ness, chaos. Every creative person is obligated to the spiritual process of perceiving unknown human development opportunities' (Br IV, 132). Kokoschka then redirects attention to musical experience and in particular to Anton von Webern.

> By chance yesterday I heard Webern's Italian Quartet Opus 28 and afterwards Beethoven's Quartet Nr 11 Opus 95. A nature is perceived and formed into an object of an artwork in late Beethoven as well as the unfinished work of the prematurely dead Webern, as it has never been formed before these two innovators. All the natural images of human emotional life – dreaming, worrying, humble devotion, tender affection and rage, deadly melancholy, yes, even strange sorrow, sound effects which should stand for themselves, based on mathematical theories or even dependent on the coincidence of electronic machines and equally from the noise of the pile of people in a world of mechanised civilisation, yes finally also folklore – are suddenly erased as though with a sponge from the board. (Br IV, 133)

Nature images of existentialist experience: Kokoschka orientates himself on these with the intention to critique civilisation. And further, and more importantly:

> Abstractions are taken from the perception of elementary forces of nature like lightning, thunder, sea breeze – or they no longer seem to be related to people. It is as though man has left nature and thus himself. And now, my dear friend, you notice the essential difference in the work of these two composers compared to the spiritual attitude of present society for which existence is meaningless. The difference is like that of snow and ashes. Both pale, under the snow it is greening, under the ashes something died.
> I am no musician, but hear from the speech of the old one, deaf Beethoven as well as that of the murdered Webern[41] breathing in ozone-rich air, sounds like grasses, stalks of reeds rubbing against

each other, harmonies as from heavily falling masses on the propor-
tionately resisting layers of air, expressive as bird song only meaningful to birds, perceptions like veil dropping upon veil from my
nakedness when nothing meaningful can be done nor known nor
seen nor heard. (Ibid)

Notice the nature references in the portraits, the incorporation of the
animal into the field of vision; in Kokoschka's work, they also represent a modern person's harking back to a connection to the nature of
his origin. The animal is the anti-abstract creature per se because the
abstract has lost one thing: the reference to instinct.

A Glimpse of Animals

Seen from an Orphean perspective, it is in any case logical that we
now switch from music to the living creature: the animal as motif in
Kokoschka's work. After all, it was Orpheus who knew how to tame
wild animals with his singing, his heavenly inspired music of nature;
he knew how to reach them on their own wavelength in order to harmoniously capture them. Kokoschka tried to reach *all* forms of living
things. As he recalled in an exchange with Heinz Spielmann, who at
the time was compiling a general interpretation of the fans Kokoschka
created for Alma Mahler[42] – they were meant to be 'love letters in
picture language', for which he attributed his inspiration to 'Flemish
books of hours' and 'Irish incunabula'. That, Kokoschka continued,
pertained particularly to the early fans, 'that don't have decorative
intent, but rather organic interweaving of man, animal, plant, spirit,
winged creature as in the Book of Kells' (Br IV, 203).

Kokoschka focused on this 'interweaving' from early on, whereby
the animal also found its way into still lifes. One thinks of the image
of a sphinx-like *Katze* (*Cat*) of 1910, the *Liebespaar mit Katze* (*Lovers
with Cat*, 1917) or the works of deer at the watering trough created
in London Zoo and the mandrill shown in his laboriously tamed
wildness, as well as the tigon (both 1926); one is also reminded of the

Clown mit Hund (*Clown with Dog*, 1948). In Scotland's Elrig he drew *Pferde in Rot* (*Horses in Red*) in front of a ruin and in Polperro, as we have seen, an allegorical crab. The 'Träumenden Knaben' are close to the fish. Animals often belong among the accessories, for example, in the *Mädchen mit Katze* (*Girl with Cat*) images, but they can also become dominant from the periphery as in the case of the painting *Mal Occhio* (*Evil Eye*, 1973/1974) in which the frog and bird simultaneously appear to be the object and the vision of the evil eye.

The still life *Putto mit Kaninchen* (*Putto with Rabbit*) has an expressive-surreal effect; the title is unsatisfactory because it ignores the cat which dominates it. Generally, this painting serves as a statement that Kokoschka has left behind any Jugendstil ornamentation and anticipates the explosiveness of colour in later work. In addition, it is an allegorical representation of the fragility of his relationship with Alma. Let us first view this picture for what it is and what it represents. The rabbit and cat are of a related style both in colour and in respect of the broad brushstrokes. The colouration indicates a tiger cat, whose light markings are even more prominent in the rabbit's coat pattern. Relegated to the picture's left edge by a bare tree trunk, but distinct and thus kept noticeably bright, is the putto, pensively reclining, turned away from both animals, its facial expression decidedly un-angelic, instead grim with wide-open eyes that seem almost threateningly alive. The background is kept dark; one might imagine an extinct volcano in the soaring mountain, a hint at a group of houses that seem deserted in the reddish-brown hues. A table-like and thus still-life-like construct, equally hinted at, occupies the right foreground. The point of this picture is that the objects of this *nature morte* are absolutely essential. The tiger cat in particular gives the painting a sense of movement atypical for a still life in multiple respects; the powerful tail is upright, the left paw turned in and the head turns towards the rabbit; an attentive communication between the two animals seems to develop, from which the putto totally withdraws. Alone the bare, crookedly looming trunk is sufficient for imagining, the *nature morte* or dead nature of a still life, which is juxtaposed against the cat's concentrated life dynamic.

The presence of an animal can also have an ironic function, for example, the chaperoning dog in the portraits of Adele Astaire (1926) and the nude paintings of Elza Temáry (1926/1927). Irony and deadly seriousness determine the interplay of animal presence and bestial politics in the political allegory *Das rote Ei* of 1940/1941. The stolen, wounded chicken has laid a red egg on the negotiating table in Munich in 1938 against the background of a Prague skyline and, with difficulty, flies away. A large cat lounges under the table as an allegory of France – like the English lion – while the two dictators pant for the egg. The cat seems to look through the table from beneath as a mouse sits on the table's edge: Czechoslovakia as a sacrifice to the Munich Agreement, beleaguered by power-hungry figures.

In Scotland during the Second World War, Kokoschka focused more on fish, sheep, cows and game birds. Among his works from 1943/1944, the watercolours *Abgeschossene Wildente* (*Shot-down Mallard*) and *Toter Fasan* (*Dead Pheasant*) are especially impressive. They become emblems of senseless death; their ability to fly and their colourfulness are seen to be sacrificed to an absurd lust for killing.

The animal in Kokoschka's paintings can epitomise the animalistic in life, as do the animal images of a Delacroix – the artfully or sense-lessly sacrificed creature. It is in no way an accessory; the artist has deemed it portrait worthy. We cannot help – and, according to Koko-schka, are not meant to be able to do otherwise – but see in *Mandrill* and *Tigon* portraits of equal worth to those of humans. In 1926 Koko-schka saw them as sovereigns of their respective species imprisoned in the zoo.

Art as Power Symbol: Portraits of Politicians

I must paint Gandhi before he dies [...], I have to paint this picture which may lead to a turning of thinking if it is elevated to a saintly icon and distributed a hundred thousand-fold through reproduc-tion. Only I alone can paint such a godlike man today, who sac-rifices himself for world peace, who has more authority than all governments of the world together, without having to rely on a state

police, concentration camp, army, navy, bank capital or civil serv-
ants as instruments of power. He is a miracle! Only one cannot wait
until he has starved to death or until the Russo-American conflict
has made minds so daft that an appeal to the human, godly idea of
brotherhood falls on deaf ears. (Br III, 192)

That is how Kokoschka described and rationalised the politician's portrait, which was meant to become his most important in the Hotel Bellevue in Sierre in September 1947. As we know, it did not come to that
because a Hindu nationalist assassinated Gandhi only four months
later. In the meantime, Kokoschka painted the portrait of Winterthur
art patron Werner Reinhardt, the owner of the castle tower in Muzot
and erstwhile Rilke benefactor.

Kokoschka would always find the essence at the end when the
'picture is almost finished', as he admitted in the letter. At the same
time, he revealed the secret of his art in matters of landscape portrait
– he had just painted the Matterhorn in all its majesty. This 'painting' came out completely differently, 'as transparent as glass with many
sudden, ambush-like colourful surprises and enormous depth and
height. These effects are based on a clear axis positioning, visual focus
in its intersection under the picture's horizon' (Br III, 191). In intense
phases of work such as this, portraits and landscapes by Kokoschka
could literally go hand in hand. Next to the Reinhardt portrait he also
painted the *Rhonelandschaft* (*Rhone Landscape*).

We have already encountered this phenomenon in Kokoschka's
work in different ways; from time to time he felt forced to paint the
powerful or at least influential, a tendency which grew stronger in his
later work not least because *they* sought him out in order to be painted
by the erstwhile 'super rascal'. The aura of the powerful and the aura
of the artist overlapped. What we have already discussed in the cases
of Masaryk and Maisky continued with greater strength after 1950 –
Kokoschka encountered the greats of politics on equal terms.

'Perhaps I shall paint Hindenburg,' Kokoschka once speculated –
as we recall – at the Berlin Hotel Adlon in January 1926 (Br II, 149).
After all, he then painted an Arab tribal chieftain, the Marabout. Now,

in the first half of December 1950, he painted the portrait of Theodor Heuss on the Viktorshöhe in the Office of the Federal President in Bonn on the Rhine. He attested to the Bundespräsident that he was 'ideal as a model' (Br III, 246). The model, however, ascribed quite a bit more to the artist: 'They were delightful hours,' Heuss reported in a letter at the end of January 1951. 'The spirit of old Austria was visiting. Some who see the painting are enthusiastic, others do not think it is me. Kokoschka himself says that he wanted to capture the "teacher".' Heuss astutely judges Kokoschka.

> I personally consider Kokoschka to be probably the most important figure of all in contemporary painting since the death of Edvard Munch and was delighted when people had the idea that I should let myself be painted by him for a museum. The picture is wonderfully colourful. It is certainly not just Heuss, but also Kokoschka. Every portrait is a statement about the painter himself, after all what would be our interest in portraits of the past. Certainly not only the model, of whom we often do not know anything, but the portraitist.[43]

Though there is no evidence that Kokoschka also discussed Comenius with Heuss, as he once did with Masaryk, we can nevertheless surmise that the great Czech thinker and humanist did come up. In a speech at the Institute for Foreign Relations in 1951, Heuss called for an 'elementary school for dealing with foreign countries' to be established. And what followed sounded very much like Kokoschka–Comenius: 'this intercourse with foreign countries is a far too beautiful, creative and productive matter as that we should force it into a world view mould of the usual sort.'[44]

Kokoschka clearly also took a political position as a result of his portraits of Theodor Heuss and the mayor of Hamburg, Max Brauer, and later of Konrad Adenauer, Ludwig Erhard and Chancellor Helmut Schmidt (a profound admirer of Kokoschka's who invited him to accompany him on his China trip in 1975 – which Kokoschka had to decline due to the state of his health. 'Max Frisch filled your place with dignity', Schmidt reported to him afterwards).[45] It was the same with his portraits of Israeli politicians, the 'Jerusalem Faces' – from Prime Minister Golda Meir to the Mayor of Jerusalem, Teddy Kollek. That Kokoschka was influenced can be clearly discerned from the correspondence, which he often carried on with the politicians he painted after their sittings. For the most part – as long as one sets aside the portraits of Adenauer and Erhard – they reflect acknowledgements of a left-leaning liberal European who cared about nothing more than to prevent 'European youth' possibly becoming 'cynical' of any conception of an ideal Europe', as he wrote to his friend the Social Democrat member of the Bundestag Adolf Arndt on 3 June 1952 from Zurich (Br III, 265).

The worry over Europe in the days of the Cold War occupied Kokoschka as much as the continued existence of the state of Israel, which connected him as much to Axel Springer as to those of the Jerusalem portraits. He even supported the Israel Fund in Paris (Br IV, 196). He appropriately gave great credit to Adenauer for his commitment to German–Israeli reconciliation.

Kokoschka had no illusions about Britain's politics towards Europe. British policy would never 'promote, much less tolerate a European Union of States', he opined in June 1952; and, in a letter to Theodor Heuss of 2 December 1953, Kokoschka cited the different path taken since the English Reformation under Henry VIII as the underlying reason for this. Britain has become 'parochial', marginalised and provincial, 'which almost leads to a forgetting of the shared destiny with Europe there today' (Br IV, 13). By contrast he saw the European issue as an ongoing task: 'Being European means to fight the barbarian within oneself again and again [...]', we read in a letter of Kokoschka's to Max Brauer of March 1958 (Br IV, 78).

These portraits alone show that they had been painted by an artist who was still highly politically aware and engaged. Kokoschka's portraiture had long since ceased to focus on the tubercular nobility as it once was in the sanatorium in Leysin, but rather on worldly wise politicians. The prematurely moribund belonged to his past as a portraitist, even if their images had brought him fame; now he was interested in the politicians who were still decisive in their advanced years. However, this did not preclude his painting a 'Mädchen mit Katze' and a couple with the title *Der verschmähte Liebhaber* (*The Rejected Lover*, 1966) in the meantime; this motif was deep-seated. Yet two triptychs formed the actual backdrop to the work of his later period – to the portrait of the *Seemannsbraut* (*Sailor's Bride*, 1967/1968) as well as to the (Hamburg) *Sturmflut* (*Storm Tide in Hamburg*, 1962), to *TIME, Gentlemen, Please* (1971/1972) and to *Ecce Homines* (*Behold Humanity*, 1972) – namely *Die Prometheus Saga* (1950) and, most importantly, *Die Thermopylen* (1954). This, his most important image sequence, could also have the title 'Herodotus Narrates', as the narration had become more important than ever to him. From Sierre, he wrote to his sister in Prague in May 1947 that he was working into the night 'on stories' that he rewrote again and again 'until I believe that they are satisfying to me'. Because 'I cannot risk that I show weakness in this area, where I am an outsider or intruder to the public' (Br III, 188). When his volume of tales appeared under the title *Spur im Treibsand* (*Tracks in the Quicksand*) in 1956, Kokoschka would endorse himself to his old girlfriend Anna Kallin in a letter: '[...] No one today writes, narrates like this!!!' (Br IV, 18). He was correct in this in every sense, even if the sentence is reminiscent of Richard Wagner's comment on a sketch for *Tristan und Isolde*: 'Nevertheless let it be said: no one is better than me.'[46]

Despite repeatedly insisting he had nothing to say about his art, Kokoschka would comment most thoroughly on the two triptychs. In addition, the Herodotus figure remained important enough to him that he provided a Herodotus illustration for the title page of the *Times Literary Supplement* of 13 October 1961 on the main topic 'European Exchanges'. Kokoschka's neo-humanistic belief was behind this. Europe could not really exist without its mythological legacy and the consciousness tied up in it.[47] In his sketches Kokoschka presents the narrating historian Herodotus as a marginal figure with self-portrait-like features. In the finished painting the soothsayer Megistias appears in place of Herodotus (and Kokoschka).

Portrait of a Myth: The Thermopylae

'Tell Sparta, we, whose record meets thine eye, / Obey'd the Spartan laws – and here we lie!'[48] This distich from Friedrich Schiller's elegy *Der Spaziergang* (*The Walk*, 1795) inspired like no other the tragiheroic re-Hellenisation of German cultural consciousness.[49] It recalls the attempted defence of the narrow pass at Thermopylae by 300 Spartans, 700 Thespians and 400 Thebans under the command of King Leonidas of Sparta against the Persian superpower, who heavily outnumbered them. Only the Theban contingent survived. Usually mention is only made of Leonidas and his Spartans. The Greeks under Themistocles were more successful in the ensuing naval battle at Salamis.

In his *Histories*, Herodotus describes the Persian military parade in gigantic dimensions, particularly to allow the achievements of the numerically far inferior Greek units to shine through all the more brightly.

(National) myths want to be retold again and again. Their fictionalisation begins in this case with Herodotus' device of declaring the erstwhile exiled king of Sparta, Damaratus, a confidant and advisor to the Persian King Xerxes. On Leonidas' side, the soothsayer Megistias is notable for his prediction of the certain catastrophe and yet remaining with his king. Herodotus now claims in his report to know the names of all 300 fallen Spartans; he thus emphasises their individuality, which was not to be obliterated by their demise.

Applied to Germany, the Thermopylae myth is seen as the heroic sacrifice for the fatherland, though it had a dubious career. Next to the so-called Nibelungen loyalty, the Thermopylae became a metaphor for perseverance in National Socialist propaganda, for example, in Hermann Göring's radio address of 30 January 1943 shortly before the capitulation of the 6th Army in Stalingrad: 'Should you come to Germany, then report that you saw us fight in Stalingrad, as the law, the law for the security of our people commanded.'[50] And still in February 1945 Hitler compared the situation of the Reich with the Thermopylae: 'One is reminded of Leonidas and his three hundred Spartans.'[51]

What of that had reached Kokoschka in exile? Had he perhaps read Heinrich Böll's short story *Wanderer, kommst du nach Spa...* (*Wanderer, Come You to Spa...*) which exploded the Thermopylae myth like no other text? In it, a young, heavily wounded soldier is admitted to a temporary military hospital somewhere in Germany in a town that is threatened to fall under sustained fire. He has to suffer through murderous pain and febrile delirium, but he recognises the improvised operating theatre as the art studio of his old humanist grammar school. Still written on the board in his handwriting is: 'Wanderer, come you to Spa...' He himself is as mutilated (he has lost both arms and his right leg) as his sentence of long ago. One final word of support is rendered to him, the war casualty, by the former caretaker from whom he once purchased his breaktime milk.[52]

Was Kokoschka familiar with the hero painting, Jacques-Louis David's *Léonidas aux Thermopyles* (1814), which shows the Spartan as a naked (meaning: pure), but helmeted hero?

Unlike the poetic place of cultural memory, visual portraits of myths consist of individual portraits. Through them, the artist says the same as Herodotus when he claims to have known all the fallen Spartans by name; in the mythological dressing-up, the individual counts. In his often reworked *Bekenntnis zu Hellas* (*Confession to Hellas*, 1961–1967), Kokoschka complains of the 'hecatombs of young people', which must fall victim to a 'false politics of world wars', 'before they are offered the chance to mature' (DSW III, 307). He may also have created his Thermopylae triptych in their memory, especially because the individual person certainly appears in it – with a face or faceless, as with the impaled child in the third picture. One is reminded, in spite of oneself, of Ossip Mandelstam's great phrase: 'Above us barbaric skies, and yet we are still Hellenes',[53] except that Kokoschka's triptych reverses this relationship. In his three-part painting the sky seems to have a consistently Greek brightness, regardless of what barbarism is taking place under it.

Nevertheless, this triptych is not lacking in lighter effects, for example, the bright bucolic landscape in the left leaf of the painting, from which Leonidas takes his leave as he does from his wife before heading off into the unimaginable horror. He carries a symbolic eye on his shield, which is meant to protect him and seems to represent clairvoyance. In the background of the middle picture, essentially the battle picture, the shining light of Apollo appears as the scorned yet unmistakable bearer of hope and, in the right leaf, the spiritual icon of freedom has loosed its chains and escapes the horror – half an Apollo, half an Orpheus, whom the bloodhounds can no longer harm. We see two naked, pure shining lights to which the erstwhile charisma of Leonidas has transferred itself. In the brightness of the background of the third painting, the naval battle of Salamis that will free Greece is already unfolding.

From a structural conception perspective, a certain similarity to that of the painting *Léonidas aux Thermopyles* is evident, except that David's naked Leonidas becomes Kokoschka's naked Apollo and the genius of freedom. The hopeful brightness of the background is found in both. Kokoschka, however, designs a three-part narrative scene consisting of Leonidas, Apollo and Freedom, wherein the middle part reveals a more heterogeneous trinity: Megistias, the traitorous fool Ephialtes and the seemingly naïve young warrior whom the traitor will deceitfully trick.

The question remains why Kokoschka chose this loaded myth in Herodotus' lore, particularly at that point in time (1953/1954). That his triptych found a home in a lecture theatre at Hamburg University says just as much as the fact that the conductor Wilhelm Furtwängler (with his own archaeological knowledge that he had from his father, the renowned archaeologist Adolf Furtwängler, and his friend Ludwig Curtius) apparently behaved in front of these three paintings in Kokoschka's Villa Delphin in a similar way to Georg Trakl in his time in front of Kokoschka's *Windsbraut*: mutely contemplating or mumbling to himself.

Obviously, Kokoschka referenced the fears and scarcely dared hopes in the early years of the Cold War with this painting. Even if it were inappropriate to project the East–West conflict of the time onto the triptych, it really cannot be detached from this background. The parallel contrast for Herodotus between culture and barbarism can be seen

in Kokoschka's painting, his baroque colour and shape intensity contrasting with the shining light but also through the goblin-like figure
of Ephialtes, the traitor in the ranks of the Spartans. Almost mis-
chievously, Kokoschka noted a trick in the treatment of well-known
motifs.

> In sketches based on ancient times it is occasionally recommended
> to give the object a slight twist, to give it a turn in order to bring
> forth a mood to the sense buried in the antique document which
> classicist rules keep hidden from the composer. (DSW III, 308)

His Silenus-like Ephialtes embodies such a 'twist'; this one is meant –
as previously mentioned – to have preoccupied Wilhelm Furtwängler
in particular. ('Mutely he watched Kokoschka until he had painted the
traitor Ephialtes.')[54]

With the *Thermopylae* Kokoschka had portrayed a perilous period,
totally without a heroic ethos (the departing Leonidas bidding farewell to wife and country in the left leaf does so without any form of
heroism), also without Böll-like radicalism in the appraisal of the
legacy of this myth but simply preserving the set mythological con-
figurations, infused with surprising signs of hope.

Perhaps the most impressive personal appraisal of Kokoschka's
mythological picture composition was provided by his old friend Paul
Westheim. From his Mexican exile, he wrote to Kokoschka in April
1955.

> Dear Ko!
> I thank you for the impressive Thermopylae folio. [...] What great
> work, what grandiose vision! Painting which offers all the magic,
> the sensuality, the riches of the metier. I was deeply touched by the
> position that your preface underlines: the barbarity of the so will-
> ingly glorified victor. One wants to shout repeatedly at those and
> their great public who are captivated by hero glorification that there
> can be no victor without those who are plunged into misery and
> despair as a result of the victory. Van Gogh, who was such a great

man, once wrote: 'That which costs human lives I find barbaric, and I do not respect that.' And that was not yet the time of the ideologues, human lives still had a value.

Well, there you have it, the Greeks and their belief in man as the measure of all things? One can also see that another way. With that principle they enthroned the gods of old Asia and made them a décor of life. This rationalism, which believed it could be lifted above the magical-mythical powers, certainly served 'progress'. But can one ask whether that was precisely the beginning of barbarisation?

The new triptych is evidence of an unending productivity. 'Full of character internally', as, I believe, old Dürer once said. My congratulations.

Warmest

Your Westheim[55]

Kokoschka felt understood. This feeling applied in an even more objective sense to the meaning the art critic Walter Kern ascribed to this triptych; Westheim's reference to the folio related to the edition provided by Kern, *Oskar Kokoschka, Thermopylae*: a triptych with texts by Kokoschka and Kern for this three-part colossal painting.[56] During the development of *Thermopylae*, he was also able to exchange thoughts on purely technical questions with Kern. As is well known, the craftsmanship, the knowledge of materials and process, remained the vital underpinnings of Kokoschka's creative efforts to the end. It soon became apparent that the *Thermopylae*, quite literally, blistered – which is to say that little bubbles appeared in the paintwork. What to do? The confidant Kern in Winterthur had advice. On 5 December 1953, he recommended the following.

In the meantime you have received a little bottle of Rembrandt Retouching-Varnish. I had it sent from Zurich. I would recommend you scrape off the blistered spots on your large canvas with a palette knife and perhaps afterwards work it a bit with pumice stone. Then apply the varnish with a brush. It dries immediately. I am certain that you can then paint on it. It is a somewhat tedious effort with such a large canvas and it will take several little bottles. However, should the varnish prove itself, I will happily have a number of additional little bottles sent to you after you give it a try. It would be regrettable if the wonderfully conceived canvas could not be taken further.[57]

The technique is believed to have helped. What had been created there could rightly be termed an allegory of the period of time in which barbaric and humane behaviours met. In his reflections on the *Thermopylae*, Kokoschka addressed his primary objective without beating around the bush: to reinstate the sophist separation of aesthetic and ethic. He begins his thoughts with a sensational question: 'Why did the Persian despot [Xerxes] allow the corpse of Leonidas to be mutilated and nailed to the cross by the guards?' (DSW III, 321). At the same time he was concerned with the question of what Herodotus wanted to achieve with his account of the battle at the Thermopylae in the seventh book of his *The Histories*.[58] The question was also relevant to Kokoschka himself because, in freely visualising Herodotus' description, he also made the Greek historian's intention his own. Kokoschka found:

A barbarian is without history and also timeless which is why he also belongs to every era, including ours. A time in which fortitude, love of freedom, humanity sound suspicious because they do not produce a standardised mass mentality. In the totalitarian state one logically liquidates the carrier of such character traits. (DSW III, 322)

Ten years after the end of the Second World War, Kokoschka spoke of the 'cynical pride of the Western World about their own self-destruction; our soul sees their picture in an art that has its mission in the gloating rejection of all that was previously held to be humanitarianism. It reflects the image of our state of mind' (ibid). With that he meant less his *Thermopylae*, but rather – once again – abstractions as a sign of Modernism.

In his interpretation, Walter Kern emphasised Kokoschka's intention to achieve a moral-pedagogical effect with this painting trio. At the same time, however, he showed that this work gave precedence to art in an impressive verbal picture.

> The moral idea comes apart in the creative idea, dissolves like salt in water, thus becoming invisible to the eye, but it does not remain hidden to the sense of taste. The narration dissolves and now appears, accessible to the eye and sensibility, as a gestalt.[59]

In that year (1955), incidentally, Kokoschka also received Hermann Melville's novel *Bartleby* (1853/1856) for Christmas from Kern, whose publishing house had brought it out in a new edition. *Bartleby* is the story of a man who rejects life; he settles into his office at a law firm on Wall Street, copies contracts day in, day out, no longer leaves the office and is finally led away by the police. He is a person without an actual biography and the crassest possible counter-figure to Kokoschka. Towards the end of the story it appears that Bartleby had previously worked in a deadletter office – Gogol and Kafka sent greetings. And Walter Kern seriously believed that this novel would have meaning for Kokoschka. He seemed to know the *Thermopylae* painting better than its creator at this point in time.

Minor Digression: When Graham Sutherland Painted Winston Churchill in 1954

Originally Kokoschka wanted to paint all four, the Greats: Stalin, Truman, de Gaulle and Churchill. As we know, that did not happen, which his friend and confidant in Vienna, Communist City Counsellor for Culture Viktor Matejka, profoundly regretted: 'They are missing so to speak from the biography of the artist, the person, the poet, the writer, the politician Oskar Kokoschka.'[60] It is certain that Kokoschka was spared quite a bit as a result because he had it comparatively easy with the politicians that he did paint. The work with

Heuss led to true friendship. Friendly relationships also developed with Theodor Körner, Konrad Adenauer and Teddy Kollek.

This type of collaboration between model and artist was by no means a matter of course, as is shown by the example of Graham Sutherland, the greatest portraitist in England in the post-war period (both artists, by the way, died in 1980, Sutherland on 17 February and Kokoschka five days later). A first difference between the two is easily identified. Sutherland sought out the powerful while, by contrast, the powerful and famous went out of their way to find Kokoschka. When Agatha Christie requested that Kokoschka paint her portrait, he let the gallerist and *homme de lettres* Wolfgang Georg Fischer (who acted as intermediary between them) know that it would cost the world-famous crime novelist quite a bit; Kokoschka also shared a missive from Adenauer according to which Graham Sutherland (who apparently had also attempted to obtain a portrait commission from Christie) 'usually brings two photographers when he paints a portrait' (Br IV, 215). In Kokoschka's view, this was the most reprehensible thing that could be said about another artist. It is unclear whether he knew why Sutherland had begun to act that way, the reason being his work on the disastrous – in Churchill's view – portrait of the statesman in the autumn of 1954. The episode, which has entered into the history of the portrait as *causa Sutherland*,[61] is retold here because it shows how problem-laden painting a portrait can be, particularly when the sitter is not only a great statesman but also thinks of himself as competent in matters of painting.

The portrait was commissioned by the House of Commons to celebrate Churchill's eightieth birthday on 30 November 1954. The sittings took place at Chartwell, Churchill's estate in Kent. The autumnal light conditions were less advantageous for Sutherland's work compared with those of the spring-like Lake Como in the Villa La Collina from which Kokoschka's Adenauer portrait profited. In addition, Sutherland was having to cope with a decidedly moody, surly model, which is why the photographs of Churchill by Elsbeth Juda became indispensable to Sutherland's work.

Churchill disliked the portrait – to such an extent that he let

Sutherland know it was not presentable for this occasion. At the beginning of the first sitting Churchill had even asked his portraitist: 'How will you paint me? As a bulldog or as an angel?' The face then resembled more the bulldog. Broad, immovably he sits there, the feet as if cut off, no Hero of the Nation, more like a cantankerous, apparently truculent prime minister with time etched indelibly in his face. A head sketch of Churchill, also drawn by Sutherland, has a decidedly more artistically challenging impact.

Despite Churchill's considerable reservations, the painting was revealed during a ceremony in Westminster Hall in front of both Houses of Parliament and was ridiculed by Churchill in his address as an obvious sign of 'modern art'. Sutherland had to endure this abuse in front of the BBC's rolling cameras as he sat in the back row of the VIP gallery.

But there was worse to come. Contrary to Parliament's plan, this painting did not find a permanent place in Westminster; rather, at the urging of Churchill's wife Clementine, it was burned in the garden at Chartwell. One tries to imagine a Churchill portrait by Kokoschka and the aged prime minister's comments on it. Michael Hamburger dedicated a three-part lyrical monologue, *Dead Artist to Dead Statesman*, based on the *causa Sutherland*, to the problem with Modernism and the – public – handling of it. The second part confronts this complex unrestrainedly with hypotheses and questions, which determined the discourse on Modernism then (in the 1950s) and still does today.

> The work, the person, the name –
> What chasms divide them!
> A silent maker sits at the daily table,
> His only care those lines that he cannot trace,
> Words that he cannot join, sounds never heard
> Until they come to him from the place never searched,
> The place that's beyond all searching –
> [...]
> Or the man, still fleshed and placed,

Is called upon to do this or that
On the strength of his name;
And asks himself: Is it I?
Will the work move the hand again
It made use of before?
Which, for my sort, 'modern',
Makes commissions a thorough rehearsal
For the ghostly part that's yours now and mine.
'Modern'? What can it mean or matter
To us who are out of time?
You, a holiday painter, chose Provence
For landscapes done in the wake
Of paintyers once 'modern' who worked there.
Worked, not relaxed. That's where the difference lies –
And, no holiday stateman, you knew it [...].[62]

What is Modernism? Is triumph over modernity inherent in the creative work of Modernism? Is such a victory even necessary or simply a rhetorical-polemical gesture? The modestly talented landscape painter named Winston S Churchill openly condemned an artist who, in addition to Jacob Epstein, John Piper, Barbara Hepworth and Francis Bacon, could be seen at the Biennale in Venice, in London and New York, and was represented at the Festival of Britain in 1951. Sutherland did not even hold with the abstract artists or extreme Modernists; rather, his Churchill portrait shows an inscrutable realism that nevertheless denies his subject any colourfulness of life, meaning exactly that creative element that Kokoschka was able to incomparably evoke in his portraits. Sutherland worked with puritanical simplicity in the expression; Kokoschka had dared to do something different in his portraits and landscapes – and that even more so after 1945 – a revival of the baroque in the language of colour. This correlates to his disaffection with the development of Modernism, whose exponent he himself had been in his early years.

7

Portrait of the Older Artist as Educator, or Schools of Seeing

'How nice it is that you, in particular, are giving youth new inspiration through such a school of seeing which they will eventually not limit just to seeing but to the entire young person.' This opinion was offered in a letter to Kokoschka by the previously mentioned businessman, painter, art critic and author Walter Kern (1898–1966), at the time guest lecturer in the history of modern art at St Gallen and director of a printing company in Winterthur, Switzerland. Kern would leave behind an important collection of letters and manuscripts as he was in friendly correspondence with Hans Arp, Max Ernst, Hermann Hesse, Robert Walser and Jakob Haringer. His 1955 study of Kokoschka's *Thermopylae* triptych was to be considered among the most important interpretations of a single work by this artist. He even acted as an intermediary when questions were at issue of where and under what conditions Kokoschka's colossal painting would be taken on by the city of Hamburg. He would do the same for Kokoschka in another conversation on the issue that plagued him about 'non-objective art', against which his School of Seeing would also take a stand. It was not unusual for Kokoschka to attract false friends or requests for support from minor artists because of his vehement opposition to non-objectiveness. Hence the complaint from the Baden-Baden painter Hans Münch that the artists' guild there, which had dedicated itself to the avant-garde, denied him the right to give lectures against the abstract. He even asked Kokoschka to publicly defend his little polemic pamphlet *Der Denkfehler der gegenstandslosen Kunst* (*The Fallacy of*

Non-objective Art, 1960), which was met with silence. Walter Kern referred to Münch as a person with 'definitely Kohlhaas-like features' to Kleist-fan Kokoschka, which was definitely intended as double-edged praise and likely also interpreted as such by Kokoschka.

Progressive Restoration, or in the Middle of the Loss

Basically, Kokoschka despised nothing more than dogmatism in matters of art. At times, however, even his anti-dogmatism could take on dogmatic (read: 'Kohlhaas-like') characteristics. There was hardly an essay or letter in the 1950s and 1960s in which Kokoschka did not polemicise against abstractionism. Subliminally the vehemence of his reaction against the abstract may have been a result of the trauma of his condemnation by the National Socialist pseudo-cultural policy, which pilloried his art as 'degenerate'. Now he saw a cabal at work, consisting of art critics –notably the most important proponent of Abstract Modernism after 1945, Will Grohmann (1887–1968)[1] – gallerists and art dealers who dismissed any hint of concreteness or realism as vulgar and old-fashioned. Kokoschka dismissed the credo of Non-Objectivism – and thus, for example, the work of Willi Baumeister[2] – as inhuman. In doing so he seemed to ignore that abstract artists were also the targets of Hitler's art policy. He further overlooked the fact that numerous works by Non-Objective and socially critical artists were represented at the first *Allgemeinen Deutschen Kunstausstellung* (*General German Art Exhibition*) after the war, in Dresden in 1946, as well as at the first 'documenta' in Kassel (1955).[3]

Grohmann, whom Kokoschka knew from his Dresden days, determinedly championed the artistic efforts of artists such as Ernst Ludwig Kirchner, Karl Schmidt-Rottluff, Otto Dix, Paul Klee and Wassily Kandinsky – particularly through his exemplary artist monographs which he had begun with his work on the drawings of Kirchner in Dresden in 1924. Nevertheless, there was contact and mutual respect between Kokoschka and this representative of the abstract artists' faction, as a letter of December 1951 demonstrates. Grohmann had

spoken positively of a Kokoschka retrospective in Berlin and even suggested he produce Alban Berg's opera *Wozzeck* in Berlin. The review
had given Kokoschka 'comfort in restoring his reputation after the
Nazi period', and producing the opera by his late friend 'would actually interest me very much' (Br III, 258). Even though nothing came of
it, the exchange of letters demonstrates that not all bridges between
him and the abstract community had been burned. Kokoschka might
even have declared himself in agreement with Paul Klee's by-then-
famous phrase: 'Art does not reflect the visible, rather it makes matters
visible'.[4] He may have been familiar with it as Kasimir Edschmid published it in his collection of artists' quotes in 1920. But it was about
the *how* of making things visible. Abstract art, including Klee's, which
originated in the identity of the colour,[5] was and remained for Kokoschka a betrayal of all things human. However, Kokoschka did not
participate in the bitter arguments about the value of figurative and
abstract painting between Grohmann and Karl Hofer, the chairman
of the Deutschen Künstlerbund, which was re-founded after the war.
Just how fiercely they locked horns over this is illustrated by the tragic
climax in 1955 when the frequently long-suffering Hofer died of a
stroke shortly after such a confrontation.[6]

   After his Expressionist beginnings, Hofer tended more towards the
'New Objectivity', to use the term coined by Gustav Friedrich Hart-
laub in 1925 (but which left unclear what the former 'old' objectivity
might have been). At the time, Hofer's painting was modelled on the
naturalistic landscape painting of the 19th century, though it was not
without stylised features, as, for example, expressed in his painting
Tessiner Landschaft (*Tessin Landscape*, 1925/1927). This put him in the
company of Christian Arnold, Ivan Babij and Caro Mense, but quite
distant from Kokoschka's liberal treatment of landscapes which tended
more towards offering colours to a landscape or allowing the colours
to become the landscape. Also the portrait art of the New Objectivity from Franz Lenk to Hanna Nagel, from Conrad Felixmüller to
Rudolf Schlichter, Bruno Voigt and Herbert Fischer-Greising does
not offer a hint of comparability in its clichéd precision to the free-
handed portrait composition of Kokoschka. No wonder, then, that he

was biased only on his own account and avoided academy disputes. If there were to be an academy, then it should be his own, an endeavour that he was soon able to realise in the form of the 'Internationale Sommerakademie in Salzburg' ('International Summer Academy in Salzburg') with his School of Seeing, which opened its doors in 1953. For as uncompromisingly as Kokoschka railed against Non-Objectivity in modern art (incidentally he found himself in agreement on this with the young, wild sculptor, graphic artist and author Günter Grass), the legacy of the New Objectivity was too objective for him.

Kokoschka's opinions in the post-war period were not lacking in contradictions. Thus, he took to the field against the sexualisation of culture (which given his own past was quite hypocritical). He increasingly held Schiele's art to be pure pornography. Yet how about his own drawing *Liegender Akt* (*Reclining Nude*) of 1953, or even in this respect to his early work? Did not a piece like *Mörder Hoffnung der Frauen*, in particular, demonstrate how the yearning for sexual fulfilment – at the cost of erotic stimulation – can suddenly turn into crime? Did it not show in word and picture that the sexual in all forms absorbs cultural sophistication?[7] It can in no way be called a late self-edit in Kokoschka's case – for example, in his memoir *Mein Leben*.

They have been described often enough, the mood and emotional swings in post-war Europe – alternating between despair and euphoria. Conservative cultural pessimism and attempted restoration – of what exactly usually remained unclear – resembled sensibilities after 1918. Yet unlike after the First World War the national consciousness was worn out. The new ideal in the West was reconstruction and European integration, preferably under the auspices of a Christian humanism. The Occident should no longer perish as per Spengler's precept, but rather become the place of new consciousness; meanwhile the art historian Hans Sedlmayr[8] from Burgenland, who was sympathetic to National Socialism, bemoaned the 'lost centre' in the arts, which he called *Verlust der Mitte* (*Art in Crisis*), in a fundamental study drafted during the Nazi period in Vienna and published in Salzburg in 1948. It became the new bible in conservative circles. Sedlmayr saw it as a 'pathography of Modernism'.[9] Incidentally, he repeatedly tried to persuade Kokoschka to give a lecture in Munich – later also through his student Dieter Henrich. The famously infamous art historian flattered the world-famous artist in a letter of 28 October 1955 – of course, without success.

> You could do much good here and be a counter-weight. It is also time that the art historians hold their peace and that the young people for once learn and listen without intermediation how a great artist thinks about art. A few sentences from you would have a greater impact than all the palaver.[10]

The knowledge of the Shoah, the destruction of Europe by the Second World War, the threat of atomic devastation, the East–West split and the related danger of a third, final world war created a cauldron of fear that far exceeded any conventional concepts of evil and the humanly possible. To re-orientate oneself aesthetically, or to continue to develop oneself creatively against this literally infernal background, seemed downright frivolous on the one hand and yet critical on the other for artists who felt compelled to reintroduce humanist values through art. This identifies a third reason for Kokoschka's increased interest in the representation of the human face, but also for his renewed exploration of the mythological world. That Kokoschka turned to Altdorfer's painting *Alexanderschlacht* (*The Battle of Alexander at Issus*) as well as the mechanistic people pictures by Giuseppe Arcimboldo in this 'epoch of preparation for the apocalyptic end of the world' may be considered logical.

Sedlmayr's study *Verlust der Mitte* may have provided the impetus for the first of the Darmstadt Conversations (1950) on the Mathildenhöhe about *Das Menschenbild in unserer Zeit* (*The Image of Man in Our Times*), but what motivated Kokoschka was the sense of having to work in the midst of a loss of traditions and values. His efforts with regard to *Arcimboldi* (1951) and *Altdorfers 'Alexanderschlacht'* (1956) offer his most impressive reflections on this. They also summarise the essence of what could be labelled Kokoschka's progressive restoration in art: a political yet somewhat leftish version of creative or conservative revolution of Hofmannsthal provenance, an aesthetic hybrid of leftist humanism and a visually influenced understanding of development that grasps the gaze as insight into the perspectives of being.

Both texts are based on a critique of abstract technique in modern art in an almost ritualistic manner wherein Kokoschka's more nuanced arguments allow more precise insights into the reasons for his position. His reflections on Giuseppe Arcimboldo (1527–1593), the Milanese patriarch of Surrealism in the service of Emperor Rudolf II, 'the Alchemist on the throne of the Habsburgs', show Kokoschka's vehement discomfort at a mechanistic concept of man. What the Milanese artist created in puzzle pictures for the Imperial cabinet of curiosities on the Hradčany in Prague was supplemented there by a large collection of 'bizarre paintings by Hieronymus Bosch' (DSW III, 103). Incidentally, the collector in Kokoschka had also built up a kind of 'cabinet of curiosities' in his Villa Delphin in Villeneuve.[11] The collector's items, often made of wood, ranged from five Indian deities, a Maori patu (flat club), a fragment of a Neolithic female figurine to a donkey with a swaying head. Yet Kokoschka largely collected with future pictures in mind, objects he incorporated in his artistic compositions.

In contrast, according to Kokoschka, in Arcimboldian Surrealism the person has become 'the sum of tangibility', such that he 'is what he eats as it were and its total represents what is there or what he produces' (DSW III, 102). In such art life is only imaginable as an 'as if'. Kokoschka's main concern runs: 'Surrealist art has obliterated the person from the picture, just as the totalitarian state performs its functions, as if the person did not exist' (DSW III, 101). The painting is no longer a 'state of mind' in Arcimboldo; rather, it is reduced to a bricolage of things: 'if in Arcimboldo the image of man consists of a mass of things which an apparent coincidence brought together, then we are more likely to think of the depersonalisation of man in the machine age in which he roughly results from the assembly line of non-stop industrialisation' (DSW III, 103). Thus, art is assigned to a study of the masses rather than to anthropology, an opinion that Kokoschka shared with H G Adler, Elias Canetti and Hermann Broch, but also with Ortega y Gasset. As diverse as their formulations may have been in the detail (ranging from Broch's mass hysteria to Adler's concentration camp experiences and Ortega's mobilisation of the masses), they all developed a theory of mass psychology or a critique of this term.

The consequence of such an image of man, as Arcimboldo suggests through his paintings, is – according to Kokoschka – a behaviour, which places 'objectivity above compassion with man'. In conclusion Kokoschka references Arcimboldo's life-time achievement, a 'theory of the colour scale of tones', and he adds, not being terribly concerned with historical accuracy: '[...] which inspired a Frenchman to build a colour piano during the French Revolution' (DSW III, 108). It was actually as follows: Louis-Bertrand Castel (1688–1757), a French Jesuit and mathematician, designed, in addition to other colour instruments, the theory for a colour piano (*Clavecin oculaire*) around 1722. At each keystroke translucent backlit silk ribbons were meant to appear. But it was only after Castel's death that the Englishman Arthur Morley actual constructed the so-called *ocular harpsichord*, in London in 1757. It consisted of a box containing hundreds of small lights set upon a harpsichord which through mechanical coupling would light up with a keystroke.[12] Alexander Skrjabin created his colour piano on this foundation, where acoustic sounds triggered colour projections. It is likely that Kokoschka was familiar with these developments, also as a result of the written material for Kandinsky's stage composition *Der gelbe Klang* (*The Yellow Sound*, 1912), which he could find in the publication *Der Blaue Reiter* (*The Blue Rider*).

Why is this important in connection with Kokoschka? Because the sound values of colours were on Kokoschka's mind as well and explain why he postulated musical analogues in his writings, particularly in the 1950s, which, as mentioned in the preceding chapter, orientated themselves on the trio of Bach–Beethoven–Schönberg (Mozart remained a special phenomenon and thus unrivalled). With this he apparently wished to establish an all-encompassing relationship with creative traditions, which characterises Kokoschka's later work as a whole – where later work refers to pictorial work as well as stage design, essays, correspondence and literary efforts, including the belated reworking of the *Comenius* drama.

In his essay, *Das Auge des Darius* (*The Eye of Darius*, 1956), Koko-schka tells how on a Sunday in bombed-out Munich he saw the *Alex-anderschlacht* by Altdorfer 'in the "bomb-proof" Haus der Kunst built by Hitler which withstood the destruction' (DSW III, 87). He had in mind the following question and in some ways posed it to the paint-ing: 'What is reality, where does it begin and how is it constrained?' Abstract Art, according to Kokoschka, evades this fundamental ques-tion. And because of this, he despises it.

> Today's modern master creating abstract work, in contrast to the artists of the past, approaches his work with an empty head, await-ing inspiration neither from his becoming conscious of his self nor from the sensory perception of objective reality around him, rather of an activity already beyond reason which begins to surprise him as a manifestation of his subconsciousness. (DSW III, 86)

Altdorfer's *Alexanderschlacht*, commissioned during the first Ottoman occupation of Vienna (1529), now seems to Kokoschka to be the literal antithesis to this denial of reality. Altdorfer depicts an historic event, the Battle at Issus 333 BC, less in the allegorical sense but rather as an example of how an historical event can become a quasi-landscape through art. Altdorfer clearly paints from the elevated point of view of the observer – the wide-ranging perspective, the dissolving of the horizon line in the windswept but clouded sky, which corresponds to the contrasting movements of the battlefield chaos. In this way, the distancing and commitment of the glance are brought into a tense reciprocal relationship because the distance creates the wish to liter-ally move closer to the painting and to what is taking place, whilst at the same time he also provides an overview, such as the 'Eye of Darius' might have been granted in the midst of the battle. Interestingly, Koko-schka titled his essay with this expression without, however, commit-ting himself to this eye in the text.

Seen historically, the Battle at Issus, Alexander's victory over the Persians, represents the reversal of fortunes at the Battle of Ther-mopylae of 480 BC. And it is likely or at least seems reasonable that

Kokoschka thought of his visual experience of seeing Altdorfer's *Alexanderschlacht* when composing the *Thermopylae* triptych. However, the decisive difference is that he created a type of close-up view, which denies the observer the possibility of distancing themselves.

And yet Kokoschka celebrates this – as he says – first baroque painting 'as a work of ultimate painting' (DSW III, 88). This painting is ultimate because in it and in the 'observer' the 'quelling, overflowing, amazement and agglomeration of the material itself, [the] growth and burgeoning of the vegetation, the roar of the water, snaking and branching out of rock and boulders, the hurricane-like tension and discharge in the atmosphere as in a catastrophe of nature itself' remain potent in retrospect. And further, it: 'Strips bare all that which is possible to express in the language, and what today is called "subject matter" only begins its independent existence in the composition, its taking shape' (DSW III, 89). The material becomes form, according to Kokoschka, through which the painting is not so much setting a process in motion as being the process itself.

In the next step of the debate Kokoschka compares Altdorfer's picture construction in an overall creative sense with a musical composition.

> Something is battling for the developing form like in a fugue in this work, however it derives from ultimate vision and opens other areas of reality than what the eye of the named illuminated painter has opened. The *progression of time* in which the motifs wrestling with each other arrive at a harmonious resolution in a musical fugue has become the *picture's contents*. (DSW III, 89)

Kokoschka saw a contrapuntal process at work in Altdorfer's picture composition. The specificity of this analogue is revealed when Kokoschka names the particular fugue he has in mind: Beethoven's Große Fuge in B-Flat Major Op 133. He speaks of the 'individual, stubbornly assertive bars' at the beginning of this composition, in which 'two thought categories' express themselves, 'two settings, a thought and a show act', hence a binary focus, just as Kokoschka himself used for his city- and landscape paintings. These 'two settings' and 'measures of value' represent – according to Kokoschka – the 'antinomy of the drama of the world' that found its expression in Altdorfer's *Alexander-schlacht* (ibid).

As confident as Kokoschka's own further creative development in the direction of a cheerful later style, rich in colour variations, may have seemed, his interventions in the aesthetic debates of the time happened in an ideological mine field. That led to his receiving occasional praise from problematic quarters, for example, from Alois Melichar, an Austrian composer and conductor of the Franz Schreker school who enjoyed success composing film music under National Socialism and attempted to conceal his role in the cultural policy of the brownshirts after 1945.[13] Kokoschka is promoted to a leading figure of an aesthetic revisionism in Melichar's polemic *Überwindung des Modernismus* (*Victory over Modernism*, 1954),[14] which, incidentally, was among Otto Dix's reading material in Hemmenhofen. Melichar argued that it was only the across-the-board demonisation of Expressionism, the 'atonalism and abstractionism' in National Socialism that helped these art styles to a new life after 1945, because in Berlin, the 'most progressive city on the continent' around 1930, these styles were already 'art historically dead'.[15] This sweeping judgement requires discernment because after 1945 the appreciation of Expressionism began only haltingly. In the GDR, for example, condemnation of this art style continued. Georg Baselitz put on record that his assumed instructor, Schmidt-Rottluff, was 'completely isolated' and the legacy of the 'Brücke', that legendary association of Expressionists founded by Kirchner, Heckel and Schmidt-Rottluff in Dresden in 1905, played no role whatsoever anymore.[16]

Incidentally, Melichar was also quite harsh about the Viennese *homme de lettres* Hans Weigel, whom he referred to as a 'little Viennese hack' kitted out with 'ruthless wrath and a remarkable nerve for humiliation', inclined to plagiarism and nefarious denunciation. Melichar took particular offence at the Viennese spokesman for a new avant-garde such that he labelled Furtwängler as a 'conductor's stand whore', who did not direct any new compositions but only prostituted himself with Beethoven and Brahms symphonies.[17]

Melichar dealt in depth with Will Grohmann's influential study *Bildende Kunst und Architektur* (*Fine Arts and Architecture*), published by Suhrkamp in 1953, especially with the pages dedicated to Kokoschka. In it, Grohmann pays the artist an ambiguous compliment that no artist talks as 'unrestrainedly' as he. The rhetorical final question in Grohmann's Kokoschka section sounds no less sardonic, even condescending: 'He is a unique case, a contradiction of our times, a Delacroix reborn or baroque. What would happen if one allowed this new baroque to stand next to the neo-classicism in music?'[18]

Grohmann's question, why Kokoschka 'suddenly' was deemed a success again after 1945 and where the fascination with his work might originate, was answered by Melichar without beating about the bush: '[...] because Kokoschka is a real, genuine painter and his great ability is to give expression to our times using legitimate, intact artistic means! It is in *his* paintings and not in the puerile paint gimmicks of abstract stuffy men that posterity will find the great themes of our times, their signatures, their woes and convulsions!'[19]

One might agree with Melichar in one respect. Grohmann's attacks on Kokoschka, Heckel or Chagall were comparable with the denigration of Stravinsky, Prokofiev, Egk and von Einem through the new music aesthetic, whose biggest proponent was Theodor W Adorno. *Die Philosophie der neuen Musik* (*The Philosophy of New Music*), which also contained his taking general account of the 'restorative' Stravinsky, became the guiding principle for a music movement of atonal abstraction. Adorno could forgive Richard Strauss no more than Stravinsky that they had not become atonal after *Salomé* and *Elektra*, or *Le Sacre du Printemps*, just as Grohmann at best ridiculed Kokoschka's dogged concretism.

It would have been difficult to speak of 'intact artistic means' (in the sense of Melichar's fairly abstract contemplation), never mind the problematic aesthetic category of the legitimate. Kokoschka was and remained disabled, as it were, except that the damage to his artistic means and life experience expressed itself differently; it often took on allegorical forms, as in his painting of 1946/1947, *Zirkus oder Die Entfesselung der Atomenergie* (*Circus or The Unleashing of*

Atomic Energy). Here, too, Kokoschka spoke, if not 'unrestrainedly' as Grohmann claimed, then rather with clarity. He achieved such an intense vividness in this painting that it turned itself into the symbolic: a clown holds a large key like a prop in his hand. With it he has opened the tiger's cage as if for a lark. The tiger – not yet the logo for a particular brand of petrol – represents accumulated atomic energy which has now been set free. The family of jugglers seems unaware and unsuspecting. Only the white dove of peace takes frightened flight in the face of the threat.[20]

A School of Seeing

What comes from the nadirs of fruitless quarrelling about the Modernist art trap? A change of direction, although it has been known since Kafka that it only benefits the catty opponent. A new viewing direction, a change of perspective or an increase in focal points? Who or what lies in wait for our eyes under an altered optic of any kind? And more importantly: are we still master, or mistress, of our glances, or are they being directed? Can they wander if need be or are they even capable of focusing? Do colour intensities, compression of forms, create unexpected perspectives? Or might we stumble on certain angles and potentially injure ourselves?

Kokoschka's pedagogic ethos worked through Eros who, by Kokoschka's own account, revealed himself in 'four infatuations': '[...] my infatuation with people, my infatuation with the work, my infatuation with composition, my infatuation with life.'[21] This love of life even helped him to resist thoughts of suicide. Among the infatuations that stimulated him was the somewhat transparently profane enthusiasm of the ageing artist for his 'dollies'. Summer upon summer, from all over the world, they flocked to Kokoschka's academy on the Hohensalzburg, and the prospect of their proximity (young sparks were, of course, no less welcome!) allowed him take on this task for a decade starting in 1953, which, despite bureaucratic hurdles, never became a drudgery for him. One such 'dolly' from northern England, representing very many, still raved months after completing her summer academy in a letter to Kokoschka.

> Everything that I ever wanted to know about you and 'life' you unveiled for me, when you said: 'Open your eyes and experience the *shock of life*.' However, regardless of your being very old, you are still the symbol of life. That does not mean that I see you as a saint with a halo – you are far more complex and at the same time modest. PS I love you very much (but also myself).[22]

For art, or more precisely a fortress for artistic talent, that is what the Internationale Akademie Salzburg created by Kokoschka might have called itself. Something of this bastion-like thinking also lives on in the architecture of the Museum der Moderne on the Mönchsberg, which opened in 2004, as it resembles an exposed high bunker, which unsuccessfully wants to elevate itself to eye level with the Hohensalzburg.

With his experiment in opening a 'school for seeing' – a centre for the senses – at the Salzburg summer academy and establishing this 'school' to run in parallel with the Festival, Kokoschka finally fulfilled an early dream: to develop new ways of seeing by teaching observation. His approach was definitely grounded in theory. The leading Irish philosopher George Berkeley's perception theory of 1709/1733, *A New Theory of Vision*, in which he establishes a correlation between sight and touch, was particularly important for the emphatically tactile artist Kokoschka. It must also have stood to reason for Kokoschka that Berkeley took this new theory of seeing as the basis for his foundational *Treatise Concerning the Principles of Human Knowledge* (1710). A further important catalyst for Kokoschka was to be found in Albert Erich Brinckmann's study *Welt der Kunst* (*World of Art*), published in 1953, which sweepingly asserts: 'Fine art is for us all an experience through the eyes first and foremost. The sense of vision, and through it the appeal to the whole intellectual man, is the prerequisite for recognition, understanding and appreciation of the wonderous world of art.'[23]

That Kokoschka could not have implemented this project without his Salzburg gallerist and friend Friedrich Welz, who functioned as the inspiration and 'secretary' of the academy, is better known than the latter's compromising behaviour during the 'großdeutsche Zeit' (Nazi era).[24] And, again, one must ask oneself – not without trepidation in the case of Kokoschka's friendly relationship with Welz: what did the artist know of the highly dubious wheeling and dealing of one of his most important agents during the Nazi period? Was he really not aware or did he not wish to know that his friend Welz opened the travelling exhibition *Die Straßen des Führers* (*The Führer's Streets*) as early as April 1938 (in celebration of the ground-breaking for the construction of the Reichsautobahn at the Walserberg); that he liaised closely with the new Nazi power in the 'Ostmark' in matters of art policy and in 1940 organised a Makart exhibition under the auspices of Hermann Göring; and that he bought up art in occupied Paris on behalf of Baldur von Schirach, which suggests the concept of compulsory purchases?[25] Or did Kokoschka believe Friedrich Maximilian Welz's lifelong lie, as, incidentally, did the American officers who released him from the Glasenbach camp after only a few weeks of internment in May 1945?

In that context, how should one judge Welz's support for witnesses of 'degenerate art' on the occasion of the Kärntner Kunstschau in 1941? Was it a sign of boldness and the temptation to test his standing with the powers that be? Or did he suddenly see future opportunities for investment in these works? How much of Welz's dubious behavious reflects back on Kokoschka, and even on the concept of the School of Seeing? Did Welz intend the markedly international reach of the summer academy to be a self-exoneration? How credible was it that one of the leading art dealers of the National Socialist regime could transform into the meritorious promoter of culture and art publisher in Austria's Second Republic, which in its first forty years was indisputably a state of deniers and quick-change artists.[26] The *causa* Welz is truly complex. It is hardly well known, for example, that Kokoschka and Welz had met as early as the summer of 1934. In the first exhibition curated by Welz in his Salzburg 'art shop' (later the Galerie Welz), *Österreichische Kunst der Gegenwart* (*Contemporary Austrian Art*), the young gallerist showed Kokoschka's painting *Mutter und Kind* (*Trudl mit der Nô-Maske*) (*Mother and Child; Trudl with the Noh Mask*), as well as *Wiener Landschaft mit Mädchen* (*Vienna Landscape with Girl*). In following years Kokoschka was represented in Welz's gallery with, amongst others, the paintings *Orpheus und Eurydike* (1917), *London* (1926), *Steinfigur im Garten* (*Stone Figure in the Garden*, 1933), *Amaryllis* (1933) and *Das Tanzpaar* (*The Dance Couple*, 1913). In 1977 Welz recalled this first encounter with Kokoschka and his mother Maria Romana, who died a few weeks later, in Wien-Liebhartstal.

> [...] I did not know much about Kokoschka's personality, just what was said about him in Vienna. Since his great successes in Berlin and Dresden the vicious attacks had fallen silent and given way to respectful recognition.
>
> From the first moment a warm connection was made. The room on the first floor was not particularly spacious, the not-yet-completed painting *Der Besuch* (*The Visitor*) stood on the easel, books were on the shelves, in a small display case along the wall were mostly small figurines of animals and idols probably collected on travels to Egypt and Asia Minor. The room made a cosy impression, despite a certain untidiness. An old lady, Kokoschka's mother, entered and asked if she might bring coffee. Kokoschka declined and indicated grinning to an almost full whisky bottle with which we wished to start, he claimed. [...] A spontaneous fascination emanated from his personality. He spoke of his mother, whom he loved above all else, made fun of himself whilst his face took on a somewhat mischievous look. His eyes looked at me searchingly as if seeking to determine my innermost secrets. I sat across from Kokoschka, repeatedly challenged to drink. I could not keep up with his tempo, I was not yet accustomed to hard spirits. Kokoschka became more and more loose and soon came to speak of the political situation in Austria at the time. The Dollfuß regime, the Home Guard seemed of great concern to him.[27]

Welz was adept at dealing with people, something he certainly had in common with Kokoschka, who was eighteen years his senior. The latter confirmed in a congratulatory letter on the occasion of 'his' gallerist and friend's sixtieth birthday (1963) that Welz, despite his impaired vision due to an accident, still truly understood how to 'see' (Br IV, 147). Kokoschka could not have overlooked that this erstwhile beneficiary of the National Socialist Aryanisation of art owned by Jewish Austrians stood in stark contrast to his communist advocate Viktor Matejka. Yet, it can by no means be ruled out that Matejka even advised the exiled artist to re-establish contact with Welz. Much remains speculation, supposition and guesswork on this. And because it would be all too easy to judge here without knowing the exact circumstances, we decline to do so.

In contrast, however, this much is certain. In the conservative to reactionary atmosphere of Salzburg in the 1950s[28] it was no mean feat to found a School of Seeing that was intended to do more than teach the handling of optical illusions. Kokoschka left no doubt as to the meaning of his undertaking: 'I am founding the Internationale Akademie in Salzburg in the sense of the European vision of a world that surrounds us all our lives as the living legacy from the past and that at the same time re-emerges in the creative moment in every talented being.'[29] That sounded unambiguously culturally conservative and seamlessly merged with what the city and state of Salzburg wished for. Yet, he continued, it depended on making young people aware that they learned 'with their own eyes.'

To see the world as a product of imagination and thus as the result of self-determination in visual matters and idiosyncratic optics – this amounted to an acknowledgement and invitation to non-conformism. What Kokoschka wished to teach was the 'lightning-quick' capturing of human movements – and that with watercolours because they cannot be corrected. In so doing he brought an understanding of experiential art into play, which was clearly reminiscent of the aesthetic debates around 1900, especially the aesthetic category of experience. Should it be viewed as ironic that the pedagogic watchword for a new way of seeing was being promulgated by an artist plagued by myopia? Has this sight-deficiency even been sufficiently appreciated up to now? Kokoschka only occasionally addressed it, and then more in passing, as in a letter to Heinz Spielmann of October 1972 in which he admitted that he could not see the capitols of the churches of Burgundy, 'especially in Vézelay due to my near-sightedness' (Br IV, 245). Considering that the artist was photographed in all manner of circumstances after 1950, he nevertheless managed to avoid being captured wearing spectacles. One might speculate that the clear lack of contour sharpness in many of his later paintings may have been due to the impairment of his eyesight. To make an artistic virtue of this cardinal optical weakness unquestionably speaks to Kokoschka's special ability.

As far as the School of Seeing was concerned there were organisational difficulties, as well as specific conditions for Kokoschka that needed ironing out. Here friend Welz proved himself to be an 'honest broker' who, of course, went in to bat for an artist of world renown, whose closeness to leftist thought was not unknown. The man who had the communist Viktor Matejka as an advocate in Vienna was not easy to defend as the arts gatekeeper of the Christian Occident to the conservative state governor of Salzburg, and later federal chancellor, Josef Klaus. Yet Welz seemed to broadly succeed even at this feat, and that despite the fact that Klaus must have been particularly sensitive as a result of the '*causa* Bertolt Brecht' of 1950/1951. In April 1950 Brecht had been compensated in advance with the granting of Austrian citizenship, on the sponsorship of Gottfried von Einem, in return for his future participation in the Salzburg Festival. However, in 1951 Brecht chose to move to the German Democratic Republic; Klaus and the Festival directors held the composer von Einem responsible for Brecht's behaviour and could not forgive him. Absurdly, von Einem was expelled from the Festival's board of trustees because of this controversy.[30]

Against this embarrassing background Salzburg did not want to get involved once more with a politically dubious loose cannon. Fittingly, Welz was able to present Kokoschka to the Salzburg authorities as the Lord Privy Seal of German-speaking European humanism, of whom no Brecht-like defection was to be expected and whose conception of art was by now grounded in absolute conservatism.

Kokoschka's Salzburg School of Seeing obviously belonged in the context of a de facto re-establishing of the Salzburg Festival after 1945 – initially under US protection. Its early protagonists were Gottfried von Einem, Oscar Fritz Schuh and Caspar Neher; its renaissance began spectacularly with the premiere of the opera *Danton's Tod* (*Danton's Death*) by Gottfried von Einem on 6 August 1947.[31] Learning to hear and see – the latter by means of the stage design by Brecht's friend Neher – were particularly merged in this production. One had kept a look out for a new Hofmannsthal for this new Salzburg Festival,[32] thought at first to have found him in Brecht, then hoped to find him in Kokoschka's circle, even though Kokoschka never really wanted to consider his School of Seeing as part of the Festival. As we know, nothing was more important to him than distance and creative independence.

Though the authorities on the Salzach did not meet Kokoschka's demand that accommodation be provided for him and Olda (and possibly also for brother Bohuslav), the Festung Hohensalzburg was made available to him for the summer academy. In turn, Kokoschka committed himself for July/August each year, and insisted on selecting and recruiting the instructors for the different classes – he regarded them as his assistants even if they were professors. In subsequent years this process led to growing tensions between the authorities and him as having the final word.[33] In no time, however, Kokoschka's claims about the effectiveness of his project dimmed. Consequently we read in a recently discovered letter, written in English in April 1955 to the sociologist Margareta Berger-Hammerschlag, whom he must have known in Vienna prior to the First World War, that the 'purely technically orientated civilisation' leads to a loss of face for mankind. Increasingly they lose their ability to 'see with their own eyes'. And further, modern forms of education 'offer the individual experience and thinking from second hand as well as visual clichés'. In contrast, mature insights should be derived, so Kokoschka continues, from independent seeing.[34]

As to the view of Salzburg, which he would open to the students of seeing from 1953, Kokoschka had completed the prototype painting in

1950. No modern painting of Salzburg gave such long-lasting shape to the myth of this city.[35] Salzburg, seen from the Kapuzinerberg, rises in front of the eye as a harmonious ensemble of houses and churches, the Mönchsberg and the Untersberg, the Festung Hohensalzburg and the twilit sky. The Salzach seems directionless, almost like standing water. It is as if this city is celebrating itself in all its baroque colourfulness. People do not even seem to be necessary, as the architectural ensemble and nature merge in this painting to transcend all.

The view of Linz five years later is different in that the city – practically marginalised – becomes a broad horizon line and the foreground defined by nature and agriculture with the wide Danube draws the main focus. Linz made him morose, as he wrote from there to his sister Berta in Prague, in April 1955. He could not paint the city in the style of his Salzburg picture. 'The view is so boring that I was properly despairing on the first day.' There follows a (for him unusual) description of view and picture.

> Deep below, parallel to the picture's edge, is the Danube, above that long, wide, green meadows, on the left the almost American industrial plants, but far in the background, in the centre, only see-able in miniature, the city, on the right far in the back the docks with barren trees that frame the picture. I have never seen anything so boring, but I shall make something out of it. (Br IV, 47 f)

The emphatic barrenness of this cityscape is reminiscent of early landscapes; it even has something of the desolation of his *Ungarischen Landschaft* (*Hungarian Landscape*) of 1908, if there were not interspersed light effects that actually create the appeal of this painting. The painting titled *Linz* rather shows a city in the process of disappearing. Nature has absorbed it. Linz has the effect of a static picture, and that despite an icy wind blowing on the high ground from where he is painting the scene of a marginalised city in April 1955, 'and the canvas' seems to 'wobble like a glider' (Br IV, 47).

The prerequisite for stylistic variety in painting is a multiplicity of perspectives, which in turn can only arise from the opening and

practising of observation. Ever since Rilke's fictional character Malte
Laurids Brigge postulated in the Paris of the early 20th century that
he had learned to see – or the metropolis on the Seine had taught him
to see – the consciousness in Modernism has orientated itself on this
discovery as an imperative. Kokoschka's multi-perspective paintings
of the Vienna Staatsoper, the Cologne Rhine riverfront, the inside of
Cologne Cathedral, and even of divided Berlin, as well as his views
of Lake Geneva and Delphi, demonstrate one thing: this artist could
become a teacher of seeing and was not tiring at his advanced age;
he continued to see himself as a student of seeing, trying new angles,
exploring insights and outlooks, lending colours their own perspectives and repeatedly giving expression to the amazement of the seen.

What was special about the School of Seeing, however, was that
Kokoschka knew how to guide students to see as individuals and at
the same time to comprehend this seeing as a communal experience. In
the psychology of seeing, this approach, namely the 'limiting of views
as a model for human sight', might now be regarded as pioneering.[36]
And more. Kokoschka's approach confirmed the findings of the Polish
theoretician Ludwik Fleck.

> He who stands in front of something new, whether a futuristic
> picture, alien landscape or even in front of a microscope for the first
> time, 'does not know what he is meant to see'. He searches for simi-
> larities to the known, overlooking precisely the new, incomparable,
> specific. He, too, must first learn to see.[37]

Except that Kokoschka only allowed the categorisation of seeing – in
other words, the search for similarities – within limits. It was significant for him, however, to be able to communicate the problem, *what*
one should see and *how* one should present (not express!) it. The necessity of the School of Seeing, Kokoschka had no doubt, derived from
the narrowing view through National Socialist propaganda. *Open your
own eyes* thus became Kokoschka's motto for his summer school (Br
IV, 30), which he – unlike the Salzburg cultural authorities – never
wanted to see turned into a permanent academy. Because that was not

what his objective was: teaching how to create art. He fundamentally rejected the academising of artistic work his entire life.

In the setting of the Salzburg enterprise, Kokoschka's letters reveal his thoughts on seeing as being as existential as creative teaching and learning material. He made no secret of the fact that seeing also had a political aspect: 'Learning seeing and insight was always at the beginning. All controversy, discord, all fracturing in the history of Europe came about when they came with theories[,] not wishing to see what is there under the sun, which is the same regardless of its rising in the East and setting in the West' (Br IV, 8). He wrote to Theodor Heuss that his intention was 'to make seeing modern again' (Br IV, 14), without abstracting from the seen. He reminds Furtwängler that he was a 'seer', as he demonstrated when he stood in front of the Thermopylae painting (Br IV, 40). Kokoschka also labelled himself as a 'seer', in all modesty, in one of the first interviews he gave in Austria after the Second World War.[38]

His School of Seeing was like a type of 'walking school for adults' to him, as he explained in August 1955, by which he meant that in this school the eye learned how to walk (Br Iv, 52). That would be all the more necessary as people were now being raised 'if anything to watch and rubberneck than to see and understand', as he says in a letter to Welz in September 1963 (in other words, after the end of his activities in Salzburg) (Br IV, 147).

On the one hand commendable, on the other inadequate, the four-volume collected letters cleverly end with a word from Kokoschka on the optical constitution of the world, which he refers to as a 'dirty nebula in the universe' after two world wars and the depressing prospect of an atomic war: 'because I am no Utopian, I do not share the optic of the futurists! Free of prejudices – for what a wonderful world is everyday life if we would just open our eyes! Unfortunately most people are only able to hear what others are saying' (Br IV, 270).

A contribution to a type of *practical* art theory came out of Kokoschka's conception for a School of Seeing. It derives from the 'wonderfulness' of everyday life, ordinary experience. The incontrovertible conclusion that man has two eyes yielded for Kokoschka, for example, the necessity for an 'elliptical composition with two vanishing points' as far as his landscape paintings were concerned. (He, of course, did not apply this insight to portraiture!) His School of Seeing was not meant to be institutionalised as a permanent academy not least because academies tended – in his opinion – to replace the 'vision' with simple 'logic' (Br IV, 226). As previously mentioned, Kokoschka styled himself as a 'man of the moment', which had a special meaning under the auspices of a 'Vision School': the students of seeing had to learn what the blink of an eye could produce, how to treat it and how to put it into practice.

The actor and later friend of Kokoschka's Will Quadflieg almost wistfully recalled the time of this 'School' whilst he was in Salzburg in July 1979 for a reading from the works of Hermann Hesse. He wrote to Kokoschka: 'How those Salzburg days with OK's "School of Seeing" were full of life and human warmth! Now the world has grown cold, worshipping ever more a monotonous perfectionism and social nonsense.'[39]

In addition, the pedagogue Eduard Spranger appropriately labelled the work of the fine artist with the expression 'working through the world of the eye' in order to thereby combat the 'world's loss in art'[40] in a thank you letter to Kokoschka for his contribution to his commemorative volume on *Die Kunst unserer Tage* (*Contemporary Art*).

There was a major retrospective of Edvard Munch's work at the Zürcher Kunsthaus at the time that Kokoschka was firming up the arrangements for his School of Seeing. Kokoschka took it as an opportunity for an extensive acknowledgment of this Norwegian Expressionist. He 'diagnosed the panicky world fear' in the belief in progress at the time in his paintings (DSW III, 168). There was already talk that Kokoschka contrasted Munch's 'symbolic Expressionism', which was based on the 'experience', with Kandinsky's (in Kokoschka's view objectionable) 'renouncement of instantaneous sensory perception' in this essay. Munch prompts the observer to look into the eyes of art.

Actually, according to Kokoschka, he learned to see from Adolf Loos. Loos taught him to 'form an image of life with my own eyes, to think of painting as a type of diary of experiences, and thus form

my future outlook on the world' (DSW III, 182). That seeing is tied
to a natural incorporation of the times or, applied differently, that we
must learn, optically, to penetrate deceits brought about by technical
progress was of primary importance in Kokoschka's vision education
programme: 'The budding, blooming of a rose can be followed in a
few minutes on film, equally the total annihilation of city of millions
with all life in that very place' (DSW III, 163). In addition, he thought
that the entertainment industry only provides 'the necessary visual
clichés' (DSW III, 232) for which only a 'receptive' but no longer creative ability is required. Kokoschka stated that 'the atrophy of the sense
of sight is characteristic of a society' 'which has adapted itself to mech-
anised civilisation' (DSW III, 231).

If one bears in mind the association in Kokoschka's thinking between
the educational project derived from Comenius, which he followed
his entire life, and the school of learning understanding, then we are
confronted with a pedagogically specific utopia of the first order. The
erstwhile international 'Volksschulbündnis auf humanitärer Grund-
lage' ('Alliance of Primary Schools on Humanitarian Foundations'),
which he had in mind around 1935, had concentrated itself on visual
learning in the educational backwater of Salzburg, which was of Goe-
the-like calibre. As such, he acknowledged in November 1947:

> I hope I will succeed in helping the youth to obtain a clearer picture
> of the world, which encourages and enables them to organise
> their lives humanely. Consequently I am acting in the sense of the
> humanist Amos Comenius, who drafted a plan for a supra-national
> primary school 300 years ago. Over time, the primary school was
> introduced everywhere, but to the wrong purpose. It is not meant
> to spread experience second-hand and knowledge from hearsay. The
> evidence for this perverse education of the people is that one speaks
> of a third world war as of a matter of course and is arming for it.[41]

In Kokoschka's conception, everyone should become a seer – in a completely non-prophetic sense of the word; as far as he was concerned,
only someone who took seriously this seeing as a form of gaining

understanding could be considered learned. For understanding art, this applied equally, whereby Kokoschka in turn demanded that it offer opportunities for insight. He was accordingly harsh about the 'art of our days', as evidenced by this unpublished text from 1957:

> The visual arts are a language in images, visible or tangible signs, a knowledge of experience-based developments, comprehensible, tangible, by which the vision of the artist becomes an experience of mutual humanity and being with the next one coming. Visual art shares with the spoken word that the content of the statement, in order to become indirect, must be expressed in obvious symbols. Visual arts also share this with music, dance, with mathematics, yes even with Morse code: that they must conform to their own laws, based on conventions, agreements. Consequently the content of visual art is not expressible according to the laws of another art.
>
> Today, for the first time in the history of mankind, contemporary art is calling for the privilege of being independent from the laws of an articulated manner of expression. [...] It seems more alarming, however, that this objectless art is being propagated in the entire world, which society admits, is only to become comprehendible through interpretation. Explanatory titles, profound theories, compelling propaganda and an entire literature as usage instructions solicit for appreciation of an art, which gets by without the image of man, without recognisable things of the human environment, without an optic experienceable by another – on the other hand, also does not want to be taken simply for decoration.[42]

From Kokoschka's legacy it clearly emerges that he planned a 'History of Seeing'. It was intended to be a human doctrine, which was meant to stem the appearance in the visual arts of the – supposed – 'dehumanisation' of artistic expression through abstraction, something he particularly lamented. The project initially had the English title 'Vision through Times'. From the notes, one gains the impression that he saw seeing as being subject to an historical process, so that it was to be determined where the visual accomplishments of specific individuals in their respective eras lay. It is revealing to trace how intensively Koko-schka worked for the verbal clarification of such a history of seeing. In these notes the thought processes that must have formed the basis for a large part of his design of the Salzburg summer academies can also be identified. Thus it appears sensible to reproduce here his most impor-tant to-date-unpublished attempts at a definition of ways of seeing, as they clearly mirror his thought process on questions of an aesthetic of seeing.

Purposeful Seeing – Utilitarian Materialism/Psychologism

Aesthetic autonomy of synthetic material, which expresses itself in that a given object, e.g., a machine, after a certain maturation period reaches a maximum of utility which at the same time in many cases means for the eye (and also for other senses) that the said object has become 'pretty' per se. In addition to the archetypes in nature perceived as 'pretty' by natural sight, a vision forms that is only influenced by nature to the extent that the materials of which the technical objects are made ultimately come from nature, an ability to see that make the requirements of technology a measure, which alters the material according to their wishes.

Seeing double, a form of split vision, occurs through the possibility of being able to apply two standards to that which is seen. The old quarrel of the utilitarian and idealist, also carried out in the indi-vidual – path to the now unlimited materialism open.

Colour photo and actual colours
Seeing at high speeds, time compression
The optical bang, without which no one can be enticed to come out from behind the stove anymore (sensationalism)
Pastel, chalk, raddle, water colour almost disappears (the parallel to this would be a book about acoustics, respectively representing the change in hearing), artificial lighting, cities at night, neon light – 'materialistic' colours.[43]

These deliberations on a categorisation of seeing and the function of colour are reminiscent of Goethe's schematisation in the area of his *Farbenlehre* (*Theory of Colours*), which included the phenomenon of 'psychological seeing' as well as his rejection of the Newtonian mechanistic light theory. It is quite bewildering to find an enthusiastic proponent of Goethe's colour theory in Kokoschka (as in William Turner in his day), precisely because the scientist as poet and poet as scientist placed the immediate experience at the centre of his argument. Kokoschka himself, in an address occasioned by an exhibition of his work in Hamburg at the end of April 1965, would conclude: 'After all, my work is nothing other than a school of seeing. I only learn from seeing. We become people when we understand.'[44]

Kokoschka's insistence on materiality, particularly in respect of schooling seeing and through sight, is remarkably reminiscent of remarks made by Karl Marx in the *Ökonomisch-philsophischen Manuskripten* of 1844 (*Economic and Philosophical Manuscripts of 1844*), namely in the section he introduces with the thesis: 'Not only in thought but with all senses man is affirmed in the objective world.' And Marx continues:

> [...] Only through the objectively unfolded richness of man's essential being is the richness of subjective human sensibility (a musical ear, an eye for beauty of form – in short, senses capable of human gratification, senses affirming themselves as essential powers of man) either cultivated or brought into being. For not only the five senses but also the so-called mental senses, the practical senses (will, love, etc.), in a word, human sense, the human nature of the senses, comes to be by virtue of its object, by virtue of humanised nature. The forming of the five senses is a labour of the entire history of the world down to the present.[45]

Only once man is allowed to be completely human, according to the essence of this Marxist orientation to the five senses, will his senses come into their own. Schiller famously argued in his epistolary treatise on the aesthetic education of man that we are only fully human – that is, we only realise our human potential – when we allow ourselves to indulge in 'playing'. Moreover, he argued that only when the five senses completely come into their own can man be completely human. One can hardly fail to also recognise in this the essence of Kokoschka's at times seemingly obsessive demands for a school of seeing and the senses.

Furthermore, literature belonged to this education for Kokoschka. This was also because this art form is difficult to express in the pure abstract. Therefore, it is important to view it in a special manner.

Seeing Literature

Kokoschka preferred to call his studio 'in the newly built little house on Lake Geneva' a 'workshop' or – as per one of his first letters written in the little villa in Villeneuve – a 'library' (Br IV, 7). The relationship between literary and visual artworks could not have been expressed more tellingly than in the spatially symbolic fusion of creating and reading. That a large portion of Kokoschka's library is preserved may thus count as a true piece of luck as it allows insights into his literary, historical, arts and cultural resources, and his reading practices and preferences.[46] Because one thing in the course of these considerations of the life and work of this artist has long become obvious: a sharp separation between Kokoschka's creative fields would be senseless. His writing and drawing often overlap. A drawing could come from a piece of writing – particularly in his letters, the word 'Schriftbild' ('script style') gains a completely specific meaning – just as he accompanied and enriched his scenic poetry with images.

We are not interested here in listing the reading matter owned by Kokoschka, the honorary member of the Max Dauthendey Society and connoisseur of Alfred Mombert's complex lyrical work, but rather the productive familiarity this artist had with literature – in other words what he saw or interpreted in writings. Remember: the literati discovered the early Kokoschka – Karl Kraus as well as Kurt Hiller and above all Else Lasker-Schüler – at the first exhibition of his work in

Berlin's Galerie Paul Cassirer, in Victoriastraße, from 11 to 21 July 1910. He painted the portraits of poets Karl Kraus, Ivar von Lücken, Walter Hasenclever and Carl Zuckmayer – and most likely also Georg Trakl; he had a lyricist for a sister and an unsuccessful author for a brother. He was intimately familiar with the psyche of the literati because he socialised with many of them (especially while exiled in England), observed them and was himself one of them.

He engaged no less intensively with literary works – and that from the perspective of a visual artist who himself had worked in a literary way from the outset. Are his drawings and lithographs of episodes in literary works comparable with their setting to music? With difficulty in their impact, as they remain mute, though they are accessible to the well-read through the totality of their visual interpretation. Because there is one thing Kokoschka's literature lithographs are not: illustrations. They are more like rearrangements, transpositions into another medium, at times even metamorphoses into a new style of statement.

Above all, there is one thing one should not forget. Literature was known to be Kokoschka's own metier. He always worked visually with literature as a poet, and as a man of letters, who at times in fact wrote more than he painted – for example, in his Prague days and also in the early London years. His literary works, the dramas and tales, as well as his memoirs, bear witness to his processing and further developing Expressionist approaches, unconventional stage work and considerable long windedness. That applies equally to his novel like self-portrayal as it does to his epic *Comenius* drama, but also to great tales, as, for example, *Ostern auf Zypern* (*Easter in Cyprus*). Particularly for this, Agatha Christie's great praise – somewhat surprisingly – must have flattered Kokoschka. In a letter of 19 May 1968, the legendary crime writer wrote him, 'Easter in Cyprus' shows a downright colourfulness in its presentation and reads like 'a picture in print'.[47] Even more surprisingly, she confessed to him that she had a 'wooden angel from Oberammergau' on her mantelpiece.[48] He attested to the reverse – which occurred seldomly enough – to contemporary painter Jack Butler Yeats (1871–1957), brother of the Irish poet, to whom he wrote: 'You alone can today tell in painting such touching stories!'[49] That was in reference to Yeats' painting *The Two Travellers* (1942), which in colouration, painting technique (turbulent, contrasting brushstrokes) and thematic interest in people who are connected to each other in their isolation actually shows an affinity to Kokoschka's concerns.

That the romantic novelist and art lover John Berger, himself author of works on the ways of seeing, declared in a letter to Kokoschka his intention to translate the artist's tales into English substantiates once again the affinity of this literary work to the visualisation of worldly experience.[50]

The relationship between linguistic and visual arts representation in Kokoschka's work is also discernible, for knowledgeable readers, in his memoirs. Gottfried von Einem reaffirms this in a letter of 27 September 1971, after he first places Kokoschka's *Mein Leben* in the context of his own creative principles: 'This prose is like one of your great landscapes, like one of the incredible, stupendous portraits. The courage to look at one's reflection and acknowledge it without adornment.'[51] So too Edgar Salin, the broadly educated economist and friend of Kokoschka's, after reading *Mein Leben* speaks of an 'exciting self-portrayal' of the artist.[52] Hermann Broch wished for a meeting with Kokoschka and an exchange about *Die Schlafwandler* (*The Sleep Walkers*) and *Tod des Vergil* (*Death of Virgil*).

If we visualise only the most important examples of Kokoschka's graphic treatment of literature (apart from the lithographs for numerous of his own works, those of his brother Bohuslav and for his sister Berta's poems), then the range of work after 1945 from the *Odyssee* (*Odyssey*, 1965), the biblical series *Saul und David* (1969) to Aristophanes' *Die Frösche* (*The Frogs*, 1969) and Knut Hamsun's novel *Pan* (1978) are sufficient. In addition, there are the quasi-literary lithographs of his series *Bekenntnis zu Hellas* (1964), *Apulien* (*Apulia*, 1964), *Marrakesch* (*Marrakech*, 1966) as well as the collection of the *Handzeichnungen (1906–1969)* (*Drawings*). The graphic print work edited by Hans M Wingler and Friedrich Welz was available from 1975, wherein Welz especially focused on the early prints (1906–1912) in a monograph (1977). In addition, there are the stage and costume designs for Mozart's *Zauberflöte* (*The Magic Flute*, 1954/55), for plays by Ferdinand Raimund (1960/1962) and Verdi's opera *Ein Maskenball* (*A Masked Ball*, 1969). Particular priority, however, should be given to Kokoschka's lithographic treatment of Heinrich von Kleist's tragedy *Penthesilea* (1969/1970) as well as – which is not well known –the tale *Einstein überquert die Elbe bei Hamburg* (*Einstein crosses the Elbe at Hamburg*) by Siegfried Lenz (1976).

The ten dry-point etchings for *Penthesilea* form the highlight of Kokoschka's years-long preoccupation with this drama. It is easy to believe that this goes back to his school days. It is evident that his early dramatic efforts were influenced by Kleist's pre- or hyper-Expressionist poetry. Kleist's drama might have stood as godparent to *Mörder Hoffnung der Frauen*. In addition, Kokoschka's library contains a copy of *Penthesilea* for nearly every life stage, whether as an inexpensive Reclam-booklet or a valuable special edition.[53] At one point in his work, he revealed the direct connection between his understanding of *Penthesilea* and his complex feelings for Alma Mahler. When, in the spring of 1969, he was asked to reproduce the fans he had made for Alma Mahler, he created the lithograph *Achill vor dem Abgrund, auf der Flucht vor Penthesilea* (*Achilles on the Precipice, Fleeing Penthesilea*) as a cover.[54] The dramatist Kleist seemed ubiquitous in Kokoschka's life. In exile, too, he sought Kleist material. Thus, he acquired an edition of *Amphytrion* (*Amphitryon*) at Blackwell's in Oxford, and occupied himself with *Prinz Friedrich von Homburg*, although *Penthesilea* and the power of emotions represented therein absorbed him more than anything else. And yet his intention with the *Penthesilea* illustrations 'from the outset was directed towards the dramatic and the dialogical.'[55]

In Kokoschka's estate there were notes that formed the basis for a lecture given in Hamburg in June 1951; they indicate an unqualified appreciation of Kleist's *Penthesilea*. It is practically mandatory to reproduce these notes unedited because they once again provide an insight into Kokoschka's 'stream-of-consciousness' thinking and reveal the progression and volatility of his line of reasoning. He begins his five-part presentation with an audience-friendly question of principle in order to set up the issue of mythical dimension.

1) Can the greatest German-language masterpiece – Heinrich von Kleist's *Penthesilea* – even be performed?

Play of love unto death

Glorious Achilles [who] voluntarily imprisons himself to the Amazon with her small feet, distraught by love, whom [Penthesilea let] ferocious dogs [tear apart] limb from limb, [like] Artemis her Actaeon [killed] with [an] arrow her red-haloed opponent because he saw too deeply into the heart of the other being.

The question of the humanist quality of the language, the animation of mask-like habitual expressions through the mythical play, follows. Kokoschka asks how the language of today could be given back new weight and existential depth – for example, through a tragedy like that of Kleist.

2) Who dares to look into the Medusa face of love today?

By contrast Penthesilea is a myth of the deification of the beloved other. Every myth – it must be speculation, as it was repeatedly found to be necessary to create perpetual gods.

To enliven the rigid features of the mask of the immortal with newly, from perception, created anthropomorphising. Thus the likeness of man becomes immortal through creative power.

Yet from where should appear to a language grown passive, as every normal conceptual language has gradually become, from where should a conception of the face, if the word no longer wants to become a philosophy – the language reflecting a mere superficial world?

Yet has – that this language and the causal law of the entire concept of being as time winning the upper hand in man – then the poet is superseded, world affairs become independent of <u>human action,</u>

becomes a fatality, – man himself an abstraction – for example, the economic man and the like.

If our time still had tears like Penthesilea, to whom the consciousness of human speech returns after the terrible deed and similarly also the contemplation of the face of the deified, who she could have eaten out of love.

Kokoschka further asks about the phenomenon of habituation and about the manifold exponential insanities of two world wars: do we thus see Kleist's *Penthesilea* differently? At the end of this third section Kokoschka directs himself to recite the last words of the Amazon princess Prothoe about her queen Penthesilea: 'She sank, because she bloomed too proud and strong! / The dead oak stands in the storm, / Yet it topples the healthy ones with a crash, / because it can reach into their crown.'[56] What did Kokoschka wish to say with this citation? That only the dead survive, or the illusion that everything would endlessly bloom?

3) [...] how ironic for those of us today as the sense of speech winks at us – absorbing another being out of love – does this mean: wanting to eat someone alive?

Penthesilea gives herself over to death when her senses return. The naked, objective fact is unbearable – appearance lies – not she could have murdered her beloved! Peculiar and strange – that society today tolerates this objectivity – few went mad in the face of the pathetic fact of two world wars in which civilised mankind sank lower than cannibalism.

It simply went beyond any of our ability to imagine – consciousness did not yet return because the language, the one grown passive – could not express – our action – our language syntax modified the subject like an object.

(reads out the last sentence of the drama – the last word on Prothoe)

Then Kokoschka confronts the problem of present traditional thinking on the stage, whereby he criticises the popular attempts at updating as too forced and transparent. For him, the human issue remains at the centre – as well as and especially on the stage.

4) We are still stuck deep in neo-classicism – today's stage, too, keeps to external laws – similar to the demanded unity of time and place under Louis XVIII.

We are only satisfied with a causal solution of a problem, a gender problem, social or economic trick that like a chess challenge is solvable based on specific rules of play – our stage shows methodically behaving people, the subconscious must also follow laws – a methodically behaving person consistent with the worldview of theoretical physics is a prerequisite to a planned world.

The modern playwright, who adheres to these laws, attempts in vain to breathe life into this non-existent character in that he allows him to discuss current problems, smoke a cigarette, use the telephone, fire a machine gun – on the stage.

The Greek heroes remain elevated people for us, yet they remain human! With the constancy of a housefly that will not allow itself to be swatted away, Homer compares the goodness of his Achilles without diminishing him. Heroes are allowed to scream, rant, cry because they are human and the writer experiences them as human.

Lessing compares the strolling dolls in high cothurns of classic Voltaire to Shakespeare's characters, in which he finds the mingling of the tragic with the comical unusually successful. They gain our sympathy through the effect of this contrast.

What Kokoschka labels as his 'Acknowledgement of Kleist' at the end rests on the autonomy of the (dramatic) language which is kindled by the all-too-human rather than the illustrative. Kokoschka makes use of the time-limited yet characteristic category of experience in doing so.

> 5) This inner authenticity of the experience is typical of all drama-tists of the Baroque, in England also Marlow, Webster – the Silesian school of poetry of a Hoffmannswaldau – and most notably Hein-rich von Kleist.

> If our time prefers to follow mandatory mechanistic laws to the inner freedom of our existence – we naturally also remain sceptical, where Lessing urges that painting becomes mute poetry – poetry speaking painting.

> This my acknowledgement of Kleist is equivalent to my belief in the promethean spark which preserves a human language to itself. A play about love unto death.[57]

Kokoschka's appreciation of Kleist's *Penthesilea*, with his various basic objections reaching to the (stage) aesthetic, moved the problem of humanness logically into the centre of interest. What Kokoschka left behind here in simple notes concentrates for his part on five 'pro-methean sparks', words to ignite which get by without much pathos, however carried by the acknowledgement of unconditional love, even when – as in the case of Penthesilea – it destroys. Kokoschka solves the riddle of love through the ambiguous expression 'a play about love unto death'. Because it can be read imperatively in the sense of: a play about love until death. It can also mean playing with love to the extreme end. It is obvious that these statements by Kokoschka about Kleist's agonising love tragedy stir up memories of his own need for love in the relationship with Alma Mahler. Yet in May 1961 we read in one of his letters a part that begins with an unusual (even for him) biblical 'See': 'See, how they still do not understand and do not know

"Penthesilea"' (Br IV, 188). Apparently, he wished to redress this ignorance with his graphic work on Kleist's tragedy play.

The expressive strength of his *Penthesilea* etchings leads one to forget this is a late work. Kokoschka offers scenic distillations in which dramatic movement, love mania and the felling of destruction come across as dramatically as they are subtle. This cycle may be considered the highpoint of his late graphic work on the basis of its intensity and, despite the shrill dissonance in the material, its internal consistency in the drawing of line and contour. It is particularly impressive the way in which the line of Penthesilea's inner arm and the line of the mutilated Achilles' skull become one.

Showing man deformed by the tragic mating game with death was certainly part of giving expression to humanness for Kokoschka – as in the case of his graphic *Penthesilea* efforts. That is probably why Victor Dirsztay's (1884–1935) novel *Der Unentrinnbare* (*The Inescapable*) appealed to him as early as 1923, so much so that Kokoschka furnished it with drawings. Here it is a case of the physiognomy of one attracted to the music of Gustav Mahler. The reader becomes witness to a failed listening experience of Mahler's Third Symphony in the Vienna Musikvereinssaal: '[…] the sounds soon flowed apart horribly out of tune, as if they wished to pick each other up; the ear did not perceive anything more than dissonant noise.'[58] Pursued by 'incoherent sequences of sounds', the first-person narrator flees into the motion-picture theatre, *vulgo*: cinema. There he sees himself on the screen. This ego development proves to be a cinematic event. Apparently this phenomenon and the change in medium within the novel particularly appealed to Kokoschka, as did the scene in which the I-narrator in this cinematic projection appears a second time next to himself as self-duplication, a theme that Alfred Kubin would pick up and illustrate no less impressively in 1948 on the basis of Fyodor Dostoevsky's novel *Der Doppelgänger* (*The Double*).

Seeing is to mean not accepting a matter as it is, but to create – in seeing – that matter anew and thus an alternative to the world. Seeing unleashed energies to counteract transience. And further: the painter must insist on bringing his own person into play, to bare his soul. He who denies himself will hardly discover the truth of the other because he himself has become a part of this truth. These insights are found in a little-known essay by Siegfried Lenz (*Über den Künstler Oskar Kokoschka*; *On the Artist Oskar Kokoschka*), that was added to an anniversary cassette tape which appeared on the occasion of Kokoschka's ninetieth and Lenz's fiftieth birthdays (1976).[59] It documents a further example of a stroke of luck in this artist's life rich in collaboration with authors and musicians. Lenz – his essay supports this sufficiently – had understood this older artist (by exactly forty years) precisely because he claimed that Kokoschka also understood his subject in painting. Even if Lenz shared the opinion with Kokoschka that the word should become a world image, he postulated something further in the work of this artist: 'Artists cannot accept: he [Kokoschka] raises objection to the status quo; he rejects the world as fait accompli, he takes the world and transforms it.'[60]

Kokoschka, on the other hand, opted for a 'Geschichte in drei Sätzen' ('Story in Three Sentences') by Siegfried Lenz: *Einstein überquert die Elbe bei Hamburg* (1969). With ever a keen eye for the essential, he extracted five motifs from the story as the basis for his lithographs: 'Blick über die Reling' ('View From the Ship's Railing'), 'Der alte Passagier' ('The Old Passenger'), 'Das Paar' ('The Couple'), 'Die stürtzende Frau' ('The Falling Woman') and 'Frau in Wehen' ('Woman in Labour'). Here, too, confirmation can be found for what Lenz saw in him: 'The artist opens our eyes to the meaning of the unspeakable (by which he meets with the composer).' His vision is like an uncovering, even like an intensification, while at the same time he is able – a sign of true mastery, according to Lenz – to 'subjugate' the variations of the original.

What is particularly noticeable about these lithographs – for example, in contrast to those of *Penthesilea*, but also the *Pan* cycle based on Hamsun – is the sparing use of contouring, a reductionism which often makes do with hints (not to be completely and utterly heretical with respect to Kokoschka) in that these drawings abstract from their motifs. Yet, the motifs themselves are about human, all-too-human moments: the glimpse into the wide open from an object of the transitory, the ship; age; silently loving togetherness, the couple on their way to the clinic; the disaster; the prospect of new life in agony.

There were apparently sufficient optical resonances for Kokoschka in Lenz's *Einstein* tale. Its visual beginning alone must have intuitively appealed to him: 'This here is a photograph to read, to search and rediscover in any event, because a few words are not sufficient for such a wide angle, it makes the eye voluble offers [...].' There is talk of the 'Elbe's descriptive breadth', of a 'summery harbour portrait', of the old man ('Einstein') with his 'iron-grey' (not 'ice-grey') hair who increasingly attracts the attention of the narrator and the reader, even while the heavily pregnant woman is ambushed by labour pains on the deck. At the end, we see the old man, who leaves the 'summery harbour picture' like one 'who determines for himself what a fact is?'[61] What an exit, what an end to a great little tale! Had Kokoschka felt differently about it, he would scarcely have troubled himself to work with five of its motifs and scenes. Incidentally, Lenz's only implied fate of the pregnant woman will have reminded him of his own, perhaps most important, tale of *Ann Eliza Reed* who perishes due to her pregnancy. And, in addition, Kokoschka once again found himself in his beloved Hamburg with this work: 'Always at defining moments, I always came to Hamburg', as on the occasion of an exhibition opening there on 29 April 1965 he stated and clarified: 'as the gate to the world lay in ashes. And during the flood catastrophe.'[62] And even in such a speech – passed on in an anonymous postscript – he recalled a story, a tale, in this case about a lobster who could not die. He framed it – as he so often did – with an acknowledgement and a criticism of science: '[...] opening the world, meaning opening the person, in general that was the European to me, always. [...] In fear for our lives after two world wars we fled to the moon and because we are infatuated with physics, the sciences and with mathematics.'[63]

How emphatically European Kokoschka was. As with Hofmannsthal, Joseph Roth and Stefan Zweig, this Europeanness was rooted in a specific understanding of Austria as a place of pluralistic cultural consciousness. Even if he repeatedly rejected the utopian, his hopes for Austria were a lifelong second ideal in addition to the ideal of a peace education in the spirit of Comenius: Austria as spiritual life form, this cultural utopia permeated him even when he was disappointed in, even despaired of, the state of the country. He pinned his hopes on the youth of the country at the heart of Europe. It should go without saying: he who never despaired in the land of his origin ought not to use the word 'homeland', which has been rendered almost meaningless through overuse. As Kokoschka wrote to his friend Albert Ehrenstein in November 1937, from Wittkowitz bei Mährisch-Ostrau: 'In reality there is no homeland, only customs officials with regulations from the fatherland [...]' (Br III, 57).

Austria as *Pars Pro Toto* for Seeing and a Friend's Painful Letter

And yet, Kokoschka's living environment and conceptual horizons were – despite numerous transatlantic excursions – influenced by old Austria and Europe; Theodor Heuss, as previously cited, had interpreted this quite correctly. For all the interest in the development of the Second Republic, Kokoschka's Austria was the highly cherished Europe in a nutshell. Austro-fascism appalled him precisely because it made him aware of the abandonment of humane policy. To a certain extent he conceded that Kurt von Schuschnigg attempted – in despair – to create a new civilising of Austrian politics. He formulated his letter of 3 August 1937 to the Austrian chancellor as a petition for the legal protection of an 'Austrian citizen' in a follow-up to Hitler's Munich speech on the opening of the exhibition defaming Modernism *Entartete Kunst* (*Degenerate Art*) on 19 July 1937. As mentioned previously, he petitioned 'his' chancellor on the basis of the Cultural Agreement between the 'Austrian Federal State and the German Reich' of 1936, 'to stand up to the German Reich's government for the publishing of crafted artistic work' (Br III, 54). In light of the 'current pogrom-mood dominating against modern artwork in Germany', which leads one to expect a 'picture storm' and a large-scale 'cleansing action', he demanded that the Austrian government take 'diplomatic steps' to protect him and his work.

Had Kokoschka really misread the political realities or did he seriously believe Schuschnigg would apply himself and take up his case?
However one may evaluate this intervention from a personal perspective, it is the legal position in the artist's argument that is once again
apparent. The question of citizenship, which he was aware of through
his future father-in-law, became toxic for him at the time. After his
emigration to Czechoslovakia, Kokoschka had considered applying
for citizenship of the country as early as 1935. According to Czech law
at the time, this would have meant relinquishing his Austrian citizenship. The Constitution of the Republic of 1933 did not entertain the
possibility of dual citizenship. Kokoschka was Austrian and wished to
remain so; he remained so until the bitter end of the First Republic.
Just three days after the 'Anschluss' Kokoschka submitted his application for Czech citizenship to the authorities. The authorities soon
granted his application on 21 July 1938. He now officially belonged
to the people of Comenius, and was also provided with the 'right of
domicile in the City of Prague'. He remained Czech and thus also a
'friendly alien' in his English exile until he took British citizenship in
1947 – primarily to make travel easier.

Kokoschka's view of Austria was clouded and permanently burdened by the early hostilities he had to endure in Vienna. Yet his work
was definitely shown sympathy. As late as May 1937 – and thus two
months before the defamation exhibition *Entartete Kunst* in Munich
– the Österreichische Museum für Kunst und Industrie in Vienna
showed the first great retrospective of his work on Austrian soil with
no fewer than thirty-eight paintings as well as sixty-four drawings and
graphics from all of Kokoschka's creative periods. It would be another
ten years before there would be an even more extensive retrospective
in Basel, which Kokoschka himself opened with a lecture on picture,
language and writing. For his part he was dubbed on this occasion by
the newly founded weekly *Die Zeit* a 'painter with X-ray vision'.

As early as March 1937, the curator at the Kunsthistorischen
Museum and co-founder of the Gesellschaft zur Förderung moderner
Kunst (Society for the Furtherance of Modern Art) Ernst Buschbeck
(1889–1963; he emigrated to London in 1939) turned to Kokoschka

with the following missive, which demonstrates in what high regard the artist was held in Austria prior to the 'Anschluss'.

> Dear Herr Professor!
> I do not know whether you are aware that the Austrian government together with the Direction des Musées Nationaux will stage a very large, representative exhibition of Austrian art in Paris this spring from 24 April to 13 June. It would naturally be of great importance to us to see you well and amply represented there, which is not all that easy as the exhibition, which Moll is staging of you in the Secession is taking place at the same time in part. Now Frau Wolf-Knize would make the portrait of mathematician Janikowski which is in Paris available to us, perhaps also others that can be found here. She would only provide these, however, if she is secure in your consent because she does not wish to do anything that might cause you discomfort. I would therefore beg of you sincerely not to deny us your permission this time to exhibit your pictures: it would be most unfortunate if a representative exhibition of Austrian art from the Middle Ages onward, to which we are incidentally also contributing a vast number of the best in state ownership, were to remain without a worthy representation of your art. I would also like to note that we of course would not exhibit anything that Moll would like for his exhibition and will only proceed in consultation with him.[64]

Incidentally Kokoschka looked on Austria in 1937/1938 similarly to the young Golo Mann, who reflected on the 'Anschluss' in the magazine *Mass und Wert* in June 1939: 'The fate of the Austrian body politic was sealed in 1918, not 1938; the Allied Powers, not Hitler, were its executioners.' The rump state Little Austria was an artificial entity. Yet:

> even the artificial can flourish with clever, moral leadership; perhaps something could have been done with this Austrian state in the context of a new Central European order. It was left to its own fate; tragic due to its previous history, lovable for its landscape and the character of its inhabitants; it lives on in poverty and revolutionary

convulsions. The inevitable [the union with the German Reich] eventually happened, despite repeated interdictions; it is an histori- cal fact that the German–Austrian land borders had all but disap- peared around 1929.[65]

Golo Mann definitely showed sympathy for Schuschnigg, the chancel- lor fighting a losing battle.

> Though the hapless heir of a system not erected by him, Herr von Schuschnigg presumably recognised that his little state, in order to stand fast against the big one, had to differentiate itself from Germany above all morally [...]. Only in the last weeks before the catastrophe could one reaffirm the resistance of the Austrian state with a clear conscience. In greatest danger, its leader found humane language which his predecessors should have never relinquished; there is always something touching when a person, stripped bare of all foreign help, defends something *different* and *better* against a dreadful superior power to the very end.[66]

Many of these insights are consistent with allusions Kokoschka made about Austria at the time and later. As with his own psyche, that of his country of origin was damaged too. Beyond his multi-faceted Come- nius project, Kokoschka continued to occupy himself with the Hab- sburg Empire of the first half of the 17th century and its European legacy. After all, Comenius' education project grew out of the Habs- burg ideals they passed on to the world.

It is, of course, noticeable that Austrian landscapes are not promi- nently represented in Kokoschka's work, apart from the cityscape por- traits of Salzburg and Linz, as well as those of the Wiener Staatsoper. Urban life in Vienna was Carl Moll's domain. As an artist Kokoschka ignored other Austrian cities. He left the Attersee to Klimt and the Wolfgangsee to the tourists. He preferred the Alps in Switzerland. And yet he notes in November 1947: 'I would like to live in Vienna again', recognising, however, the need to go to the USA first, 'where in the six largest museums' collective exhibitions of my paintings are taking place.'[67] That was intended as a broad hint of his intentions to resettle, whereas his relationship with Vienna after 1945 was principally shaped by education: 'It always delights me in Vienna when I see that the youth so depends on me as the teacher, promoter and protector I see myself as.'[68] We have previously spoken of his efforts on behalf of Vienna's starving children. At the end of October 1947 he tried to organise prostheses via the USA for young Austrians disabled in the war. These are examples of Kokoschka's humanism in practice.

In addition to Viktor Matejka, Kokoschka had another *honest* loyal friend in Vienna in Ludwig Münz, the aforementioned director of the Gemäldegalerie der Akademie der bildenden Künste (Picture Gallery of the Academy for Fine Arts). Münz made the following radio announcement on 6 March 1948.

For the first time after a long pause, Kokoschka's paintings are again on public view in the context of this exhibition and everyone who visits this exhibition can form their own opinion of what Kokoschka means for Austrian art.

The homeland did not always make it easy for Oskar Kokoschka, who is deeply attached to it, as important and startling as his work is. There were persecutions, derisions from the first exhibition and the Nazi-regime branded him as degenerate. It is an honorific title, because even at this year's Biennale in Venice the art of the Austrian Kokoschka, next to that of another 'degenerate' artist, Van Gogh, will provide testimony to the greatness, grandeur and integrity of European art. The exhibited works here, which will also be shown at the Biennale, encompass in particular those created in his youth in Austria. For us, who fought for Kokoschka at the time, they have lost nothing of their immediacy, expressiveness of line and colourful liveliness. They remain true documents of deep, human conception.[69]

Münz would prove to be important to Kokoschka in yet another respect. On 3 December 1955 he would write his artist friend one of the harshest letters that, to my knowledge, ever reached him, which the artist nevertheless apparently took note of without responding. In it Münz urgently warns him of false friends, by which he primarily means Friedrich Maximilian Welz. Kokoschka should pay more particular attention to whom he engages with, the more so when dealing with former National Socialists. Kokoschka had visited Vienna from 4 to 8 November 1955 and was present at the re-opening of the Vienna Staatsoper that began with a new production of Beethoven's *Fidelio*. On this occasion, a special delight was bestowed on him: the Vienna Secession Retrospective also opened its doors at this time, honouring Kokoschka with the exhibition of forty-eight paintings, and sixty-five watercolours and prints. Münz references it a month later when he writes:

> Your stay in Vienna, as happy as you may be with your external success, brought some disappointment in more than one respect to those people who always and in more difficult times than now defended you and found for humanity and purity. You must allow an old friend, who stood by you in much more critical moments, to articulate this clearly. You surely have the right to surround yourself with people who seem to be most useful at the moment. For me, however, it will always remain a deeply shattering experience that Oskar Kokoschka, who fights for humanity, surrounds himself with people who so grievously sinned against this humanity.[70]

Münz became even more explicit.

> I had already said to you in Villeneuve that I reject a person like Herr Welz who used the anti-Semitism in the Hitler period to gain advantage. He Aryanised artworks. It would have been nobler – it appears to me – if you had rejected this relationship out of hand. Dr Grimschitz also paid homage to these teachings of anti-Semitism. The defence and battle for human existence is at least as important as the defence of every piece of art. At the time and later, Professor Novotny reproached Grimschitz on how Grimschitz did not protect the noble Dr Blauensteiner who worked under him at the

Austrian Gallery. Blauensteiner fell as a tank driver in Russia [...] It is possible that Grimschitz has now converted – maybe. But it pains me deeply that one of my few still living old friends believes that it is possible to forget such old ties. Believe me, neither Karl Kraus, nor Adolf Loos, Peter Altenberg nor Arnold Schönberg would have any sympathy for your new friends![71]

The Carinthian art historian and museum director Bruno Grimschitz (1892–1964), to whom Münz alludes here and whom Kokoschka presumably met again in connection with the Secession Retrospective, was one of the primary actors in the Aryanisation of private Viennese art collections, as director of the Austrian Gallery (1939–1945). Although he was relieved of all his offices in 1945, he nevertheless regained his teaching certificate at the university ten years later, which he retained until one year prior to his death.[72] It is that 'Dr Grimschitz' to whom Kokoschka refers in a letter of 3 March 1935 because a 'higher authority' explained to him: 'Kokoschka? But no one speaks of him in Austria' (Br III, 17). One may conclude from this that even then Kokoschka must have been quite familiar with Grimschitz.

Now Münz strikes out even further, wherein it becomes clear that his bluntness may also have been justified by the internal Viennese conflicts between Academy and Secession.

I have fought for your art repeatedly as in my youth after my return to Austria in far more difficult times than today and had pushed through against strongest opposition that the central focus of the exhibition 'European Art Yesterday and Today' would be rooms in which your work would be shown next to that of Liebermann, Corinth and Käthe Kollwitz, and then a main room with Munch. The Academy, as I had already told you in Villeneuve, would have staged a very different celebration and exhibition for you, even if you now praise the exhibition of the Secession to high heaven.

[...]

It also seemed my duty, and let me say this at the end, as Max Liebermann and Alfred Ehrenstein are dead, that as perhaps the last surviving Jewish friend from your youth, to speak with total clarity about what has me distraught today. Your life consists – and that is what was so great until now – of the fact that you have always found the way back from serious errors, impossible situations and I am convinced that you will find the way back to yourself again now, and will create works out of renewed consciousness that will allow one to forget again how easily you tied yourself to people who in the horrific Hitler period were only too ready to play along and draw benefit from it. – Personally, I do not have any kind of feeling of revenge against any of these people. On the contrary, I wish each of these people that he finds his honest livelihood. But I am opposed to Oskar Kokoschka surrounding himself with people, who for example are only affiliated with the VdU [Verband der Unabhängigen (The Federation of Independents) – a German nationalist and national-liberal political party] rag, the *Salzburger Nachrichten*. The condemnation of all manner of racial fanaticism, no matter how camouflaged it may appear, is part and parcel of true peace.

There are moments in life when only the friend with innermost conviction must have the strength and courage to openly tell the truth to a friend, no matter how important he may be as an artist.[73]

Furthermore, Münz condemns the project of the equally Nazi-tainted Linz gallerist Gurlitt to found a Kokoschka archive, and deems the Salzburg Summer Academy a 'Salzburg Theatre of Doom' which 'in a deeper sense [is] a calamity' for Kokoschka. Münz likely also appealed to Kokoschka's conscience in such a manner because he himself had to suffer under the malign presence of Nazi thinking in Vienna. Two years after this letter Münz succumbed to heart failure. His widow wrote a moving note of thanks to Kokoschka on 14 April 1957 which reveals that Kokoschka had interceded with the education minister for the criminally shabby treatment to which Münz had been exposed. He, the leading art historian, had been lured from London to Vienna in 1947 with false promises, and he led the Picture Gallery of the Academy there for the wages of a tram conductor. Maria Münz was unambiguous; the pressures brought to bear by the Ministry and worries about his insufficient income had driven her husband to his death – incidentally in Munich at a major Rembrandt conference. Maria Münz continued:

> I have often thought in recent days of the time in 1940, I was visiting you, Ludwig was [interned] on the Isle of Man, Olda's parents had just arrived from Czechoslovakia. You and your wife lived somewhere in St John's Wood in a little flat on the ground floor. At the time you had also spontaneously written to Churchill about Ludwig and a couple of other friends, protesting the injustice [of internment].[74]

Incidentally, Kokoschka had been equally successful with the British authorities in securing the release from an internment camp of Alfred Sohn-Rethel, who thanked him for it in a letter of 30 January 1941.[75] It is hardly surprising that the same behaviour by the Austrian authorities, as revealed in respect of Münz, must have dimmed Kokoschka's image of post-war Austria. Yet efforts were now slowly being made for Kokoschka in Vienna. The municipal authorities of the City of Vienna wrote to him on 16 September 1948:

> Most esteemed Master!
> The signatories of this letter would like to take up a suggestion of University Lecturer Dr Fritz Novotny under the auspices of Executive City Councillor Victor Matejka and arrange an exhibition of your latest work in the rooms of the Historischen Museums der Stadt Wien in City Hall. The City of Vienna hopes it will not meet with refusal if it invites the most important artist in contemporary painting, who began his rise to this rank from our city, to show his work to the broad public [...].[76]

They further suggested, on the urging of the then president of the Wiener Musikverein Rudolf Gamsjäger, who emerged as an ardent Kokoschka admirer, that a Kokoschka exhibition should take place on classical music's hallowed ground, and in the 'Year of Mozart', 1956, in particular. They even had in mind a personal appearance of the artist in the Great Hall of the Musikverein. Friend Matejka beckoned: 'Your paintings are now in a true musical setting, it is the ancestral home of Furtwängler in Vienna, the view out to the Karlskirche continues all the way to Cologne.' Yet Kokoschka made his excuses and preferred to stay on the Rhine, where he painted the interior of Cologne Cathedral and, from typical heights, a soon-to-be-celebrated view of the war-ravaged city.

In between – it was March 1951 – the City of Vienna wanted to bestow the Ring of Honour on the world-famous artist. However, 'jewellery' of this sort held little interest for Kokoschka. Matejka personally advised him to decline the lesser honour and did so with words that require no further comment.

[By now] so many simpletons and idiots in the course of the decades, some at 50, some at 55 and 60, have received the Ring of the City of Vienna, such that it means the total debasement of the character and accomplishment of an O K, if one now bestows this third-class honour on him. I already summoned everything for your 60th birthday to convince the most senior city dimwits of who this O K is and his extraordinary accomplishments. I made them aware that the only Honorary Citizen in the creative arena since 1918 was Richard Strauss, in other words a foreigner. That is proof for how little the Viennese are capable of truly appreciating their own countrymen.[77]

In October of 1951 Kokoschka had re-established ties with Franz Theodor Csokor to effect performances of his plays in Vienna. However, Csokor was himself embittered in view of various rejections. The Burgtheater had only recently turned down his *Pilatus* drama, for example. He expressed himself no less unambiguously than Matejka in his response to Kokoschka: 'Well, you know the Austrians through thorny paths frequently spiced with trip-ups!'[78]

What particularly delighted Kokoschka was the honorary membership of the Austrian PEN-Club, which was bestowed on him at the instigation of Hilde Spiel (whom he, who could never miss an opportunity for a pun, liked to call 'My Dear Playmate' since 'Spiel' means 'game' in German).

However, post-war Austria also gained respect in Kokoschka's eyes, particularly the manner in which the country accepted more than 50,000 Hungarian refugees after the 1956 uprising. According to Kokoschka in a further letter to Theodor Heuss (referring to the Austrian chancellor Julius Raab):

> what distinguishes the old Catholic culture of humanity from the cultural drivel of contemporary society: that one does not stick one's head in the sand, not exist day-to-day with the others 'without me', that the fellow human being is not an abstraction, whatever the communist pacesetters amongst the culture apostles may wish to propagate. (Br IV, 68)

One more thing should be added. The sharpness with which Kokoschka dealt with Austria is explained in most cases by his disappointed love for her difficult heritage, which he never ceased to associate with Europe's core values – most importantly respect for culture. Europe threatened to give up on itself, primarily in the face of the Americanisation of its culture, which – the more frequently he went there after 1945 – became ever more objectionable to him. He commented to Wolfgang Fischer in March 1964, not shying away from drastic comparisons:

> We will soon be making a book, in order to leave a few traces of a more humane past visible for an even darker, more barbaric future. This American devastation of the physical and moral, Hiroshima, pornography and drip art [he aims at Jackson Pollock with this comment] gnaws [...] too deeply into the flesh of Europe's society, and Asia grinningly awaits stewing the European missionary, or what remains edible despite all paralysis in the sausage boiler. (Br IV, 155)

However, that should not be a reason to freeze in fear, but rather one should continue to cultivate one's garden with Voltaire's *Candide*. Austria remained such a garden to him. That is also why his School of Seeing could only be founded there, a *tangible* utopia, if there ever was one.

Austria after 1945 – for Kokoschka this primarily meant a new backdrop for the presentation of his art, no matter how dubious the characters of its protagonists like Welz and Gurlitt may have been. Austria, that became the locus of his School of Seeing in the baroque setting of Salzburg. Austria, namely Vienna, also meant difficult nego-tiations in matters of the restitution of the parental home in Wien-Liebhartstal to his brother Bohuslav. Here he painted the portrait of Vienna's first post-war mayor, Theodor Körner, and formed a belated friendship with Bruno Kreisky, whose accomplishments as a mediator on the world political stage he admired as much as his appreciation for art. Austria, that, however, was also the land of his wounds. We do not know whether he ever looked up the places of his early activities again, his former studio and the places of his Alma, who had long since lived in New York. In Vienna he thought of her, and particularly in April 1960, because he suggested to his so-often coiling 'Anaconda', Gitta Perl-Wallerstein, that she rang Alma on his behalf, in order to make her a little jealous. Alma still wrote him the 'hottest letters' – almost every week (which was a gross exaggeration!). Incidentally, Koko-schka signed the letter to Gitta with the comment: 'I love you and kiss you everywhere' (Br III, 106). One may assume that Olda, who was increasingly responsible for his correspondence, was not present when he wrote this.

Which memories arose there for Kokoschka? Did he have to hand the photograph of him in Dresden in 1921 with the young Gitta Waller-stein? They could have been father and daughter, the yearned-for but denied beloved child. The elegant, relaxed artist; the girl, a budding dancer, with the big bow in her hair, an indicative gesture with the right hand. He is the girl's portraitist, who painted her in blue, Koko-schka's bluest picture of that year, the blue of the Elbe and the sky, which carries over onto Gitta's little dress and her eyes, interlaced with a somewhat dark green, contrasting with the very bright face and lips, which necessarily cover the suggested buckteeth; the arms and hands give away the child's sense of movement. Gitta remembers this Easter in Dresden when she was ten and a half.

> His especially beautiful, manly appearance, the shimmering iridescence which was inherent to him as a result of his intensity, his joy in playfulness, his laughter, as a result of 'seeing things', 'being touched by things' which most people, 'normal' people had overlooked, always made him seem unique to me. His almost spooky ability to read a person's innermost made the greatest impression on me.[79]

The blue with which Kokoschka surrounded his little Gitta was not the blue of the Expressionists, nor the blue of *Der Blaue Reiter* (*The Blue Rider*). But it may have been related to that blue which Ernst Bloch wrote about around that time (1919) in *Geist der Utopie* (*Spirit of Utopia*), a blue into which he wanted to build in order to search for the 'true, real', 'where the simply actual disappears'.[80] Or is this already an indication of an ominous anticipation of that ambiguous blue we read about in Ilse Aichinger's *Die größere Hoffnung* (*The Greater Hope*)?

> The sky laughed sky blue. But they would no longer allow themselves to be deceived! This clear, innocent blue, the blue of the sky, the blue of the gentian and the blue of the Blue Dragoons mirrors the blackness of space in the ball of the sun, this endless, inconceivable blackness beyond the borders![81]

All the same, the optimistic and abysmal, the raised glance and pensiveness, in a visual interplay of photograph and portrait – it may have come back to Kokoschka when he reconnected with Gitta Perl-Wallerstein in April 1960. However, do memories allow hope or does even hope fade with them?

In Comenius' Name: An Afterlife During a Lifetime

If one thinks of only the first decade after the Second World War, then there are no other words to describe Kokoschka's impact than world presence. He creates his later works nearly everywhere and he is represented everywhere: from Venice to New York, from Vienna to Boston. The painting *Prometheus-Sage* (*Prometheus Legend*) creates as much of a furore at the 26th Biennale in Venice as the *Thermopylae* do later. Italy, in particular, seeks him out, and he seeks out the infinite Italian artwork with repeated study visits to Venice, Florence and Rome. Hence, it is hardly surprising that in 1949 Michelangelo Masciotta produces an important monograph on Kokoschka – in addition to Paul Westheim, Hans Platschek, Edith Hoffmann and James S Plaut – a further great overview of his life and work.

Yet from 9 September 1953, the day he moved into his little villa in Villeneuve, this place became his first and last actual home. One can still sense how it continues to be present, this view from the garden of Villa Delphin to the glittering Lake Geneva, even if one is elsewhere. Heat shimmers over Montreux and the Château Chillon swirl in front of the eye.

As Rilke wrote in his cryptic, undated text *Das Testament* in the winter of 1920/1921 at Schloss Berg am Irchel in the canton of Zurich: '[...] The view gained influence.' So, too, here, halfway up above the lake, is a view that was to be painted by Kokoschka many times; as early as 1923, from Blonay, he managed two – dark – views of Lake Geneva; in 1956 the cheerful colour lithograph *Genfer See Landschaft* (*Lake Geneva Landscape*) emerged and three years later the painting *Genfer See* (*Lake Geneva*), in which the perspective avoids the city of Montreux and the focus is on nature, apart from a ship which functions as a type of reference to human civilisation. The mood in these paintings of Lake Geneva is reminiscent of a verse in Friedrich Hölderlin's poem *Abendphantasie* (*Evening Fantasy*, 1799): 'In my old age, leave me peaceful and serene.'[1] That seems to be how Kokoschka wished it after a more-than-stormy life out in the world.

This landscape is such that one can imagine that Kokoschka might have only painted *it* from then on, teasing out secrets with pencil and brush from his favourite place in the garden, a grotto where he often indulged in a whisky. It must have reminded him of his sojourns in Scotland, of the great – to him ever-more-threatening – outside world. This scenery at Lake Geneva was more akin to an oversized yet tranquil internal space which offered him colours of every shade and of a lush southerly flora.

'How much I would rather still be twenty and "notorious" than 70 and "famous"', Kokoschka admitted in a thank you letter to the 'revered, dear head of state' Theodor Heuss. And with typical conceit, he added:

> Then the young ladies still saw something other in me than simply the painter who, like Don Quixote, tilted against the shepherds of 'abstract' artists and made a fool of himself with it, as who can win against the herd instinct of time which is consistent with the technologically civilised mass man! Praise God, though, it is great fun to remain an errant knight, and so I also thank in particular the few upstanding in the land, particularly you, dear friend, who keep their noses held high in the intellectual struggle. (Br IV, 61)

The errant knight of Villeneuve la Mancha sensed that he was in the process of surviving himself. Yet, from the outside, this did not worry him all that much. However, it is abundantly clear from this comment that he noted the risk that his striving or railing against abstraction in art made him seem like a crank and opened him up to ridicule.

Apart from that there was no cause for complaint with respect to his impact on young ladies as he still encountered some who recognised him in the best sense. The most impressive example of this came from the author Luise Rinser (1911–2002), who wrote to Kokoschka the arguably most insightful fan letter in his later years. It was written on 5 September 1950 and again one can only cite it in full.

Dear Herr Kokoschka

You said I should send you something of my work. You said it out of politeness, but perhaps also out of interest in something that has been created in Germany today. Perhaps you like my writing style. I wrote my first book in 1940; it was published by S Fisher (I am also there again now) – then I was banned and eventually (after years of starvation) locked up, and if the war had not ended, I would not be alive here today as I had a difficult trial at the Volksgerichtshof Berlin for 'high treason' (resistance movement). That was not pretty, particularly as I had two small children whose father (he was a student of Hindemith's) was killed in action in Russia in 1942.

So here you have one of the typical fates. (I am also familiar with yours and know how poorly it went for you in your emigration, as for many of my best friends. He, whom 'Jan Lobel' is dedicated to, took his own life out of disappointment in the 'peace' when he returned to G as an American in 1946.)

Now, to me – I am working. It struck me to the core when I heard you say to one of the dumb reporters yesterday: 'To be the first to see the cracks in the wall, long before the others, that is the responsibility of the artist.' You already saw the cracks decades ago, I know that from your portraits. Your first picture that I truly loved though it frightened me was the portrait of Karl Kraus with the two so different halves of the face.

I am delighted to have now seen you in person. You are like your paintings. You have eyes that see through and through, also into the depraved, but the eyes themselves are totally pure. That is odd next to each other: childishness and this extremely keen gaze. (But it is not that odd, they belong together.)

Your Luise Rinser[2]

Kokoschka may have been less impressed by Rinser's gift, her 1948 novella *Jan Lobel aus Warschau (Jan Lobel from Warsaw)*, than by her letter – despite the words of praise that Carl Zuckmayer found for her. This is because the first-person narrator is a 'female artist' who in the last weeks of the war falls in love with a concentration camp prisoner who has escaped from a transport, but reveals nothing of her art or her artistic talents. Instead she hires herself out as a gardener. Only occasionally would her talent for seeing have met Kokoschka's expectations, for example, in places such as this one:

> Barely had the last drop fallen when the evening light broke through the clouds in a fan of rays. The garden glowed in a deep, juicy green from which the fallen jasmine petals shimmered like yellow cream [...] The light trembled in a thousand drops on branches and tips of leaves.[3]

There would be no lack of major retrospectives in the following decades; Kokoschka remained a magnet far into the 1980s and a central figure in the global art trade. Since then it has become quieter around his legacy, which is surprising given the freshness, the immediacy that speaks from his art – especially from his later work. One should learn to appreciate again the tensions which bore fruit in this artist, namely those between the early avant-garde and a conservative visualism. An aesthetic dialectic of elucidation on the requirements of human existence in an age of global threats arose from his work.

Something of this insight permeates the young Thomas Bernhard's critique of an exhibition of Kokoschka's 'newest works' in the weißen Saal of the Residenz in Salzburg in the summer of 1955. He admires Kokoschka's portrait of Pablo Casals, whom he counts among the 'warriors for this our earth' with the cello as 'weapon'. 'Casals: that means remaining unwavering, immutable. That means loving creation despite the bitterness. This powerful painting says all of that.' Then again, Bernhard says of this: 'This is where the colour became a philosophy and the philosophy became the question of mankind.'[4] Bernhard sees 'the monumental tryptic *Thermopylae*' more critically, regarding it as 'not quite mastered'.

The wild colours of human chaos: the fictional annihilation of all culture. Even if it represents his worldview, Kokoschka has not attained the wisdom of, for example, Picasso's latest drawings in the image [...]. It is the horrors of modern hell that flicker through the three over-dimensional paintings, green, red and yellow. The most captivating is the middle piece with the soothsayer Megistias who foretold the demise of the Greeks. This triptych consists of three great attempts. Perhaps the final conclusion is still on the great artist's agenda?[5]

In contrast he considered the views of London and of Linz complete, whereas he believed the exhibition could have totally and readily done without the 'more or less meaningless sketches for the stage designs for this year's *Zauberflöte* (*The Magic Flute*)'.[6] It is comforting to think, though highly unlikely, that Kokoschka was a reader of the Catholic weekly *Die Furche* (*The Furrow*) in which this fierce critique by the young yet completely unknown author appeared.

The period of the late great retrospectives began with the Salzburg exhibition – right across Europe all the way to Japan; though it made sense that the most comprehensive retrospective took place in the heart of the German–Austrian–Swiss corner, in Bregenz, in the Künstlerhaus there (1976). The elder Kokoschka developed into an eminent audience-friendly, marketable phenomenon. Television discovered him. Interviews, documentaries; Kokoschka arrives in Pöchlarn; Kokoschka here; Kokoschka there. He always appears as a citizen of the world with expansive gestures and strong dialectical tint to his speech. Sage, somewhat naïve, shrewd; he appears to television audiences with this picturesque mixture. What he has to say about the monstrosity of the machine in the present could also have been said by a Silesian weaver at the time of revolts against the mechanical loom around 1845. And at the same time, his undiminished efforts for humane conduct, which equally come across in these television recordings, touch the (artistic) struggle for the appreciation of the individual in an age of ideologically re-armed advanced civilisation.

In addition, in the public consciousness, Kokoschka became a

Picasso alternative, as even he styled himself. What did he accuse his notoriously energetic Catalonian rival of? Superficiality. Others certainly also saw it that way, for example, the important sculptor and graphic artist Gerhard Marcks (1889–1981), who commented on Kokoschka's *Thermopylae* paintings in a letter to Ernest Rathenau in December 1958 as follows: 'I thought they were great and, in any event, can better take them to my heart than Picasso's Guernica.'[7] Unquestionably, though, Kokoschka's aversion to Picasso bordered on obsessive. His long-term friend Ernst Rathenau went so far as to advise Olda Kokoschka and Elisabeth Furtwängler to exercise a moderating influence on their husband and friend in this respect and to restrain him from criticising Picasso in public.

> Years ago I swore to OK not to say anything more against Picasso. The paintings of the blue and pink periods as well as many graphic sheets are amongst the greatest that our century has produced. I thus find that such news items are detrimental to OK.[8]

It therefore must have especially irked Kokoschka that another friend, with whom he had been in particularly warm correspondence for some time, the author, translator and art historian Benno Geiger, sent him a postcard of Picasso's *Colomba* (*The Dove*), a plucked dove of peace, from Venice in May 1957. The later photo, which shows Kokoschka with a clay dove around which he has placed his hands protectively, comes across as a response to Picasso's helpless messenger of peace. And one of Kokoschka's students, Michaela Krinner (1915–2006), later created a hand-coloured etching of a dove swooping down.

Kokoschka also dared much for art in his old age. No structure was too precarious for him to climb it with his painting tools. Even a crane basket could serve him as a lookout, in order to – around June 1961 – paint Hamburg harbour scenes. In general, in fact, this gateway to the world rising from fire storm and ruin appealed to him. It was always essential to Kokoschka to gain height at any cost. Thus he painted the view from the Hamburg (and Berlin) high-rise of the Axel Springer publishing house. In Hamburg he not only supervised the installation of his *Thermopylae* triptych at the University in September 1958, but also created the mosaic series *Ecce Homines* for the ruins of the St Nicholas Church, which he personally delivered in April 1974. It was in Hamburg that – due to the pioneering effort of Heinz Spielmann – Kokoschka's literary and essayistic works in four volumes appeared (1973/1974). And it was also in Hamburg that he followed the filming of his *Comenius* play.

And again, and above all: Amos Comenius. Though the red threads in Oskar Kokoschka's works are many, none is redder than the one that is interwoven in the Comenius complex. One gains the definite impression that Kokoschka made Comenius' (1668) warning words to the London Royal Society his own: never to forget 'the higher knowledge'. According to Comenius, this contained a pantheistic empirical principle, which he by no means understood as only a formula of faith: 'God is a being and yet everything, He is everything and yet one.'

It speaks to the concern for his – literary – efforts that Kokoschka returned to his *Comenius* play and fundamentally reworked it in 1972, having, as we recall, begun it in Prague in 1936–1938 and believed it finished at the time. Among Kokoschka's drama creations, *Comenius* represents a one-off. Nothing about this play is reminiscent of this artist-author's Expressionist beginnings, nothing of *Träumenden Knaben*, nothing of *Mörder Hoffnung der Frauen*, of *Hiob* or the *Brennenden Dornbusch*, or even of *Orpheus und Eurydike*. If one thinks of Kokoschka's plays, then it is usually only of those that belong to his tempestuous early work. *Comenius*, however, is a mature work in four acts with picture-like scenes, whereby Kokoschka repeatedly poses the question of what genre his play belongs to.

Edgar Salin's answer to Kokoschka's question, whether his *Comenius* play is truly a play and thus capable of being staged, aims at the essence of this piece and therefore also at its author's view of history.

> The question arose because I found many places that are spiritually moving, but hardly suitable to the stage. In my opinion, the whole should not be played on the stage, rather it would be a really terrific template for one of the great Italian film directors. If one of

these were to take up the spiritual element as well as the political element and have great actors present it, then 'Comenius' would be the enduring, exciting depiction of the dissolution of the Habsburg Empire, exciting not only due to the force of the scenes, but exciting primarily because something is seen here which – I believe – no historian ever realised with this incisiveness: namely that the Habsburg Empire and also the Holy Roman Empire of German nations broke apart not starting with Franz Josef and with the First World War, but already in the Thirty Years' War and already with Charles V, the last great Habsburg, and that it basically belongs amongst the wonders of the world that these fragments then managed to endure another four centuries.[9]

Comenius belongs to the genre of closet dramas, as, for example, Thomas Mann's *Fiorenza*, which does not mean that these plays cannot be staged. Rather they challenge theatrical editing or even film adaptation, as befell this Kokoschka drama 1973/1975 – although not to its detriment. Stanislav Barabáš produced this television play for the Zweite Deutsche Fernsehen. Kokoschka provided his own lithographic cycle, and expressive room and scene designs. It was only with this that he brought his *Comenius* opus to completion. A walk through this play shows that, with it, Kokoschka succeeded in giving his core interests in art, education and politics an interpretable shape. Just as the *Thermopylae* and *Ecce Homines* in many respects represent his pictorial legacy, the same can be said of *Comenius* in a literary sense. In the process, however, Kokoschka did not succumb to the temptation to idealise his Comenius. On the contrary, he shows the problems of his idealism in an increasingly illusion-less time, the travails of an emigrant existence of this sage from Moravia, which he was only able to survive through his commitment to hope for a more peaceful, more humane future through education.

The play has, corresponding to the four acts, four main settings: the inside of the Wiener Hofburg with Capuchin Crypt and the Amalienburg; the Moravian-Silesian provincial town Fulnek; the royal residence in Stockholm; and Rembrandt's studio in Amsterdam. We dive into the world of religious wars, dynastic intrigues (the quarrel between the Habsburg cousins Mathias and Ferdinand), and the Defenestration in Prague; we hear the people's voices in Moravia, and are witnesses to the political manoeuvring of the Swedish queen; we learn quite a bit about the betrayal of Bohemia, which was robbed of its independence in the Peace of Westphalia, and experience a tense domestic scene involving the artist of artists, Rembrandt van Rijn. And Comenius is always present, even if not in the first act, where he is only mentioned incidentally towards the end, though by Wallenstein who asks himself whether Comenius might not be correct in the end, 'to teach the brethren of Bohemia to read the Gospel of peace' (DSW I, 209; Mitchell, 193). The first act is dominated by the conversation between Ferdinand, who eliminates his related rival Mathias, and the 'Court Jew' Shylock, his barber who reports without illusion on the condition of the Jews as the embodiment of the 'guilty conscience' of the powerful. Add to that the rancour over Ferdinand's impending marriage to Eleonore of Mantua. It is the court world just before the outbreak of the Thirty Years' War to which Drabik also belongs, a jester and ventriloquist, who in conversation with his dummy excels at providing the actual truth about political conditions in the Holy Roman Empire of the German Nation. We gain a brief impression of Wallenstein's manoeuvring and Ferdinand's determination now that he has eliminated Mathias to create 'order' again in Bohemia and Moravia with bloody means, and in the name of the Holy Church.

In the second act, we discover – after a leap of ten years – more details about the desperate situation of the reformers in Bohemia and Moravia, who are now being mercilessly persecuted and have either become refugees or are about to. Comenius appears along with a blind girl whom he has adopted, but he loses sight of her in the chaos of escape and continues to search for her. He calls to his brethren in faith: 'Like the Jews, our lot is to be scattered to the four winds. A premonition tells me I will never again tread the ground I came from. I must become a citizen of the world' (DSW I, 236; Mitchell, 214). Comenius, echoing the famous words of Moses, sees the Promised Land but fears he will no longer be able to enter it; however, he learns that the Swedes

wish to grant him political asylum, though he formulates his fundamental belief earlier in conversation with *young* people who demand
drastic action, which shows how little he is inclined to support reform
for reform's sake.

> The Saviour is still being crucified, even if the translated Bible can
> be bought at the fair. Brother! Let us reflect on this freedom in the
> new spirit of the modern age. The common man can be taught to
> read and write, but his mind still bears calluses from the past. Are
> we not all the same, human beings fleeing to a new age, which will
> not become home to us until people learn reason. Animals can be
> tamed, shall man along remain a murderer? (DSW I, 237; Mitchell,
> 215–216)

At the Swedish court, however, Comenius discovers that they want
to give him the title of an 'Educator in Sweden' and that his ideas
of a peaceful accord between the people have spread to the other
state leaders. But the Bohemia of the Reformed is lost. Sweden has
made peace with Habsburg, recognises Cardinal Richelieu's and thus
France's interests in Europe and does not wish to oppose the Counter-
Reformation any longer.

Here, too, Comenius was not to stay – not here in Paris, where
Richelieu approves his plan to build a school of pan-sophistry, nor in
London, though he also commands great respect there; ever-changing
political conditions thwart his continuous effort. At the end we see
him with Rembrandt who is, by commission of Comenius' spiritual
brethren, to paint his portrait. As if by coincidence the portrait comes
about, one of the great late works of the drunken Master; yet the actual
theme of this important fourth act is the human, all-too-human.

We experience Rembrandt with his Hendrickje Stoffels who
manages his impoverished household and provides him with sexual
satisfaction when he is overcome by depression. The *Nachtwache* (*The
Night Watch*) 'is on the easel, darkly glowing in a shaft of storm-shot
light', as the stage direction states. The great artist suffers from vision
problems: 'I can already see pink elephants in the picture. As if my

own eyes were betraying me!' (DSW I, 254; Mitchell, 229). It is the primal fear of the artist, that his vision deceives him, of the composer that he becomes deaf, of the author that his writing freezes.

What follows is the great conversation between Comenius and Rembrandt, who – completely in Kokoschka's style – paints his portrait while speaking, without making a fuss about it. In doing so, Rembrandt proves himself well versed in the Bible if not much of a believer. The language of the Bible is an artistic standard for him: 'The way the most fantastical as well as the most heart-warming stories are told with all the graphic power of the word makes it clear to us that art should not be used to prettify or disguise things' (DSW I, 259; Mitchell, 234). Rembrandt also proves himself an informed reader of Comenius' writings, who for his part compares himself with the immortal Jew: 'For over forty years now I've been wandering from land to land, like Ahasuerus, preaching to deaf ears, unrecognised, and homesick for the country where I was born and where I have been forgotten' (DSW I, 263; Mitchell, 236). If Comenius holds the 'Light of Reason' high in order to find the way out of the 'labyrinth of the world', then Rembrandt works with visions of light and shadow, gradations of darkness and light. While Comenius seems to resign himself in the end ('The dawn of the human spirit was indeed a mirage that left the thirsty people to die in the desert'; DSW I, 264; Mitchell, 237), Rembrandt advises astonishing pragmatism: 'Accept the world the way it is!' (DSW I, 265; Mitchell, 238).

Comenius compares himself to a Jew so often that one considers him to be one: 'You can trust me', he says to a girl who vividly reminds him of his lost adopted daughter, Christl, 'even though I don't wear a Jew's patch. My foreign dress is cause enough for people to throw stones at me. You're a clever girl, Hannah? or Christl? Do you understand? Nowadays they play with people just as a child satisfies its curiosity playing with a toy until it breaks' (DSW I, 268; Mitchell, 240).

The Watch then arrest Comenius in Rembrandt's studio because 'as a Jew' he is illegally in Amsterdam without permission and is not wearing the 'yellow patch on his coat', as is prescribed for Jews. The indignant Rembrandt, who is still working on the *Nachtwache* and thus on figures who now violently disturb his domestic peace, chooses not to complain about this arbitrary behaviour. After Comenius is led away, Rembrandt continues to paint in the dark, namely the likeness of the mysterious girl from the ghetto whom he shares with Comenius to some extent. That, according to Kokoschka's theatre version, is how the famous girl with the chicken got into the picture of the *Nachtwache*.

The girl's – or child's – voice comments: 'In your picture I am there as witness to his compassion, showing to all what being human means' (DSW I, 272; Mitchell, 243). The shunned, the outcast, the girl from the ghetto sees herself, at least in Rembrandt's painting, as being protected by the militia, who have taken Hannah's or Christl's actual protector, the supposed Jew Comenius, into custody. The paradox of secular circumstances pervades Kokoschka's drama to the end. To this day it appears to have lost nothing of its relevance and topicality – quite the opposite.

It was due to his long life and extensive body of work that Kokoschka's legacy was established during his own lifetime. He remained true to his likeness until the end. A few years prior to his death he once again drew himself with lithographic chalk – this after recovering from an eye operation, as if he wanted to prove to himself that he was able to continue to have an uninterrupted view of himself. His facial features remain as unmistakable as his powerful hand. It was the year in which the death of his younger brother Bohuslav, the unsuccessful writer, left him deeply shaken. He apparently needed self-reaffirmation.

There were then only six years between a flood of obituaries and the essays to mark the 100th anniversary of his birth. Nature almost arranged it that the day of his death fell close to his birthday, 22 February and 1 March respectively. Wulf Schön celebrated him as a 'magician of colour' and remembered the 'painter with X-ray vision'; Clara Menck showed fascination with Kokoschka's long journey from 'enfant terrible to classic', spoke of the 'terrible marvel' of his work and grasped that in his work he once again declared man as the measure of all things, as Romeo Giger wrote in his notable appraisal on his 100th birthday. Giger accurately saw, especially in Kokoschka's landscapes, the locus of humanity, even if they usually showed no people.

> Kokoschka's landscapes are not anonymous and hostile to life as in those Expressionists who have dedicated themselves to a destructive nihilism without hope; his painting draws its strength from the fundamental conviction that it is possible to 'regain humanity' [...] and to free oneself from the Dionysian barbarism of a hopeless worldview.'[10]

Peter Sager recalls, in his thoughtful portrayal of Kokoschka's work and impact, a phrase used by the English art critic Herbert Read, that his 'Expressionism in reality was an embittered Humanism'. Incidentally, the art critic had dedicated his book *The Creative Nature of Humanism* to the artist: '[I]n token of my never-ending admiration of his creative Humanism.'[11] Sager then summed up Kokoschka's impact in the apposite sentence: 'Here an artist once again dared a world concept, with baroque pleasure for the eyes and universal appeal.'[12] How impressive, if not overwhelming, this daring of a 'world concept' is, shown by the full appraisal of Kokoschka arranged by the Tate Gallery in London in 1986, which was then also shown in Zurich and New York. Until the great retrospectives in Wolfsburg (2014) and in Regensburg and Prague (2014/2015), this exhibition in London, conceived as all-encompassing, had a sense of legacy about it, which also applied to the accompanying, standard-setting catalogue and broad media coverage supplied by Richard Calvocoressi.

Their thrust was: here *once again* someone has dared that which was considered nearly impossible, namely to assert advocacy for humanness in art and to create this humanity anew. The art historian and later director of the Hamburg Kunsthalle, Werner Hoffman, had acknowledged to the artist during his lifetime:

> You have set the myth of nature against the historicity and the moral responsibility of man – you have reminded the individual of his ethical obligation again – you have clarified the vague

motivating forces in the light of the human and given Eros a human form![13]

In his appraisal on the artist's 100th birthday, Hoffman posited that Kokoschka's life's work consisted of 'wandering pictures'. In the course of six decades, a 'painted travelogue' was thus created. Hoffmann took the motto for his article from the artist's *Comenius* play: 'Yes, I am a refugee, driven from border to border for forty years, by the good citizens who may safely cower behind the heater, timidly recoiling as if from a plague victim.'[14] He also pointed out that in September 1886, the year of Kokoschka's birth, Nietzsche completed the preface to the second volume of his work *Menschliches, Allzumenschliches* (*Human, All Too Human*). It deals with subjectivity's doubt about the expressiveness of modern art. However, the opposite of such scepticism manifests itself in the work of Kokoschka, the pictorial, literary *and* political: humaneness speaks through this work; it summoned up his own mythos and shaped him through the never-paling colours and forms.

Hindsight

Backward glances are retrospective ones, attempts to look through the window of time into the space of a life without ever being able to fathom it. At times you feel like an inquisitive child who presses their face against a windowpane in order to see what is happening inside. In some respects Georg Trakl's poem *Die Nacht* was my window pane as it became apparent that an ever-increasing interest in Oskar Kokoschka was growing out of my preoccupation with this poet; it so happens that this poem was written at the time of the *Windsbraut* painting, in a period of the most intense connection between both artists.

At some point, so it seems, a world citizen is born in every province, one who feels driven out, who grows beyond himself and who becomes a guide in his metier everywhere he appears – in the case of Kokoschka a sage of the possibilities in the visual arts which unsettles, shakes up, leaving no one indifferent, in the name of humaneness.

Three things on these travels with Kokoschka proved particularly surprising: his political awareness; his not infrequent aggressive treatment of artistic traditions; and the simultaneous playfulness and fury, all of which have left deep imprints on his work. Kokoschka, a maker of art, was no stranger to 'cultural animosity', which Hölderlin once attributed to the pre-Socratic Empedocles.

Kokoschka felt driven back to the ancient origins of culture through the use of colours and shapes, especially because he lived through two catastrophes of civilisation brought about and manipulated by politicians, and because his living and loving were severely tested. He who only sees in Kokoschka the villa owner of Villeneuve, who could work in a beautiful landscape and affluence, in worldwide demand as one of the greatest artists of his time, overlooks the essence: Kokoschka drew to the end as one who has been drawn.

Anyone who was intimately involved with him, his wife Olda primarily, had to endure quite a bit, for example, his 'irrepressible rage' (Olda), his erratic behaviour, his eccentric opinions and his endless dalliances. But those were the colours of his life; no one recognised that more clearly than his perceptive wife, who grew and grew in my estimation whilst I worked on this book. It was she who made the life-saving exile in London possible; it was she who created a domestic environment for him, which supported his somehow wild work that, even when he created softly coloured idylls of Lake Geneva, had something turbulent about them under the surface.

And Trakl's poem, which sings out and describes an extreme horror, which sounds so like a hymn and has such an unfathomable effect, repeatedly came up whilst I researched this account of a life's opus. It became clear to me that Trakl had not just written a poem in the context of Kokoschka's painting, but with it captured the substance of this artist's life and work. These lyrical motifs were and became Kokoschka's visual motifs, too. And the ever-shifting moods of this poem always caught up with Kokoschka again. What one wouldn't give to be able to see his portrait of Trakl, which may hang somewhere in the USA or is forgotten in a suitcase. And so this book can only end in that its readers absorb this poem of Trakl's or, yet more effective, quietly read it to themselves.

Georg Trakl
Night

You I sing wild craggy chasms
In tempest night
Towering mountains;
You grey towers
Brimming with hellish grimaces,
Fiery beasts,
Coarse ferns, firs,

Crystal flowers.
Unending torment,
That you hunted down God
Gentle spirit,
With deep sighs in cascading waters,
In swaying firs.

Golden flicker the fires
Of nations around.
Drunken with death
Over blackened cliffs
Plunges the fervid whirlwind.
The glacier's
Blue wave,
And the bell in the valley
Resounds with might:
Flames, curses
And the dark
Games of lustfulness,
Heaven is stormed
By a petrified head.[1]

This, too, was painted with vivid words, written in abrupt script, with pencil and ink. Kokoschka could have provided the poem with colour samples, as he framed some texts, allowing it to darkly shine. He, too, was *rugged*, the visual artist and author. He had come to know the *tempest night*; the *hellish grimaces*, the *fiery beasts* became his motifs, the animalistic, at times refined to *games of lustfulness*, only there can be no talk of the 'heads' that he portrayed as being *petrified*. Quite the contrary: they have remained alive, characterful, permeated by complementary and contrasting colour values. She, however, remained with him, attached herself to him: the *Windsbraut*, Almschi, the Mahler woman. She, his erstwhile 'Windsbraut', Alma Mahler-Werfel, published the first edition of her long-awaited memoirs in 1958, six years before her death, where she goes so far as to say, on page 286, the following: 'Before Kokoschka, I had been married to an abstraction when I was still half a child. But with Franz Werfel, everything I might have wished for on earth had been fulfilled.' The 'abstraction' of a person refers to Gustav Mahler. Kokoschka represents the reference point between the before and after. Werfel, on the other hand, is the fulfilment. In his copy, Kokoschka noted, as if still in conversation with her: 'so be satisfied with it.' It should not remain unmentioned that there are no books by Werfel to be found in his estate's library.

However, in his poem, Trakl saw the 'Windsbraut' as 'drunken with death' – not him, the artist who lies by her in the painting. *She* plunges over 'blackened cliffs', not he. Nevertheless, in life as in art, both survived the plunge over the cliffs, each in their own way.

Hölderlin articulated the yet deeper truth about the state of matters of life in the last stanza of *Hyperions Schicksalslied* (*Hyperion's Song of Destiny*), which Trakl knew and Kokoschka suspected.

> But we are fated
>   To find no foothold, no rest
>   And suffering mortals
>   Dwindle and fall
>   Headlong from one
>   Hour to the next,
>   Hurled like water
>   From ledge to ledge
>   Downward for years to the vague abyss.[2]

Notes

Dedication

1. Henrik Ibsen, *When We Dead Awaken: a Dramatic Epilogue in 3 Acts*, transl by William Archer (London: 1900) <www.gutenberg.org/files/4782/4782-h/4782-h.htm>.

Foundations, or the Journey to an Achievement of the Century

1. Oskar Kokoschka, *Mein Leben*, ed and contrib Remigius Netzer (Munich: 1971), p 31. Hereafter cited in the text with the abbreviation ML and page number.
2. Compare this to the masterly study by Roberto Calasso, *Das Rosa Tiepolos*, transl from the Italian by Reimar Klein (Munich: 2010).
3. Hilde Burger (ed), *Hugo von Hofmannsthal – Harry Graf Kessler, an Exchange of Letters 1898–1929* (Frankfurt am Main: 1968), Nr 12.
4. Oskar Kokoschka, *Briefe I-IV. Vol. IV*, ed by Olda Kokoschka and Heinz Spielmann (Düsseldorf: 1988), p 222. Hereafter cited in the text with the abbreviation Br and volume and page numbers.
5. Carl Einstein, *Die Kunst des 20. Jahrhunderts* (Berlin: 1926), p 144 (the chapter dedicated to Kokoschka is found in the double-columned, large-format pp 147–149).
6. Ibid.
7. Ibid, p 148.
8. Max Dauthendey, 'Norsland in allen Farben', in *Max Dauthendey, Frühe Prosa*. From handwritten unpublished work, ed by

Hermann Gerstner in collaboration with Edmund L Klaffki (Munich/Vienna: 1967), p 225.

9. *Ernst Barlach, Dramen: Der Tote Tag*, ed by Helmar Harald Fischer (Munich/Zurich: 1988), p 162. Thomas Mann appraised this play in 1924: 'A tragedy of the man, the son of gods, that will forever remain a mummy's boy to jealously clinging Earth'; ibid, p 12.

10. *Oskar Kokoschka, Das schriftliche Werk in vier Bändern*, ed by Heinz Spielmann (Hamburg: 1973–1976), Vol IV, p 116. Hereafter cited in the text with the abbreviation DSW, volume and page numbers.

11. Thomas Anz, Michael Stark (eds), *Expressionismus. Manifeste und Dokumente zur deutschen Literatur* (Stuttgart: 1982), p 685 f.

12. Alfred Lichtwark, *Übungen in der Betrachtung von Kunstwerken nach Versuchen mit einer Schulklasse*, ed by Lehrervereinigung zur Pflege der künstlerischen Bildung (Dresden: 1898). Kafka recommends Lichtwark's work in a letter of 26 September 1916 to Felice Bauer in connection with their own pedagogic efforts in the Jewish People's Home in Berlin in *Franz Kafka, Briefe an Felice und andere Korrespondez aus der Verlobungszeit*, ed by Erich Heller and Jurgen Born, 2nd edition (Frankfurt am Main: 2009), p 709.

1: The Journey

1. Oskar Kokoschka, *Das schriftliche Werk in vier Bändern*, ed by Heinz Spielmann (Hamburg: 1973–1976), Vol III, p 251. Hereafter cited in the text with the abbreviation DSW, volume and page numbers.

2. Br, I, 10 (letter dated 11 August 1909).

3. Hugo von Hofmannsthal, *Gesammelte Werke in zehn Einzelbänden: Reden und* Aufsätze II (1914–1924), ed by Bernd Schoeller, in consultation with Rudolf Hirsch (Frankfurt am Main: 1979), pp 55–68.

4. See Heinz Spielmann, *Oskar Kokoschka. Leben und Werk* (Cologne: 2003), p 14. Nietzsche's *Ecce Homo* translated by Mark Daniel Cohen, 'Nietzsche – A Selection of Poems in Translation', *Hyperion*, Vol II, issue 4, December 2007, p 9, <www.nietzschecircle.com/N_poetry_MDC1.pdf>; *Dionysus Dithyrambs* transl by James Luchte © James Luchte, 2010, *The Peacock and the Buffalo: The Poetry of Nietzsche*, Continuum Publishing, used by permission of Bloomsbury Publishing Plc.

5. Elias Canetti, *Party im Blitz. Die englischen Jahre*, from the estate, Kristian Wachinger (ed), with postscript by Jeremy Adler (Munich/Vienna: 2003), p 168.

6. Spielmann, *Oskar Kokoschka*, p 108.

7. Stefan Zweig, *Die Welt von Gestern. Erinnerungen eines Europäers*, 38th edition (Frankfurt am Main: 2010), pp 15–44.

8. See among others Michiko Mae, Elisabeth Scherer (eds), *Nipponspiration – Japonismus und japanische Populärkultur im deutschsprachigen Raum* (Vienna/Cologne/Weimar: 2013).

9. Oskar Kokoschka, *Plays and Poems*, transl by Michael Mitchell (Riverside, CA: 2001), p 4. Hereafter cited in the text as Mitchell with page number.

10. See, in particular, Inga Rossi-Schrimpf, George Minne, *Das Frühwerk und seine Rezeption in Deutschland und Österreich bis zum Ersten Weltkrieg* (Weimar: 2012).

11. Hans Maria Wingler, *Kokoschka-Fibel* (Salzburg: 1957), p 22.

12. Christian Brandstätter (ed), *Die Welt von Gestern in Farbe* (Vienna: 2009).

13. Franz Pfeuffer, 'Die neue Franzensbrücke über den Donau-Canal in Wien', *Zeitschrift des Österreichischen Ingenieur- und Architekten-Vereins*, 18 (1900).

14. Pjotr A Fürst Kropotkin, *Moderne Wissenschaft und Anarchismus* (Berlin: 1904). A copy with numerous annotations can be found in Kokoschka's bequest library in the Oskar Kokoschka-Zentrum in the archive of the Universität für angewandte Kunst Wien.

15. Ibid, p 41.

16. See Willi Reich, Alban Berg. *Leben und Werk* (Munich/Zurich: 1985), p 24.

17. Egon Friedell, *Ecce Poeta* (Berlin: 1912), p 22 f. The presentation copy can be found in Kokoschka's bequest library.

2: Determination and Confusion

1. Johann Amos Comenius, *Orbis Sensualium Pictus*, ed by Johann Kühnel, facsimile of the original of 1658 (Leipzig: 1910). A copy can be found in Kokoschka's bequest library in the Oskar Kokoschka-Zentrum in the archive of the Universität für angewandte Kunst Wien. I thank the director, Frau Dr Bernadette Reinhold, for the reference and access. Translation by Charles Hoole, 1658, as found in C W Bardeen (ed), *The Orbis Pictus of John Amos Comenius* (Syracuse, NY: 1887).

2. See Ernst Klee, *Das Kulturlexikon zum Dritten Reich. Wer war was vor und nach 1945* (Frankfurt am Main: 2007), pp 249–253.

3. Johann Wolfgang von Goethe, *Werke, Hamburger Ausgabe*, ed by Erid Trunz (Munich: 1988), Vol III, p 159, v 5106/5107. Hereafter cited in the text with the abbreviation HA, volume and page numbers. Transl by A S Kline (2003), <goethe.holtof.com/faust/FaustIIActISceneItoVII.htm>.

4. Quoted by Hermann Köstler, 'Oskars guter Geist. Zum Tod von Olda Kokoschka', *Neue Zürcher Zeitung* (26 June 2004).

5. Elias Canetti, *Party im Blitz. Die englischen Jahre*, from the estate, Kristian Wachinger (ed), with postscript by Jeremy Adler (Munich/Vienna: 2003), p 168.

6. Ibid.

7. Köstler, *Oskars guter Geist*.

8. Canetti, *Party im Blitz*, p 166.

9. Alma Mahler-Werfel, *Mein Leben*, foreword by Willy Haas (Frankfurt am Main: 1980), p 50.

10. Quote from Elana Shapria, *Style and Seduction: Jewish Patrons, Architecture and Design in the Fin de Siècle Vienna* (Lebanon,

NH: 2016) p 191. A hand-written entry by Kokoschka is beside the drawing.

11. Karl Kraus, *Worte in Versen* (Leipzig: 1916). The presentation copy is in the artist's bequest library.

12. For the issues Kraus/Kokoschka, see Régine Bonnefoit, Bernadette Reinhold, 'Die Nachlassbibliothek von Oskar Kokoschka – neue Perspektiven in der Kokoschka-Forschung' in *Spur im Treibsand. Oskar Kokoschka neu gesehen. Briefe und Bilder*, ed by Régine Bonnefoit and Ruth Häusler (Petersberg: 2010), pp 35–61, in particular pp 46–48.

13. Walter Muschg, 'Von Trakl zu Brecht' in *Die Zerstörung der deutschen Literatur und andere Essays*, ed by Julian Schütt and Winfried Stephan, with a postscript by Julian Schütt (Zurich: 2009), p 690.

14. The only examples cited are the films *Die Windsbraut* (2001) by Bruce Beresford, *ALMA* by Paulus Manker (2007) and the novel by Hilde Berger, *Ob es Haß ist, solche Liebe? Oskar Kokoschka und Alma Mahler* (Vienna/Cologne/Weimar: 2008).

15. See in particular Oliver Hilmes, *Witwe im Wahn* (Munich: 2004), p 34 ff.

16. Translated by A S Kline (2004), <www.poetryintranslation.com/ PITBR/German/Goethepoems.php#anchor_Toc74652106>.

17. Heinz Spielmann, *Oskar Kokoschka. Leben und Werk* (Cologne: 2003), p 140.

18. Henning Mankell, *Treibsand. Was es heißt, ein Mensch zu sein*, transl from the Swedish by Wolfgang Butt (Vienna: 2014), p 103.

19. Heinz Spielmann, *Oskar Kokoschka. Leben und Werk* (Cologne: 2003).

20. Alma Mahler-Werfel, *Mein Leben*, p 53.

21. Ibid.

22. Heinz Spielmann, *Oskar Kokoschka. Die Fächer für Alma Mahler* (Hamburg: 1969), p 30.

23. Lines from Trakl's poem transl by Max Wickert, *The Poems of Georg Trakl*, 2009.

24. See Rüdiger Görner, *Georg Trakl. Dichter im Jahrzehnt der Extreme* (Vienna: 2014), particularly pp 176–180.

25. Wolfgang Schneditz, 'Kokoschkas Erinnerungen an Trakl', *Die Presse* (Vienna: 21 October 1950) Nr 42, p 6.

26. Georg Trakl, *Dichtungen und Briefe*, ed by Walther Killy and Hans Szklenar, 2nd expanded edition (Salzburg: 1987), Vol I, p 475. English translation by A S Kline, <poetryintranslation. com/PITBR/German/FaustIIActISceneItoVII.php>.

27. Ibid, p 499.

28. Klaus Manger, 'Trakl und die "Franziska Kokoschkas"', *Neue Zürcher Zeitung* (3/4 August 1985), Nr 177, pp 47–48.

29. Marie Luise Kaschnitz, *Gesammelte Werke*, ed by Christian Büttrich and Norbert Miller, Vol 5: *Die Gedichte* (Frankfurt am Main: 1987), p 245 f.

30. Ibid, Vol VII: *Die essayistische Prosa*, p 279. See also Brigitte Raitz (ed), '"Ein Wörterbuch anlegen". Marie Luise Kaschnitz zum 100. Geburtstag', with an essay by Ruth Klüger, *Marbacher Magazin* (95/2001), pp 102–104 (Eintrag Windsbraut).

31. Alma Mahler-Werfel, *Mein Leben*, p 49.

32. Ibid, p 50.

33. Ibid, p 55.

34. August Stramm, *Du. Liebesgedichte* (Berlin: 1916), p 5. See also the edition August Stramm, *Die Dichtungen. Sämtliche Gedichte, Dramen, Prosa*, ed and postscript by Jeremy Adler (Munich: 1990), pp 28–29. Transl by Isham Cook, www.ishamcook. com, <ishamcook.files.wordpress.com/2011/11/august-stramm-poems-19881.pdf>.

35. The copy can be found in Kokoschka's bequest library.

36. Zentralbibliothek Zürich, Nachlass Kokoschka, Sig 271.4.

37. Ibid.

38. Ibid, Sig 346.18.

3: Wartime Art

1. See British Library, Postcard by Adolf Loos about Oskar Kokoschka's injury, <www.bl.uk/collection-items/kokoschka>.
2. August Stramm, *Du. Liebesgedichte* (Berlin: 1916), p 110. Author's translation.
3. Estate of Leonard Forster, Box 130: Oskar Kokoschka, Senate House Library, London.
4. First discussed by Leonard Forster, 'An Unpublished Letter from Rilke to Kokoschka', *German Life & Letters* 15 (1961) 1, pp 21–24, here p 21.
5. Herman Meyer, 'Die Verwandlung des Sichtbaren. Die Bedeutung der modernen bildenden Kunst für Rilkes späte Dichtung' in Rüdiger Görner (ed), *Rainer Maria Rilke. Wege der Forschung*, Vol 638 (Darmstadt: 1987), pp 131–184, here p 156.
6. Ibid, p 156 f.
7. Rainer Maria Rilke, *Werke. Kommentierte Ausgabe in vier Bänden*, Vol 2: *Gedichte 1910 bis 1926*, ed by Manfred Engel and Ulrich Fülleborn (Frankfurt am Main/Leipzig: 1996), p 548. Including the poem, pp 148–151.
8. Rainer Maria Rilke, *Haßzellen, stark im größten Liebeskreise. Verse für Oskar Kokoschka*, ed Joachim W Storck (Marbach: 1988), p 13.
9. Rilke, *Werke*, Vol 2, pp 148 and 149 (V 1 and V 31 f). Author's translation.
10. Ibid, p 150 (V 45–48). Author's translation.
11. Ibid (V 53–56). Author's translation.
12. Ibid (V 57–60). Author's translation.
13. Stramm, *Die Dichtungen*, p 97; transl by Isham Cook, www.ishamcook.com, <https://ishamcook.files.wordpress.com/2011/11/august-stramm-poems-19881.pdf>
14. Albrecht Scholz, 'Ärzte und Patienten in Dresdner Naturheilsanatorien', *medizin – bibliothek – information* 4 (2004), Nr 1, pp 13–19.
15. George Grosz, *Ein kleines Ja und ein großes Nein* (Hamburg: 1955), p 135.

16. Donata Kaman, *Theater der Maler in Deutschland und Polen* (Münster: 2001), p 102 f.

17. Camill Hoffmann, 'Kokoschkas Dichtung und Theater', *Das Kunstblatt* (Jahrgang 1917), Nr 7, pp 219–221, here p 221.

18. Hugo Zehder, 'Dresdner Theater', *Tägliche Rundschau*, 6 June 1917.

19. Camill Hoffmann, 'Kokoschkas Bildnisse und Phantasien', *Die Dame* (1917), Nr 3, pp 6–7, here p 7.

20. See Gertrud Pott, *Die Spiegelung des Sezessionismus im österreichischen Theater* (Vienna: 1975), pp 46–56; Kaman, *Theater der Maler in Deutschland und Polen*, pp 104–107.

21. Knut Hamsun, *Pan. Aus Leutnant Thomas Glahns Papieren*, novel, transl from the Norwegian by Ingeborg Keel and Aldo Keel, afterword by Aldo Keel (Zurich: 2009), p 193.

22. Adalbert Stifter, *Der Nachsommer*, with an afterword and selected bibliography by Uwe Japp, annotations and chronology by Karl Pörnbacher (Düsseldorf/Zurich: 2005), p 89.

23. Ibid, p 89 f.

24. See Ingrid Mesterton et al (eds), *Ernst Josephson. 1851–1906 Bilder und Zeichnungen* (Bonn: 1979).

25. See important study by Judith E Bernstock, *Under the Spell of Orpheus: The Persistence of a Myth in Twentieth-Century Art* (Carbondale, IL: 1991).

26. See Reinhard Kapp, 'Zum Stand der Bearbeitung des Orpheus-Stoffes in den zwanziger Jahren' in Jürg Stenzl (ed), *Ernst Křenek, Oskar Kokoschka und die Geschichte von Orpheus und Eurydike*. Ernst Křenek-Studien, Vol 1 (Schliengen: 2005), pp 33–47.

27. Letter from Oskar Kokoschka to Ernst Křenek dated 17 July 1923. Sig IN 220.969 in der Wienbibliothek im Rathaus der Stadt Wien. Cited with kind permission of Dr Marcel Atze.

28. Der Herkules. Cassel, 4 December 1926. The critiques are collected in the Ernst Křenek-Institut, Krems.

29. Ernst Křenek, *Im Atem der Zeit. Erinnerungen an die Moderne*, transl from the American English by Friedrich Saathen, revised transl by Sabine Schulte (Vienna: 2012), p 458.

30. Ibid.

31. Ibid, p 459.

32. Ibid, p 471.

33. Letter dated 6 January 1923. Sig IN 220.968. Wienbibliothek im Rathaus Wien.

34. Křenek, *Im Atem der Zeit*, p 473.

35. See the equally material, rich and readable study by Insa Fooken, *Puppen – heimliche Menschenflüsterer. Ihre Wiederentdeckung als Spielzeug und Kulturgut* (Göttingen: 2012) (I owe this reference to Frau Dr Elisabeth Kohler, Mainz).

36. See Nathan J Timpano, *Constructing the Viennese Modern Body: Art, Hysteria, and the Puppet* (New York: 2017), p 167 f.

37. E T A Hoffmann, *Der Sandmann. Historisch-kritische Edition*, ed by Kaltërina Latifi (Frankfurt am Main: 2011), p 114. For the interpretation see Latifi ('Das ganze ist eine sattsam ausgeführte Allegorie' in *Täuschung und Enttäuschung des Lesers in E. T. A. Hoffmanns Sandmann*), ibid, pp 149–178, esp p 171 ff.

4: Pre-Schooling Vision

1. See Fritz Löffler, 'Dresdner Sezession Gruppe 1919', *Expressionismus: die zweite Generation 1915–1925* (Munich: 1989), p 61–83; Fritz Löffler, Emilio Bertonati, Joachim Heusinger von Waldegg (eds), *Dresdner Sezession 1919–1923*, Ausstellungskatalog, Galleria del Levante (Munich/Milan: 1977).

2. Heinrich von Kleist, *Sämtliche Werke und Briefe in vier Bänden*, ed by Ilse-Marie Barth, Klaus Müller-Salget, Stefan Ormanns and Hinrich C Seeba, Vol 4: *Briefe von und an Heinrich von Kleist 1793–1811* (Frankfurt am Main: 1997), p 221 (Nr 47), letter of 4 May 1801.

3. Ibid, p 172 (Nr 33), letter of 29 and 30 November 1800.

4. See the subtle appraisal by Karl-Markus Gauß, *Wann endet die Nacht. Über Albert Ehrenstein – ein Essay* (Zurich: 1986).

5. Albert Ehrenstein, *Werke*, ed by Hanni Mittelmann, Vol V:

Aufsätze und Essays (Göttingen: 2004), p 226. Author's translation.

6. Ibid, p 229.

7. On the Venice myth and its attraction for German-speaking artists and writers, see especially Klaus Bergdolt, *Deutsche in Venedig. Von den Kaisern des Mittelalters bis zu Thomas Mann* (Darmstadt: 2011).

8. The catalogue for the great retrospective of 1986 *Oskar Kokoschka 1886–1980* at the Tate Gallery London misleadingly translates this section of the letter incorrectly: '[...] *unless* you stay at the Ritz [...]'; The Tate Gallery (London: 1986), p 347.

9. Josef Bard, 'The Leading Expressionist. Oskar Kokoschka in London', *The Forum* (September 1927), pp 410–416.

10. Edith Wharton, *In Morocco* (London: 1920, new edition 1927).

11. George Padmore, *Afrika unter dem Joch der Weissen* (Erlenbach-Zurich/Leipzig: 1937).

12. Abd el Krim, *Memoiren. Mein Krieg gegen Spanien und Frankreich*, transl by Artur Rosenberg (Dresden: 1927).

13. According to Heinz Spielmann, Br II, p 326, notation to p 278.

14. Compare Armin A Wallas, *Albert Ehrenstein. Mythenzerstörer und Mythenschöpfer* (Munich: 1994), in particular chapter XIII: 'Der Weg zum Matriarchat', pp 485–516.

15. As also Yahya Elsaghe in his otherwise-readable introduction to Johann Jakob Bachofen, *Mutterrecht und Urreligion*, ed and newly introduced by Yahya Elsaghe, 7th revised edition (Stuttgart: 2015), pp ix–lxv.

16. E H Gombrich, 'Kokoschka in his Time', lecture given at the Tate Gallery on 2 July 1986 (London: 1986), p 9.

17. Victor Freiherr von Weizsäcker, *Seelenbehandlung und Seelenführung nach ihren biologischen und metaphysischen Grundlagen betrachtet* (Gütersloh: 1926), p 57.

18. Sigmund Freud, *Studienausgabe*, Vol 9: *Fragen der Gesellschaft, Ursprünge der Religion*, ed by Alexander Mitscherlich, Angela Richards and James Strachey (Frankfurt am Main: 2000), pp 287–444 (1st edition Vienna: 1913).

19. See Gombrich, *Kokoschka in his Time*, p 21.

20. Hans Vaihinger, *Die Philosophie des Als Ob. System der theoretischen, praktischen und religiösen Fiktionen der Menschheit auf Grund eines idealistischen Positivismus*, with supplement on Kant and Nietzsche (Berlin: 1911). On the basis of the 9th and 10th editions, a so-called people's edition was released in 1923. A school edition for Prussian grammar schools as well as translations into twelve languages explain the broad dissemination of Vaihinger's philosophy of 'as if' and the search for meaning in scientific fictions.

21. Ibid, p 11. See also the research volume by Matthias Neuber (ed), *Beiträge zu Hans Vaihingers 'Philosophie des Als Ob'* (Würzburg: 2014).

22. Thomas Mann, *Tagebücher 1933–1934*, ed by Peter de Mendelssohn (Frankfurt am Main: 1977), p 294.

23. *Der Wiener Kunstwanderer*, Offizielles Organ der Notgemeinschaft für Kunst und Schrifttum in Österreich, 1 (1933), Issue 10 (November), pp 4–26.

24. See article on Thomas Mann by Marina Rauchenbacher, *Handbuch der Kunstzitate: Malerei, Skulptur, Fotografie in der deutschsprachigen Literatur der Moderne*, Vol 2, ed by Konstanze Fliedl, Marina Rauchenbacher and Joanna Wolf (Berlin/Boston, MA: 2011), pp 517–521.

25. See the foundational study by Katrin Bedenig-Stein, *Nur ein 'Ohren- mensch'? Thomas Manns Verhältnis zu den bildenden Künsten* (Bern (inter alia): 2001). On the research literature, see 'Thomas Mann', *Handbuch der Kunstzitate*, p 521.

26. *Der Wiener Kunstwanderer*, p 5.

27. Thomas Mann, *Tagebücher 1933–1934*, p 245.

28. Thomas Mann, *Gesammelte Werke in dreizehn Bänden*. Vol X: *Reden und Aufsätze 2.* (Frankfurt am Main: 1990), p 915 f (on Oskar Kokoschka). Hereafter page citations in the text refer to this volume and edition.

29. Thomas Mann, *Tagebücher 1933–1934*, p 249.

30. Thomas-Mann-Archiv (TMA), Zürich. Sig: B-II-KOKO-1. Reprinted with kind permission of the TMA.

31. Ibid, p 324.

32. Jutta Hülsewig-Johnen (ed), *Oskar Kokoschka. Emigrantenleben. Prag und London 1934–1953*, Catalogue for 1994/1995 exhibition in the Bielefelder Kunsthalle and the Nationalgalerie Prag (Bielefeld: 1994), esp Werner Haftmann, *Oskar Kokoschka – Exil in der Tschechoslowakei und Großbritannien* (II Prag), pp 55–74.

33. Joseph Roth, 'Prag. Spaziergang in einer verzauberten Stadt (1932)', *Frankfurter Allgemeine Sonntagszeitung* (25 November 2012), Nr 47, p 57.

34. Régine Bonnefoit, 'Oskar Kokoschkas pazifistisches und politisches Engagement in Prag', *Stifter-Jahrbuch* (2015), NF 29, pp 161–188. Bonnefoit places great emphasis on not labelling the Prague years as 'exile', which is correct when seen purely from a legal perspective, but was viewed differently by Kokoschka himself.

35. See Christiane Heuwinkel, 'Die sichtbare Welt. Oskar Kokoschka und Jan Amos Comenius' in Jutta Hülsewig-Johnen, *Oskar Kokoschka. Emigrantenleben*, pp 91–98.

36. See Silvio Vietta, *Die Weltgesellschaft. Wie die abendländische Rationalität die Welt erobert und verändert hat* (Baden-Baden: 2016), p 31 f.

37. Raoul Hausmann, 'Rückkehr zur Gegenständlichkeit in der Kunst', *Dada Almanach 1920*, pp 147–151.

38. See esp Heiko Christians, 'Gesicht, Gestalt, Ornament. Überlegungen zum epistemologischen Ort der Physiognomik zwischen Hermeneutik und Mediengeschichte', *Deutsche Vierteljahrsschrift für Literaturwissenschaft und Geistesgeschichte* (2000) 74 (1), pp 84–110.

5: Exile in England

1. See 'Max Beckmann', <www.kunstzitate.de/bildendekunst/manifeste/beckmann1938>.

2. Edith Hoffmann-Yapou, *Kokoschka: Life and Work* (London: 1947), p 223. Author's translation.

3. See Marian Malet, 'Oskar Kokoschka and the Freie Deutsche Kulturbund: The "Friendly Alien" as Propagandist', in *'I didn't want to float; I wanted to belong to something': Refugee Organizations in Britain 1933–1945*, ed by Anthony Grenville and Andrea Reiter, *The Yearbook of the Research Centre for German and Austrian Exile Studies*, Vol 10 (London: 2008), pp 49–66. For an overview of the work by the Deutsche Kulturbund, see the fundamental study by Charmian Brinson and Richard Dove, *The Continuation of Politics by Other Means: The Free German League of Culture in London, 1939–1945* (Middlesex: 2010).

4. The most comprehensive study of Uhlman to date was undertaken by Anna Plodeck, *The Making of Fred Uhlman: Life and Work of the Painter and Writer in Exile*, 2 Vol, Dissertation (Courtauld Institute of Art, University of London: 2004).

5. See the detailed paper by Anna Müller-Härlin, 'Rebellious and Supportive: The Collector Michael Croft and Artists in Exile in Great Britain' in Andrew Chandler, Katarzyna Stoklosa, Jutta Vinzent (eds), *Exile and Patronage: Cross-cultural Negotiations Beyond the Third Reich* (Berlin: 2006), pp 45–54.

6. Fred Uhlman, *The Making of an Englishman* (London: 1960), p 208.

7. See Heinz Spielmann, 'Oskar Kokoschka in Prag und England' in Hülsewig-Johnen (ed), *Kokoschka, Emigrantenleben. Prag und London 1934–1953*, Catalogue for 1994/1995 exhibition in the Bielefelder Kunsthalle and the Nationalgalerie Prag (Bielefeld: 1994), pp 177–189, esp pp 182–188.

8. Uhlman, *The Making of an Englishman*, pp 213–214.

9. See Rüdiger Görner, 'Reality as Fiction or Fashioning of the Self: Fred Uhlman – The Artist as Writer' in Nicola Baird (ed),

The Making of an Englishman: Fred Uhlman – A Retrospective (London: 2018), pp 102–119.

10. Zentralarchiv Zürich, Nachlass Kokoschka, Sig 312.8.

11. See Anna Müller-Härlin, 'Die Artists' International Association und "refugee artists"', in Grenville and Reiter (eds), *'I didn't want to float; I wanted to belong to something'*, pp 27–48, here p 38.

12. See the standard work by A J Sherman, *Island Refuge. Britain and Refugees from the Third Reich 1933–1939* (Berkeley and Los Angeles, CA: 1973); Ronald Stents, *A Bespattered Page? The Internment of His Majesty's 'Most Loyal Enemy Aliens'* (London: 1980); Connery Chappell, *Island of Barbed Wire: Internment on the Isle of Man in World War Two* (London: 1984); as well as Colin Holmes, *John Bull's Island: Immigration and British Society 1871–1971* (Abingdon: 1988).

13. See Panikos Panayi, *The Enemy in Our Midst: Germans in Britain During the First World War* (London (inter alia): 1991).

14. Zentralbibliothek Zürich, Nachlass Kokoschka, Sig 325.3.

15. Zentralbibliothek Zürich, Nachlass Kokoschka, Sig 364.

16. Ibid.

17. Letter to J P Hodin of 3 October 1939; J P Hodin, 'Einige frühe Briefe Kokoschkas aus der Emigration', *Literatur und Kritik*, Issue 128 (September 1978), pp 458–462, here p 459.

18. Ibid, p 460. This existentially relevant passage is strangely omitted in the four-volume correspondence edition (Br III, p 98 f).

19. Silvia Höller (ed), *Hilde Goldschmidt, 1897–1980. Zwischen Kokoschka, Exil und Kitzbühel* (Innsbruck/Vienna: 2005).

20. Josef Paul Hodin, *Spuren und Wege. Leben und Werk der Malerin Hilde Goldschmidt* (Hamburg: 1974).

21. Werner Haftmann, 'Oskar Kokoschka. Exil in der Tschechoslowakei und Großbritannien' in Hülsewig-Johnen (ed), *Kokoschka, Emigrantenleben*, pp 27–45, here p 38.

22. Ibid, p 44.

23. See Spielmann, *Kokoschka in Prag und England*, p 185.

24. Hoffmann-Yapou, *Kokoschka: Life and Work*, p 234.

25. Lun Yu, *Gespräche* (Düsseldorf/Cologne: 1975), Book 12, Section 1, p 121. See commentary by Wolfgang Mieder, '"Nichts sehen, nichts hören, nichts sagen". Die drei weisen Affen', *Kunst, Literatur, Medien und Karikaturen* (Vienna: 2005).

26. Hoffmann-Yapou, *Kokoschka – Life and Work*, p 236.

27. See Richard Calvocoressi, 'Kokoschka und Schottland' in Hülsewig-Johnen (ed), *Kokoschka, Emigrantenleben*, pp 153–159, here p 155.

28. It has only been possible to grasp Ivan Maisky's meaning through the publication of a diary selection: *Die Maiski-Tagebücher. Ein Diplomat im Kampf gegen Hitler, 1932–1943*, ed by Gabriel Gorodetsky, transl by Karl Heinz Siber (Munich: 2016). See the introduction 'Der Werdegang eines sowjetischen Diplomaten', pp 32–60, as well as esp 'Ende einer Ära: Maiskis Abberufung', pp 761–784, which also references Kokoschka's portrait and accompanying circumstances, pp 766–769.

29. Cited with kind permission of the Tate Gallery Archive, Sig TGA 844/2–41.

30. Ibid.

31. Ibid.

32. Cited by James Stourton, *Kenneth Clark: Life, Art and Civilization* (London: 2016), p 208.

33. All comments cited with kind permission of the Tate Gallery Archive, TGA 844/2–41.

34. Paul Westheim, *Oskar Kokoschka*, 2nd edition (Berlin: 1925; 1st edition: 1918).

35. Ibid, p 15.

36. Ibid, pp 21 and 50.

37. Ibid, p 99.

38. Ibid, p 100.

39. Ibid, p 79.

40. See the retrospective in the Hamburger Kunsthalle on the occasion of Kokoschka's 100th birthday; Serge Sabarsky, *Oskar Kokoschka. Die frühen Jahre 1906–1926. Aquarelle und*

Zeichnungen, with contributions by Werner Hofmann and Willi Hahn (Munich: 1986), p illus 1–8.

41. Hülsewig-Johnen (ed), *Kokoschka, Emigrantenleben*, pp 170, 171.

6: The Portrait as a Form of Representation

1. Johann Wolfgang von Goethe, 'Der Sammler und die Seinigen', *Werke*, Hamburg edition, Vol 12, ed by Erich Trunz (Munich: 1988), p 85.

2. Barbara Honigmann, *Das Gesicht wiederfinden. Über Schreiben, Schriftsteller und Judentum* (Munich/Vienna: 2006), p 137 f and p 139.

3. Ibid, p 93 f.

4. 'Anselm Haverkamp im Interview mit Juliane Rebentisch und Susanne Leeb', *Latenzzeit. Die Leere der fünfziger Jahre. Texte zur Kunst*, 12 (2003), Heft 50, pp 45–53, here p 50.

5. Carl Einstein, *Die Kunst des 20. Jahrhunderts* (Berlin: 1926), p 145.

6. Ibid, p 146.

7. Albert Soergel, *Dichtung und Dichter der Zeit. Eine Schilderung der deutschen Literatur der letzten Jahrzehnte. NF: Im Banne des Expressionismus*, 5th edition (Leipzig: 1927), p 737.

8. Cited by Hanno Rauterberg, 'Architektur und Verbrechen', *Die Zeit* (13 August 2015), Nr 31.

9. Cited by ibid. Compare especially to Christopher Long, *Der Fall Loos* (Salzburg: 2014).

10. Michael Navratil, '"Den Schauer des Mythos neu schaffen". Die kreative Rezeption von Nietzsches "Geburt der Tragödie" in der Wiener Moderne', *Sprachkunst* XLII (2011), second half, p 268 (pp 245–269, on Kokoschka esp pp 262–268).

11. Erich Mühsam, *Tagebücher 1910–1924*, ed and postscript by Chris Hirte, 2nd edition (Munich: 1995), p 37.

12. Georg Simmel, *Aufsätze und Abhandlungen 1901–1908*, Vol 1, Complete edition, Vol 7, ed by Rüdiger Kramme, Angela

Rammstedt and Ottheim Rammstedt (Frankfurt am Main: 1995), pp 321–332, the citations pp 321–325.

13. Ibid, pp 36–42, here p 37.

14. Ibid, p 38.

15. Ibid.

16. For research see overview by Maraike Bückling (ed), *Die phantastischen Köpfe des Franz Xaver Messerschmidt* (Munich: 2006).

17. Harry Graf Kessler, *Tagebücher 1918 bis 1937*, ed by Wolfgang Pfeiffer-Belli (Frankfurt am Main/Leipzig: 1996), p 551 f.

18. Wingler, *Kokoschka-Fibel*, pp 46, 116.

19. Otto F Best (ed), *Theorie des Expressionismus* (Stuttgart: 1978), pp 68–73, here p 68.

20. Jacob Burckhardt, 'Das Porträt in der Malerei', *Werke*, critical complete edition, Vol 6 (Munich: 2000), pp 147–281. See also Manuel Gasser, *Das Selbstbildnis. Gemälde grosser Meister* (Zurich: 1961); Stephen Greenblatt, *Renaissance Self-Fashioning: From More to Shakespeare* (Chicago, IL: 1980); as well as Ulrich Pfisterer, Valeska von Rosen (eds), *Der Künstler als Kunstwerk. Selbstporträts vom Mittelalter bis zur Gegenwart* (Stuttgart: 2005). Inexplicably this representative volume has no reference to Kokoschka.

21. Citation by Pfisterer, von Rosen (eds), *Der Künstler als Kunstwerk*, p 13.

22. Friedrich Gundolf, *Heinrich von Kleist* (Berlin: 1922), p 87.

23. Régine Bonnefoit, Roland Scotti (eds), *Oskar Kokoschka. Wunderkammer/Cabinet de curiosités* (Göttingen: 2011).

24. See esp Jean Starobinski, *Porträt des Künstlers als Gaukler. Drei Essays*, transl from the French by Markus Jakob (Frankfurt am Main: 1985).

25. Georg Wilhelm Friedrich Hegel, *Vorlesungen über die Ästhetik, erster und zweiter Teil*, ed and introduction by Rüdiger Bubner (Stuttgart: 1977), p 662.

26. See Oskar Kokoschka, *Städtebilder und Landschaften*, introduction by Walter Urbanek (Munich: 1990).

27. Véronique Mauron, *Werke der Oskar Kokoschka-Stiftung*, transl from the French by Kathrin Braunschweig-Geller, Pascal Steenken and Heike Gieche Wenger (Vevey: 1994), p 208 f.

28. See Wolfgang Kemp (ed), *Der Betrachter ist im Bild. Kunstwissenschaft und Rezeptionsästhetik* (Berlin: 1991).

29. Heinz Spielmann, *Oskar Kokoschka, Lebensspuren. Ausgewählte Gemälde, Aquarelle, Zeichnungen der Kokoschka-Stiftung Vevey aus den Jahren 1906 bis 1976. Mit unveröffentlichten Gesprächen des Künstlers aus dem Jahre 1966* (Flensburg: 1992), p 33.

30. See catalogue: *The Passionate Eye: Impressionist and Other Master Paintings from The E. G. Bührle Collection* (Zurich/Munich: 1990). The informative article by Margit Hahnloser-Ingold, Emil Georg Bührle, 'A Student of Art History Turned Industralist and Art Collector', ibid, pp 17–34, typically enough contains no information of any kind about the type of Bührle's businesses. The exhibition 'Von Dürer bis van Gogh', with an accompanying document showing Bührle's connections to National Socialist clients, mounted in the Kölner Wallraf-Richartz-Museum from 23 September 2016 to 29 January 2017 was quite a bit more detailed and honest. See also the superb catalogue for the exhibition: *Von Dürer bis van Gogh. Sammlung Bührle trifft Wallraf* (Stuttgart: 2016).

31. Ibid, image 85.

32. Iwan Goll/Claire Goll, *Briefe*, with an introduction by Kasimir Edschmid (Mainz and Berlin: 1966), p 48.

33. Ibid, p 49.

34. Zentralbibliothek Zürich, Nachlass Kokoschka, Sig 336.41.

35. Zentralbibliothek Zürich, Nachlass Kokoschka, Sig 316.27.

36. All citations by Gottfried von Einem, ibid.

37. Régine Bonnefoit, 'Kokoschka, la musique et les musiciens', in R B (ed), *Kokoschka et la musique* (Vevey: 2007), p 30.

38. Spielmann, *Lebensspuren*, p 13.

39. Bonnefoit, 'Kokoschka, la musique et les musiciens', p 44.

40. Yehudi Menuhin, *Unvollendete Reise. Lebenserinnerungen*, transl

by Isabella Nadolny and Albrecht Roeseler, 6th edition (Munich: 1976), p 238 f.

41. Webern was accidentally shot by a US soldier on 15 September 1945 in Mittersill bei Zell am See. The fatal shots were fired during a raid on Webern's house; his son-in-law was suspected of black marketeering.

42. Heinz Spielmann, *Oskar Kokoschka. Die Fächer für Alma Mahler* (Hamburg: 1969).

43. Both citations in Eberhard Pikart in collaboration with Dirk Mende, *Theodor Heuss. Der Mann. Das Werk. Die Zeit*, publications by the Schiller Nationalmuseums, Nr 17, ed by Bernhard Zeller (Stuttgart: 1967), p 339.

44. Citation by Hildegard Hamm-Brücher, *Kulturbeziehungen weltweit. Ein Werkstattbericht zur Auswärtigen Kulturpolitik*, 2nd edition (Munich/Vienna: 1980), p 24 f.

45. Letter by Helmut Schmidt of 9 December 1975. Zentralbibliothek Zürich, Nachlass Kokoschka, Sig 314.44. When the Kokoschka mosaic in the Hamburg Nicolai Church Tower was dedicated one year later, Schmidt offered him terms that normally would have been intended only for guests of the state: 'You have, seen through the eyes of Hamburg's citizens, through your pictures painted in Hamburg, but especially also due to the portraits of Theodor Heuss, Max Brauer and Konrad Adenauer, in a way become a part of Hamburg – to say nothing of the fact that in all of Germany and also in Hamburg there are many admirers of your art, who revere you and would welcome you as a guest of this city.'

46. Richard Wagner, *Tristan und Isolde*, facsimile of the author's handwritten manuscript, ed and annotated by Ulrich Konrad (Kassel: 2012) (Sig A II a 5).

47. See Katja Schneider, Stefan Lehmann (eds), *Oskar Kokoschkas Antike. Eine europäische Vision der Moderne*, with contributions by Régine Bonnefoit, Diana Furtwängler, Andreas Gutsfeld, Stephan Lehmann, Christian Mileta, Heinz Spielmann and Peter Weidmann (Munich: 2010), as well as esp on the *Thermopylen*:

Heinz Spielmann, *Oskar Kokoschka. Leben und Werk* (Cologne: 2003), pp 402–405.

48. Friedrich Schiller, *The Poems and Ballads of Schiller*, transl Sir Edward Bulwer Lytton, Bart. (Leipzig: 1844) p 142.

49. See the impressive overview essay which also cites the relevant research literature by Mischa Meier, 'Die Thermopylen – "Wanderer, kommst Du nach Spa(rta)'" in Elke Stein-Hölkeskamp, Karl-Joachim Hölkeskamp (eds), *Die griechische Welt. Erinnerungsorte der Antike* (Munich: 2010), pp 98–113.

50. Ibid, p 98 f.

51. Ibid, p 99.

52. Heinrich Böll, *Wanderer, kommst du nach Spa... Erzählungen.* 43rd edition (Munich: 2007), pp 45–56.

53. Ralph Dutli, *Meine Zeit, mein Tier. Ossip Mandelstam. Eine Biographie*, 2nd edition (Zurich: 2003), p 182.

54. Spielmann, *Oskar Kokoschka* (2003), p 405.

55. Zentralbibliothek Zürich, Nachlass Kokoschka, Sig 390.7.

56. Oskar Kokoschka/Walter Kern, *Thermopylae. Ein Triptychon* (Winterthur: 1955).

57. Zentralbibliothek Zürich, Nachlass Kokoschka, Sig 337.3.

58. Complete reproduction in the translation by Theodor Braun as supplement in Kokoschka/Kern, *Thermopylae*, pp 1–6 (pieces 201–238).

59. Ibid, p 8.

60. Barbara Wally, 'Neue Aspekte zur Gründungsgeschichte der Sommerakademie: Kokoschkas "Schule des Sehens" im Kunstkontext der 50er Jahre' in Barbara Wally (ed), *Oskar Kokoschka in Salzburg. Die Gründung der Internationalen Sommerakademie für Bildende Kunst. Vor fünfzig Jahren* (Salzburg: 2003), pp 9–62, here p 45.

61. See Simon Schama, *The Face of Britain: The Nation through its Portraits* (London: 2015), pp 1–21.

62. Michael Hamburger, 'Toter Maler an toten Staatsmann. Deutsch von Hanno Helbling,' in Lea Ritter-Santini (ed), *Mit den Augen*

geschrieben. Von gedichteten und erzählten Bildern (Munich: 1991), p 254.

7: Portrait of the Older Artist as Educator, or Schools of Seeing

1. See Martin Schieder, 'Der Kritiker ist für die Kunst. Will Grohmann und die Moderne, 1914–1968' in Regula Krähenbühl (ed), *Avantgarden im Fokus der Kunstkritik. Eine Hommage an Carola Giedion-Welcker (1893–1979)* (Zurich: 2011), pp 205–222; Konstanze Rudert (ed), *Will Grohmann. Im Netzwerk der Moderne*, catalogue for the exhibition in the Staatlichen Kunstsammlungen – Kunsthalle im Lipsiusbau Dresden (Munich: 2012); Konstanze Rudert (ed), *Will Grohmann. Texte zur Kunst der Moderne* (Munich: 2012); Konstanze Rudert (ed), *Zwischen Intuition und Gewissheit. Will Grohmann und die Rezeption der Moderne in Deutschland und Europa 1918–1968* (Dresden: 2013).
2. See Brigitte Pedde, *Willi Baumeister 1889–1955. Schöpfer aus dem Unbekannten* (Berlin: 2013); Jörg-Heiko Bruns, *Willi Baumeister* (Dresden: 1991). For the foundation of Baumeister's impact see the study by Wolfgang Kermer (ed), 'Der schöpferische Winkel – Willi Baumeisters pädagogische Tätigkeit', *Beiträge zur Geschichte der Staatlichen Akademie der Bildenden Künste Stuttgart*, Vol 7 (Ostfildern-Ruit: 1992).
3. Barbara Wally, 'Neue Aspekte zur Gründungsgeschichte der Sommerakademie: Kokoschkas "Schule des Sehens" im Kunstkontext der 50er Jahre' in Barbara Wally (ed), *Oskar Kokoschka in Salzburg. Die Gründung der Internationalen Sommerakademie für Bildende Kunst. Vor fünfzig Jahren* (Salzburg: 2003), p 40.
4. Paul Klee, 'Schöpferische Konfession', *Tribüne der Kunst und der Zeit. Eine Schriftensammlung*, Vol XIII, ed by Kasimir Edschmid (Berlin: 1920), p 28.
5. 'The paint has me. I do not need to chase after it. It has me

forever. That is the purpose of the perfect moment: the paint and I are one. I am a painter.' *Tagebücher 1898–1918*, ed by Felix Klee (Cologne: 1957), p 307.

6. Christine Fischer-Defoy (ed), *Ich habe das Meine gesagt! – Reden und Stellungnahmen von Karl Hofer zu Kunst, Kultur und Politik in Deutschland 1945–1955* (Berlin: 1995).

7. See Frank Krause, *The Phallic Woman as Sacred Mother in Plays by Kokoschka and von Unruh: Ritualistic Body Phantasms in Expressionist Approaches to Gender*, Performance Research Pamphlets, Nr 5 (London: 2014).

8. See biography of Sedlmayrs, esp Gert Kerschbaumer, Karl Müller, *Begnadet für das Schöne. Der rot-weiß-rote Kulturkampf gegen die Moderne* (Vienna: 1992), p 178 f.

9. See Wally, *Neue Aspekte*, p 38.

10. Zentralbibliothek Zürich, Nachlass Kokoschka, Sig 374.8.

11. See Régine Bonnefoit, Roland Scotti (eds), *Oskar Kokoschka. Wunderkammer/Cabinet de curiosités* (Göttingen: 2011).

12. Corinna Caduff, 'Fantom Farbenklavier. Das Farbe-Ton-Verhältnis im 18. Jahrhundert oder Vom Einspruch gegen das clavecin oculaire und seinen ästhetischen Folgen', *Zeitschrift für deutsche Philologie* 121 (2002), pp 481–509; Albert Wellek, 'Farbenharmonie und Farbenklavier. Ihre Entstehungsgeschichte im 18. Jahrhundert', *Archiv für die gesamte Psychologie* 94 (1935), pp 347–375.

13. See Fred K Prieberg, *Musik im NS-Staat* (Frankfurt am Main: 1982), p 22 f.

14. Alois Melichar, *Überwindung des Modernismus. Konkrete Antwort an einen abstrakten Kritiker* (Vienna/Frankfurt am Main/London: 1954).

15. Ibid, p 32.

16. Christine Eichel, 'Heimatkunde. Interview mit Georg Baselitz', *Cicero* 1 (2010), pp 110–119, here p 115.

17. Ibid, p 34.

18. Ibid, p 46.

19. Ibid, p 47.

20. Heinz Spielmann, *Oskar Kokoschka. Leben und Werk* (Cologne: 2003).
21. Zentralbibliothek Zürich, Nachlass Kokoschka, Sig 5.34.
22. Zentralbibliothek Zürich, Nachlass Kokoschka, Sig 313.9.
23. Bonnefoit, Reinhold, *Die Nachlassbibliothek von Oskar Kokoschka*, p 46.
24. Fundamental to this is Gert Kerschbaumer, *Meister des Verwirrens. Die Geschäfte des Kunsthändlers Friedrich Welz* (Vienna: 2000); Barbara Wally (ed), *Oskar Kokoschka in Salzburg. Die Gründung der Internationalen Sommerakademie für Bildende Kunst. Vor fünfzig Jahren* (Salzburg: 2003), pp 9–62; therein Robert Hoffmann, 'Goldene Jahre oder falsche Fuffziger? Salzburg um 1953', pp 71–90.
25. See esp Kerschbaumer, *Meister des Verwirrens*.
26. See Oliver Rathkolb, *Die paradoxe Republik. Österreich 1945–2015*, updated and expanded revised edition (Vienna: 2005 and 2015).
27. *Ausblick – Rückblick II. Österreichische klassische Moderne und Kunst nach 1945*, ed by Franz Eder, Galerie Welz (Salzburg: 2000), p 8.
28. More detail in Kerschbaumer, Müller, *Begnadet für das Schöne*; also Oliver Rathkolb, *Die paradoxe Republik*, p 348 f.
29. Wally, *Neue Aspekte*, p 54.
30. The reasons for this scandal are covered in depth in Joachim Reiber, *Gottfried von Einem. Komponist der Stunde null* (Vienna: 2017), pp 64–73.
31. See Reiber, ibid, esp pp 9–27.
32. On Hofmannsthal's paramount importance to the establishment of the Festspiele, see esp Norbert Christian Wolf, *Eine Triumphpforte österreichischer Kunst. Hugo von Hofmannsthals Gründung der Salzburger Festspiele* (Salzburg: 2014).
33. More detail on this in ibid, pp 50–60.
34. Letter from Oskar Kokoschka to Margareta Berger-Hammerschlag of 2 April 1955, University of London, Senate

House Library/Archive. Cited with kind permission of Ms Andrea Ludowisy.

35. See Robert Hoffmann, *Mythos Salzburg. Bilder einer Stadt* (Salzburg/Munich: 2002).

36. See Helmut Pape, 'Wir können nur gemeinsam sehen. Die Verschränkung der Blicke als Modell humanen Sehens' in Horst Bredekamp, John M Krois (eds), *Sehen und Handeln. Berliner Schriften für Bildaktforschung und Verkörperungsphilosophie*, Vol 1 (Berlin: 2011), pp 117–140.

37. Ludwik Fleck, *Denkstile und Tatsachen*, ed by Sylwia Werner and Claus Zittel (Berlin: 2010), p 53.

38. Oskar Kokoschka, 'Ich bin ein Seher', *Österreichisches Tagebuch* (28 November 1947), Zentralbibliothek Zürich, Nachlass Kokoschka, Sig 5.12.

39. Zentralbibliothek Zürich, Nachlass Kokoschka, Sig 363.9.

40. Zentralbibliothek Zürich, Nachlass Kokoschka, Sig 379.10.

41. Oskar Kokoschka, 'Ich bin ein Seher'.

42. 'Die Kunst unserer Tage' (1957), Zentralbibliothek Zürich, Nachlass Kokoschka, Sig 5.14

43. Zentralbibliothek Zürich, Nachlass Kokoschka, Sig 5.25.

44. Zentralbibliothek Zürich, Nachlass Kokoschka, Sig 5.34.

45. Karl Marx, 'Ökonomisch-philosophische Manuskripte' ('Pariser Manuskripte' 1844), MEW Vol 40 (Berlin: 2005), p 541 f. Translated by Martin Milligan, revised by Dirk J Struik, contained in *Marx/Engels, Gesamtausgabe*, Abt 1, Vol 3, <www.marxists.org/archive/marx/works/download/pdf/Economic-Philosophic-Manuscripts-1844.pdf>.

46. Fundamental to this is Bonnefoit, Reinhold, *Die Nachlassbibliothek von Oskar Kokoschka*, pp 35–62.

47. Zentralbibliothek Zürich, Nachlass Kokoschka, Sig 312.21.

48. Ibid, letter of 18 July 1977.

49. Zentralbibliothek Zürich, Nachlass Kokoschka, Sig 36.23 (letter of 11 November 1956).

50. Letter from John Berger to Kokoschka of 7 February 1960, Zentralbibliothek Zürich, Nachlass Kokoschka, Sig 307.8.

51. Zentralbibliothek Zürich, Nachlass Kokoschka, Sig 316.27.

52. Zentralbibliothek Zürich, Nachlass Kokoschka, Sig 369.29.

53. Perhaps he owned the following edition: Heinrich von
    Kleist, *Penthesilea. Ein Trauerspiel*, numbered special edition
    (Stuttgart: 1923), produced in the Graphischen Werkstätten der
    Württembergischen Staatlichen Kunstgewerbeschule Stuttgart.
    In the following edition he underlined: Heinrich von Kleist,
    Penthesilea, Reclam-edition (Leipzig: 1927): Achilles, 21st
    entrance: 'Yes. But a whim sacred to her / demands that I should
    fall by her sword in battle; / Not even in love can she embrace
    me'. Author's translation.

54. Lise Lotte Möller, *Kokoschkas Radierungen zu 'Penthesilea'. Eine
    Einführung* (Frankfurt am Main: 1970), p 8; also Günter Busch,
    Kokoschkas Radierfolgen (Frankfurt am Main: 1970).

55. Möller, *Kokoschkas Radierungen zu 'Penthesilea'*, p 20.

56. Heinrich von Kleist, *Sämtliche Werke und Briefe in vier Bänden*,
    ed by Ilse-Marie Barth, Klaus Müller-Salget, Stefan Ormanns and
    Hinrich C Seeba, Vol 2: *Rahmen 1808–1811* (Frankfurt am Main:
    1997), p 256.

57. Zentralbibliothek Zürich, Nachlass Kokoschka, Sig 5.30.

58. Victor Dirsztay, *Der Unentrinnbare*, novel, with illustrations by
    Oskar Kokoschka (Munich: 1923), p 67.

59. Published by Hoffmann and Campe in Hamburg.
    Staatsbibliothek Munich/Handschriftenabteilung, Sig 2. L. sel
    III. 414-1.

60. Ibid.

61. Siegfried Lenz, *Einstein überquert die Elbe bei Hamburg.
    Erzählungen* (Munich: 1978), pp 73–81.

62. Zentralbibliothek Zürich, Nachlass Kokoschka, Sig 5.34.

63. Ibid.

64. Zentralbibliothek Zürich, Nachlass Kokoschka, Sig 303.36.

65. Golo Mann, *Zeiten und Figuren. Schriften aus vier Jahrzehnten*
    (Frankfurt am Main: 1979), p 8.

66. Ibid, p 9.

67. Zentralbibliothek Zürich, Nachlass Kokoschka, Sig 5.12.

68. Ibid.
69. Zentralbibliothek Zürich, Nachlass Kokoschka, Sig 353.20.
70. Ibid.
71. Ibid.
72. See Monika Mayer, 'Bruno Grimschitz und die Österreichische Galerie 1938–1945. Eine biografische Annäherung im Kontext der aktuellen Provenienzforschung' in Gabriele Anderl, Alexandra Caruso (eds), *NS-Kunstraub in Österreich und die Folgen* (Innsbruck: 2005), pp 59–79.
73. Zentralbibliothek Zürich, Nachlass Kokoschka, Sig 353.20.
74. Ibid.
75. Zentralbibliothek Zürich, Nachlass Kokoschka, Sig 376.6.
76. Zentralbibliothek Zürich, Nachlass Kokoschka, Sig 349.15.
77. Ibid.
78. Zentralbibliothek Zürich, Nachlass Kokoschka, Sig 357.24 (letter of 7 October 1951).
79. *Oskar Kokoschka, Gitta Wallerstein, 1921*, ed by Kulturstiftung der Länder und Staatliche Kunstsammlungen Dresden. *Albertinum. Patrimonia* 380 (Dresden: 2015), p 14. See also Michael Zajonz, 'Mädchen in Blau. Oskar Kokoschkas Kinderporträt "Gitta Wallerstein" kehrt nach Dresden zurück', *Arsprototo* 10 (2014) Issue 3, pp 42–45.
80. Ernst Bloch, *Geist der Utopie*, 1st edition (Frankfurt am Main: 1969), p 9.
81. Ilse Aichinger, *Die größere Hoffnung*, novel, 1st edition (Amsterdam: 1948), p 141.

In Comenius' Name: An Afterlife During a Lifetime

1. Translated by Maxine Chernoff and Paul Hoover, *Selected Poems of Friedrich Hölderlin* (Oakland, CA: 2008).
2. Zentralbibliothek Zürich, Nachlass Kokoschka, Sig 367.6.
3. Luise Rinser, *Jan Lobel aus Warschau: Erzählung*, 18th edition (Frankfurt am Main: 2012), p 45.

4. Thomas Bernhard, *Der Wahrheit auf der Spur. Reden, Leserbriefe, Interviews, Feuilletons*, ed by Wolfram Bayer, Raimund Fellinger and Martin Huber (Berlin: 2011), p 24.

5. Ibid.

6. Ibid, p 25.

7. Zentralbibliothek Zürich, Nachlass Kokoschka, Sig 364.

8. Ibid, letter of 26 January 1971.

9. Zentralbibliothek Zürich, Nachlass Kokoschka, Sig 357.24.

10. Romeo Giger, 'Der Mensch ist das Mass der Dinge. Zum 100. Geburtstag von Oskar Kokoschka', *Neue Zürcher Zeitung* (28 February 1986), p 39.

11. Herbert Read, *The Creative Nature of Humanism* (Zurich: 1958). The presentation copy is in Kokoschka's Nachlassbibliothek.

12. Peter Sager, 'Alter Wilder. Großer Oskar. Ein Porträt', *ZEIT Magazin*, Nr 9 (21 February 1986), pp 20–31, here p 26.

13. Private letter to Kokoschka, ibid, Zentralbibliothek Zürich, Nachlass Kokoschka, Sig 442.6.

14. Werner Hofmann, 'Der irrende Ritter', *Die Zeit* (28 February 1986).

Hindsight

1. Georg Trakl, 'Night' from *Poems and Prose*, transl by Alexander Stillmark (Libris/Angel Books, London, 2001).

2. Friedrich Hölderlin, *Selected Poems and Fragments*, transl by Michael Hamburger, ed by Jeremy Adler, with a new preface and an introduction by Michael Hamburger (London: 1998), p 27.

Bibliography

Many translations are courtesy of Oskar Kokoschka, *Plays and Poems*, transl by Michael Mitchell (Riverside, CA: 2001), used by permission of Ariadne Press.

Aichinger, Ilse, *Die größere Hoffnung*, novel, 1st edition (Amsterdam: 1948).

Anz, Thomas and Michael Stark (eds), *Expressionismus. Manifeste und Dokumente zur deutschen Literatur* (Stuttgart: 1982).

Bachofen, Johann Jakob, *Mutterrecht und Urreligion*, ed and new introduction by Yahya Elsaghe, 7th revised edition (Stuttgart: 2015).

Bard, Josef, 'The Leading Expressionist. Oskar Kokoschka in London', *The Forum* (September 1927).

Barlach, Ernst, *Dramen: Der Tote Tag*, ed and foreword by Helmar Harald Fischer (Munich/Zurich: 1988).

Bedenig-Stein, Katrin, *Nur ein 'Ohrenmensch'? Thomas Manns Verhältnis zu den bildenden Künsten* (Bern: 2001).

Bergdolt, Klaus, *Deutsche in Venedig. Von den Kaisern des Mittelalters bis zu Thomas Mann* (Darmstadt: 2011).

Berger, Hilde, *Ob es Haß ist, solche Liebe? Oskar Kokoschka und Alma Mahler* (Vienna/Cologne/Weimar: 2008).

Bernhard, Thomas, *Der Wahrheit auf der Spur. Reden, Leserbriefe, Interviews, Feuilletons*, ed by Wolfram Bayer, Raimund Fellinger and Martin Huber (Berlin: 2011).

Bernstock, Judith E, *Under the Spell of Orpheus. The Persistence of a Myth in Twentieth-Century Art* (Carbondale, IL: 1991).

Best, Otto F (ed), *Theorie des Expressionismus* (Stuttgart: 1978).

Bloch, Ernst, *Geist der Utopie*, 1st edition (Frankfurt am Main: 1969).

Böll, Heinrich, *Wanderer, kommst du nach Spa... Erzählungen*, 43rd edition (Munich: 2007).

Bonnefoit, Régine, 'Kokoschka, la musique et les musiciens' in *Kokoschka et la musique*, ed by Régine Bonnefoit (Vevey: 2007).

_____, 'Oskar Kokoschkas pazifistisches und politisches Engagement in Prag', *Stifter-Jahrbuch*, NF 29 (2015), pp 161–188.

_____ and Bernadette Reinhold, 'Die Nachlassbibliothek von Oskar Kokoschka – neue Perspektiven in der Kokoschka-Forschung', *Spur im Treibsand. Oskar Kokoschka neu gesehen. Briefe und Bilder*, ed by Régine Bonnefoit and Ruth Häusler (Petersberg: 2010), pp 35–61.

_____ and Roland Scotti (eds), *Oskar Kokoschka. Wunderkammer/Cabinet de curiosités* (Göttingen: 2011).

Brandstätter, Christian (ed), *Die Welt von Gestern in Farbe* (Vienna: 2009).

Brinson, Charmian and Richard Dove, *The Continuation of Politics by Other Means: The Free German League of Culture in London, 1939–1945* (Middlesex: 2010).

Bruns, Jörg-Heiko, *Willi Baumeister* (Dresden: 1991).

Bückling, Maraike (ed), *Die phantastischen Köpfe des Franz Xaver Messerschmidt* (Munich: 2006).

Bührle Collection, *The Passionate Eye: Impressionist and Other Master Paintings from the collection of Emil G. Bührle, Zurich* (Zurich/Munich: 1990).

Burckhardt, Jacob, 'Das Porträt in der Malerei', *Werke. Kritische Gesamtausgabe*, Vol 6 (Munich: 2000), pp 147–281.

Burger, Hilde (ed), *Hugo von Hofmannsthal – Harry Graf Kessler, an Exchange of Letters 1898–1929* (Frankfurt am Main: 1968), Nr 12.

Busch, Günter, *Kokoschkas Radierfolgen* (Frankfurt am Main: 1970).

Caduff, Corinna, 'Fantom Farbenklavier. Das Farbe-Ton-Verhältnis im 18. Jahrhundert oder Vom Einspruch gegen das clavecin oculaire und seinen ästhetischen Folgen', *Zeitschrift für deutsche Philologie* 121 (2002), pp 481–509.

Calasso, Roberto, *Das Rosa Tiepolos*, transl from the Italian by
Reimar Klein (Munich: 2010).

Canetti, Elias, *Party im Blitz. Die englischen Jahre*, published
posthumously, ed by Kristian Wachinger with an afterword by
Jeremy Adler (Munich/Vienna: 2003).

Chappell, Connery, *Island of Barbed Wire: Internment on the Isle of
Man in World War Two* (London: 1984).

Christians, Heiko, 'Gesicht, Gestalt, Ornament. Überlegungen zum
epistemologischen Ort der Physiognomik zwischen Hermeneutik
und Mediengeschichte', *Deutsche Vierteljahresschrift für
Literaturwissenschaft und Geistesgeschichte* 74 (2000) 1, pp 84–110.

Cohen, Mark Daniel, 'Nietzsche – A Selection of Poems in
Translation', *Hyperion*, Vol II, issue 4 (December 2007).

Comenius, Johann Amos, *Orbis Sensualium Pictus*, ed by Johann
Kühnel, facsimile of the original from 1658 (Leipzig: 1910).

_____,*The Orbis Pictus of John Amos Comenius*, transl by Charles
Hoole (1658), this edition published by C W Bardeen (Syracuse,
NY: 1887), <www.gutenberg.org/files/28299/28299-h/28299-h.
htm>.

Dauthendey, Max, 'Norsland in allen Farben', *Frühe Prosa*, from the
handwritten estate, ed by Hermann Gerstner in collaboration with
Edmund L Klaffki (Munich/Vienna: 1967).

Der Wiener Kunstwanderer, Offizielles Organ der Notgemeinschaft
für Kunst und Schrifttum in Österreich. 1 (1933), Heft 10
(November), pp 4–26.

Dirsztay, Victor, *Der Unentrinnbare*, novel, with illustrations by
Oskar Kokoschka (Munich: 1923).

Dutli, Ralph, *Meine Zeit, mein Tier. Ossip Mandelstam. Eine
Biographie*, 2nd edition (Zurich: 2003).

Eder, Franz (ed) for Galerie Welz, *Ausblick – Rückblick II.
Österreichische klassische Moderne und Kunst nach 1945* (Salzburg:
2000).

Ehrenstein, Albert, *Werke*, ed by Hanni Mittelmann, Vol V: *Aufsätze
und Essays* (Göttingen: 2004).

Eichel, Christine, 'Heimatkunde. Interview mit Georg Baselitz', *Cicero* 1 (2010), pp 110–119.

Einstein, Carl, *Die Kunst des 20. Jahrhunderts* (Berlin: 1926).

Fischer-Defoy, Christine (ed), *Ich habe das Meine gesagt! – Reden und Stellungnahmen von Karl Hofer zu Kunst, Kultur und Politik in Deutschland 1945–1955* (Berlin: 1995).

Fleck, Ludwik, *Denkstile und Tatsachen*, ed by Sylwia Werner and Claus Zittel (Berlin: 2010).

Fliedl, Konstanze, Marina Rauchenbacher, Joanna Wolf (eds), *Handbuch der Kunstzitate: Malerei, Skulptur, Fotografie in der deutschsprachigen Literatur der Moderne*, Vol 2 (Berlin/Boston, MA: 2011).

Fooken, Insa, *Puppen – heimliche Menschenflüsterer. Ihre Wiederentdeckung als Spielzeug und Kulturgut* (Göttingen: 2012).

Forster, Leonard, 'An unpublished letter from Rilke to Kokoschka', *German Life & Letters* 15 (1961) 1, pp 21–24.

————, Estate, Box 130, Senate House Library London.

Freud, Sigmund, *Studienausgabe*, Vol 9: *Fragen der Gesellschaft, Ursprünge der Religion*, ed by Alexander Mitscherlich, Angela Richards and James Strachey (Frankfurt am Main: 2000), pp 287–444 (1st edition, Vienna: 1913).

Friedell, Egon, *Ecce Poeta* (Berlin: 1912).

Gasser, Manuel, *Das Selbstbildnis. Gemälde grosser Meister* (Zurich: 1961).

Gauß, Karl-Markus, *Wann endet die Nacht. Über Albert Ehrenstein – ein Essay* (Zurich: 1986).

Giger, Romeo, 'Der Mensch ist das Mass der Dinge. Zum 100. Geburtstag von Oskar Kokoschka', *Neue Zürcher Zeitung* (28 February 1986), p 39.

Goethe, Johann Wolfgang v, *Werke. Hamburger Ausgabe*, Vol 12 (Munich: 1988).

Goll, Iwan and Claire Goll, *Briefe*, with a foreword by Kasimir Edschmid (Mainz/Berlin: 1966).

Gombrich, E H, 'Kokoschka in his Time', lecture given at the Tate Gallery, 2 July 1986 (London: 1986).

Görner, Rüdiger, *Georg Trakl. Dichter im Jahrzehnt der Extreme* (Vienna: 2014).

_____, 'Reality as Fiction or: Fashioning of the Self. Fred Uhlman – The Artist as Writer' in *The Making of an Englishman: Fred Uhlman – A Retrospective*, ed by Nicola Baird (London: 2018), pp 102–119.

Greenblatt, Stephen, *Renaissance Self-Fashioning: From More to Shakespeare* (Chicago, IL: 1980).

Grosz, George, *Ein kleines Ja und ein großes Nein* (Hamburg: 1955).

Gundolf, Friedrich, *Heinrich von Kleist* (Berlin: 1922).

Haftmann, Werner, 'Oskar Kokoschka. Exil in der Tschechoslowakei und Großbritannien' in *Oskar Kokoschka. Emigrantenleben. Prag und London 1934–1953*, ed by Jutta Hülsewig-Johnen, Catalogue for the 1994/1995 exhibition in the Bielefelder Kunsthalle und Nationalgalerie Prag (Bielefeld: 1994), pp 27–45.

Hamburger, Michael, 'Toter Maler an toten Staatsmann', transl by Hanno Helbling, *Neue Zürcher Zeitung* (18 May 1990, Foreign Edition No 113).

Hamm-Brücher, Hildegard, *Kulturbeziehungen weltweit. Ein Werkstattbericht zur Auswärtigen Kulturpolitik*, 2nd edition (Munich/Vienna: 1980).

Hamsun, Knut, *Pan. Aus Leutnant Thomas Glahns Papieren*, novel, transl from the Norwegian by Ingeborg Keel and Aldo Keel, afterword by Aldo Keel (Zurich: 2009).

Hausmann, Raoul, 'Rückkehr zur Gegenständlichkeit in der Kunst', *Dada Almanach* (1920).

Haverkamp, Anselm, 'Interview mit Juliane Rebentisch und Susanne Leeb', *Latenzzeit. Die Leere der fünfziger Jahre. Texte zur Kunst*, 12 (2003), Issue 50, pp 45–53.

Hegel, Georg Wilhelm Friedrich, *Vorlesungen über die Ästhetik. Erster und zweiter Teil*, ed and introduction by Rüdiger Bubner (Stuttgart: 1977).

Heuwinkel, Christiane, 'Die sichtbare Welt. Oskar Kokoschka und Jan Amos Comenius' in *Oskar Kokoschka. Emigrantenleben. Prag und London 1934–1953*, ed by Jutta Hülsewig-Johnen (Bielefeld: 1994), pp 91–98.

Hilmes, Oliver, *Witwe im Wahn* (Munich: 2004).

Hodin, Josef Paul, 'Einige frühe Briefe Kokoschkas aus der Emigration', *Literatur und Kritik* (September 1978), Issue 128, pp 458–462.

_____, *Spuren und Wege. Leben und Werk der Malerin Hilde Goldschmidt* (Hamburg: 1974).

Hoffmann, Camill, 'Kokoschkas Bildnisse und Phantasien', *Die Dame* (1917), Issue 3, pp 6–7.

_____, 'Kokoschkas Dichtung und Theater', *Das Kunstblatt. Jahrgang 1917*, Issue 7, pp 219–221.

Hoffmann, E T A, *Der Sandmann. Historisch-kritische Edition*, ed by Kaltërina Latifi (Frankfurt am Main: 2011).

Hoffmann, Robert, *Mythos Salzburg. Bilder einer Stadt* (Salzburg/Munich: 2002).

Hofmann, Werner, 'Der irrende Ritter', *Die Zeit* (28 February 1986).

Hoffmann-Yapou, Edith, *Kokoschka: Life and Work* (London: 1947).

Hofmannsthal, Hugo von, *Gesammelte Werke in zehn Einzelbänden: Reden und Aufsätze II (1914–1924)*, ed by Bernd Schoeller in consultation with Rudolf Hirsch (Frankfurt am Main: 1979).

Hölderlin, Friedrich, *Sämtliche Werke und Briefe in drei Bänden*, ed by Jochen Schmidt (Frankfurt am Main: 1994).

_____, *Selected Poems of Friedrich Hölderlin*, transl by Maxine Chernoff and Paul Hoover (Oakland, CA: 2008); excerpts at <labos.ulg.ac.be/cipa/wp-content/uploads/sites/22/2015/07/20_chernoff.pdf>.

Höller, Silvia and Hilde Goldschmidt (eds), *1897–1980. Zwischen Kokoschka, Exil und Kitzbühel* (Innsbruck/Vienna: 2005).

Holmes, Colin, *John Bull's Island: Immigration and British Society 1871–1971* (Abingdon: 1988).

Honigmann, Barbara, *Das Gesicht wiederfinden. Über Schreiben, Schriftsteller und Judentum* (Munich/Vienna: 2006).

Hülsewig-Johnen, Jutta (ed), *Oskar Kokoschka. Emigrantenleben. Prag und London 1934–1953*. Catalogue for the 1994/1995 exhibition in the Bielefelder Kunsthalle und Nationalgalerie Prag (Bielefeld: 1994).

Ibsen, Henirk, *When We Dead Awaken: a Dramatic Epilogue in 3 Acts*, transl by William Archer (London: 1900).

Kafka, Franz, *Briefe an Felice und andere Korrespondenz aus der Verlobungszeit*, ed by Erich Heller and Jürgen Born, 11th edition (Frankfurt am Main: 2009).

Kaman, Donata, *Theater der Maler in Deutschland und Polen* (Münster: 2001).

Kapp, Reinhard, 'Zum Stand der Bearbeitung des Orpheus-Stoffes in den zwanziger Jahren' in *Ernst Křenek, Oskar Kokoschka und die Geschichte von Orpheus und Eurydike. Ernst Křenek-Studien*, ed by Jürg Stenzl, Vol 1 (Schliengen: 2005), pp 33–47.

Kaschnitz, Marie Luise, *Gesammelte Werke*, ed by Christian Büttrich and Norbert Miller, Vol 5: *Die Gedichte* (Frankfurt am Main: 1987).

_____, *Gesammelte Werke*, ed by Christian Büttrich and Norbert Miller, Vol 7: *Die essayistische Prosa* (Frankfurt am Main: 1987).

Kemp, Wolfgang (ed), *Der Betrachter ist im Bild. Kunstwissenschaft und Rezeptionsästhetik* (Berlin: 1991).

Kermer, Wolfgang, 'Der schöpferische Winkel – Willi Baumeisters pädagogische Tätigkeit' in *Beiträge zur Geschichte der Staatlichen Akademie der Bildenden Künste Stuttgart*, ed by Wolfgang Kermer. Vol 7 (Ostfildern-Ruit: 1992).

Kerschbaumer, Gert, *Meister des Verwirrens. Die Geschäfte des Kunsthändlers Friedrich Welz* (Vienna: 2000).

_____ and Karl Müller, *Begnadet für das Schöne. Der rot-weiß-rote Kulturkampf gegen die Moderne* (Vienna: 1992).

Kessler, Harry Graf, *Tagebücher 1918 bis 1937*, ed by Wolfgang Pfeiffer-Belli (Frankfurt am Main/Leipzig: 1996).

Klee, Ernst, *Das Kulturlexikon zum Dritten Reich. Wer war was vor und nach 1945* (Frankfurt am Main: 2007).

Klee, Paul, 'Schöpferische Konfession', *Tribüne der Kunst und der Zeit. Eine Schriftensammlung*, Vol XIII, ed by Kasimir Edschmid (Berlin: 1920).

_____, *Tagebücher 1898–1918*, ed by Felix Klee (Cologne: 1957).

Kleist, Heinrich von, *Penthesilea. Ein Trauerspiel. Nummerierte Vorzugsausgabe*. Produced by the Graphischen Werkstätten der Württembergischen Staatlichen Kunstgewerbeschule Stuttgart (Stuttgart: 1923).

_____, *Penthesilea. Reclam-Ausgabe* (Leipzig: 1927).

_____, *Sämtliche Werke und Briefe in vier Bänden*, ed by Ilse-Marie Barth, Klaus Müller-Salget, Stefan Ormanns and Hinrich C Seeba (Frankfurt am Main: 1997).

Kokoschka, Oskar, Brief an Ernst Křenek on 17 July 1923, Sig IN 220.969 in the Wienbibliothek im Rathaus der Stadt Wien.

_____, *Briefe in vier Bänden*, Vol I, ed by Olda Kokoschka and Heinz Spielmann (Düsseldorf: 1984 ff), p 10 (11 August 1909).

_____, *Das schriftliche Werk in vier Bänden*, Vol IV, ed by Heinz Spielmann (Hamburg: 1973–1976).

_____, *Gitta Wallerstein, 1921*, published by Kulturstiftung der Länder und Staatliche Kunstsammlungen Dresden, Albertinum, *Patrimonia* 380 (Dresden: 2015).

_____, *Mein Leben*, in collaboration with and foreword by Remigius Netzer (Munich: 1971).

_____, Nachlassbibliothek in the Oskar Kokoschka-Zentrum of the Universität für angewandte Kunst Wien.

_____, Documentary estate in Zentralbibliothek Zürich: Sammlung Kokoschka.

_____, *Städtebilder und Landschaften*, introduction by Walter Urbanek (Munich: 1990).

_____ and Walter Kern, *Thermopylae. Ein Triptychon* (Winterthur: 1955).

_____, *Plays and Poems*, transl by Michael Mitchell (Riverside, CA: 2001).

Köstler, Hermann, 'Oskars guter Geist. Zum Tod von Olda Kokoschka', *Neue Zürcher Zeitung* (26 June 2004).

Kraus, Karl, *Worte in Versen* (Leipzig: 1916).

Krause, Frank, *The Phallic Woman as Sacred Mother in Plays by Kokoschka and von Unruh: Ritualistic Body Phantasms in*

Expressionist Approaches to Gender, Performance Research Pamphlets, No 5 (London: 2014).

Křenek, Ernst, *Im Atem der Zeit. Erinnerungen an die Moderne*, transl from the American English by Friedrich Saathen, revised transl by Sabine Schulte (Vienna: 2012).

Krim, Abd el, *Memoiren. Mein Krieg gegen Spanien und Frankreich*, transl by Artur Rosenberg (Dresden: 1927).

Kropotkin, Pjotr A Fürst, *Moderne Wissenschaft und Anarchismus* (Berlin: 1904).

Lenz, Siegfried, *Einstein überquert die Elbe bei Hamburg. Erzählungen* (Munich: 1978).

Lichtwark, Alfred, *Übungen in der Betrachtung von Kunstwerken nach Versuchen mit einer Schulklasse*, pub der Lehrervereinigung zur Pflege der künstlerischen Bildung (Dresden: 1898).

Löffler, Fritz, 'Dresdner Sezession Gruppe 1919', *Expressionismus: die zweite Generation 1915–1925* (Munich: 1989).

_____, Emilio Bertonati and Joachim Heusinger von Waldegg (eds), *Dresdner Sezession 1919–1923*, exhibition catalogue Galleria del Levante (Munich/Milan: 1977).

Lun Yu, *Gespräche* (Düsseldorf/Cologne: 1975), Book 12, Section 1, p 121.

Mae, Michiko and Elisabeth Scherer (eds), *Nipponspiration – Japonismus und japanische Populärkultur im deutschsprachigen Raum* (Vienna/Cologne/Weimar: 2013).

Mahler-Werfel, Alma, *Mein Leben*, foreword by Willy Haas (Frankfurt am Main: 1980).

Malet, Marian, 'Oskar Kokoschka and the Freie Deutsche Kulturbund: The "Friendly Alien" as Propagandist', in *'I didn't want to float; I wanted to belong to something': Refugee Organizations in Britain 1933–1945'*, ed by Anthony Grenville and Andrea Reiter, *The Yearbook of the Research Centre for German and Austrian Exile Studies*, Vol 10 (2008), pp 49–66.

Manger, Klaus, 'Trakl und die "Franziska Kokoschkas"', *Neue Zürcher Zeitung* (3/4 August 1985), No 177, pp 47–48.

Mankell, Henning, *Treibsand. Was es heißt, ein Mensch zu sein*, transl from the Swedish by Wolfgang Butt (Vienna: 2014).

Mann, Golo, *Zeiten und Figuren. Schriften aus vier Jahrzehnten* (Frankfurt am Main: 1979).

Mann, Thomas, *Gesammelte Werke in dreizehn Bänden,* Vol X: *Reden und Aufsätze 2* (Frankfurt am Main: 1990).

_____, *Tagebücher 1933–1934,* ed by Peter de Mendelssohn (Frankfurt am Main: 1977).

Marx, Karl, 'Ökonomisch-philosophische Manuskripte ("Pariser Manuskripte" 1844)'. *MEW,* Vol 40 (Berlin: 2005), p 541 f. (Translated from the German text by Martin Milligan, revised by Dirk J Struik, contained in Marx/Engels, Gesamtausgabe, Abt. 1, Bd. 3. Corrections were made of typographical errors and the author's obvious slips when preparing the Russian edition, 1956; transcribed in 2000 for marxists.org by Andy Blunden; proofread and corrected by Matthew Carmody, 2009. <www.marxists.org/archive/marx/works/download/pdf/Economic-Philosophic-Manuscripts-1844.pdf>.)

Mauron, Véronique, *Werke der Oskar Kokoschka-Stiftung,* transl from the French by Kathrin Braunschweig-Geller, Pascal Steenken and Heike Gieche Wenger (Vevey: 1994).

Mayer, Monika, 'Bruno Grimschitz und die Österreichische Galerie 1938–1945. Eine biografische Annäherung im Kontext der aktuellen Provenienzforschung' in *NS-Kunstraub in Österreich und die Folgen,* ed by Gabriele Anderl and Alexandra Caruso (Innsbruck: 2005), pp 59–79.

Meier, Mischa, 'Die Thermopylen – "Wanderer, kommst Du nach Spa(rta)"' in *Die griechische Welt. Erinnerungsorte der Antike,* ed by Elke Stein-Hölkeskamp and Karl-Joachim Hölkeskamp (Munich: 2010), pp 98–113.

Melichar, Alois, *Überwindung des Modernismus. Konkrete Antwort an einen abstrakten Kritiker* (Vienna/Frankfurt am Main/London: 1954).

Menuhin, Yehudi, *Unvollendete Reise. Lebenserinnerungen,* transl by Isabella Nadolny and Albrecht Roeseler, 6th edition (Munich: 1976).

Mesterton, Ingrid et al (eds), *Ernst Josephson. 1851–1906. Bilder und Zeichnungen*, Städtisches Kunstmuseum (Bonn: 1979).

Meyer, Herman, 'Die Verwandlung des Sichtbaren. Die Bedeutung der modernen bildenden Kunst für Rilkes späte Dichtung' in *Rainer Maria Rilke. Wege der Forschung*, ed by Rüdiger Görner, Vol 638 (Darmstadt: 1987), pp 131–184.

Long, Christopher, *Der Fall Loos* (Salzburg: 2014).

Möller, Lise Lotte, *Kokoschkas Radierungen zu 'Penthesilea'. Eine Einführung* (Frankfurt am Main: 1970).

Mühsam, Erich, *Tagebücher 1910–1924*, 2nd edition, ed and afterword by Chris Hirte (Munich: 1995).

Müller-Härlin, Anna, 'Die Artists' International Association and "refugee artists"' in *'I didn't want to float; I wanted to belong to something': Refugee Organizations in Britain 1933–1945*, ed by Anthony Grenville and Andrea Reiter, *The Yearbook of the Research Centre for German and Austrian Exile Studies*, Vol 10 (2008), pp 27–48.

_____, 'Rebellious and Supportive: The Collector Michael Croft and Artists in Exile in Great Britain' in *Exile and Patronage: Cross-cultural Negotiations Beyond the Third Reich*, ed by Andrew Chandler, Katarzyna Stoklosa and Jutta Vinzent (Berlin: 2006), pp 45–54.

Muschg, Walter, 'Von Trakl zu Brecht' in *Die Zerstörung der deutschen Literatur und andere Essays*, ed by Julian Schütt and Winfried Stephan, with an afterword by Julian Schütt (Zurich: 2009).

Navratil, Michael, '"Den Schauer des Mythos neu schaffen". Die kreative Rezeption von Nietzsches "Geburt der Tragödie" in der Wiener Moderne', *Sprachkunst* XLII (2011), 2nd half, pp 245–269.

Neuber, Matthias (ed), *Beiträge zu Hans Vaihingers 'Philosophie des Als Ob'* (Würzburg: 2014).

Nietzsche, Friedrich, *Dionysus Dithyrambs* transl by James Luchte in *The Peacock and the Buffalo: The Poetry of Nietzsche* (London, Continuum Publishing: 2010).

Padmore, George, *Afrika unter dem Joch der Weissen* (Erlenbach-Zurich/Leipzig: 1937).

Panayi, Panikos, *The Enemy in our Midst: Germans in Britain During the First World War* (London/New Delhi/New York/Sydney: 1991).

Pape, Helmut, 'Wir können nur gemeinsam sehen. Die Verschränkung der Blicke als Modell humanen Sehens' in *Sehen und Handeln. Berliner Schriften für Bildaktforschung und Verkörperungsphilosophie*, Vol 1, ed by Horst Bredekamp and John M Krois (Berlin: 2011), pp 117–140.

Pedde, Brigitte, *Willi Baumeister 1889–1955. Schöpfer aus dem Unbekannten* (Berlin: 2013).

Pfeuffer, Franz, 'Die neue Franzensbrücke über den Donau-Canal in Wien', *Zeitschrift des Österreichischen Ingenieur- und Architekten-Vereins*, 18 (1900).

Pfisterer, Ulrich and Valeska von Rosen (eds), *Der Künstler als Kunstwerk. Selbst-porträts vom Mittelalter bis zur Gegenwart* (Stuttgart: 2005).

Pikart, Eberhard in collaboration with Dirk Mende, *Theodor Heuss. Der Mann. Das Werk. Die Zeit.* Veröffentlichungen des Schiller Nationalmuseums, Nr 17. Pub Bernhard Zeller (Stuttgart: 1967).

Plodeck, Anna, *The Making of Fred Uhlman: Life and Work of the Painter and Writer in Exile*, 2 Vol, Dissertation (Courtauld Institute of Art, University of London: 2004).

Pott, Gertrud, *Die Spiegelung des Sezessionismus im österreichischen Theater* (Vienna: 1975).

Prieberg, Fred K, *Musik im NS-Staat* (Frankfurt am Main: 1982).

Raitz, Brigitte (ed), '"Ein Wörterbuch anlegen". Marie Luise Kaschnitz zum 100. Geburtstag. Mit einem Essay v. Ruth Klüger', *Marbacher Magazin* 95/2001, pp 102–104.

Rathkolb, Oliver, *Die paradoxe Republik. Österreich 1945–2015*, updated and new edition (Vienna: 2005 and 2015).

Rauterberg, Hanno, 'Architektur und Verbrechen', *Die Zeit*, No 31 (13 August 2015).

Read, Herbert, *The Creative Nature of Humanism* (Zurich: 1958).

Reiber, Joachim, *Gottfried von Einem. Komponist der Stunde null* (Vienna: 2017).

Reich, Willi, *Alban Berg. Leben und Werk* (Munich/Zurich: 1985).

Rilke, Rainer Maria, *Haßzellen, stark im größten Liebeskreise. Verse für Oskar Kokoschka*, ed by Joachim W Storck (Marbach: 1988).

_____, *Werke. Kommentierte Ausgabe in vier Bänden*, Vol 2: *Gedichte 1910 bis 1926*, ed by Manfred Engel and Ulrich Fülleborn (Frankfurt am Main/Leipzig: 1996).

Rinser, Luise, *Jan Lobel aus Warschau. Erzählung*, 18th edition (Frankfurt am Main: 2012).

Ritter-Santini, Lea (ed), *Mit den Augen geschrieben. Von gedichteten und erzählten Bildern* (Munich: 1991), pp 253–255.

Rossi-Schrimpf, Inga, *George Minne. Das Frühwerk und seine Rezeption in Deutschland und Österreich bis zum Ersten Weltkrieg* (Weimar: 2012).

Roth, Joseph, 'Prag. Spaziergang in einer verzauberten Stadt (1932)', *Frankfurter Allgemeine Sonntagszeitung*, No 47 (25 November 2012), p 57.

Rudert, Konstanze (ed), *Will Grohmann. Im Netzwerk der Moderne*, catalogue for exhibition in the Staatlichen Kunstsammlungen – Kunsthalle im Lipsiusbau Dresden (Munich: 2012).

_____ (ed), *Will Grohmann. Texte zur Kunst der Moderne* (Munich: 2012).

_____ (ed), *Zwischen Intuition und Gewissheit. Will Grohmann und die Rezeption der Moderne in Deutschland und Europa 1918–1968* (Dresden: 2013).

Sabarsky, Serge, *Oskar Kokoschka. Die frühen Jahre 1906–1926. Aquarelle und Zeichnungen*, with contributions by Werner Hofmann and Willi Hahn (Munich: 1986).

Sager, Peter, 'Alter Wilder. Großer Oskar. Ein Porträt', *ZEIT Magazin*, No 9 (21 February 1986), pp 20–31.

Sandy, Mark, '"The Last Great Romantic": Nietzsche's Romanticism

Out of the Spirit of Decadence' in *Decadent Romanticism 1780–1914*, ed by Kostas Boyiopoulos and Mark Sandy (Abingdon: 2015).

Schama, Simon, *The Face of Britain: The Nation through its Portraits* (London: 2015).

Schieder, Martin, 'Der Kritiker ist für die Kunst. Will Grohmann und die Moderne, 1914–1968' in *Avantgarden im Fokus der Kunstkritik. Eine Hommage an Carola Giedion-Welcker (1893–1979)*, ed by Regula Krähenbühl (Zurich: 2011), pp 205–222.

Schiller, Friedrich, *The Poems and Ballads of Schiller*, transl Sir Edward Bulwer Lytton, Bart. (Leipzig: 1844).

Schneditz, Wolfgang, 'Kokoschkas Erinnerungen an Trakl', *Die Presse*, No 42 (Vienna, 21 October 1950), p 6.

Schneider, Katja and Stefan Lehmann (eds), *Oskar Kokoschkas Antike. Eine europäische Vision der Moderne*, with contributions by Régine Bonnefoit, Andreas and Diana Furtwängler, A Gutsfeld, Stephan Lehmann, Christian Mileta, Heinz Spielmann and Peter Weidmann (Munich: 2010).

Scholz, Albrecht, 'Ärzte und Patienten in Dresdner Naturheilsanatorien', *medizin – bibliothek – information 4* (2004), No 1, pp 13–19.

Shapria, Elana, *Style and Seduction: Jewish Patrons, Architecture and Design in the Fin de Siècle Vienna* (Lebanon, NH: 2016).

Sherman, A J, *Island Refuge: Britain and Refugees from the Third Reich 1933–1939* (Berkeley and Los Angeles, CA: 1973).

Simmel, Georg, *Aufsätze und Abhandlungen 1901–1908*, Vol 1, Gesamtausgabe, Vol 7, ed by Rüdiger Kramme, Angela Rammstedt and Ottheim Rammstedt (Frankfurt am Main: 1995).

Soergel, Albert, *Dichtung und Dichter der Zeit. Eine Schilderung der deutschen Literatur der letzten Jahrzehnte*, NF: *Im Banne des Expressionismus*, 5th edition (Leipzig: 1927).

Spielmann, Heinz, *Oskar Kokoschka. Die Fächer für Alma Mahler* (Hamburg: 1969).

_____, *Oskar Kokoschka. Leben und Werk* (Cologne: 2003).

_____, *Oskar Kokoschka, Lebensspuren. Ausgewählte Gemälde,*

Aquarelle, Zeichnungen der Kokoschka-Stiftung Vevey aus den Jahren 1906 bis 1976. Mit unveröffentlichten Gesprächen des Künstlers aus dem Jahre 1966 (Flensburg: 1992).

_____, 'Oskar Kokoschka in Prag und England' in *Oskar Kokoschka. Emigrantenleben. Prag und London 1934–1953*, ed by Jutta Hülsewig-Johnen, catalogue for the 1994/1995 exhibition in the Bielefelder Kunsthalle and the Nationalgalerie Prag (Bielefeld: 1994), pp 177–189.

Starobinski, Jean, *Porträt des Künstlers als Gaukler. Drei Essays*, transl from the French by Markus Jakob (Frankfurt am Main: 1985).

Stents, Ronald, *A Bespattered Page? The Internment of His Majesty's Most Loyal Enemy Aliens* (London: 1980).

Stifter, Adalbert, *Der Nachsommer*, with an afterword and selected bibliography by Uwe Japp, comments and chronology by Karl Pörnbacher (Düsseldorf/Zurich: 2005).

Stourton, James and Kenneth Clark, *Life, Art and Civilization* (London: 2016).

Stramm, August, *Du. Liebesgedichte* (Berlin: 1916).

_____, *Die Dichtungen. Sämtliche Gedichte, Dramen, Prosa*, ed and afterword by Jeremy Adler (Munich: 1990).

_____, *Selected Poems*, transl by Isham Cook (1988), www.ishamcook.com, <ishamcook.files.wordpress.com/2011/11/august-stramm-poems-19881.pdf>.

Timpano, Nathan J, *Constructing the Viennese Modern Body: Art, Hysteria, and the Puppet* (New York: 2017).

Trakl, Georg, *Dichtungen und Briefe, Vol I*, ed by Walther Killy and Hans Szklenar, 2nd expanded edition (Salzburg: 1987).

_____, *Poems and Prose – A Bilingual Edition*, transl from the German and with an introduction and notes by Alexander Stillmark (Libris/Angel Books, London: 2001).

_____, *The Poems of Georg Trakl*, transl by Max Wickert (2009), <www.outriderspoetryproject.com/uploads/4/6/1/4/4614234/trakls_collected_poems.pdf>.

Uhlman, Fred, *The Making of an Englishman. Erinnerungen eines deutschen Juden*, ed by and transcribed from English by Manfred Schmid (Zurich: 1998).

Vaihinger, Hans, *Die Philosophie des Als Ob. System der theoretischen, praktischen und religiösen Fiktionen der Menschheit auf Grund eines idealistischen Positivismus. Mit einem Anhang über Kant und Nietzsche* (Berlin: 1911).

Vietta, Silvio, *Die Weltgesellschaft. Wie die abendländische Rationalität die Welt erobert und verändert hat* (Baden-Baden: 2016).

Wallas, Armin A, *Albert Ehrenstein. Mythenzerstörer und Mythenschöpfer* (Munich: 1994).

Wally, Barbara, 'Neue Aspekte zur Gründungsgeschichte der Sommerakademie: Kokoschkas "Schule des Sehens" im Kunstkontext der 50er Jahre' in *Oskar Kokoschka in Salzburg. Die Gründung der Internationalen Sommerakademie für Bildende Kunst. Vor fünfzig Jahren*, ed by Barbara Wally (Salzburg: 2003), pp 9–62.

Weizsäcker, Victor Freiherr von, *Seelenbehandlung und Seelenführung nach ihren biologischen und metaphysischen Grundlagen betrachtet* (Gütersloh: 1926).

Wellek, Albert, 'Farbenharmonie und Farbenklavier. Ihre Entstehungsgeschichte im 18. Jahrhundert', *Archiv für die gesamte Psychologie*, 94 (1935), pp 347–375.

Westheim, Paul, *Oskar Kokoschka*, 2nd edition (Berlin: 1925; 1st edition 1918).

Wharton, Edith, *In Morocco* (London: 1920, new edition 1927).

Wingler, Hans Maria, *Kokoschka-Fibel* (Salzburg: 1957).

Wolf, Norbert Christian, *Eine Triumphpforte österreichischer Kunst. Hugo von Hofmannsthals Gründung der Salzburger Festspiele* (Salzburg: 2014).

Zajonz, Michael, 'Mädchen in Blau. Oskar Kokoschkas Kinderporträt "Gitta Wallerstein" kehrt nach Dresden zurück', *Arsprototo* 10 (2014), Issue 3, pp 42–45.

Zehder, Hugo, 'Dresdner Theater', *Tägliche Rundschau* (6 June 1917).

Zweig, Stefan, *Die Welt von Gestern. Erinnerungen eines Europäers*, 38th edition (Frankfurt am Main: 2010).

Internet sources

Archer, William (transl), <www.gutenberg.org/files/4782/4782-h/4782-h.htm> (*When We Dead Awaken*, Henrik Ibsen).

British Library, <www.bl.uk/collection-items/kokoschka> (postcard by Adolf Loos).

Kline, A S, <goethe.holtof.com/faust/FaustIIActIScenesItoVII.htm> (*Faust Part II*, Goethe).

Kline, A S, <www.poetryintranslation.com/PITBR/German/Goethepoems.php#anchor_Toc74652106> (*Selected Poems*, Goethe).

<www.kunstzitate.de/bildendekunst/manifeste/beckmann1938.htm> (lecture by Max Beckmann, 1938).

Mitchell, James, <www.babelmatrix.org/works/de/H%C3%B6lderlin%2C_Friedrich/Hyperions_Schicksalslied/en/4793-Hyperion_s_Song_of_Destiny> ('Hyperion's Song of Destiny', Friedrich Hölderlin).

Acknowledgements: A Word of Thanks

Much is owed to books. To whom or what a book is owed, based on the wisdom of a Latin saying, often has its own quite specifically delineated story. Gratitude is owed in the first place to the idea of even daring this book. It was, as it were, to rethink this only sparsely documented relationship between Georg Trakl and Oskar Kokoschka and to repeatedly follow and explore those Rilke words that applied to the ambivalent relationship of this 'expressionist'. Out of this came the notion of attempting a study of this century-spanning artist which would combine the monographic thematic with the biographic, a parallel to *Rainer Maria Rilke. Im Herzwerk der Sprache* (1987) and *Georg Trakl. Dichter im Jahrzehnt der Extreme* (2014); in other words a trilogy of the artistic in which the word new was to become visible and the visible had an opportunity to speak in an atypical manner. Read: these books are grateful to each other. That they could be published under the auspices of the Zsolnay Verlag in Vienna may appear appropriate in hindsight; yet precisely therein lies an especially fortunate coincidence, which is based as much in the name of this traditional house as in the commitment of its director Herbert Ohrlinger and the professional expertise in editing in the guise of Bettina Wörgötter, who looked after all three books. That this has become a rarity in today's publishing business obligates the author all the more to special gratitude.

Even if the giving of thanks may now tend towards a listing, it should be emphasised that without the following who are to be thanked, this book simply would not have come into being. They provided essential assistance in numerous, yes, unmistakable ways, whether with advice and material sourcing, suggestions or cross-references which proved indispensable: Aglaja Kempf, Conservatrice de la Fondation Oskar Kokoschka in the Musée Jenisch in Vevey; Dr Hildegund Amanshauser, Sommerakademie Salzburg; Andrea Meyer-Ludowisy, Senate House Library London; Ruth Häusler, Rainer Walter as well as the team in the reading room of the Handschriftenabteilung der Zentralbibliothek Zürich; Marcel Atze, Wienbibliothek im Wiener Rathaus; Bernadette Reinhold, Director of the Oskar Kokoschka Zentrum at the Universität für angewandte Kunst Wien; Dr Antje Müller, Ernst Křenek-Institut in Krems an der Donau; the team in the reading room of the archives of Tate Britain, London; as well as Franz Eder, Galerie Welz in Salzburg.

This English edition would not exist without my constructive translators, Debra S Marmor and Herbert A Danner, as well as the unfailing commitment of Haus Publising in the shape of Barbara Schwepcke and Harry Hall. Warmest thanks to all.

Naturally, no one is owed more thanks than Oskar Kokoschka himself, for his life and his work. For art criticism must never forget one thing: it must ultimately always serve the valuation of its subject. Even if in the best case and demanded by Friedrich Schlegel, critique should also become art and – in return – art become critique, in reality critique can only flirt with becoming art. D H Lawrence gave us the adage, the critic has the task of protecting the work from its originator. That may pertain to some artists, but certainly not to Kokoschka, whose life and work desire to be illuminated mutually. Goethe's great affirmation: 'Whatever the case, life, it is good', should be given the addendum: 'in particular through its art'.